QUANTITATIVE METHODS FOR FINANCE AND INVESTMENTS

QUANTITATIVE METHODS FOR FINANCE AND INVESTMENTS

John L. Teall and Iftekhar Hasan

© 2002 by John L. Teall and Iftekhar Hasan

Editorial Offices:
108 Cowley Road, Oxford OX4 1JF, UK
  Tel: +44 (0)1865 791100
Osney Mead, Oxford OX2 0EL, UK
  Tel: +44 (0)1865 206206
350 Main Street, Malden, MA 02148-5018, USA
  Tel: +1 781 388 8250
Iowa State Blackwell Publishing USA Press, a Blackwell Publishing company, 2121. State
  Avenue, Ames, Iowa 50014-8300, USA
  Tel: +1 515 292 0140
Blackwell Munksgaard, Nørre Søgade 35, PO Box 2148, Copenhagen, DK-1016, Denmark
  Tel: +45 77 33 33 33
Blackwell Publishing Asia, 54 University Street, Carlton, Victoria 3053, Australia
  Tel: +61 (0)3 9347 0300
Blackwell Verlag, Kurfürstendamm 57, 10707 Berlin, Germany
  Tel: +49 (0)30 32 79 060
Blackwell Publishing, 10, rue Casimir Delavigne, 75006 Paris, France
  Tel: +331 5310 3310

First published 2002 by Blackwell Publishers Ltd, a Blackwell Publishing company

Library of Congress Cataloging-in-Publication Data

Teall, John L., 1958–
  Quantitative methods for finance and investments / John L. Teall and Iftekhar Hasan.
    p. cm.
  Includes bibliographical references and index.
  ISBN 0-631-22338-X (alk. paper) — ISBN 0-631-22339-8 (pbk. : alk. paper)
    1. Finance—Mathematical models.   2. Investments—Mathematical models.   I. Hasan,
  Iftekhar.   II. Title.
  HG106 .T4 2002
  332′.01′5118—dc21   2001043228

A catalogue record for this title is available from the British Library.

Set in 10 on 12 pt Photina
by Graphicraft Limited, Hong Kong

For further information on
Blackwell Publishers, visit our website:
www.blackwellpublishers.co.uk

Dedicated to Polly Mitchell

CONTENTS

PREFACE

One of the most intriguing and captivating aspects of finance is its application of mathematics. Unfortunately, most faculty in finance find that this reliance on mathematics prompts too many business students to approach finance with great dread. Even many of our finance majors approach their studies with apprehension and fail to comprehend many of the more subtle aspects of the subject material. Fortunately, most university students, despite their lack of confidence, really do have the quantitative skills necessary to understand finance through the M.B.A. level. In many cases, only relatively minor preparation or review is needed to provide the student with the groundwork and confidence required to study finance. The purpose of our text is to provide M.B.A. and undergraduate finance students this opportunity to update basic mathematics skills for basic business finance and investments courses.

The level of mathematics reviewed in this text does not extend beyond first-year linear algebra, statistics, and calculus, with the possible exception of a brief introduction to differential equations in chapter 9. This is consistent with the level of mathematics required for finance concentrations in most M.B.A. and undergraduate business programs. Most students will not require an intense instruction in high-school level mathematics. Hence, we offer only brief reviews of mathematics at these lowest levels and only those that are most important for studying finance (chapters 2 and 3). We then introduce three chapters on the mathematics of time value, return, and risk (chapters 4–6). Chapters 7–9 provide more detailed reviews and finance applications of college-level linear mathematics and calculus. The organization of the text is generally by mathematics topic followed by finance applications. Exceptions to this include those chapters devoted to time value, return, and risk measures, portfolio analysis and elementary options mathematics. Spreadsheet applications are provided in many of the chapter appendices, and exercises are provided for all but the first chapter. The exercises are solved in the end-of-text appendix A.

This text can be used as prerequisite or parallel reading for most introductory business finance texts, such as Ross, Westerfield, and Jordan (2001), Brealey and Myers (2000), and Brealey, Myers, and Marcus (1995), and most basic investments texts, including Bodie, Kane, and Marcus (1999). It may also serve as foundation reading for more advanced texts, such as Teall (1999), Neftci (1996), Pliska (1997), Hull (2000), and Elton and Gruber (1995).[1] This book can also be used as a primary text for an undergraduate or M.B.A. course such as "Quantitative Methods for Finance," intended to improve finance students' mathematics skills. Finally, the book may serve as a primary or secondary text for a prerequisite M.B.A. mathematics course covering elementary linear mathematics and calculus for business students.

The authors welcome your comments and suggestions regarding this book. Professor Teall can be contacted by e-mail at jteall@pace.edu or jteall@juno.com or by using contact information available on his web page at http://webpage.pace.edu/jteall. Professor Hasan can be contacted by e-mail at hasan@adm.njit.edu.

John L. Teall and Iftekhar Hasan
August 2001

[1] References are provided on pages 222–3.

ACKNOWLEDGMENTS

We have been fortunate to have had a number of students, colleagues, and friends assist and provide guidance in the preparation of this book. Michael Dang, Hyangbab Ku, and T. J. Wu all strengthened our book with useful comments and corrections on earlier versions of the manuscript. Al Bruckner, Elizabeth Wald, and especially Geoffrey Palmer, provided wonderful editorial support. Our old friends Ed Downe, Peter Knopf, and John Knopf contributed encouragement and advice throughout the various stages of writing this book. Miriam Vasquez dispensed irrepressible needling and stole drafts of the text manuscript to pass on to students, yet continues to be a good friend. Anne, who never forgets having been left out of the acknowledgments of an earlier book and Emily, whose Pocahontas game shares disk space with preliminary drafts of this book, ensured that the various publisher deadlines would not be met prematurely. They have earned eternal gratitude for the delightful manner in which they accomplished this.

CHAPTER ONE
INTRODUCTION AND OVERVIEW

1.1   THE IMPORTANCE OF MATHEMATICS IN FINANCE

Finance is an immensely exciting academic discipline and a most rewarding professional endeavor. However, ever-increasing sophistication of financial markets, design of financial securities, and computational technology has heightened the business practitioner's need for understanding of mathematics. In order to understand and participate in financial decision-making, students and practitioners of finance need to be familiar with the basic tools and techniques used in more formal analysis of financial problems. Mathematics is among the most important of these tools. In addition to being crucial to the analysis of financial problems, mathematics is a language that is most useful for communication of financial concepts, techniques, and results. Yet many of us approach mathematics very tentatively, feeling overwhelmed by its apparent complexity and insecure about our own preparation to understand and apply the variety of useful tools available to us. In many cases, our preparation for handling financial analysis merely requires a review of mathematics that we may have been quite comfortable with in the past; in others, we may need to learn new tools and techniques in mathematics. This book aspires to facilitate review and presentation of more elementary mathematics concepts sufficient to understand many of the most interesting concepts in financial analysis. The vast majority of students of finance require at least some review of mathematics tools, and most will be surprised at how quickly they can be grasped with relatively little dedication and effort.

A few students will question the need to understand mathematics and its application to finance. One challenge occasionally posed in the finance classroom, "Don't they have computers that do this?", can be difficult to confront convincingly. Nevertheless, computers cannot actually understand what types of problems can be solved with what types of technique. Computers are capable only of performing unthinking operations exactly as they are programmed, without any ability to criticize the suitability of solution technique or to understand the implications of the results that they generate. The computer user or financial analyst must formulate the problem, determine the solution technique, and interpret the computer output. This essentially relegates the role of the computer to mindlessly performing routine and perhaps repetitive computations in exactly the manner specified by its user. The user should understand all of the aspects of the problem and its results, and must also be able to determine the usefulness of the results and apply them. Hence, an analyst, perhaps working in conjunction with other analysts and professionals, must understand the problem, formulate a solution, and interpret the results. In a sense, the computer cannot solve mush of the problem itself; not only must someone know enough to communicate to it exactly what to do, but most of the analytical work must be left to thinking and understanding humans.

Financial analysis is performed in intensely competitive and uncertain environments, bringing together many individuals, businesses, governments, and other institutions. These participants in markets interact with one another over many periods of time, which can be presumed to be infinitely divisible. Numerous sources of uncertainty abound and information derives from the unexpected as well as the expected. While this complex financial environment is most fascinating and exciting, its analysis can be most confounding, requiring application of many branches of mathematics, ranging from simple arithmetic, algebra, and calculus to stochastic processes, numerical methods, wave theory, and nonlinear dynamics. This book presents the most essential mathematical technique and its applications to financial analysis. The level of presentation of this book might be considered to be either prerequisite or parallel to that of an introductory business finance or investments course.

1.2 MATHEMATICAL AND COMPUTER MODELING IN FINANCE

Financial analysis starts with the construction of *financial models*. A model is an artificial or idealized structure describing the relationships among variables or factors. All of the methodology in this book is intended to facilitate the development, implementation, and analysis of financial models to solve financial problems. For example, the elementary mathematics presented in chapters 2 and 3 is integral to almost any serious financial analysis. The valuation models in chapter 4 provide a groundwork for making investment and budgeting decisions, while the more sophisticated option pricing models in chapter 10 enable us to grasp the essentials for understanding derivative instruments. The use of models is important in finance because the direct analysis of actual markets is extraordinarily complex. For example, a thorough valuation of a stock should require us to understand everything about the economy, political arena, human psychology, and so on that could have an impact on that stock's value. This thorough understanding is simply impossible; it is much more practical to construct a valuation model that accounts for only the most important factors. Models provide the analyst the opportunity to simplify real-world circumstances to a construct that can be easily be manipulated and understood. Financial decision-makers frequently use existing models or construct new ones that relate to the types of decisions they wish to make.

The aim of a financial model is to simulate or behave like a real financial situation. Analysts who create financial models exclude "real-world" conditions that have only minor impact on the results of their decisions. Instead, analysts focus on those factors that are most relevant to their situations. The most important conditions retained by analysts for model-building along with those ignored for sake of simplicity form the basis for the set of assumptions for the model. In most cases, analysts must make unrealistic assumptions in order to simplify their models and make them easier to work with. The simplest models building on more restrictive simplifying assumptions can be adapted to more life-like scenarios by relaxing the most unrealistic assumptions. The best financial models are those that appropriately account for the most significant factors affecting financial decisions, are simple enough be practical and easy to work with, and are useful for predicting actual financial results. Models that predict actual financial outcomes most accurately are most useful. Unfortunately, accuracy and simplicity in the construction of financial models often conflict with each other. Some degree of inaccuracy in the model must usually be tolerated in order to maintain its ease of use and analysis. The appropriate tradeoff between accuracy and simplicity is a problem constantly faced by the financial analyst.

This book is concerned with both theoretical and practitioner-oriented models. The book's primary focus is the mathematics and quantitative technique required to create and analyze financial models. Theoretical models are created to explain financial markets and scenarios; practitioner-oriented empirical models are intended to be applied to actual business situations. The financial analyst may construct and use a theoretical model to provide a framework for decision-making and then use a practitioner-oriented model to apply the theory. Analysts also use models to measure phenomena in financial markets and scenarios and to evaluate financial results. This book will emphasize practical applications of the most essential models.

In many cases, mathematics-based financial models are readily adaptable to computer spreadsheet programs. Computer spreadsheets and structured programs are most important in financial analysis because of frequent time-consuming and complex computations. At present, the most popular of the spreadsheet programs is Excel™. This spreadsheet appears on the user's computer screen as an array of columns and rows, where numbers, formulas, labels, or other code can be entered. Ease of use and ability to handle enormous numbers of computations are among the advantages of computer-based spreadsheet analysis over a calculator-based analysis. The authors recommend that the reader take every opportunity to use spreadsheets to aid to the understanding of the models presented here. Spreadsheet examples are developed in several chapter appendices in this text to illustrate financial applications.

1.3 MONEY, SECURITIES, AND MARKETS

Money is anything that is commonly accepted in exchange for goods and services. Money is a measure of value, a store of value and, as just suggested, a medium of exchange. Financial assets (including money) are contracts or certificates indicating financial claims. A *security* is a financial asset that can be purchased or sold in financial markets. For example, a corporate *bond* is a security that indicates a claim by its owner (the investor or bondholder) on a specified series of interest payments and principal repayment by the firm which issued the bond. The corporation is obligated to make payments to the bondholder as specified by the bond contract. A share of corporate *stock* is a residual claim; that is, shareholders have a right to receive all cash flows (according to a schedule determined by the firm) which remain in the corporation after obligations to all other claimants have been satisfied. Shareholders also have the right to direct certain discretionary activities of the firm. Corporations and other business enterprises issue securities for the purpose of raising money to engage in business activities; investors may be willing to purchase securities in order to receive cash flows associated with these business activities. Markets exist for securities enabling investors to buy, sell, or trade securities. Among these markets are exchanges and over-the-counter markets for stocks and bonds and networks of financial institutions engaged in the trade of derivative instruments and other securities. An understanding of these markets is crucial to successful investing in the securities that trade in them.

Corporate issues are made either to specific investors (private placements, e.g., a bank note) or to the general public (public placements, e.g., publicly traded common stock). Primary markets for securities are the markets of original issue; by participating in these markets, corporations sell their own securities to raise money. Thus, a corporation may raise money by issuing or selling securities in primary markets. *Investment banks* are financial institutions whose function is to assist corporations in the placement of their securities to investors. Investment banks provide advice and other assistance to firms concerning the marketing and pricing new issues. Advertisements (sometimes called "tombstone ads") related to primary market offerings may be seen in financial publications such as the *Wall Street Journal*. Secondary markets exist for many previously issued securities. Secondary markets provide liquidity for primary market participants. That is, secondary markets provide the opportunity for original purchasers of securities to sell their securities before they mature, expire or cease generating payments from the corporations. The New York Stock Exchange and other exchanges provide secondary markets for many corporate issues. Issues not traded on exchanges are traded in the "over-the-counter" markets – markets for all publicly traded securities not listed on exchanges. The National Association of Security Dealers Automated Quotation System (NASDAQ) is among the most visible components of the over-the-counter markets.

In addition to the markets for corporate securities, there exist well-developed markets for a variety of instruments created by other types of issuers. For example, the federal government raises money through the sale of U.S. Treasury issues, including Treasury bills, Treasury notes, and Treasury bonds. These are all debt securities indicating that the United States government has borrowed money from their original purchasers. Such treasury instruments, particularly those of shorter term to maturity, are often regarded to be free of many of the risks associated with other issuers of debt instruments. The United States Treasury is a very reliable debtor and there is a very well developed market for treasury issues. State and local governments issue municipal bonds (the term "muni" does apply to state issues as well as to municipal issues) which often confer certain income tax advantages. A variety of other institutions offer securities, including nonprofit institutions, mutual funds, and government agencies. There even exist active markets for instruments representing claims on other securities (derivative instruments). *Derivative instruments* include *options* and *futures contracts*. The value of a derivative instrument is derived from the value of another security or asset. An option contract provides its owner the right to buy or sell another security or asset at a specified price on or before a given date. The owner of the option contract may choose whether he wishes to exercise his right to buy or sell. A forward or futures contract obligates its participants to execute an agreed-upon transaction at a later date. All of these different types of instruments, securities, and markets will be discussed in greater detail later in this text.

1.4 TIME VALUE, RISK, ARBITRAGE, AND PRICING

Perhaps the single most important and difficult type of problem in finance is how to value or price an asset, particularly when its cash flow stream is unpredictable and/or lengthy. A variety of tools exists for these types of problems, providing us with different perspectives on value. Two of the most important valuation tools are based on the concepts of *present value* and *relative value*.

Present value recognizes that the worth to an investor of cash flows to be received at a later date is less than the worth of those to be received earlier due to the following:

1 *Inflation.* The purchase power of money tends to decline over time.
2 *Risk.* We never know with certainty whether we will actually realize the cash flow that we are expecting. In a sense, "the bird in the hand is worth two in the bush."
3 The option to either spend money now or defer spending it is likely to be worth more than being forced to defer spending the money.

Present-value methodologies typically involve predicting a cash flow or computing an expected or "most likely" cash flow and dividing it by a factor that accounts for the timing and risk of the cash flow, as well as other potentially important factors. Present-value models are emphasized in chapter 4.

The most important alternative to present-value methodologies is relative valuation. The relative valuation methodologies attempt to locate or devise other securities or combinations of securities whose values are already known and value the asset under consideration relative to those whose values are known. These methodologies make use of the "Law of One Price," which states that an asset whose cash flow structure is identical to that of another asset or combination of assets must be priced identically to the other asset or combination. This law derives from the activity known as arbitrage which, in its classic case, is the simultaneous purchase and sale of the same asset. For example, if gold is selling in Chicago markets for $400 per ounce and in New York markets for $410 per ounce, a classic arbitrage opportunity exists. That is, an investor has an opportunity to earn a riskless profit by engaging in arbitrage activities. In this case, the investor would purchase gold in Chicago for $400 per ounce and simultaneously sell it in New York for $410. This results in a $10 profit per "round trip" transaction. The transactions involve no risk, since both the selling and purchase prices are known. Furthermore, no initial net investment is required, because the transactions offset each other; the proceeds of the sale are used to finance the purchase. Thus, if a classic arbitrage opportunity exists, an investor will have the opportunity to make a riskless profit without investing any of his own money. If the laws of supply and demand are not impeded by market inefficiencies, investors will flock to exploit this opportunity. Their buying pressure in Chicago markets will force the Chicago price to rise; their selling pressure in New York markets will force the New York price down. Buying and selling pressure will persist until the prices in the two markets are equal. Thus, classic arbitrage opportunities are not likely to persist long in unimpeded free markets. More generally, arbitrage might refer to the near simultaneous purchase and sale of portfolios generating similar cash flow structures. The accuracy of relative valuation models depends on the extent to which securities with known values can be located or combined to resemble the asset under consideration. Arbitrage and relative valuation models are emphasized in chapters 7 and 10.

1.5   The Organization of this Book

This text seeks to provide the reader a level of competence and confidence for the application of elementary mathematics to financial analysis. This book might be used as prerequisite or supplemental reading for an introductory M.B.A.-level finance or investments course. Chapters 2 and 3 provide reviews of topics of elementary mathematics and definitions required for the most basic quantitative applications to finance. These chapters might be regarded as reviews of mathematics at the high-school level with applications specific to business and finance. Particular applications of a particular topic will follow the description of the mathematical topic in this and in other chapters. Certain sections in these two chapters may contain material that is new to some readers. This is particularly true with the applications. Chapters 4, 5, and 6 cover time value of money and measures of return and risk for securities and portfolios. The emphasis of these chapters is relevant mathematics and the level of rigor in these chapters might be comparable to that of an introductory business finance course. Chapter 7 delivers an introduction to matrix algebra along with a number of applications in finance. This chapter and chapter 8 on differential calculus are likely to be most helpful to students enrolled or planning to enroll in an M.B.A.-level investments or portfolio management course. Chapter 8 also provides a large number of applications of differential calculus to finance. Chapter 9 discusses rudiments of integral calculus, differential equations, and a few simple applications to finance, which may be particularly helpful to students planning to enroll in a derivatives course. This chapter could be skipped for those students wishing to move directly into the elementary option pricing mathematics presented in chapter 10. There are appendices at the ends of many chapters and at the end of the text. Some of these appendices are intended to demonstrate spreadsheet applications of the mathematical models. Included in the end-of-text appendices are detailed solutions to end-of-chapter exercises, a z-table, and a list of notation definitions. A glossary of terms follows the text appendices.

This book is designed to enable a student to understand a given topic by reading specific background material without the need to start at the beginning and read all the material prior to a given topic. Generally, reading the previous section (except for the first section in each chapter) will be sufficient background for the reader to comprehend any given section or application unless additional "Background readings" are listed. In many instances, the reader will already be familiar with the material covered in the "Background readings" for a section or application. In some instances, listed "Background readings" may themselves require additional background reading.

CHAPTER TWO
A REVIEW OF ELEMENTARY MATHEMATICS: FUNCTIONS AND OPERATIONS

2.1 INTRODUCTION

This chapter contains a review of some of the most basic mathematics functions and operations required for financial analysis. Anyone interested in pursuing study in finance should be very comfortable working through the material in this chapter (and chapter 3) prior to enrolling in an introductory finance course. Most of the concepts presented in the early part of this chapter will likely have been covered during the reader's high-school (or junior high-school) math sequence; however, many students will benefit from a review. Some readers will wish to merely skim this material before progressing to subsequent chapters. Readers with weaker mathematics preparation may find sections and applications followed by an asterisk (*) somewhat more difficult. Such readers may prefer to work through relevant exercises at the ends of the various chapters before spending too much time with this material. In some cases, the more difficult material may be skipped entirely.

Students in any introductory or intermediate finance course must be comfortable working with material in sections 2.2 through 2.8. Hence, students should be certain that they are comfortable with this material before attempting any study in finance. Other sections may be important as well, even in many introductory finance courses, depending on the reader's interests or exact course or program content. For example, material in section 2.9 will be needed by students planning study of material related to portfolio management, section 2.10 will be needed by students planning study in interest rate theory or fixed income management, and the remainder of the chapter will be needed by students interested in the pricing of options contracts and other derivatives.

2.2 VARIABLES, EQUATIONS, AND INEQUALITIES

Mathematics is the primary language of financial model-building, while variables, functions, equations, and inequalities are the building blocks of financial models. A *variable*, usually represented as a letter or group of letters, denotes a quantity that can be assumed from a given set of numbers. A *function* is a rule that assigns to each element x of a set X a unique element y of a set Y. For example, the following reads "y is a function of x":

$$y = f(x), \tag{2.1}$$

where y is a dependent variable and x is an independent variable. The variable y may also be expressed as a function of a series of independent variables. Such a function might be described more explicitly by specifying a particular mathematical operation to define the rule relating the sets. For example, we could write one example of the above functional relationship as

$$y = 3x + 4.$$

In this equation, we used two arithmetic operations, multiplication and addition. An *equation* such as the one we just considered is a statement that two mathematical expressions are equal, while an inequality states that one expression is greater than (>) or less than (<) another.

2.3   EXPONENTS

After the four basic arithmetic operations, exponentiation is the most commonly used operation in finance. Exponents enable us to express a repetitive series of multiplications or divisions in a concise form. They are particularly useful in finance where we frequently need to evaluate a large number of payments extending over many years. Exponents are also useful for expressing various types of "roots" of numbers or variables. Exponents are sometimes referred to as "powers."

Consider the function $y = 3^2$, which reads "y equals three squared" or "y equals three to the power two." The value of y is $3 \cdot 3 = 9$. We refer to the "power" 2 as the exponent of 3. More generally, we may write functions of the following form:

$$y = x^n, \tag{2.2}$$

where n represents the exponent for variable x. If n is a positive integer (a whole number greater than zero), it is an exponent referring to the number of times minus one the variable x is to be multiplied by itself. Thus, for example, if n were to equal 4, y would equal $x \cdot x \cdot x \cdot x = x^4$; that is, x is multiplied by itself three times. Clearly, it is more efficient to write x^4 than $x \cdot x \cdot x \cdot x$. Where $y = x^n$ and x is 3 and n is 4, $y = 3^4 = 81$.

The exponent n can also be a fractional or negative number. A negative exponent associated with x means that y is the inverse of x^n; that is, $y = x^{-n}$, which is the inverse of x^n:

$$y = x^{-n} = \frac{1}{x^n}. \tag{2.3}$$

Thus, $x^{-1} = 1/x$ and $x^{-2} = 1/x^2$. If $y = 4^{-2}$, then $y = 1/4^2 = 1/16$. Note that one may multiply any term by its inverse to obtain 1. For example, $x^2 \cdot x^{-2} = x^2 \cdot 1/x^2 = 1$. If n is a fractional value, y requires finding the "nth root" of x:

$$y = x^{1/n} = \sqrt[n]{x}. \tag{2.4}$$

Thus, $x^{1/2} = \sqrt{x}$ (the square root of x equals $x^{1/2}$) and $x^{1/3} = \sqrt[3]{x}$. For example, $4^{1/2} = 2$ and $64x^{1/3} = 4$. Furthermore, if $y = x^{m/n}$, then $y = \sqrt[n]{x^m}$. For example, if $y = 4^{3/2}$, $y = 8$. If $y = x^{-m/n}$, then $y = 1 \div \sqrt[n]{x^m}$.

When the exponent of a real number equals zero, the function has a value equal to one; that is, $x^0 = 1$ for any real x. The product of any base x with exponents n and m equals the base x with an exponent equal to the sum of the original exponents; that is, $x^n x^m = x^{n+m}$. For example, $y = 4^3 \cdot 4^2 = 4^{3+2} = 1{,}024$. Finally, $(x^n)^m$ equals x^{nm}.

APPLICATION 2.1: INTEREST AND FUTURE VALUE (A more complete presentation of this material is provided in chapter 4)

Suppose we deposit \$100 into a bank account paying interest at an annual rate of 5% compounded annually.[1] The total amount in our account after one year will be \$105, or 1.05 times our original deposit amount of \$100:

$$\$100 \cdot 1.05 = \$105.$$

If we left our \$105 in the account for a second year, our account would have a future value of \$105 · 1.05 = \$110.25. Thus, our account will have a future value of $\$100 \cdot 1.05^2$:

$$\$100 \cdot 1.05 \cdot 1.05 = \$100 \cdot 1.05^2 = \$110.25.$$

More generally, our account will have a future value of $\$100 \cdot 1.05^n$, where n is the number of years that the account will accumulate interest. Again, the concepts of interest and future value are dealt with more extensively in chapter 4.

We can use negative exponents to determine how much we would have to deposit now to obtain a given future value in the future. Suppose we wished to make a deposit now into a savings account paying 5% interest such that the amount in the account in two years were \$100. Thus, how much would we have to deposit now to obtain a given future value in two years? We find the solution to this problem as follows: $\$100 \cdot 1.05^{-2} = \$90.70$. This problem can be written

$$\$100 \cdot 1.05^{-2} = \frac{\$100}{1.05^2} = \$90.70.$$

---

[1] Compound interest means that interest accrues on accumulated interest on loans as well as principal.

2.4 THE ORDER OF ARITHMETIC OPERATIONS AND THE RULES OF ALGEBRA
(Background reading: section 2.3)

Many equations require combinations of different types and series of operations. Mathematicians use well-established rules for sequencing operations in more complicated equations, which may be summarized as follows:

A Operations within innermost sets of parentheses (or brackets) are performed first. After operations within innermost sets of parentheses are performed, operations may be performed within sets moving to outer levels, until operations within the outermost level are performed. For example, consider the expression: $10 \cdot \{[3 + (6 \cdot 4)] \cdot [5 \cdot (7 + 11)]\}$. This expression simplifies to $10 \cdot \{[3 + (24)] \cdot [5 \cdot (18)]\}$, and further simplifies to $10 \cdot \{[27] \cdot [90]\} = 10 \cdot \{2{,}430\} = 24{,}300$.

B Varying types of operations within a given level of parentheses are performed in the following order:
1 Exponents.
2 Multiplication and division (do these in any order).
3 Addition and subtraction (do these in any order).

Consider the equation $y = 12 + 4 \cdot 2^3$. This equation simplifies to $y = 12 + 4 \cdot 8 = 12 + 32 = 44$. The following equation may be simplified using a combination of rules A and B above:

$$y = 3 + \{4[3(2 \cdot 6 + 1) + 2(4 + 3 \cdot 4^{(1+2)}) + 7]^2\} + 3\{2 + [4 \cdot 2^3 \cdot (3 + 5^2)(2 + 4)]\},$$

$$y = 3 + \{4[3(12 + 1) + 2(4 + 3 \cdot 4^{(3)}) + 7]^2\} + 3\{2 + [4 \cdot 2^3 \cdot (3 + 25)(6)]\},$$

$$y = 3 + \{4[3(13) + 2(4 + 3 \cdot 64) + 7]^2\} + 3\{2 + [4 \cdot 8 \cdot (28)(6)]\},$$

$$y = 3 + \{4[39 + 2(4 + 192) + 7]^2\} + 3\{2 + [5{,}376]\},$$

$$y = 3 + \{4[39 + 2(196) + 7]^2\} + 3\{5{,}378\},$$

$$y = 3 + \{4[39 + 392 + 7]^2\} + 16{,}134,$$

$$y = 3 + \{4[438]^2\} + 16{,}134 = 3 + \{4 \cdot 191{,}844\} + 16{,}134$$
$$= 3 + 767{,}376 + 16{,}134,$$

$$y = 783{,}513.$$

Notice that in the earlier formulations of the equations, higher levels of parentheses are distinguished with brackets [ ] and braces { }.
Now, consider the following equation:

$$PVA = \$1{,}000 \cdot \left[\frac{1}{0.05} - \frac{1}{0.05 \cdot (1 + 0.05)^5} \right].$$

This equation, which is used for evaluating series of cash flows over time (see section 4.9 for more details on its application) can be simplified and solved as follows:

$$PVA = \$1,000 \cdot \left[\frac{1}{0.05} - \frac{1}{0.05 \cdot (1 + 0.05)^5} \right] = \$1,000 \cdot \left[\frac{1}{0.05} - \frac{1}{0.05 \cdot (1.05)^5} \right]$$

$$= \$1,000 \cdot \left[\frac{1}{0.05} - \frac{1}{0.05 \cdot 1.27628} \right] = \$1,000 \cdot \left[\frac{1}{0.05} - \frac{1}{0.063814} \right]$$

$$= \$1,000 \cdot \left[\frac{1}{0.05} - 15.670523 \right] = \$1,000 \cdot [20 - 15.670523]$$

$$= \$1,000 \cdot 4.329476 = \$4,329.48.$$

APPLICATION 2.2: INITIAL DEPOSIT AMOUNTS
(A more complete presentation of this material is provided in chapter 4)

Suppose that you wished to have $1,000 in your bank account in five years. Your bank account pays interest at an annually compounded rate of 10% or 0.10. How much would you need to deposit in your account today for your balance to be $1,000 in five years?

First, we note that the account balance $(1 + 0.10)$ times as great at any point in time as it was one year earlier because of the 10% interest rate. For example, the account will have a balance of $1,000 after five years; in four years, the account will have a balance of $909.91 (which is $1,000 ÷ [1 + 0.1]$). Furthermore, the account balance will be $(1 + 0.1)^n$ times as large as n years earlier. We know that the future value of the account will be $1000; what will be the initial deposit amount? Let X_0 represent the initial deposit amount of the account, solved for as follows:

$$X_0 = \frac{\$1,000}{(1 + 0.10)^5} = \frac{\$1,000}{(1.10)^5} = \frac{\$1,000}{1.61051} = 620.92.$$

Note the order of arithmetic operations in the above equation.

2.5 THE NUMBER e

The number e, also known as the base of the natural exponential function, has a non-repeating, nonterminating decimal value of approximately 2.7182818. The number e may be characterized more precisely as follows:

$$e = \left(1 + \frac{1}{\infty} \right)^{\infty} \approx 2.7182818. \tag{2.5}$$

Table 2.1   Computing the number e

m	$y = \left(1 + \dfrac{1}{m}\right)^{m}$	y
1	$y = (1 + 1/2)^2$	2
2	$y = (1 + 1/3)^3$	2.25
3	$y = (1 + 1/4)^4$	2.37037037
4	$y = (1 + 1/1)^1$	2.44140625
5	$y = (1 + 1/5)^5$	2.48832
6	$y = (1 + 1/6)^6$	2.521626372
7	$y = (1 + 1/7)^7$	2.546499697
8	$y = (1 + 1/8)^8$	2.565784514
9	$y = (1 + 1/9)^9$	2.581174792
10	$y = (1 + 1/10)^{10}$	2.59374246
100	$y = (1 + 1/100)^{100}$	2.704813829
1,000	$y = (1 + 1/1,000)^{1,000}$	2.716923932
100,000	$y = (1 + 1/100,000)^{100,000}$	2.718268237
10,000,000	$y = (1 + 1/10,000,000)^{10,000,000}$	2.718281694

Obviously, one cannot use the arithmetic operations described thus far to divide by infinity or raise the sum to the power infinity. However, one can replace the value for infinity with the variable m and observe what happens to the value of the function y in the following as m is replaced by integers of increasing value:

$$y = \left(1 + \frac{1}{m}\right)^{m}.$$

As m approaches infinity, y approaches the value of the number e. Table 2.1 provides computations to demonstrate how y approaches e as m approaches infinity. The number e is defined again in chapter 8. This number e is used as the base for the natural log function (discussed in the next section) and is particularly useful for computations involving continuous growth or compounding (see chapter 4).

2.6   LOGARITHMS
(Background reading: sections 2.2 and 2.5)

A logarithm is a power to which another number (called the base) must be raised to obtain a given value. For example, suppose we wish to find the power n to which 10 must be raised in order to obtain 100; that is, we wish to solve $100 = 10^n$ for n. The number 2 is the appropriate power or exponent such that $100 = 10^2$. The number 10 is our base and 2 is the logarithm (or log) of 100. Thus we say that 2 is the base ten log of 100. The base ten logs are the second most commonly used in finance.

The most commonly used log in finance is the natural log (also called a Napierian log). The base of the natural log is the number e, which as we observed in section 2.5, has a nonrepeating, nonterminating decimal value of approximately 2.7182818. The natural log is particularly useful for certain types of computations involving continuous growth or compounding (see chapter 4). If $x = \ln(y)$, we say that x is the natural log of y and $y = e^x \approx 2.718^x$. For example, the natural log of 22 is approximately 3.091 (i.e., $\ln(22) \approx 3.091$), which means that $e^{3.091} \approx 22$ or $2.718^{3.091} \approx 22$.

The following rules of operation apply to operations involving logs of a given base:

$$\log(x \cdot y) = \log(x) + \log(y),$$

$$\log(x \div y) = \log(x) - \log(y),$$

$$\log(x^y) = y \cdot \log(x).$$

Logs are useful when solving for n in exponential functions such as $y = cx^n$. If $y = cx^n$, then from the rules of operation above, the following must be true: $\ln(y) = \ln(c) + n \cdot \ln(x)$. Suppose, for example, that we wished to solve for n in the following: $50 = 3 \cdot 7^n$. We may do so by finding the logs of both sides of the equation: $\ln(50) = \ln(3) + n \cdot \ln(7)$. Solving, we obtain $3.912 = 1.0986 + n \cdot 1.9459$; $n = 1.4458$.

APPLICATION 2.3: THE TIME NEEDED TO DOUBLE YOUR MONEY
(You may also wish to read related material in chapter 4)

How long would it take to double the balance of a bank account paying interest compounded at an annual rate of 5%? For example, how long would it take $1,000 to double to $2,000 in a 5% bank account? We determine this by solving the following for n:

$$\$2,000 = \$1,000(1 + 0.05)^n.$$

First, divide both sides by 1,000 and find the natural logs of both sides, to obtain

$$\ln\left(\frac{2,000}{1,000}\right) = \ln[(1 + 0.05)^n] = n \cdot \ln(1.05).$$

We rewrite this equation to obtain

$$\ln(2) = n \cdot \ln(1.05),$$

$$0.693147 = n \cdot 0.04879.$$

We solve for n, the number of years required to double our money in the bank account, as follows:

$$\frac{0.693147}{0.04879} = n = 14.2067.$$

$1,000 must be left in this 5% bank account for 14.2067 years to double. A simple rule of thumb sometimes used by practitioners and based on this analysis is known as the *Rule of 72*. If one divides 72 (it is slightly higher than 100 times the natural log of 2) by the interest rate of the account expressed as a percentage (in this case, 5% which is slightly higher than 100 times the natural log of 1 plus the interest rate), one can *approximate* the length of time required for a bank account to double. In this case, our approximation would hold that the account would require 72/5 = 14.4 years to double.

2.7   SUBSCRIPTS

Consider the expression x_i, which might be read "x subscript i" or "x sub i." Subscripts are variables or numbers that serve to identify the variables with which they are associated. For example, in the expression $x_1 + x_2 + x_3$, which reads "x sub one plus x sub two plus x sub three," the subscripts distinguish the x variables from each other. Sometimes it is more practical to identify variables with subscripts than with different letters, especially when there are many variables or there is a well-defined order to them.

Frequently, the subscript t is used to identify time periods. For example, suppose that an investment will pay its owner $100 in one year, $200 in two years, $300 in three years, and $400 in four years. Let the variable CF_t refer to the cash flow (payment) generated by the investment for a given year t. The following table associates each cash flow with its appropriate identifying subscript:

t	CF_t
1	$CF_1 = \$100$
2	$CF_2 = \$200$
3	$CF_3 = \$300$
4	$CF_4 = \$400$

2.8   SUMMATIONS
(Background reading: sections 2.3 and 2.7)

The summation, or sigma, notation (Σ) is a "shorthand" means of expressing our intent to add a series of variables. Consider the following expression:

$$y = \sum_{i=1}^{n} x_i,$$ (2.6)

which reads "y equals the sum from i equals 1 to n of x sub i." This expression orders values of x from one (the first x) to n (the last x) and sums them. The subscript i serves as the counter (its value increases by one as we continue the operation) and the integer under the upper-case sigma (Σ) is the starting value for the order. The stopping point for the order is the superscript n. The sigma means that we will add all of the x values within the stated range.

Suppose that we wish to sum the following ordered series of variables: x_1, x_2, x_3, and x_4. There are two ways to represent this operation:

$$\sum_{i=1}^{4} x_i = x_1 + x_2 + x_3 + x_4.$$

If the series is long or involves many variables, the summation notation is a more efficient means of representing the summation operation. For most functions involving the summation notation, it will be necessary to perform another series of operations before adding. For example, consider the following:

$$z = \sum_{i=1}^{4} x_i^2 = x_1^2 + x_2^2 + x_3^2 + x_4^2,$$

which reads "z equals the sum from i equals one to four of x squared." Each of the x values must be squared before the summation takes place. Suppose, for example that $x_1 = 3$, $x_2 = 6$, $x_3 = 9$, and $x_4 = 12$. Then z would equal $3^2 + 6^2 + 9^2 + 12^2 = 9 + 36 + 81 + 144 = 270$.

APPLICATION 2.4: MEAN VALUES
(You may also wish to read related material in section 5.1)

A stock generated the following profits over a five-year period:

Year	Profit ($)
1	15
2	5
3	2
4	24
5	4

Let the subscript t represent time (years 1 through 5) and let π_t represent profit for a given year. The stopping value n for our summation will equal 5. We can determine the average or mean ($\bar{\pi}$) profit over the five-year period as follows:

$$\bar{\pi} = \frac{\sum_{t=1}^{n} \pi_t}{n} = \frac{\sum_{t=1}^{5} \pi_t}{5} = \frac{15 + 5 + 2 + 24 + 4}{5} = 10.$$

The value that we have computed here is often referred to as the arithmetic mean. We simply add the observed values and divide by the number of observations.

2.9 DOUBLE SUMMATIONS
(Background reading: section 2.8)

Double summations are very useful when working with variables that are to be paired and ordered for operations. The double summation notation is very useful for concisely representing many of the types of long and repetitive series of operations that arise in finance. The subscript notation can be generalized to denote a variety of character-istics associated with a variable. For example, consider the following array or matrix of numbers on the left, which can be identified by row and column numbers given in the array on the right:

$$\begin{bmatrix} 7 & 4 & 9 \\ 6 & 4 & 12 \\ 3 & 2 & 17 \end{bmatrix} \begin{bmatrix} a_{1,1} & a_{1,2} & a_{1,3} \\ a_{2,1} & a_{2,2} & a_{2,3} \\ a_{3,1} & a_{3,2} & a_{3,3} \end{bmatrix}$$

Each of the numbers in the first matrix is associated with a variable $a_{i,j}$, where the first subscript i represents the row of element $a_{i,j}$ and j represents the column of element $a_{i,j}$. Each of the three elements in a given row will have the same i subscript; each of the elements in a given column will have the same j subscript. For example, since the num-ber 12 is in the second row and third column, it is identified with variable $a_{2,3}$. Suppose that we wished to add the elements in the three rows and columns. We could add ele-ments across the top row, then across the second row and then across the bottom row and finally add the three row totals. This operation is equivalent to

$$y = \sum_{i=1}^{3} \sum_{j=1}^{3} a_{i,j} = [a_{1,1} + a_{1,2} + a_{1,3}] + [a_{2,1} + a_{2,2} + a_{2,3}] + [a_{3,1} + a_{3,2} + a_{3,3}],$$

$$y = \sum_{i=1}^{3} \sum_{j=1}^{3} a_{i,j} = [7 + 4 + 9] + [6 + 4 + 12] + [3 + 2 + 17],$$

$$y = \sum_{i=1}^{3} \sum_{j=1}^{3} a_{i,j} = [20] + [22] + [22] = 64.$$

We started with row 1 ($i = 1$) and summing the three variables in row 1. With $i = 1$, we set $j = 1$, $j = 2$, and $j = 3$ in order. We summed the three variables $a_{1,1}$, $a_{1,2}$, and $a_{1,3}$ to obtain 20. When we completed the summation in the first row, we moved to the second row, setting i equal to 2. With $i = 2$, we set $j = 1$, $j = 2$, and $j = 3$ in order. We summed the three variables $a_{2,1}$, $a_{2,2}$, and $a_{2,3}$ to obtain 22. We then repeated this operation for the third row. Finally, we summed the three row totals $20 + 22 + 22$ to obtain 64.

2.10 PRODUCTS
(Background reading: section 2.8)

The product, or $\prod$, notation provides a "shorthand" expression multiplying together a series of variables. Consider the following expression:

$$y = \prod_{i=1}^{n} x_i,$$

which reads "y equals the product from i equals 1 to n of terms labeled x sub i." This expression orders values of x from one to n and multiplies them. The subscript i serves as the counter (its value increases by one as we continue the operation) and the integer under the upper-case pi ($\prod$) is the starting value for the order. The stopping point for the order is the superscript n. The pi means that we will multiply together all of the x values.

Suppose that we wish to multiply the following ordered series of variables: x_1, x_2, x_3, and x_4. There are two ways to represent this operation:

$$\prod_{i=1}^{4} x_i = x_1 \cdot x_2 \cdot x_3 \cdot x_4.$$

If the series is long or involves many variables, the product notation is a more efficient means of representing the multiplication operations. For many functions involving the product notation, it will be necessary to perform another series of operations before multiplying. For example, consider the following:

$$z = \prod_{i=1}^{3} x_i^2 = x_1^2 \cdot x_2^2 \cdot x_3^2,$$

which reads "z equals the product from i equals one to three of x squared." Each of the x values must be squared before the multiplication takes place.

APPLICATION 2.5: GEOMETRIC MEANS
(Background reading: application 2.4)

Geometric means are particularly useful for situations involving compound interest, returns, or growth. The geometric mean of a series is computed as the nth root of the product of the series

$$\bar{x}_g = \sqrt[n]{\prod_{i=1}^{n} x_i}. \qquad (2.7)$$

For example, suppose the value of a $1,000 security held by an investor grew by 10% in its first year and 20% in its second year, but lost 30% in its third year. Its final value would be determined as follows:

$$V_3 = 1,000 \cdot [(1 + 0.10) \cdot (1 + 0.20) \cdot (1 - 0.30)] = 924.$$

The arithmetic mean return on this investment is computed to be 0 ([0.10 + 0.20 − 0.30] ÷ 3 = 0), although we saw in the above equation that the investment actually lost value. This discrepancy is due to the fact that the arithmetic mean return does not account for the compounding of growth before the year it lost value. The geometric mean return, computed as follows, will account for the compounding of growth:

$$\bar{x}_g = \sqrt[3]{(1 + 0.10) \cdot (1 + 0.20) \cdot (1 - 0.30)} = \sqrt[3]{1.1 \cdot 1.2 \cdot 0.7} = \sqrt[3]{0.924} = 0.974.$$

We see that, on average, the investment will be 0.974 as large in each of the three years than in the previous year; thus, the geometric mean growth rate is computed as $1 - 0.974 = -0.026$.

APPLICATION 2.6: THE TERM STRUCTURE OF INTEREST RATES
(Background reading: application 2.5)

The term structure of interest rates is concerned with the change in interest rates on debt securities resulting from varying times to maturity on the debt. For example, it may be concerned with explaining why the interest rate on debt maturing in one year might be 4% versus 7% for debt maturing in 20 years. Generally, at a given point in time, we observe longer-term interest rates exceeding shorter-term rates, although this is not always the case (for example, the years 1980–3). There are several theories which attempt to explain relationship between long- and short-term interest rates. Among the best known is the Pure Expectations Theory, which states that long-term spot rates (interest rates on loans originating now) can be explained as a product of short-term spot rates and short-term forward rates (interest rates on loans committed to now but actually originating at later dates). For example, if we borrow now for three years at 5%, the three-year spot rate equals 5%. If we commit now with a bank to borrow in one year at 8% for one year, the one year forward rate for one year equals 8%. Thus, we may write $y_{0,3} = 0.05$ and $y_{1,2} = 0.08$, where the first subscript represents the year in which the loan is originated and the second subscript represents the year in which the loan is repaid. Where $y_{t,m}$ is the rate on a loan originated at time t to be repaid at time m, the Pure Expectations Theory defines the relationship between long- and short-term interest rates as follows:

$$(1 + y_{0,n})^n = \prod_{t=1}^{n} (1 + y_{t-1,t}). \tag{2.8}$$

Thus, the long-term spot rate $y_{0,t}$ is defined as the nth root of the product of the one-period spot rate $y_{0,1}$ and a series of one-period forward rates $y_{t-1,t}$ minus one. That is, the long-term spot rate equals the geometric mean of the short-term (one-year) spot and forward rates minus one.

Consider an example where we can borrow money today for one year at 5%; $y_{0,1} = 0.05$. Suppose that we are able to obtain a commitment to obtain a one-year loan one year from now at an interest rate of 8%. Thus, the one-year forward rate on a loan originated in one year equals 8%. According to the Pure Expectations Theory, we compute the two-year spot rate as follows:

$$(1 + y_{0,2})^2 = \prod_{t=1}^{2} (1 + y_{t-1,t}) = (1 + 0.05)(1 + 0.08) = 1.134,$$

$$y_{0,2} = (1 + 0.05)(1 + 0.08)^{1/2} - 1 = \sqrt{1.134} - 1 = 0.0648944.$$

2.11 FACTORIAL PRODUCTS
(Background reading: section 2.10)

Factorial products are very useful for determining numbers of possible combinations of objects and for working through different types of probability distributions. A factorial product ($n!$) is defined as follows:

$$n! = n \cdot (n - 1) \cdot (n - 2) \cdot (n - 3) \cdot \ldots \cdot 2 \cdot 1 = \prod_{i=0}^{n-1} (n - i). \qquad (2.9)$$

For example, $5! = 5 \cdot 4 \cdot 3 \cdot 2 \cdot 1 = 120$.

Suppose that we wished to purchase five given stocks one at a time. How many possible orderings of transactions are there? There are five different stocks that we could purchase first. Given our first purchase, there are four different stocks that we could purchase second. Thus, there are $5 \cdot 4 = 20$ possible orderings for the first two purchases. Then, there are three possible orderings for the third purchase, given our first two purchases. This process continues until we notice that there are $5! = 5 \cdot 4 \cdot 3 \cdot 2 \cdot 1 = 120$ possible orderings for the five stock purchases. Thus, $n!$ represents the number of potential orderings or permutations of a series of n events. We will make extensive use of factorial products later when we discuss probability and option pricing. We also note that $0! = 1$ and that $69! \approx 1.7112 \cdot 10^{98}$.

APPLICATION 2.7: DERIVING THE NUMBER e
(Background reading: section 2.5)

The number e was defined in section 2.5 and approximated at 2.718. A second definition which is often quite useful in finance and probability computations is given as follows:

$$e = \sum_{i=0}^{\infty} \frac{1}{n!} = \frac{1}{1} + \frac{1}{1} + \frac{1}{2} + \frac{1}{6} + \frac{1}{24} + \frac{1}{120} + \ldots \qquad (2.10)$$

2.12 PERMUTATIONS AND COMBINATIONS
(Background reading: section 2.11)

A permutation of a set of objects is an ordered arrangement of some or all of the objects in the set. In section 2.11, we demonstrated that a set of n objects can be ordered $n!$ ways. More generally, a set of r objects taken from a set of n objects can be ordered $_nP_r$ ways where $_nP_r$ is defined as follows:

$$_nP_r = \frac{n!}{(n-r)!} = n(n-1)(n-2)\cdots(n-r+1). \tag{2.11}$$

For example, suppose that an investor wishes to purchase 5 stocks from 12 in a particular industry. Suppose that she will select 5 stocks from the 12 and then enter purchases in sequence one at a time. How many possible orderings (permutations) of 5 purchases from an industry of 12 must she select from? This number is determined as follows:

$$_nP_r = {}_{12}P_5 = \frac{12!}{(12-5)!} = \frac{479,001,600}{5,040} = 95,040.$$

There are 12 possible selections for the first stock, 11 for the second, 10 for the third, and so on:

$$_nP_r = {}_{12}P_5 = 12\cdot 11\cdot 10\cdot 9\cdot 8 = 95,040.$$

We have determined the possible number of orderings of stock purchases; now we will determine the number of possible combinations of stocks. We will now assume that the purchase order for the five stocks combines all five stocks, rather than assume five separate sequential purchase orders. Where $_nP_r$ represented the number of orderings of sequential purchases, $_nC_r$ (which reads "n choose r") will represent the number of possible combinations irrespective of order:

$$_nC_r = \binom{n}{r} = \frac{n!}{r!(n-r)!} = \frac{_nP_r}{r!}. \tag{2.12}$$

In our example, there will be 792 possible combinations of 12 stocks from which the investor can select 5:

$$_{12}C_5 = \binom{12}{5} = \frac{12!}{5!(12-5)!} = \frac{12\cdot11\cdot10\cdot9\cdot8\cdot7\cdot6\cdot5\cdot4\cdot3\cdot2\cdot1}{(5\cdot4\cdot3\cdot2\cdot1)\cdot(7\cdot6\cdot5\cdot4\cdot3\cdot2\cdot1)}$$

$$_{12}C_5 = \binom{12}{5} = \frac{12\cdot11\cdot10\cdot9\cdot8}{5\cdot4\cdot3\cdot2\cdot1} = \frac{95,040}{120} = 792.$$

EXERCISES

2.1. Solve each of the following for y:

(a) $y = 5^2$;   (e) $y = 5^{-2}$;   (i) $y = 5^{1/2}$;   (m) $y = 5^{3/2}$;
(b) $y = 5^3$;   (f) $y = 5^{-3}$;   (j) $y = 5^{1/3}$;   (n) $y = 5^{-1/3}$;
(c) $y = 5^4$;   (g) $y = 5^{-4}$;   (k) $y = 5^{1/4}$;   (o) $y = 5^{3/4}$;
(d) $y = 25^2$;   (h) $y = 25^{-2}$;   (l) $y = 25^{1/2}$;   (p) $y = 25^{3/4}$.

2.2. Solve each of the following for y:

(a) $y = 5^2 \cdot 5^{-2}$;   (e) $y = 5^{1/2} \cdot 5^{3/2}$;
(b) $y = 5^3 \cdot 5^{-3}$;   (f) $y = 5^{1/3} \cdot 5^{-3}$;
(c) $y = 5^4 \cdot 5^{-4}$;   (g) $y = 5^{1/4} \cdot 5^{3/4}$;
(d) $y = 25^2 \cdot 25^{-2}$;   (h) $y = 25^{1/4} \cdot 25^{3/4}$.

2.3. Solve the following for FV: $FV = 50(1 + 0.3)^4$.

2.4. Solve the following for PV: $PV = 180(1 + 0.2)^{-0.5}$.

2.5. Simplify the following:

(a) $y = 4x^3 \cdot 6(5x + 7x)$;
(b) $y = 7(2x^2 + 3x - 5x^2) + 4x$;
(c) $y = 25 + \{2x[3x + 4(x + 5)^2 \cdot 6] - 5\} - 7x^2$.

2.6. Solve each of the following for y:

(a) $y = 9(4(7 + 3^2)^2)^{0.5} + 6^3 \cdot 5(2 + 7)$;
(b) $y = ((7 + 2^4)(3^3 \cdot 4^2 + 2)^3)^{-0.5}$.

2.7. Solve the following for PVA:

$$PVA = \$250 \cdot \left[\frac{1}{0.08} - \frac{1}{0.08 \cdot (1 + 0.08)^7} \right].$$

2.8. Find the following natural logs:

(a) $\ln(0.000001)$;   (d) $\ln(1.1)$;   (g) $\ln(3)$;   (j) $\ln(1,000)$.
(b) $\ln(0.5)$;   (e) $\ln(2.7)$;   (h) $\ln(10)$;
(c) $\ln(1)$;   (f) $\ln(2.718)$;   (i) $\ln(100)$;

2.9. Determine how long it takes to double the money in a bank paying interest compounded annually at each of the following rates:

(a) 0.03;   (c) 0.07;   (e) 0.12;
(b) 0.05;   (d) 0.10;   (f) 0.15.

2.10. Work through each of the parts of problem 2.9 using the Rule of 72.

2.11. The future value of an account whose interest is compounded can be approximated with the following future-value formula:

$$FV_n = PV \cdot e^{rn}.$$

A simple rule used by practitioners holds that the length of time that it takes for an account to double when interest is compounded equals 0.72 divided by the interest rate (expressed as a decimal). Demonstrate this rule to be approximately correct using the future-value equation expressed above.

2.12. Demonstrate that the number e is the future value of a 10-year account with an initial deposit of $1 and an interest rate of 0.10 compounded continuously.

2.13. Consider the following series:

t	X
1	15
2	25
3	35
4	45

(a) Identify each of the variables X with a subscript t.
(b) What is the value of $\sum_{t=1}^{4} X_t$?
(c) What is the value of $\sum_{t=1}^{4} 3X_t$?
(d) What is the value of $\sum_{t=1}^{4} 3X_t^2$?
(e) What is the value of $\prod_{t=1}^{4} 3X_t^2$?
(f) What is the arithmetic mean of X_t?
(g) What is the geometric mean of X_t?

2.14. Let $w_1 = 0.4$, $w_2 = 0.5$, and $w_3 = 0.1$. Furthermore, the following table (or "matrix") provides values for $x_{i,j}$:

$$\begin{bmatrix} 7 & 4 & 9 \\ 6 & 4 & 12 \\ 3 & 2 & 17 \end{bmatrix}.$$

(a) Compute $\sum_{i=1}^{3} w_i$.
(b) Compute $\sum_{i=1}^{3} \sum_{j=1}^{3} w_i w_j x_{i,j}$.

2.15. Suppose that the one-year spot rate $y_{0,1}$ of interest is 5%. Investors are expecting that the one-year spot rate one year from now will increase to 6%; thus, the one-year forward rate $y_{1,2}$ on a loan originated in one year is 6%. Furthermore, assume that investors are expecting that the one-year spot rate two years from now will increase to 7%; thus, the one-year forward rate $y_{2,3}$ on a loan originated in two years is 7%. Based on the pure expectations hypothesis, what is the three-year spot rate?

2.16. Solve the following for FV: $FV = \sum_{t=1}^{4} 25(1 + 0.10)^t$.

2.17. Solve each of the following for x:

(a) $x = 8!$;
(b) $x = 9!$;
(c) $x = 0!$.

2.18. Solve each of the following:

(a) $_6P_4$;   (d) $_6C_4$;
(b) $_4P_4$;   (e) $_4C_4$;
(c) $_8P_2$;   (f) $_8C_2$.

APPENDIX 2.A   AN INTRODUCTION TO THE EXCEL™ SPREADSHEET

This appendix is intended to introduce the reader to a few of the bare essentials for working with spreadsheets such as Excel™, Lotus™, and Quattro®Pro. We will emphasize Excel here, because it is currently the best-selling spreadsheet program, but most of these basics will also apply to other spreadsheet programs as well. Excel is an electronic spreadsheet program designed to perform mathematics, statistics, and financial computations as intended by the user. The spreadsheet is a rectangular array comprising cells that are organized into rows identified by numbers and columns identified by letters. Normally, when one loads a new Excel file, the cursor is initiated in cell A1, the uppermost and leftmost cell on the spreadsheet. Arrow keys on the keyboard can be used to move the cursor about the screen.

The user creates a spreadsheet file by moving the cursor to appropriate cells and making entries with the keyboard or mouse. Three of the most important types of entries are values, labels, and formulas. Suppose, for example, that I wished to compose a simple income statement for a firm. The firm had $1,000 in sales and $600 in costs. I could enter labels in column A to identify the numbers and formula that I will enter in column B. As we see in table 2.A.1, I enter labels in cells A1, A2, and A3 for Sales, Costs and Profits. We enter numbers in cells B1 and B2 for Sales and Costs. In cell B3, I enter in the formula =b2-b3 to calculate profits.

The user should be aware of a few spreadsheet conventions. Label entries either begin with a letter or an apostrophe. Number entries begin with a number, decimal sign, plus

Table 2.A.1 A simple income statement example

	A	B
1	Sales	1000
2	Costs	600
3	Profits	=b2-b1

	A	B
1	Sales	1000
2	Costs	600
3	Profits	400

What you enter   What appears on your screen.

Table 2.A.2 A simple formula example

	A	B
1	Coefficient	3
2	Base	4
3	Exponent	2
4	Result	=b1*b2^b3

	A	B
1	Coefficient	3
2	Base	4
3	Exponent	2
4	Result	48

What you enter   What appears on your screen

sign, or minus sign. Formula entries can begin with an equals sign or a number. The sign for the multiplication operation is * and the exponent operation is ^. Thus, 3 times 4 squared would be entered in the spreadsheet as 3*4^2. If the user wished to allow the coefficient, base and exponent to vary, he could create a spreadsheet like that in table 2.A.2. I enter numerical values for my coefficient, base, and exponent in cells B1, B2, and B3. The result to my equation is obtained by typing the formula =b1*b2^b3 into cell B4. Now, the user may change values in cells B1, B2, and B3 to obtain the result for any equation of the form $y = cx^n$.

To edit a formula or other entry, the user may move the cursor to the appropriate cell and left click, then move the cursor to the Formula Bar near the top of the screen (the entry in the cell should appear there). One can edit the cell in the Formula Bar. To save a worksheet file, the user may either click the diskette icon near the top of the screen or click File in the top left-hand corner, then Save As and follow instructions. To print a file, the user may either click the printer icon near the top of the screen or click File in the top left-hand corner, then Print and follow instructions. One exits by clicking the X button in the top right-hand corner of the screen. The Escape key (Esc) in the upper left-hand corner of the keyboard may sometimes be used to block an action that has been initiated.

Among the most useful functions for finance applications in Excel is the Paste Function (f_x) on the toolbar near the top of the screen. This function will return a menu of categories of formulas including financial, statistical, math, and trig functions. Work through the menu and follow instructions to use a particular function. Function definitions and help can be obtained by clicking Help or a question mark button on a page or pallette.

Perhaps the best way to learn how to use a spreadsheet is simply to experiment. Modern electronic spreadsheets are menu-driven. Menus and toolbars near the top of the screen will provide many options and categories of commands and functions. One of the most important things to remember while working is to *save frequently* and to back up your spreadsheet files, because accidents frequently occur that can cause you to lose work.

CHAPTER THREE
A REVIEW OF ELEMENTARY MATHEMATICS: ALGEBRA AND SOLVING EQUATIONS

3.1 ALGEBRAIC MANIPULATIONS
(Background reading: section 2.4)

Algebraic manipulations are series or combinations of arithmetic operations on equations. The usual purpose for manipulating an equation is to solve for a given variable. Two types of manipulations will be used throughout this text:

1 *Addition or subtraction.* Here we either add or subtract a constant, variable or another equation to the equation we wish to manipulate.
2 *Multiplication.* Here we multiply (or divide) the equation by a constant (other than zero) or a variable.

These operations may usually be applied in any sequence or combination. In order to maintain the equality stated by an equation, we must perform the same series of arithmetic operations on both sides of the equality.

Suppose that we wished to solve the following for x: $24 = 15 + 2x$. We may subtract a constant (15) from both sides of the equation to obtain: $24 - 15 = 2x$, or $9 = 2x$. We may also divide both sides of our new equation by a constant (2) to obtain: $4.5 = x$. We now have successfully solved our original equation for x.

Consider the following example:

$$900 = \frac{1,000}{1+r}.$$

We may solve for r by first multiplying both sides of the equation by $(1 + r)$ to obtain $900(1 + r) = 1,000$. Next, divide both sides of the equation by 900 to obtain $(1 + r) = 1,000/900 = 1.1111$. Finally, subtract 1 from both sides of the equation to obtain $r = 0.1111$.

Next, consider a slightly more complex equation:

$$900 = 500 + \frac{500}{(1+r)^2}.$$

To solve this equation for x, subtract 500 from both sides:

$$900 - 500 = \frac{500}{(1+r)^2}.$$

Simplify the left side and find the positive square root of both sides:[1]

$$\sqrt{400} = \frac{\sqrt{500}}{1+r}.$$

Continue to rewrite as follows:

$$\sqrt{400}(1+r) = \sqrt{500},$$

$$r = \frac{\sqrt{500}}{\sqrt{400}} - 1 = \frac{22.36068}{20} - 1 = 0.118034.$$

Geometric expansions

If your algebra is particularly "rusty," you may wish to work through a few of the exercises following this chapter and applications 3.1 through 3.3 before proceeding with this example, applying a technique known as a geometric expansion. In any case, suppose that we wished to solve the following equation for x: $1 = 0.5 + 0.5x + 0.5x^2 + 0.5x^3 + 0.5x^4 + 0.5x^5$. It will not be possible in this example to isolate x by itself on one side of the equation with everything else on the other side; that is, this equation has no closed form solution for x. We will need to find another solution algorithm or substitute values for x until we find one that works. However, this substitution process may be substantially simplified by reducing the length of the original equation. One method for reducing the length of this equation is to first multiply both sides by our variable (x) to obtain: $x = 0.5x + 0.5x^2 + 0.5x^3 + 0.5x^4 + 0.5x^5 + 0.5x^6$. If we subtract our original equation from our new equation, we are able to cancel a number of terms, thus simplifying the equation:

$$
\begin{array}{rll}
x = & 0.5x + 0.5x^2 + 0.5x^3 + 0.5x^4 + 0.5x^5 + 0.5x^6 \\
-1 = & -0.5 - 0.5x - 0.5x^2 - 0.5x^3 - 0.5x^4 - 0.5x^5 \\
\hline
(x-1) = & -0.5 + 0.5x^6
\end{array}
$$

---

[1]   A positive number will have two square roots, one positive and one negative. We should take care to use the appropriate value to solve our equation. In finance examples, positive square roots will more frequently (although not always) provide the more meaningful solution than the negative square root.

Notice again how subtracting the equations canceled a number of terms. Our equation is much less cumbersome now. We have performed this procedure, known as a geometric expansion, to simplify our original equation. To simplify it further, we add 1 to both sides, to obtain $x = 0.5 + 0.5x^6$, or $0.5x^6 - x = -0.5$. This is probably the simplest form of our original equation (although the process of simplifying it did change the solution set for the equation, as we will see later). We may now substitute values for x until we find one (or more) that will work. As $0.5x^6 - x$ approaches -0.5 with our substituted values for x, our substituted values will approach the true value for x. In this example, we will find that our solution for x is approximately 0.5086603917. Verify this by substituting 0.5086603917 for x in our original equation. Although our original equation has only one solution (0.5086603917), our simplified equation created with the geometric expansion does have a second solution (check the value $x = 1$). We should be careful to test our solutions when we perform complicated algebraic manipulations, since our final simplified equations do not always retain the same values as our original equations. We will provide a more complete description of geometric expansions in section 3.4, discuss finance applications of the geometric expansion in chapter 4, and consider applications of substitution methods in chapter 5.

APPLICATION 3.1: PURCHASE POWER PARITY

An important concept in international finance is that a given commodity must sell for the same price (after adjusting for currency prices) in two countries. Of course, this law must be adjusted for differences in costs of providing the commodity, taxes, and so on. One well known (though somewhat tongue-in-cheek) test of the purchase power parity is the "Big Mac Standard," popularized by *The Economist*. McDonald's Corporation's Big Mac hamburgers are generally regarded to be more or less identical all over the world. If purchase power parity holds, then the Big Mac should sell for the same price in each country. For example, in the April 9, 1994 issue, *The Economist* reported that the Big Mac cost $2.30 in a U.S. restaurant. The Big Mac cost £1.81 in the U.K. At the then prevailing exchange rate of $1.46/£, the dollar equivalent cost was $2.64; the British pound appeared overvalued by approximately 15%. In Thailand, the Big Mac cost Baht 48. At an exchange rate of Baht 25.3/$, this represented a dollar cost of $1.90 per Big Mac. The Baht appeared undervalued by 17%. Thus, the Law of One Price did not hold with respect to Big Macs. However, one must note that Big Macs are not easily exported out of countries where they are underpriced; thus, it is difficult for markets to adjust to purchase power parity violations. As we suggested earlier, this relationship among prices account for differences in taxes, subsidies, labor, and other production costs.

Suppose that we expected that purchase power parity should hold between the United States and Canada. Assume that the exchange rate between U.S. dollars and Canadian dollars is *CanD*1/*USD*0.64. That is, one dollar Canadian will purchase 0.64 dollars U.S. If *USD*2.30 purchases one Big Mac in the U.S., how much should a Big Mac cost in Canada? This problem is formulated as follows:

$$CanD\ Big\ Mac\ Cost = USD2.30 \cdot \frac{CanD1.00}{USD0.64} = 2.30 \cdot 1.5625 = CanD3.59375.$$

Now, consider an example involving three currencies concerning cross rates of exchange. Assume that 2.5 Swiss francs are required to purchase one U.S. dollar. If 0.64 U.S. dollars are required to purchase one Canadian dollar, how many Canadian dollars are required to purchase ten Swiss francs? If we assume that purchase power parity holds, how many Swiss francs are required to purchase one Big Mac? First, we will determine the Canadian dollar/Swiss franc exchange rate as follows:

$$SFr \ per \ CanD = 2.5 SFr \ per \ USD \div \frac{CanD1.00}{USD0.64} = 2.5 \div 1.5625 = SFr1.6.$$

Thus, $10/1.6 = 6.25$ Canadian dollars are required to purchase ten Swiss francs. In Switzerland, one Big Mac should cost 2.5 *SFr per USD* times *2.30 USD* per Big Mac, or *SFr*5.75, when purchase power parity holds.

APPLICATION 3.2: FINDING BREAK-EVEN PRODUCTION LEVELS

Suppose that a firm produces a product that can be sold for a price of $P = \$10$ per unit such that its total annual revenues equals $TR = PQ = 10Q$. The variable Q represents the number of units of the product produced and sold by the firm. Further suppose that the firm incurs two types of costs in its production process, fixed and variable. Fixed costs FC include overhead expenditures totaling $\$100,000$ per year. Variable costs VC incurred by the firm include raw materials and direct labor. These costs are $\$6$ per unit produced. Total variable costs are simply the product of variable costs per unit VC and total production output Q. The firm's profit function is defined as follows as total revenues minus the sum of fixed and variable costs:

$$\pi = P \cdot Q - (FC + VC \cdot Q) = 10Q - (100{,}000 + 6 \cdot Q).$$

We can observe from the above equation that if the firm were to maintain an output level $Q = 0$, its profit would equal $-100{,}000$ due to its fixed costs. As the firm's output (and sales level) Q increases, profits π will increase. The firm's break-even production level is determined by solving for Q when profits π equal zero:

$$0 = 10Q - (100{,}000 + 6 \cdot Q).$$

First, we will add 100,000 to both sides:

$$100{,}000 = 10Q - 6Q.$$

Next, note that $10Q - 6Q = 4Q$; so that we will divide both sides of the above equation by 4, to obtain

$$100{,}000 \div 4 = Q^* = 25{,}000,$$

where Q^* is the break-even production level (the asterisk does not represent a product symbol here). Thus, the firm must produce 25,000 units to recover its fixed costs in order to break even. More generally, the following expression can be used to determine the break-even production level when the firm has linear revenue and cost functions:

$$Q^* = \frac{FC}{P - VC}.$$

The above expression is derived algebraically as follows:

$$0 = PQ^* - (FC + VC \cdot Q^*),$$

$$FC = PQ^* - VC \cdot Q^* = Q^*(P - VC).$$

Finally, divide both sides of the above equation by $P - VC$ to solve for Q^*.

APPLICATION 3.3: SOLVING FOR SPOT AND FORWARD INTEREST RATES
(Background reading: sections 1.3 and 2.10, and application 2.6)

Application 2.6 described the long-term interest rate as a geometric mean of the short-term spot rate and a series of short-term forward rates of interest. If current long- and short-term spot rates of interest are known, we may be able to solve algebraically for forward rates of interest. Suppose, for example, that the one-year spot rate of interest equals 8% ($y_{0,1} = 0.08$) and the two-year spot rate equals 12% ($y_{0,2} = 0.12$). What would these spot rates imply about the one-year spot rate anticipated one year hence? That is, what is the one-year forward rate on a loan originated one year from now? Given the pure expectations structure discussed in application 2.6, we wish to solve for $y_{1,2}$ in the following:

$$(1 + y_{0,2})^2 = (1 + y_{0,1})(1 + y_{1,2}) = (1 + 0.12)^2 = (1 + 0.08)(1 + y_{1,2}).$$

We can solve algebraically for the one-year forward rate $y_{1,2}$ by dividing both sides of the above equation by $1 + 0.08$, then subtracting 1 as follows:

$$\frac{(1 + 0.12)^2}{1 + 0.08} = 1 + y_{1,2},$$

$$\frac{(1 + 0.12)^2}{1 + 0.08} - 1 = y_{1,2} = 0.16148.$$

3.2 THE QUADRATIC FORMULA
(Background reading: section 3.1)

A *quadratic* equation is an equation of order two; that is, the highest exponent in the equation is two. The usual form of the quadratic equation written in polynomial form (in descending order of exponents) is $0 = ax^2 + bx + c$, where a, b, and c are coefficients. Note that the x^2 appears first, the x term second, and the constant third on the right side of the equation. Consider the following example: $2 = 5x^2 + 10x$. We subtract 2 from both sides and express this equation in polynomial form (set equal to zero and write it in descending order of exponents) as follows: $0 = 5x^2 + 10x - 2$. Now, we will generalize this equation by changing its numerical coefficients to variables. If we let $a = 5$, $b = 10$, and $c = -2$, we write this equation as $0 = ax^2 + bx + c$. This is a more general form of a quadratic equation. A useful formula known as the quadratic formula for solving a quadratic equation for the variable x is given as follows:

$$x = \frac{-b \pm \sqrt{b^2 - 4ac}}{2a}.$$

We can use this formula to solve for x when $b^2 \geq 4ac$. When $b^2 > 4ac$, we will obtain two real solutions for x, and when $b^2 = 4ac$, we will obtain one real solution. When $b^2 < 4ac$, there will be no real solution for x. Substituting in values from our original example for a, b, and c, we obtain the following two solutions for x:

$$x = \frac{-10 \pm \sqrt{10^2 - 4 \cdot 5 \cdot (-2)}}{2 \cdot 5} = \frac{-10 \pm \sqrt{100 - (-40)}}{10} = \frac{-10 \pm \sqrt{140}}{10}$$

$$= \frac{-10 \pm 11.83216}{10} = \frac{1.183216}{10} \text{ and } \frac{-21.83216}{10} = 0.1183216 \text{ and } -2.183216,$$

where $\pm$ signifies two operations: add terms following the $\pm$, and then, as a separate operation, subtract terms following the $\pm$.

APPLICATION 3.4: FINDING BREAK-EVEN PRODUCTION LEVELS
(Background reading: application 3.2)

Suppose that a firm's price and per-unit variable costs are functions of sales and output levels. For example, as the firm sells additional units, its market may become saturated and the price it receives for each additional unit of production may drop. Consider a firm whose price function is related to sales: $TR = 10 - 0.00001Q$. Total revenues equal the product of price and output $PQ = 10Q - 0.00001Q^2$. In addition, assume that this firm's per-unit variable costs increase with production: $4 + 0.00002Q$. Further, assume that this firm's fixed costs equal \$100,000, such that total costs equal $100,000 + 4Q + 0.00002Q^2$. Thus, the firm's profit function, total revenues minus total costs, is given by

$$\pi = 10Q - 0.00001Q^2 - (100,000 + 4Q + 0.00002Q^2),$$

which simplifies to

$$\pi = -0.00003Q^2 + 6Q - 100,000.$$

Note that the terms are arranged in descending order of exponents for Q. Our coefficients for this quadratic equation are $a = -0.00003$, $b = 6$, and $c = -100,000$. We can solve for the break-even production level by setting π equal to zero using the quadratic formula, as follows:

$$Q = \frac{-6 \pm \sqrt{6^2 - 4 \cdot (-0.00003) \cdot (-100,000)}}{2 \cdot (-0.00003)} = \frac{-6 \pm \sqrt{36 - (12)}}{-0.00006} = \frac{-6 \pm \sqrt{24}}{0.00006}$$

$$= \frac{-6 \pm 4.89898}{-0.00006} = \frac{-10.89898}{-0.00006} \text{ and } \frac{-1.10102}{-0.00006} = 181,633.33 \text{ and } 18,350.33 \text{ units.}$$

Either of the above production levels will enable the firm to break even with a profit level equal to zero (the arithmetic may round to a slightly different figure).

APPLICATION 3.5: FINDING THE PERFECTLY HEDGED PORTFOLIO

Certain parts of this example are fairly technical and not covered until chapter 5. However, the algebra application is still useful and, if you wish to avoid the more technical part of the discussion, you may simply skip to the equation beginning with zero. If you choose to read on, think of a portfolio as a combination of two or more securities with given proportions. The assets may provide for an opportunity to hedge risk through diversification. In certain extreme cases, two risky assets can be combined to hedge out all of the risk in the portfolio. Our problem here is to determine what proportions of total investment should be put into each of the assets.

Suppose that an investor wishes to combine two risky stocks into a portfolio that is perfectly safe. This perfectly safe combination of two risky stocks is actually possible if the two stocks' returns or profits are perfectly inversely correlated. This means that two risky stocks can be combined into a riskless portfolio if one of the securities always does well when the second security performs poorly and if the second security performs well whenever the first security performs poorly. There is a formula that can be used to measure the risk of a portfolio (also called portfolio variance, or σ_p^2) whose two securities' returns are perfectly inversely correlated:

$$\sigma_p^2 = (\sigma_1^2 + \sigma_2^2 + 2 \cdot \sigma_1 \cdot \sigma_2)w_1^2 - (2\sigma_2^2 + 2 \cdot \sigma_1 \cdot \sigma_2)w_1 + \sigma_2^2,$$

where σ_1^2 is the risk or variance of the first stock, σ_2^2 is the risk or variance of the second stock, and w_1 is the proportion of the portfolio invested in the first stock. The terms σ_1 and σ_2 are simply the square roots of the variances of the two stocks' returns (also known as standard deviations).

Now, suppose that the stocks' variances or risk levels are $\sigma_1^2 = 0.01$ and $\sigma_2^2 = 0.0324$. What must be the proportion of the investor's money invested in stock 1 (w_1) for the portfolio to be riskless? We shall assume that the remainder of the portfolio will be invested in stock 2. We want to find that w_1 value that will set portfolio variance equal to zero. We rewrite the above equation as follows:

$$0 = (0.01 + 0.0324 + 0.036)w_1^2 - (0.0648 + 0.036)w_1 + 0.0324,$$

$$0 = 0.0784w_1^2 - 0.1008w_1 + 0.0324.$$

We need to solve this equation for w_1 using the quadratic formula. This is accomplished as follows:

$$w_1 = \frac{-b + \sqrt{b^2 - 4ac}}{2a}, \qquad \text{where } a = 0.0784, b = -0.1008, \text{ and } c = 0.0324.$$

We fill in our coefficients' values to determine the proportion of the investor's money to be invested in stock 1:

$$w_1 = \frac{0.1008 \pm \sqrt{-0.1008^2 - 4 \cdot 0.0784 \cdot 0.0324}}{2 \cdot 0.0784} = \frac{0.1008 \pm \sqrt{0}}{0.1568} = 0.64286.$$

The value under the square root sign (radical) will be zero. Hence, there will be only one value for $w_1 = 0.64286$. Therefore, we find that the portfolio is riskless when $w_1 = 0.64286$. Thus, 64.286% of the riskless portfolio should be invested in stock 1 and 35.714% of the portfolio should be invested in stock 2. There will be more discussion of risk and portfolio mathematics in chapters 5 and 6.

3.3 SOLVING SYSTEMS OF EQUATIONS THAT CONTAIN MULTIPLE VARIABLES
(Background reading: section 3.1)

Systems of linear equations with multiple variables are often solved algebraically using the addition method. This method uses addition and multiplication principles. In order to use this method to solve the system completely, we normally must have the same number of equations as variables. That is, for two variables, we need two equations, for three variables, we need three equations, and so on.

For a two-variable system, we simply add or multiply the equations to cancel out or eliminate one variable. We then solve for the second variable, and plug it into either equation to solve for the first variable which we originally canceled. Consider the following two-equation system:

$$0.05 = 0.05x + 0.12y, \tag{A}$$

$$0.08 = 0.10x + 0.30y. \tag{B}$$

This system is easily solved by eliminating one of the unknown variables, x or y. One easy way to accomplish this is to multiply the first equation by -2, then add the two equations. This will enable us to eliminate the x variable. First, multiply both sides of (A) by -2,

$$-2 \cdot 0.05 = -2 \cdot 0.05x + -2 \cdot 0.12y,$$

which gives us the following equation:

$$-0.10 = -0.10x + -0.24y.$$

We then add this equation to our original equation (B):

$$
\begin{array}{rl}
-0.10 = & -0.10x + -0.24y \\
+0.08 = & 0.10x + 0.30y \\
\hline
-0.02 = & 0 + 0.06y
\end{array}
$$

Now we can easily solve for y:

$$0.06y = -0.02,$$

$$y = -0.02/0.06,$$

$$y = -0.333.$$

Now that we have found y, we can easily solve for x. This can be done by substituting -0.333 for y into either of our original equations:

$$0.05 = 0.05x + -0.333 \cdot 0.12,$$

$$0.05 = 0.05x + -0.04,$$

$$0.05x = 0.09,$$

$$x = 0.09/0.05,$$

$$x = 1.8.$$

To check our solution, we can also substitute -0.333 for y into our original second equation (B) to ensure that we obtain a value of 1.8 for x:

$$0.08 = 0.10x + 0.30 \cdot (-0.333),$$

$$0.10x = 0.18,$$

$$x = 1.8.$$

Solving systems of equations for three unknown variables is quite similar to solving for two variables. Solving a system of three variables requires three equations. We will attempt to substitute an equation for one of the variables and reduce the three equations to a two-equation system. When the system is reduced to two equations with two variables, we will solve just as we did in the previous example. Consider the following three-equation, three-variable example:

$$0.05 = 0.04x + 0.09y + 0.15z, \tag{A}$$

$$0.15 = 0.08x + 0.12y + 0.10z, \tag{B}$$

$$0.30 = 0.12x + 0.06y + 0.25z. \tag{C}$$

To begin, we solve one equation for x. We could have started with any other variable, but x in this example is eliminated slightly more easily. Solving the first equation for x results in the following:

$$0.04x = 0.05 - 0.09y - 0.15z,$$

$$x = 0.05/0.04 - 0.09y/0.04 - 0.15z/0.04,$$

$$x = 1.25 - 2.25y - 3.75z.$$

Now we substitute for x (our revised version of equation (A)) into the other two equations:

$$0.15 = 0.08(1.25 - 2.25y - 3.75z) + 0.12y + 0.10z, \tag{B1}$$

$$0.30 = 0.12(1.25 - 2.25y - 3.75z) + 0.06y + 0.25z. \tag{C1}$$

Simplifying these two equations results in the following:

$$0.05 = -0.06y - 0.20z, \tag{B2}$$

$$0.15 = -0.21y - 0.20z. \tag{C2}$$

Now we have two equations with two variables. This is solved exactly as our first example. Multiply the first equation by -1 and then add the two equations:

$$\begin{aligned} -0.05 &= 0.06y + 0.20z && \text{(B3)} \\ +\quad 0.15 &= -0.21y - 0.20z && \text{(C3)} \\ \hline 0.10 &= -0.15y \end{aligned}$$

$$y = -0.66667.$$

Now substitute for y in either equation (B3) or (C3) and solve for z:

$$0.05 = -0.06 \cdot (-0.66667) - 0.20z,$$

$$z = -0.05.$$

Finally, we have solved for y and z, and we can substitute these values into any of our three original equations to solve for x:

$$0.15 = 0.08x + 0.12 \cdot (-0.66667) + 0.10 \cdot (-0.05),$$

$$x = 2.9375.$$

These values for x, y, and z can be substituted into any of the other two original equations to verify our results.

APPLICATION 3.6: PRICING FACTORS

An investor has a theory that oil company stock prices are a function of the Dow Jones Industrial Average and the price of a gallon of gasoline. The investor believes that no other factors affect prices and that if the *DJIA* and gas prices were zero, stock prices would be zero. For example, Greaser Company stock is currently selling for $32.20 per share and Slick Oil Company stock is currently selling for $63.30 per share. The investor has determined that a one-point change in the Dow Jones Industrial Average (*DJIA*) changes the stock price of the Greaser Company by 0.01 and changes the price of the Slick Oil Company by 0.02. Thus, the sensitivity (often called beta) of Greaser Company stock to the *DJIA* equals 0.01 and the sensitivity or beta of the Slick Oil Company to the *DJIA* equals 0.02. A one cent change in the price of gasoline changes the stock price of the Greaser Company by $2 and changes the price of the Slick Oil Company by $3. Thus, the sensitivity or beta of Greaser Company stock to the gas price equals 2 and the sensitivity or beta of the Slick Oil Company to the gas price equals 3. In fact, the investor uses the following equations to price the Greaser and Slick Oil Companies:

$$P_G = \$32.20 = 0.01 \cdot DJIA + 2 \cdot (Gas\ Price), \qquad (A1)$$

$$P_S = \$63.30 = 0.02 \cdot DJIA + 3 \cdot (Gas\ Price). \qquad (B1)$$

By solving these two equations simultaneously, we are able to value the two factors that affect oil company stock prices, *assuming that the investor's theory is correct*. We will first multiply equation (A1) by 2, to obtain:

$$2 \cdot P_G = \$64.40 = 0.02 \cdot DJIA + 4 \cdot (Gas\ Price). \qquad (A2)$$

Now, subtract equation (B1) from equation (A2):

$$P_G = \$1.10 = 1 \cdot (Gas\ Price). \qquad (C1)$$

Thus, the price of a gallon of gasoline must be $1.10. We find the level of the Dow Jones Industrials Average by plugging $1.10 for (*Gas Price*) into either equation (A1), (B1), or (A2). We find that *DJIA* = 3,000.

APPLICATION 3.7: EXTERNAL FINANCING NEEDS
(Background reading: section 3.3)

Consider the Albert Company, whose financial statements are given in tables 3.1 and 3.2. The firm's Earnings Before Interest and Tax (*EBIT*) level is projected to be $300,000 next year. This *EBIT* level (sometimes referred to as Net Operating Income) represents the sum of funds available to pay interest to bondholders, taxes, dividends to shareholders, and earnings to retain. The firm has previously borrowed $600,000 by issuing bonds which will require $50,000 in interest payments. Management expects the firm to remain in the 40% corporate income tax bracket and pay out one

Table 3.1   Albert Company financial statements

Income statement, this year		Pro-forma income statement, next year	
Sales (*TR*).............................	$500,000	Sales (*TR*)...................................	$700,000
Cost of Goods Sold......................	200,000	Cost of Goods Sold......................	300,000
Gross Margin..............................	300,000	Gross Margin..............................	400,000
Fixed Costs..................................	100,000	Fixed Costs..................................	100,000
EBIT...	200,000	*EBIT*...	300,000
Interest Payments	50,000	Interest Payments	_____
Earnings Before Taxes.................	150,000	Earnings Before Taxes.................	
Taxes (@ 40%)............................	60,000	Taxes (@ 40%)............................	_____
Net Income After Tax	90,000	Net Income After Taxes	
Dividends (@ 33%)	30,000	Dividends (@ 33%)	
Retained Earnings.......................	60,000	Retained Earnings.......................	_____

Balance sheet, December 31, this year

ASSETS		LIABILITIES AND EQUITY	
Cash...	$100,000	Accounts Payable.......................	$100,000
Accounts Receivable...................	100,000	Accrued Wages	50,000
Inventory.....................................	100,000	Current Liabilities.......................	150,000
Current Assets.............................	300,000	Bonds Payable............................	600,000
Plant and Equipment..................	700,000	Equity	250,000
Total Assets	1,000,000	Total Capital...............................	1,000,000

Pro-forma balance sheet, December 31, next year

ASSETS		LIABILITIES AND EQUITY	
Cash...	$140,000	Accounts Payable.......................	$140,000
Accounts Receivable...................	140,000	Accrued Wages	70,000
Inventory.....................................	140,000	Current Liabilities.......................	210,000
Current Assets.............................	420,000	Bonds Payable............................	
Plant and Equipment..................	980,000	Equity	_____
Total Assets	1,400,000	Total Capital...............................	1,400,000

third of its after-tax earnings in dividends. However, since the firm's production level is expected to increase next year, management has determined that each asset account must also increase by 40%. Assets currently total $1,000,000; thus, total assets must increase by $400,000. Current liabilities will also increase from its present level of $150,000 by 40% to $210,000. The firm pays no interest on its current liabilities. Managers have already decided to sell bonds at an interest rate of 10% to provide any external capital necessary to finance the asset level increase. Management's problem is to determine how much additional capital to raise through this 10% bond issue. Based on this information, we may determine the Albert Company's external financing needs (*EFN*) for next year.

Table 3.2 Albert Company pro-forma income statement

Pro-forma income statement, next year	
Sales (*TR*)	$700,000
Cost of Goods Sold	300,000
Gross Margin	400,000
Fixed Costs	100,000
EBIT	300,000
Interest Payments	$50,000 + (0.10 \cdot EFN)$
Earnings Before Taxes	$250,000 - (0.10 \cdot EFN)$
Taxes (@ 40%)	$100,000 - (0.04 \cdot EFN)$
Net Income After Taxes	$150,000 - (0.06 \cdot EFN)$
Dividends (@ 33%)	$50,000 - (0.02 \cdot EFN)$
Retained Earnings	$100,000 - (0.04 \cdot EFN)$

Since management has determined that it must increase its asset total by $400,000, it must determine how these assets will be financed. That is, management must determine the total sum of capital required to support the change in the total asset level. Some of this necessary capital can be derived from internal sources such as retained earnings (*RE*) or current liabilities (*CL*). These sources are likely to change simultaneously with the firm's production level and provide capital directly from the increase in the firm's level of operation. For example, an increase in the firm's sales level may result directly in an increase in the firm's level of retained earnings, since revenues, variable costs, and profits can be expected to increase. Furthermore, as the firm's sales level increases, it may be reasonable to anticipate an increase in the firm's number of employees, further resulting in an increase in the firm's accrued wages level. Other current liability levels are likely to increase in a similar manner. The remaining funds must be obtained through some external source, such as the sale of long-term bonds or equity. In summary, the amount of money the firm must raise from external sources is determined by the following equation:

$$EFN = \Delta Assets - \Delta CL - RE,$$

where *EFN* is the firm's external financing need; *ΔAssets* is the anticipated change in the firm's asset level from the prior year to the year of the increased operating level; *ΔCL* is the anticipated change in the firm's current liability debt level, assuming that current liabilities change spontaneously with the firm's sales level; and *RE* is the firm's anticipated retained earnings level for the year of the increased level of operation.

Our first problem is to compute Net Income After Taxes (*NIAT*) and Retained Earnings (*RE*) for Albert next year. However, we don't know what the company's interest expenditure (*INT*) next year will be until we know how much money it will borrow (*EFN*). At the same time, we cannot determine how much money the firm needs to borrow until we know its interest expenditure (so we can solve for retained earnings). Therefore, we must solve simultaneously for *EFN* and interest expenditure (or solve simultaneously for *EFN* and *RE*).

EFN can be found with the following:

$$EFN = \Delta Assets - \Delta CL - RE,$$

$$EFN = \$400,000 - \$60,000 - RE,$$

$$EFN = \$340,000 - RE.$$

Retained Earnings (*RE*) is determined by first subtracting total interest payments (\$50,000 on existing debt plus $0.10 \cdot EFN$ for newly issued debt) from Earnings Before Interest and Taxes (*EBIT*). This difference, $\$300,000 - \$50,000 - 0.10 \cdot EFN$ results in Earnings Before Taxes (*EBT*), or taxable income. Since the corporate tax rate equals 40%, the firm realizes 60% in Net Income after Taxes (*NIAT*), or $0.6(\$300,000 - \$50,000 - 0.10 \cdot EFN) = \$150,000 - 0.06 \cdot EFN$. Since the firm pays one third of its Net Income After Taxes (*NIAT*) to shareholders in dividends, its retained earnings are 0.667 times its *NIAT*, or $RE = 0.6667(\$150,000 - 0.06 \cdot EFN) = \$100,000 - 0.04 \cdot EFN$. We have two equations to work with here, one for *EFN* and a second for *RE*:

$$EFN = \$340,000 - RE,$$

$$RE = \$100,000 - 0.04 \cdot EFN.$$

We have two equations with two unknown variables, *EFN* and *RE*. We may use the addition method discussed in section 3.3 to solve this system. Therefore, the External Financing Needs expression may be written as follows:

$$EFN = \$340,000 - (\$100,000 - (0.04 \cdot EFN)).$$

Thus, we have written an expression for *RE*, $(\$100,000 - (0.04 \cdot EFN))$, and inserted it into our expression for *EFN*. We now proceed to solve for *EFN* as follows:

$$EFN = \$240,000 + 0.04 \cdot EFN,$$

$$0.96 \cdot EFN = \$240,000,$$

$$EFN = \$250,000.$$

Our *EFN* problem is complete. We now know that the firm must borrow \$250,000. Thus, the firm's total interest payments for next year must be \$50,000 plus 10% of \$250,000, or \$75,000. Retained Earnings will be 90,000, computed by substituting 250,000 for *EFN* into the following expression for *RE*: $RE = \$100,000 - 0.04 \cdot EFN$.

3.4 GEOMETRIC EXPANSIONS
(Background reading: section 3.1)

At the end of section 3.1, we introduced the concept of the geometric expansion as a technique to simplify a polynomial consisting of a repetitive series of terms. These terms, arranged in a series of terms with a single variable and exponents arranged in descending order of exponents, are called a geometric series. A geometric expansion is an algebraic procedure used to simplify a geometric series. This procedure is most useful when the number of terms is large. Suppose that one intended to solve the following finite geometric series for S:

$$S = c + cx + cx^2 + cx^3 + \ldots + cx^n. \tag{A}$$

In this series, c is a constant, or parameter, and x is a quotient, or variable. If n is large, direct calculations on this series may be time-consuming and repetitive. Simplifying the series to reduce the number of terms may save a significant amount of time performing routine calculations. The geometric expansion is a two-stage procedure:

1 First, multiply both sides of the equation by the quotient:

$$Sx = cx + cx^2 + cx^3 + cx^4 + \ldots + cx^{n+1}. \tag{B}$$

This first step is intended to obtain a very similar type of expression with repetitive terms that will be eliminated in the second step.

2 Second, to eliminate these repetitive terms, subtract the above product (B) from the original equation (A) and then simplify the result:

$$Sx - S = cx + cx^2 + cx^3 + cx^4 + \ldots + cx^{n+1}$$
$$- c - cx - cx^2 - cx^3 - \ldots - cx^n. \tag{C}$$

The following simplification completes the geometric expansion. Notice the set of terms that should cancel when we simplify:

$$Sx - S = -c + cx^{n+1}, \tag{D}$$

$$S(x - 1) = c(x^{n+1} - 1). \tag{E}$$

Continue the process of simplification by dividing both sides by $(x - 1)$:

$$S = c\left(\frac{x^{n+1} - 1}{x - 1}\right) \quad \text{for } x \neq 1. \tag{F}$$

Consider the following example, where we set x to equal $(1 + i)$. Equations (G) and (H) will be identical:

$$S = c + c(1 + i) + c(1 + i)^2 + c(1 + i)^3 + \ldots + c(1 + i)^n, \tag{G}$$

$$S = c\left(\frac{1 - (1 + i)^{n+1}}{1 - (1 + i)}\right) = c\frac{(1 + i)^{n+1} - 1}{i}. \tag{H}$$

Thus, any geometric series where $x \neq 1$ can be simplified with the following right-hand side formula:

$$S = c + cx + cx^2 + cx^3 + \ldots + cx^{n-1} = c\frac{x^n - 1}{x - 1}. \qquad \text{(I)}$$

Geometric expansions are most helpful in time value mathematics with many periods, and in situations involving series of potential outcomes with associated probabilities. Such situations occur very frequently in finance. The geometric expansion procedure can save substantial amounts of computation time for problems involving these situations.

APPLICATION 3.8: MONEY MULTIPLIERS

Commercial banks play a most important role in the world economy. Among their important functions is their role in creating money by extending credit or loans. It may be reasonable to assume that the central bank of a country (the Federal Reserve system in the U.S.) issues a fixed amount of currency (paper money) K to the public and allows commercial banks to loan funds entrusted to them by depositors (in checking accounts, also known as demand deposits) of amount DD. Thus, businesses and consumers receive the currency from the central bank and deposit it into the commercial banking system in the form of demand deposits. Typically, the central bank requires that commercial banks hold on reserve a proportion r of their demand deposits. This reserve cannot be loaned to the general public. More specifically, commercial banks leave on deposit (or reserve) with the central bank nonloanable reserves totaling $r \cdot DD$. The bank loans the remainder. After one round of deposits and loans, money supply in the economy is determined:

$$M_1 = K + (1 - r)K \qquad \text{with a single round of deposits and loans.} \qquad \text{(A)}$$

Thus, the economy's money supply thus far consists of paper currency K issued by the government which is deposited into the bank plus proportion $(1 - r)$, which is loaned by the bank to its customers. The loaned funds are then spent and then redeposited by their recipients, allowing the process to repeat itself:

$$M_1 = K + (1 - r)K + (1 - r)^2K \qquad \text{with two rounds of deposits and loans.} \qquad \text{(B)}$$

This process can continue perpetually. Whenever funds are loaned by a commercial bank, they are spent by the borrower. The borrower purchases goods from a seller; the seller then deposits its receipts into the commercial banking system, creating more funds available to loan. However, each deposit requires that the commercial bank increase its reserve left with the central bank by the proportion r. The level of money supplied, M_1, in such a system is determined as follows:

$$M_1 = K + (1 - r)K + (1 - r)^2K + \ldots + (1 - r)^\infty K. \qquad \text{(C)}$$

K is the currency originally issued by the central bank to the public and deposited in the commercial banking system. The amount rK fulfills the initial reserve requirement and the remainder $(1 - r)K$ is loaned to the public. The public redeposits this sum back into the commercial banking system. Of the $(1 - r)K$ redeposited into the banking system, $(1 - r)(1 - r)K = (1 - r)^2K$ is available to loan after the reserve requirement is fulfilled on the second deposit. This process continues forever; that is, it continues through $(1 - r)^\infty K$. Where K is the level of currency originally issued by the central bank and r is its reserve requirement, what is the total money supply for this economy? Obviously, since series (A) above is extended through an infinite number of repetitions, its exact computation is impossible without simplification. We can determine total money supply through the following geometric expansion, where we first multiply by $1 - r$:

$$(1 - r)M_1 = (1 - r)K + (1 - r)^2K + (1 - r)^3K + \ldots + (1 - r)^{\infty+1}K. \qquad \text{(D)}$$

The coefficient $1 - r$ is analogous to c in the geometric expansions in section 3.3. We subtract equation (C) from equation (D), to obtain

$$(1 - r)M_1 - M_1 = (1 - r)^1K + (1 - r)^2K + \ldots + (1 - r)^{\infty+1}K - (K + (1 - r)^1K$$
$$+ (1 - r)^2K + \ldots + (1 - r)^\infty K), \qquad \text{where } (1 - r)^\infty K = 0, \qquad \text{(E)}$$

which simplifies to

$$(1 - r)M_1 - M_1 = -K + (1 - r)^{\infty+1}K, \qquad \text{where } (1 - r)^{\infty+1}K = 0. \qquad \text{(F)}$$

The process of simplification continues as follows:

$$rM_1 = K, \qquad \text{(G)}$$

$$M_1 = K/r, \qquad \text{(H)}$$

where we assume that K is positive and $0 < r \leq 1$. Thus, the money multiplier here equals $1/r$. Money supply M_1 is simply K/r. Thus, for example, a central bank issuing \$100 in currency with a reserve requirement equal to 10% will have a total money supply equal to \$1,000:

$$M_1 = \frac{100}{0.10} = 1{,}000. \qquad \text{(I)}$$

3.5   FUNCTIONS AND GRAPHS
(Background reading: section 2.3)

A *function* is a rule that assigns to each number in a set a unique second number. Functions may be represented by equations, graphs, or tables. An example of a "generic" functional relationship in equation form is given by $y = f(x)$, which reads

"y is a function of x." If y increases as x increases, then y is said to be a direct or increasing function of x. In the following examples, y is an increasing function of x:

(a) $y = 5x$;   (b) $y = 12x + 3$;
(c) $y = 0.9x$;   (d) $y = 3e^x$;
(e) $y = 10x^2 + 20x + 10$ (when $x > -1$);   (f) $y = 12x^3 + 2x^2$.

Functions (a), (b), and (c) are said to be linear functions. This means that graphs depicting the relationships between x and y would plot lines. In other words, the graphs or plots would be linear. Equation (d) represents an exponential function because of its use of the number e. Equation (e) represents a quadratic function because it has a single independent variable x and its exponents are integers ranging from zero to two. Equation (f) is a cubic function because its exponents are integers ranging from zero to three. If y decreases as x increases, it is said that y is a decreasing or inverse function of x. In the following examples, y is a decreasing function of x:

$$y = \frac{6}{x} \quad \text{(where } x > 0\text{)}, \qquad y = -9x + 5,$$

$$y = -3x^2 - 6x \quad \text{(where } x > -1\text{)}, \qquad y = 6e^{-x},$$

$$y = \frac{1}{7x} \quad \text{(where } x > 0\text{)}, \qquad y = -(x^2).$$

Consider the functions depicted in figures 3.1 and 3.2. To plot functions on a graph, simply solve for y in terms of x and plot corresponding coordinates on x/y axes as in the graphs depicted in figures 3.1 and 3.2. Coordinates for two points are sufficient to plot out linear functions; many other functions may require more points or other information in order to estimate placement of the appropriate curve.

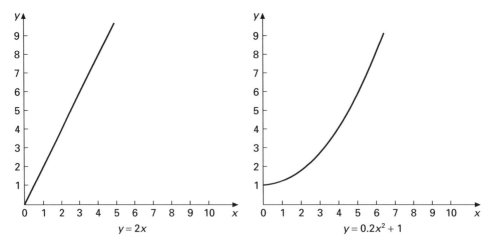

$y = 2x$ $y = 0.2x^2 + 1$

Figure 3.1 Increasing or direct functions.

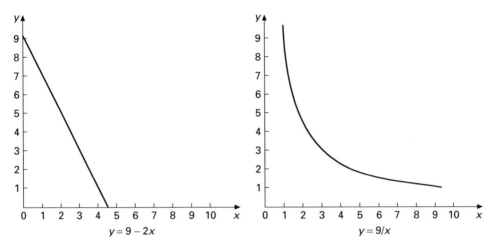

Figure 3.2 Decreasing or inverse functions.

APPLICATION 3.9: UTILITY OF WEALTH

In finance, we typically assume that individuals obtain some sort of satisfaction from acquiring wealth. In this application, we shall assume that an investor can associate some measurable level of personal satisfaction (or, in economic terms, utility) with any given wealth level. Furthermore, it is reasonable to assume that this level of utility or satisfaction increases as the investor's level of wealth increases; that is, an investor becomes more satisfied as his level of wealth increases. Next, we shall assume in this application that we can mathematically define the relationship between an investor's wealth and utility levels. Thus, utility will be characterized as a function (which will be specified precisely shortly) of the investor's level of wealth:

$$U = f(W).$$

Finally, we shall make the additional and perhaps less realistic assumption that utility is measurable and that we can specify its exact functional relationship with wealth. An example of such a utility function might be

$$U = 0.5 \cdot \sqrt{W}.$$

An investor with this utility function and whose wealth is given by W (W and $U \geq 0$) will have a utility level equal to one-half times the square root of his wealth level. Figure 3.3 represents a utility of wealth curve for this function. The investor with this particular utility of wealth function whose wealth level is \$2,000,000 would have a utility level of 1,414.21. If the investor's wealth level were to increase to \$3,000,000, his utility level would increase to 1,732.05. Clearly, this investor's utility level

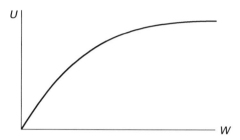

Figure 3.3   Utility of wealth. Utility-of-wealth function for risk-averse individual: $f'(W) > 0$; $f''(W) < 0$. For example, $U_W = 0.5W^{0.5}$.

increases as he becomes wealthier. There is a positive or direct relationship between the investor's wealth and utility levels. Of course, all of this is based on the rather unrealistic assumption that utility is observable and measurable. Even though the assumptions of observability and measurability may be unrealistic, utility models can be most useful in describing how investors behave and react to changing conditions. These models can also be used to demonstrate how investors react to risk, how they might value insurance policies, and how they mix bonds and stocks in portfolios.

EXERCISES

3.1.   Solve each of the following for x:

     (a) $100 = 5x + 10$;   (d) $50 = 300/5 + 5x$;
     (b) $500 = 3{,}000 - 2x$;   (e) $20 = 10 - 15/x + 25$;
     (c) $100 = 15 + 2x + 6x$;   (f) $25 - 3x = 100 - 2x + 5x$.

3.2.   Solve each of the following for x:

     (a) $100 = 90(1 + x)^2$;   (c) $100 = 90/(1 + x)^2$;
     (b) $100 = 90(1 + x)^3$;   (d) $90 = 100/(1 + x)^2$.

3.3.   Assume that $1 will purchase £0.60 and ¥108; that is, one U.S. dollar will purchase 0.6 U.K. pounds and 108 Japanese yen. Assume that goods in the three countries are identically priced after adjusting for currency exchange rates.

     (a)   What is the value of £1 in ¥?
     (b)   What is the value of ¥1 in £?
     (c)   If one ounce of gold costs $300 in the United States, what is its cost in the U.K. and in Japan?

3.4.   Smith Company produces a product that can be sold for a price of $P = \$80$ per unit such that its total annual revenues equals $TR = PQ = 80Q$. The variable Q represents the number of units of the product produced and sold by the firm. The company incurs two types of costs in its production process, fixed and variable. Fixed costs total $\$500,000$ per year. Variable costs VC are $\$50$ per unit produced. The firm's profit function is defined as follows as total revenues minus the sum of fixed and variable costs:

$$\pi = P \cdot Q - (FC + VC \cdot Q) = 80Q - (500{,}000 + 50 \cdot Q).$$

What is the firm's break-even production level?

3.5.   Suppose that the one-year spot rate $y_{0,1}$ of interest is 5%. Investors are expecting that the one-year spot rate one year from now will increase to 6%; thus, the one-year forward rate $y_{1,2}$ on a loan originated in one year is 6%. Furthermore, assume that investors are expecting that the one-year spot rate two years from now will increase to 7%; thus, the one-year forward rate $y_{2,3}$ on a loan originated in two years is 7%. Based on the pure expectations hypothesis, what is the three-year spot rate?

3.6.   Suppose that the one-year spot rate $y_{0,1}$ of interest is 5%. Investors are expecting that the one-year spot rate one year from now will increase to 7%; thus, the one-year forward rate $y_{1,2}$ on a loan originated in one year is 7%. Furthermore, assume that the three-year spot rate equals 7% as well. What is the anticipated one-year forward rate $y_{2,3}$ on a loan originated in two years based on the pure expectations hypothesis?

3.7.   Consider a firm whose price function is related to sales: $TR = 50 - 0.00002Q$. Total revenues equal the product of price and output $PQ = 50Q - 0.00002Q^2$. In addition, assume that this firm's per-unit variable costs increase with production, $20 + 0.00001Q$, and that this firm's fixed costs equal $\$500,000$, such that total costs equal $500{,}000 + 20Q + 0.00001Q^2$.

(a)   What is the firm's profit function?
(b)   What is the firm's break-even production level?

3.8.   Suppose that the risk of a portfolio is given by the following equation:

$$\sigma_p^2 = 0.25w_1^2 - 0.3w_1 + 0.09.$$

What proportion of the portfolio should be invested in asset one (w_1) so that the portfolio risk σ_p^2 equals zero?

3.9.   Solve the following for x_1 and x_2:

$$0.04x_1 + 0.04x_2 = 0.01,$$
$$0.04x_1 + 0.16x_2 = 0.11.$$

3.10. Solve the following for x and λ:

$$20x - 5\lambda = -3,$$
$$-5x - 0\lambda = -100.$$

3.11. Solve the following for x_1, x_2, and x_3:

$$962 = 100x_1 + 100x_2 + 1,100x_3,$$
$$1,010.4 = 120x_1 + 120x_2 + 1,120x_3,$$
$$970 = 100x_1 + 1,100x_2.$$

3.12. Stock A, which currently sells for \$16.80, has a sensitivity or beta with respect to GNP equal to 4 and a beta with respect to interest rates i equal to 80. Stock B, which currently sells for \$9.00, has a beta with respect to GNP equal to 2 and a beta with respect to interest rates i equal to 50. Thus, two factors drive stock prices in this economy. No other factors affect prices.

(a) Write one equation for each stock depicting the relationship between stock prices and the two explanatory variables GNP and i.
(b) Solve these two equations simultaneously to determine current GNP and interest rate levels.

3.13. The Victoria Company's financial statements are given below. Management is forecasting an increase in the company's sales level by 40% to \$1,050,000. Managers predict that this 40% sales increase will increase the firm's Cost of Goods Sold level by 50% to \$450,000. Fixed costs will remain constant at \$150,000. The firm will continue to make the \$50,000 interest payments necessary to sustain its \$600,000 in bonds outstanding. Management expects the firm to remain in the 40% corporate income tax bracket and pay out one third of its earnings in dividends. In order to sustain this 40% increase in sales, management has determined that each asset account must also increase by 40%; that is, the total must increase by \$400,000. Current Liabilities will also increase by 40%. The firm pays no interest on its current liabilities. Managers have already decided to sell bonds at an interest rate of 10% to provide any external capital necessary to finance the asset level increase. Management's problem is to determine how much additional capital to raise through this 10% bond issue. Based on this information and the company's financial statements given below, determine the Victoria Company's 2001 External Funding Needs (*EFN*).

VICTORIA COMPANY FINANCIAL STATEMENTS

Income statement, 2000		*Pro-forma income statement, 2001*	
Sales (*TR*)	$750,000	Sales (*TR*)	$1,050,000
Cost of Goods Sold	300,000	Cost of Goods Sold	450,000
Gross Margin	450,000	Gross Margin	600,000
Fixed Costs	150,000	Fixed Costs	150,000
EBIT	300,000	EBIT	450,000
Interest Payments	50,000	Interest Payments	
Earnings Before Taxes	250,000	Earnings Before Taxes	
Taxes (@ 40%)	100,000	Taxes (@ 40%)	
Net Income After Tax	150,000	Net Income After Taxes	
Dividends (@ 33%)	50,000	Dividends (@ 33%)	
Retained Earnings	100,000	Retained Earnings	

Balance sheet, December 31, 2000

ASSETS		LIABILITIES AND EQUITY	
Cash	$100,000	Accounts Payable	$100,000
Accounts Receivable	100,000	Accrued Wages	50,000
Inventory	100,000	Current Liabilities	150,000
Current Assets	300,000	Bonds Payable	600,000
Plant and Equipment	700,000	Equity	250,000
Total Assets	1,000,000	Total Capital	1,000,000

Pro-forma balance sheet, December 31, 2001

ASSETS		LIABILITIES AND EQUITY	
Cash	$140,000	Accounts Payable	$140,000
Accounts Receivable	140,000	Accrued Wages	70,000
Inventory	140,000	Current Liabilities	210,000
Current Assets	420,000	Bonds Payable	
Plant and Equipment	980,000	Equity	
Total Assets	1,400,000	Total Capital	1,400,000

3.14. Perform a geometric expansion to simplify the following series:

$$1,200 = 100(1 + x + x^2 + x^3 + \ldots + x^9).$$

What is the value of x?

3.15. The Keynesian Macroeconomic Model postulates a relationship between autonomous consumer consumption (consumption expenditures independent of income) and total income. Suppose that the following depicts the relationships among income Y, autonomous consumption $\bar{C}$, and income-dependent consumption cY:

$$Y = \bar{C} + cY. \tag{A}$$

If autonomous consumption were to increase by a given amount, this would increase income, resulting in an increase in income-dependent consumption. This would further increase income and consumption, and the process would replicate itself perpetually:

$$\Delta Y = \Delta\bar{C} + Y(c + c^2 + c^3 + \ldots + c^\infty). \tag{B}$$

Perform a geometric expansion on (B) to derive an income multiplier to determine the full amount of the change in income resulting from a change in autonomous consumption.

3.16. For each of the following, $y = f(x)$. Plot each of these four functions:

(a) $y = 10 - 0.5x$;   (c) $y = 9 + 25x$;
(b) $y = 20/3x$;   (d) $y = 8 + 0.3x^2$.

APPENDIX 3.A SOLVING SYSTEMS OF EQUATIONS ON A SPREADSHEET

(Background reading: section 3.3 and appendix 2.A)

Solving larger systems of equations containing larger numbers of variables by hand or with a calculator can be an extremely time-consuming and frustrating process. However, spreadsheets can be used quite effectively to solve systems of linear equations simultaneously. Suppose that we wished to solve the following system of two equations simultaneously for x and y using an Excel™ spreadsheet:

$$10 = 8x + 4y,$$

$$20 = 2x + 6y.$$

We have two equations with two variables, x and y, with unknown values. Notice that the numbers for each of the two equations are arranged in a particular order: solutions (10 & 20) on the left, coefficients for x (8 & 2) then coefficients for y (4 & 6). Allowing one equation per row and noting that the x coefficients line up in the first column and the y coefficients line up in the second column, insert the coefficients in the spreadsheet as follows:

	A	B	C	D	E
1	8	4			
2	2	6			
3					
4					
5					

To solve the system, we will perform a matrix invert procedure which we will discuss in chapter 7. However, the mechanics are quite simple. First, use the mouse to highlight cells A4 to B5. With most desktop computers, this means to move the cursor to cell A4, hold down the left click, and while holding the left click, move the cursor to cell B5. After releasing the left click with four cells highlighted, left click on the toolbar at the top of the screen the Paste Function button (f_x). A Paste Function menu should appear on the screen, from which you should select the MATH & TRIG submenu. In the MATH & TRIG submenu, scroll down to select MINVERSE. The MINVERSE function will prompt you for an array; you should enter A1:B2. To fill all four cells A4 to B5, simultaneously hit the Ctrl, Shift, and Enter keys. Your spreadsheet should then appear as follows:

	A	B	C	D	E
1	8	4			
2	2	6			
3					
4	0.15	-0.1			
5	-0.05	0.2			

Now, enter into cells C4 and C5 the equation solutions 10 and 20. Then highlight cells D4 and D5, left click the Paste Function key in the Toolbar, select the MATH & TRIG menu and scroll down to and select the MMULT function. Now, you will be prompted for two arrays. The first will be A4:B5 – hit the Tab key; the second array will be C4:C5. Then hit the Ctrl, Shift, and Enter keys simultaneously to fill cells D4 and D5. The result will be −0.5 and 3.5. Thus, $x = -0.5$ and $y = 3.5$. The final spreadsheet will appear as follows:

	A	B	C	D	E
1	8	4			
2	2	6			
3					
4	0.15	-0.1	10	-0.5	
5	-0.05	0.2	20	3.5	

The process of expanding this solution procedure to three or more equations and variables is quite simple. First, be certain that each equation in the system is linear (no exponents other than 0 or 1 on the variables) and that there are exactly the same number of variables as equations. Arrange the terms in the equations so that the columns contain coefficients for the same variables. In some instances, the systems cannot be solved. Reasons for this will be discussed in chapter 7. Consider the following four-equation, four-variable system:

$$10 = 8x + 4y + 2z + 10q,$$

$$20 = 2x + 4y + 1z + 12q,$$

$$30 = 0x + 4y + 2z + 16q,$$

$$40 = 5x + 6y + 8z + 20q.$$

Now, examine the following spreadsheet, which solves the system:

	A	B	C	D	E	F	G
1	8	4	2	10			
2	2	4	1	12			
3	0	4	2	16			
4	5	6	8	20			
5							
6	0.235294	-0.29412	0.147059	-0.05882	10	-1.470588	
7	-0.52941	1.578431	-1.12255	0.215686	20	1.2254902	
8	-0.11765	-0.01961	-0.15686	0.196078	30	1.5686275	
9	0.147059	-0.39216	0.362745	-0.07843	40	1.372549	

Thus, $x = -1.470588$, $y = 1.2254902$, $z = 1.5686275$, and $q = 1.372549$. This issue of solving systems of linear equations simultaneously will be revisited in chapter 7.

CHAPTER FOUR
THE TIME VALUE OF MONEY

4.1 INTRODUCTION AND FUTURE VALUE

The perspective and the organization of this chapter differs from that of chapters 2 and 3 in that topics are arranged by finance application rather than mathematics area. The mathematics tools presented in chapters 2 and 3 are applied in this chapter to closely examine the analytical aspects underlying what might be the single most important topic in finance – the *time value of money*. In this chapter, we study how investors and borrowers interact to value investments and determine interest rates on loans and fixed income securities.

Interest is paid by borrowers to lenders for the use of lenders' money. The level of interest charged is typically stated as a percentage of the *principal* (the amount of the loan). When a loan matures, the principal must be repaid along with any unpaid accumulated interest. In a free market economy, interest rates are determined jointly by the supply of and demand for money. Thus, lenders will usually attempt to impose as high an interest rate as possible on the money they lend; borrowers will attempt to obtain the use of money at the lowest interest rates available to them. Competition among borrowers and competition among lenders will tend to lead interest rates toward some competitive level. Factors affecting the levels of interest rates will do so by affecting supply and demand conditions for money. Among these factors are inflation rates, loan risks, investor intertemporal monetary preferences (how much individuals and institutions prefer to have money now rather than have to wait for it), government policies, and the administrative costs of extending credit.

4.2 SIMPLE INTEREST
(Background reading: sections 2.4, 2.7, and 4.1)

Interest is computed on a *simple* basis if it is paid only on the principal of the loan. *Compound* interest is paid on accumulated loan interest as well as on the principal. Thus, if a sum of money (X_0) were borrowed at an annual interest rate i and repaid at the end of *n* years with accumulated interest accruing on a simple basis, the total sum repaid (FV_n or *Future Value* at the end of year *n*) is determined as follows:

$$FV_n = X_0(1 + ni). \tag{4.1}$$

The subscripts *n* and 0 merely designate time; they do not imply any arithmetic function. The product *ni* when multiplied by X_0 reflects the value of interest payments to be made on the loan; the value 1 accounts for the fact that the principal of the loan must be repaid. If the loan duration includes some fraction of a year, the value of *n* will be fractional; for example, if the loan duration were one year and three months, *n* would be 1.25. The total amount paid (or, the future value of the loan) will be an increasing function of the length of time the loan is outstanding (*n*) and the interest rate (*i*) charged on the loan. For example, if a consumer borrowed $1,000 at an interest rate of 10% for one year, his total repayment would be $1,100, determined from equation (4.1) as follows:

$$FV_1 = \$1,000(1 + 1 \cdot 0.1) = \$1,000 \cdot 1.1 = \$1,100.$$

If the loan were to be repaid in two years, its future value would be determined as follows:

$$FV_2 = \$1,000(1 + 2 \cdot 0.1) = \$1,000 \cdot 1.2 = \$1,200.$$

Continuing our example, if the loan were to be repaid in five years, its Future Value would be

$$FV_5 = \$1,000(1 + 5 \cdot 0.1) = \$1,000 \cdot 1.5 = \$1,500.$$

The longer the duration of a loan, the higher will be its future value. Thus, the longer lenders must wait to have their money repaid, the greater will be the total interest payments made by borrowers.

4.3 COMPOUND INTEREST
(Background reading: sections 2.7, 3.1, and 4.2)

Interest is computed on a compound basis when the borrower pays interest on accumulated interest as well as on the loan principal. If interest on a given loan must accumulate for a full year before it is compounded, the future value of this loan is determined as follows:

$$FV_n = X_0(1 + i)^n. \tag{4.2}$$

For example, if an individual were to deposit $1,000 into a savings account paying annually compounded interest at a rate of 10% (here, the bank is borrowing money), the future value of the account after five years would be $1,610.51, determined by equation (4.2) as follows:

$$FV_5 = \$1{,}000(1 + 0.1)^5 = \$1{,}000 \cdot 1.1^5 = \$1{,}000 \cdot 1.61051 = \$1{,}610.51.$$

Notice that this sum is greater than the future value of the loan (\$1,500) when interest is not compounded.

The compound interest formula can be derived intuitively from the simple interest formula. If interest must accumulate for a full year before it is compounded, then the future value of the loan after one year is \$1,100, exactly the same sum as if interest had been computed on a simple basis:

$$FV_n = X_0(1 + ni) = X_0(1 + 1 \cdot i) = X_0(1 + i)^1 = \$1{,}000(1 + 0.1) = \$1{,}100. \quad (4.3)$$

The future values of loans where interest is compounded annually and when interest is computed on an annual basis will be identical only when n equals one. Since the value of this loan is \$1,100 after one year and interest is to be compounded, interest and future value for the second year will be computed on the new balance of \$1,100:

$$FV_2 = X_0(1 + 1 \cdot i)(1 + 1 \cdot i) = X_0(1 + i)(1 + i) = X_0(1 + i)^2,$$

$$FV_2 = \$1{,}000(1 + 0.1)(1 + 0.1) = \$1{,}000(1 + 0.1)^2 = \$1{,}210. \quad (4.4)$$

This process can be continued for five years:

$$FV_5 = \$1{,}000(1 + 0.1)(1 + 0.1)(1 + 0.1)(1 + 0.1)(1 + 0.1)$$

$$= \$1{,}000(1 + 0.1)^5 = \$1{,}610.51.$$

More generally, the process can be applied for a loan of any maturity. Therefore:

$$FV_n = X_0(1 + i)(1 + i) \cdots (1 + i) = X_0(1 + i)^n,$$

$$FV_n = \$1{,}000(1 + 0.1)(1 + 0.1) \cdots (1 + 0.1) = \$1{,}000(1 + 0.1)^n. \quad (4.5)$$

4.4   FRACTIONAL PERIOD COMPOUNDING OF INTEREST

In the previous examples, interest is compounded annually; that is, interest must accumulate at the stated rate i for an entire year before it can be compounded or re-compounded. In many savings accounts and other investments, interest can be compounded semiannually, quarterly, or even daily. If interest is to be compounded more than once per year (or once every fractional part of a year), the future value of such an investment will be determined as follows:

$$FV_n = X_0(1 + i/m)^{mn}, \quad (4.6)$$

where interest is compounded m times per year. The interpretation of this formula is fairly straightforward. For example, if m is 2, then interest is compounded on a semi-annual basis. The semiannual interest rate is simply i/m or $i/2$. If the investment is held for *n* periods, then it is held for 2*n* semiannual periods. Thus, we compute a semi-annual interest rate *i*/2 and the number of semiannual periods the investment is held 2 · *n*. If $1,000 were deposited into a savings account paying interest at an annual rate of 10% compounded semiannually, its future value after five years would be $1,628.90, determined as follows:

$$FV_5 = \$1,000(1 + 0.1/2)^{2\cdot5} = \$1,000(1.05)^{10} = \$1,000(1.62889) = \$1,628.90.$$

Notice that the semiannual interest rate is 5% and that the account is outstanding for ten six-month periods. This sum of $1,628.90 exceeds the future value of the account if interest is compounded only once annually ($1,610.51). In fact, the more times per year interest is compounded, the higher will be the future value of the account. For example, if interest on the same account were compounded monthly (12 times per year), the account's future value would be $1,645.31:

$$FV_5 = \$1,000(1 + 0.1/12)^{12\cdot5} = \$1,000(1.008333)^{60} = \$1,645.31.$$

The monthly interest rate is 0.008333 and the account is open for *m* · *n* or 60 months. With daily compounding, the account's value would be $1,648.61:

$$FV_5 = \$1,000(1 + 0.1/365)^{365\cdot5} = \$1,648.61.$$

Therefore, as *m* increases, future value increases, as in table 4.1. However, this rate of increase in future value becomes smaller with larger values for *m*; that is, the increases in FV_n induced by increases in *m* eventually become quite small. Thus, the difference in the future values of two accounts where interest is compounded hourly in one and every minute in the other may actually be rather trivial.

Table 4.1 Future values and annual percentage yields of accounts with initial $10,000 deposits at 10%

Years to maturity, *n*	Future value simple interest ($)	Future value compounded annually ($)	Future value compounded monthly ($)	Future value compounded daily ($)	Future value compounded continuously ($)
1	11,000	11,000	11,047	11,052	11,052
2	12,000	12,100	12,204	12,214	12,214
3	13,000	13,310	13,481	13,498	13,499
4	14,000	14,641	14,894	14,917	14,918
5	15,000	16,105	16,453	16,486	16,487
10	20,000	25,937	27,070	27,179	27,183
20	40,000	67,275	73,281	73,870	73,891
30	80,000	174,494	198,374	200,773	200,857
50	320,000	1,173,909	1,453,699	1,483,116	1,484,140
Annual percentage yield	Varies with *n*	0.100000	0.104713	0.1051557	0.1051709

APPLICATION 4.1: *APY* AND BANK ACCOUNT COMPARISONS

Financial institutions often have many ways of defining the terms or rules associated with their loans, accounts, and other investments. Such large numbers of terms and rules frequently lead to confusion among investors and consumers, particularly when trying to compare their various alternatives. For this reason, there exist several conventions which are intended to standardize the disclosure of these terms. For example, we have seen in the previous two sections the impact that changing the compounding intervals has on future value. Comparison between investments is more complicated when their numbers of compounding intervals differ. To simplify the comparison between loans with varying compounding intervals, it is often useful to compute *annual percentage yields*, also known as equivalent annual rates. The annual percentage yield (*APY*) represents the yield that, if compounded once per year, will produce the same future value as the stated rate *i* compounded *m* times per year:[1]

$$FV = X_0\left(1 + \frac{i}{m}\right)^{mn} = X_0(1 + APY)^n.$$

Thus, we can compute *APY* as follows:

$$APY = \left(1 + \frac{i}{m}\right)^{m} - 1. \qquad (4.7)$$

Because the annual percentage yield simplifies comparison between accounts with different compounding intervals, U.S. banks are normally required by law to disclose *APY*s along with their stated interest rates in their advertisements soliciting bank accounts. Consider an example where a savings account at bank X pays 6% interest compounded daily and a similar account at bank Y pays $6\frac{1}{4}$% interest, compounded semiannually. Which account will pay more to an investor who leaves a $100 deposit for one year? Based on equation (4.6), we can obtain the following future values:

$$FV_X = \$100\left(1 + \frac{0.06}{365}\right)^{365 \cdot 1} = \$106.18313,$$

$$FV_Y = \$100\left(1 + \frac{0.0625}{2}\right)^{2 \cdot 1} = 106.34766.$$

Thus, an account paying a stated rate of 6% compounded daily yields a future value equivalent to an account paying slightly more than 6.18% compounded annually. An account paying a stated rate of 6.25% compounded semiannually yields a future value equivalent to an account paying slightly more than 6.437% compounded annually.

---

[1] If interest is not compounded, $APY = (1 + ni)^{-n} - 1$.

Therefore, the account in bank Y is preferred to that at bank X. We can arrive at the same preference ranking by examining annual percentage yields:

$$APY_X = \left(1 + \frac{0.06}{365}\right)^{365} - 1 = 0.0618313, \qquad APY_Y = \left(1 + \frac{0.0625}{2}\right)^{2} - 1 = 0.0634766.$$

Because the account at bank Y has the higher *APY*, it is preferred. The account with the higher *APY* will produce a higher future value. However, it is not necessarily true that the account with the highest stated rate also has the highest *APY*.

A 1997 advertisement in a New York newspaper offered a five-year certificate of deposit account paying interest at an annual rate of 5.83%, compounded daily. The annual percentage yield (*APY*) on this account was advertised at 6.00%. Given these details, the future value of $100 deposited into this account can be computed to be $133.84:

$$FV = \$100(1 + 0.0583/365)^{365 \cdot 5} = \$133.84.$$

The *APY* of this account is determined as follows:

$$APY = (1 + 0.0583/365)^{365} - 1 = 0.06003.$$

The 6% *APY* advertised by the bank was approximately correct; such advertisements are often rounded slightly. In any case, the future value of this account can be determined with the 6.003% account *APY* as follows:

$$FV = \$100(1 + 0.06003)^{5} = \$133.84.$$

A $100 initial deposit into a five-year CD account paying interest at an annual rate of 5.85%, compounded quarterly, would have a future value of $133.69:

$$FV = \$100(1 + 0.0585/4)^{4 \cdot 5} = \$133.69.$$

The *APY* of this account is 0.0598, determined as follows:

$$APY = (1 + 0.0585/4)^{4} - 1 = 0.0598.$$

Note that the future value and the *APY* of the second account are lower than those of the first account – even though the stated interest rate on the second account is higher. Compounding can have a significant effect on both future value and *APY*.

4.5   CONTINUOUS COMPOUNDING OF INTEREST
(Background reading: sections 2.5 and 4.4)

If interest were to be compounded an infinite number of times per period, we would say that interest is compounded continuously. However, we cannot obtain a numerical solution for future value by merely substituting in ∞ for m in equation (4.6) – calculators have no "∞" key. In the previous section, we saw that increases in m cause the future value of an investment to increase. As m approaches infinity, FV_n continues to increase, however at decreasing rates. More precisely, as m approaches infinity ($m \to \infty$), the future value of an investment can be defined as follows:

$$FV_n = X_0 e^{in}, \tag{4.8}$$

where e is the natural log whose value can be approximated at 2.718, or derived as in section 2.5.

If an investor were to deposit $1,000 into an account paying interest at a rate of 10%, continuously compounded (or compounded an infinite number of times per year), the account's future value would be approximately $1,648.64:

$$FV_5 = \$1,000 \cdot e^{1.5} \approx \$1,000 \cdot 2.718^{0.5} = \$1,648.64.$$

The Future Value of this account exceeds only slightly the value of the account if interest were compounded daily. Also, note that continuous compounding simply means that interest is compounded an infinite number of times per time period.

4.6 ANNUITY FUTURE VALUES
(Background reading: sections 2.8, 3.4, and 4.3)

An *annuity* is a series of equal payments made at equal intervals. Suppose that payments are to be made into an interest-bearing account. The future value of that account will be a function of interest accruing on prior deposits as well as the deposits themselves. A future value annuity factor (fvaf) is used to determine the future value of an annuity. This annuity is a series of equal payments made at identical intervals. The future value annuity factor may be derived through the use of the geometric expansion procedure discussed in section 3.4. This technique is very useful for future value computations when a large number of time periods are involved. The geometric expansion enables us to reduce a repetitive expression requiring many calculations to an expression that can be computed much more quickly. Suppose that we wish to determine the future value of an account based on a payment of X made at the end of each year t for n years, where that account pays an annual interest rate equal to i:

$$FVA = X[(1 + i)^{n-1} + (1 + i)^{n-2} + \ldots + (1 + i)^2 + (1 + i)^1 + 1]. \tag{4.9}$$

The payment made at the end of the first year will accumulate interest for a total of $n - 1$ years, the payment at the end of the second year will accumulate interest for $n - 2$ years, and so on. Clearly, determining the future value of this account with equation (4.9) will be very time-consuming if n is large. The first step in the geometric expansion to simplify equation (4.9) is to multiply both of its sides by $1 + i$:

$$FVA(1 + i) = X[(1 + i)^n + (1 + i)^{n-1} + \ldots + (1 + i)^3 + (1 + i)^2 + (1 + i)]. \quad (4.10)$$

The second step in this geometric expansion is to subtract equation (4.9) from equation (4.10), to obtain:

$$FVA(1 + i) - FVA = X[(1 + i)^n - 1]. \quad (4.11)$$

Notice that the subtraction led to the cancellation of many terms, reducing the equation that we wish to compute with to a much more manageable size. Finally, we rearrange terms in equation (4.12) to obtain equations (4.12) and (4.13):

$$FVA \cdot 1 + FVA \cdot i - FVA = X[(1 + i)^n - 1] = FVA \cdot i = X[(1 + i)^n - 1], \quad (4.12)$$

$$FVA = \frac{X[(1 + i)^n - 1]}{i}. \quad (4.13)$$

Practicing derivations such as this is an excellent way to understand the intuition behind financial formulas. Understanding the derivations is necessary in order to be able to modify the formulas for a variety of more complex (and realistic) scenarios.

Consider an example applicable to many individuals who open Individual Retirement Accounts (I.R.A.'s), from which they may withdraw when they reach the age of $59\frac{1}{2}$ years. Consider an individual who makes a \$2,000 contribution to his I.R.A. at the end of each year for 20 years. All of his contributions receive a 10% annual rate of interest, compounded annually. What will be the total value of this account, including accumulated interest, at the end of the 20-year period? Equation (4.13) can be used to evaluate the future value of this annuity, where X is the annual contribution made at the end of each year by the investor to his account, i is the interest rate on the account, and *FVA* is the future value of the annuity. The future value of this individual's I.R.A. is \$114,550:

$$FVA_n = \$2,000 \frac{(1 + 0.10)^{20} - 1}{0.10} = \$114,550.$$

This future value annuity equation can be used whenever identical periodic contributions are made toward an account. Section 4.8 will present a discussion on determining the present value of such a series of cash flows. (The term "present value" is also defined later in section 4.8.)

Note that each of the above calculations assumes that cash flows are paid at the end of each period. If, instead, cash flows were realized at the beginning of each period, the annuity would be referred to as an *annuity due*. The annuity due would generate an extra year of interest on each cash flow. Hence, the future value of an annuity due is determined by simply multiplying the future value annuity formula by $(1 + i)$:

$$FVA_{n,\text{due}} = X \frac{(1 + i)^n - 1}{i}(1 + i) = X \frac{(1 + i)^{n+1} - (1 + i)}{i}. \quad (4.14)$$

From the above example, we find that the future value of the individual's I.R.A. is $126,005 if payments to the I.R.A. are made at the beginning of each year:

$$FVA_{n,\text{due}} = \$2{,}000 \frac{(1+0.10)^{21} - (1+0.10)}{0.10} = \$126{,}005.$$

APPLICATION 4.2: PLANNING FOR RETIREMENT
(Background reading: sections 2.5, 3.1, and 4.5)

Suppose that a 23-year-old accountant wishes to retire as a millionaire based on her retirement savings account. She intends to open and contribute to a tax-deferred 401k retirement account sponsored by her employer each year until she retires with $1,000,000 in that account. Would she meet her retirement goal if she deposited $10,000 into that account at the end of each year until she is 65 years of age? Assume that her account will generate an annual rate of interest equal to 5% for each of the next 42 years.

Equation (4.13) will be used to solve this problem:

$$FV_n = X \frac{(1+i)^n - 1}{i} = \$10{,}000 \cdot \frac{(1+0.05)^{42} - 1}{0.05}$$

$$= \$10{,}000 \cdot \frac{7.76159 - 1}{0.05} = \$1{,}352{,}318.$$

Now, suppose that she would like to retire as soon as possible with $1,000,000 in her account. Assuming that nothing else associated with her situation changes, what is the earliest age at which she can retire?

Now, we will use equation (4.13) to algebraically solve for n, the number of years that the accountant must wait to retire:

$$FV_n = X \frac{(1+i)^n - 1}{i}, \qquad \frac{FV_n \cdot i}{X} = (1+i)^n - 1,$$

$$\log\left(\frac{FV_n \cdot i}{X} + 1\right) = n \cdot \log(1+i), \qquad \log\left(\frac{FV_n \cdot i}{X} + 1\right) \div \log(1+i) = n,$$

$$n = \log\left(\frac{\$1{,}000{,}000 \cdot 0.05}{\$10{,}000} + 1\right) \div \log(1+0.05) = \frac{\log(6)}{\log(1.05)} = 36.72.$$

Since payments are made at the end of each year, the accountant must wait 37 years when she is 60 before she can retire as a millionaire. Note that we were able to find a closed-form solution (put n on one side alone) using simple algebra. In many time value problems, the exact placement of the exponent n will prevent us from obtaining a solution so easily.

4.7   DISCOUNTING AND PRESENT VALUE
(Background reading: section 4.3)

Cash flows realized at the present time have a greater value to investors than cash flows realized later, for the following reasons:

1   *Inflation.* The purchasing power of money tends to decline over time.
2   *Risk.* We never know with certainty whether we will actually realize the cash flow that we are expecting.
3   The option to either spend money now or defer spending it is likely to be worth more than being forced to defer spending the money.

The purpose of the present-value model is to express the value of a future cash flow in terms of cash flows at present. Thus, the present-value model is used to compute how much an investor would pay now for the expectation of some cash flow to be received in *n* years. The present value of this cash flow would be a function of inflation, the length of wait before the cash flow is received (*n*), the riskiness associated with the cash flow, and the time value an investor associates with money (how much he needs money now as opposed to later). Perhaps the easiest way to account for these factors when evaluating a future cash flow is to discount it in the following manner:

$$PV = \frac{CF_n}{(1+k)^n},$$
(4.15)

where CF_n is the cash flow to be received in year *n*, *k* is an appropriate discount rate accounting for risk, inflation, and the investor's time value associated with money, and *PV* is the present value of that cash flow. The discount rate enables us to evaluate a future cash flow in terms of cash flows realized today. Thus, the maximum a rational investor would be willing to pay for an investment yielding a $9,000 cash flow in six years assuming a discount rate of 15% would be $3,891, determined as follows:

$$PV = \frac{\$9,000}{(1+0.15)^6} = \frac{\$9,000}{2.31306} = \$3,890.95.$$

In the above example, we simply assumed a 15% discount rate. Realistically, perhaps the easiest value to substitute for *k* is the current interest or return rate on loans or other investments of similar duration and riskiness. However, this market-determined interest rate may not consider the individual investor's time preferences for money. Furthermore, the investor may find difficulty in locating a loan (or other investment) of similar duration and riskiness. For these reasons, more scientific methods for determining appropriate discount rates will be discussed later. In any case, the discount rate should account for inflation, the riskiness of the investment, and the investor's time value for money.

Deriving the present-value formula

The present-value formula can be derived easily from the compound interest formula. Assume that an investor wishes to deposit a sum of money into a savings account paying interest at a rate of 15%, compounded annually. If the investor wishes to withdraw from his account $9,000 in six years, how much must he deposit now? This answer can be determined by solving the compound interest formula for X_0:

$$FV_n = X_0(1+i)^n, \quad X_0 = \frac{FV_n}{(1+i)^n} = \frac{\$9,000}{(1+0.15)^6} = \frac{\$9,000}{2.31306} = \$3,890.95.$$

Therefore, the investor must deposit $3,890.95 now in order to withdraw $9,000 in six years at 15%.

Notice that the present-value equation (4.15) is almost identical to the compound interest formula where we solve for the principal (X_0):

$$PV = \frac{CF_n}{(1+k)^n}, \quad X_0 = \frac{FV_n}{(1+i)^n}.$$

Mathematically, these formulas are the same; however, there are some differences in their economic interpretations. In the interest formulas, interest rates are determined by market supply and demand conditions, whereas discount rates are individually determined by investors themselves (although their calculations may be influenced by market interest rates). In the present-value formula, we wish to determine how much some future cash flow is worth now; in the interest formula above, we wish to determine how much money must be deposited now to attain some given future value.

4.8 THE PRESENT VALUE OF A SERIES OF CASH FLOWS
(Background reading: sections 2.8 and 4.7)

Suppose that an investor needs to evaluate a series of cash flows. She needs only to discount each separately and then sum the present values of each of the individual cash flows. Thus, the present value of a series of cash flows CF_t received in time period t can be determined by the following expression:

$$PV = \sum_{t=1}^{n} \frac{CF_t}{(1+k)^t}. \tag{4.16}$$

For example, if an investment were expected to yield annual cash flows of $200 for each of the next five years, assuming a discount rate of 5%, its present value would be $865.90:

$$PV = \frac{200}{(1+0.05)^1} + \frac{200}{(1+0.05)^2} + \frac{200}{(1+0.05)^3} + \frac{200}{(1+0.05)^4} + \frac{200}{(1+0.05)^5} = \$865.90.$$

Therefore, the maximum price an individual should pay for this investment is $865.90, even though the cash flows yielded by the investment total $1,000. Because the individual must wait up to five years before receiving the $1,000, the investment is worth only $865.90. Use of the present-value series formula does not require that cash flows CF_t in each year be identical, as does the annuity model presented in the next section.

4.9   ANNUITY PRESENT VALUES
(Background reading: sections 3.4, 4.6, and 4.8)

The expression for determining the present value of a series of cash flows can be quite cumbersome, particularly when the payments extend over a long period of time. This formula requires that n cash flows be discounted separately and then summed. When n is large, this task may be rather time-consuming. If the annual cash flows are identical and are to be discounted at the same rate, an annuity formula can be a useful time-saving device. The same problem as discussed in the previous section can be solved using the following annuity formula:

$$PV_A = \frac{CF}{k}\left[1 - \frac{1}{(1+k)^n}\right],$$ (4.17)

where CF is the level of the annual cash flow generated by the annuity (or series). Use of this formula does require that all of the annual cash flows be identical. Thus, the present value of the cash flows in the problem discussed in the previous section is $865.90, determined as follows:

$$PV_A = \frac{\$200}{0.05}\left[1 - \frac{1}{(1+0.05)^5}\right] = \$4,000(0.2164738) = \$865.90.$$

As n becomes larger, this formula becomes more useful relative to the present-value series formula discussed in the previous section. However, the annuity formula requires that all cash flows be identical and be paid at the end of each year. The present-value annuity formula can be derived easily from the perpetuity formula discussed in section 4.11, or from the geometric expansion procedure described later in this section.

Note that each of the above calculations assumes that cash flows are paid at the end of each period. If, instead, cash flows were realized at the beginning of each period, the annuity would be referred to as an annuity due. Each cash flow generated by the annuity due would, in effect, be received one year earlier than if cash flows were realized at the end of each year. Hence, the present value of an annuity due is determined by simply multiplying the present-value annuity formula by $(1 + k)$:

$$PVA_{due} = \frac{CF}{k}\left[1 - \frac{1}{(1+k)^n}\right](1+k).$$ (4.18)

The present value of the five-year annuity due discounted at 5% is determined as follows:

$$PVA_{due} = \frac{200}{0.05}\left[1 - \frac{1}{(1+0.05)^5}\right](1+0.05) = \$4,000[0.2164738](1.05) = 909.19.$$

Deriving the present-value annuity formula

The present value annuity factor (pvaf) may be derived through use of the geometric expansion (see section 3.4). Consider the case where we wish to determine the present value of an investment based on a cash flow of CF made at the end of each year t for n years, where the appropriate discount rate is k:

$$PV_A = CF \cdot \left[\frac{1}{(1+k)^1} + \frac{1}{(1+k)^2} + \ldots + \frac{1}{(1+k)^n}\right]. \qquad (A)$$

Thus, the payment made at the end of the first year is discounted for one year, the payment at the end of the second year is discounted for two years, and so on. Clearly, determining the present value of this account will be very time-consuming if n is large. The first step of the geometric expansion is to multiply both sides of (A) by $(1 + k)$:

$$PV_A(1+k) = CF \cdot \left[1 + \frac{1}{(1+k)^1} + \ldots + \frac{1}{(1+k)^{n-1}}\right]. \qquad (B)$$

The second step in the geometric expansion is to subtract equation (A) from equation (B), to obtain:

$$PV_A(1+k) - PV_A = CF\left[1 - \frac{1}{(1+k)^n}\right], \qquad (C)$$

which simplifies to

$$PV_A(1+k-1) = PV_A(k) = CF\left[1 - \frac{1}{(1+k)^n}\right]. \qquad (D)$$

Notice that the subtraction led to the cancellation of many terms, reducing the equation that we wish to compute to a much more manageable size. Finally, we cancel the ones on the left side and divide both sides of equation (D) by k, to obtain:

$$PV_A = \frac{CF}{k}\left[1 - \frac{1}{(1+k)^n}\right]. \qquad (4.17)$$

APPLICATION 4.3: PLANNING FOR RETIREMENT, PART II
(Background reading: application 4.2 and section 4.9)

Suppose that the 23-year-old accountant from application 4.2 wishes to retire as a millionaire based on her retirement savings account, but needs to know what the present value of that million-dollar account is. If the account is open for the full 37 years, its future value will be $1,016,282, based on equation (4.13). Based on a discount rate of 5% and assuming that the account is open for 37 years, its present value is easily determined from equation (4.15) as follows:

$$PV = \frac{CF_n}{(1+k)^n} = \frac{\$1,016,282}{(1+0.05)^{37}} = \$167,112.07.$$

In present-value terms, this million-dollar account is obviously worth much less than $1,000,000. However, what is the present value of the annual series $10,000 deposits that she will make to that account? Again, based on a 5% discount rate, we determine this present value with equation (4.17) as follows:

$$PV_A = \frac{\$10,000}{0.05}\left[1 - \frac{1}{(1+0.05)^{37}}\right] = \$167,112.97.$$

Notice that the present value of contributions that she makes to the account is identical to the present value of what she will be able to retire with.

APPLICATION 4.4: VALUING A BOND

Because the present value of a series of cash flows is simply the sum of the present values of the cash flows, the annuity formula can be combined with other present-value formulas to evaluate investments. Consider, for example, a 7% coupon bond making annual interest payments for nine years. If this bond has a $1,000 face (or par) value, and its cash flows are discounted at 6%, its cash flows will be $70 in each of the nine years plus $1,000 in the tenth year. The present value of the bond's cash flows can be determined as follows:

$$PV = \frac{\$70}{0.06}\left[1 - \frac{1}{(1+0.06)^9}\right] + \frac{\$1,000}{(1+0.06)^9} = \$1,166.67(0.4081015) + \frac{\$1,000}{1.689479}$$

$$= \$476.118 + 591.898 = \$1,068.017.$$

Thus, the value of a bond is simply the sum of the present values of the cash flow streams resulting from interest payments and from principal repayment.

Now, let us revise the above example to value another 7% coupon bond. This bond will make semiannual (twice yearly) interest payments for nine years. If this bond has a $1,000 face (or par) value, and its cash flows are discounted at the stated annual rate of 6%, its value can be determined as follows:

$$PV = \frac{\$35}{0.03}\left[1 - \frac{1}{(1+0.03)^{18}}\right] + \frac{\$1,000}{(1+0.03)^{18}} = \$1,166.67(0.4126) + \frac{\$1,000}{1.7024}$$

$$= \$481.373 + 587.395 = \$1,068.768.$$

Again, the value of the bond is the sum of the present values of the cash flow streams resulting from interest payments and from the principal repayment. However, the semi-annual discount rate equals 3% and payments are made to bondholders in each of 18 semiannual periods.

4.10 AMORTIZATION
(Background reading: section 4.9)

At the beginning of this chapter, we derived the concept of present value from that of future value. Amortization is essentially a topic relating to interest, but the present-value annuity model presented in this chapter is crucial to its development. Amortization is the payment structure associated with a loan. That is, the amortization schedule of a loan is its payment schedule. Consider the annuity model from equation (4.17):

$$PV_A = \frac{CF}{k}\left[1 - \frac{1}{(1+k)^n}\right].$$ \hfill (4.17)

Typically, when a loan is amortized, the loan repayments will be made in equal amounts; that is, each annual or monthly payment will be identical. At the end of the repayment period, the balance (amount of principal remaining) on the loan will be zero. Thus, each payment made by the borrower is applied to the principal repayment as well as to interest. A bank lending money will require that the sum of the present values of its repayments be at least as large as the sum of money it loans. Therefore, if the bank loans a sum of money equal to PV for n years at an interest rate of i, the amount of the annual loan repayment will be CF:

$$CF = [PV_A \cdot k] \div \left[1 - \frac{1}{(1+k)^n}\right].$$ \hfill (4.18)

For example, if a bank were to extend a $865,895 five year mortgage to a corporation at an interest rate of 5%, the corporation's annual payment on the mortgage would be $200,000, determined by equation (4.18):

Table 4.2 The amortization schedule of a $865,895 loan with equal annual payments for five years at 5%

Year	Principal ($)	Payment ($)	Interest ($)	Payment to principal ($)
1	865,895	200,000	43,295	156,705
2	709,189	200,000	35,459	164,541
3	544,649	200,000	27,232	172,768
4	371,881	200,000	18,594	181,406
5	190,476	200,000	9,524	190,476

The loan is fully repaid by the end of the fifth year. The principal represents the balance at the beginning of the given year. The payment is made at the end of the given year, and includes one year of interest accruing on the principal from the beginning of that year. The remaining part of the payment is payment to the principal. This payment to the principal is deducted from the principal or balance as of the beginning of the following year.

$$CF = [\$865,895 \cdot 0.05] \div \left[1 - \frac{1}{(1+0.05)^5}\right] = \$200,000.$$

Thus, each year, the corporation will pay $200,000 toward both the loan principal and interest obligations. The amounts attributed to each are given in table 4.2. Notice that as payments are applied toward the principal, the principal declines; correspondingly, the interest payments decline. Nonetheless, total annual payments are identical until the principal diminishes to zero in the fifth year.

APPLICATION 4.5: DETERMINING THE MORTGAGE PAYMENT

A family has purchased a home with $30,000 down and a $300,000 mortgage. The mortgage will be amortized over 30 years with equal monthly payments. The interest rate on the mortgage will be 9% per year. Based on this data, we would like to determine the monthly mortgage payment and compile an amortization table decomposing each of the monthly payments into interest and payment toward principle.

First, we will express annual data as monthly data. Three hundred and sixty $(12 \cdot 30)$ months will elapse before the mortgage is fully paid, and the monthly interest rate will be 0.0075, or 9% divided by 12. Given this monthly data, monthly mortgage payments are determined as follows:

$$Payment = \$300,000 \div \left(\frac{1}{0.0075} - \frac{1}{0.0075(1+0.0075)^{360}}\right) = \$2,413.87.$$

Table 4.3 depicts the amortization schedule for this mortgage.

Table 4.3 The amortization schedule of a $300,000 loan with equal monthly payments for 30 years at 9% interest per annum (0.0075% per month)

Month	Beginning-of-month principal ($)	Total payment ($)	Payment on interest ($)	Payment on principal ($)
1	300,000.00	2,413.87	2,250.00	163.87
2	299,836.13	2,413.87	2,248.77	165.10
3	299,671.03	2,413.87	2,247.53	166.34
4	299,504.69	2,413.87	2,246.29	167.58
5	299,337.11	2,413.87	2,245.03	168.84
⋮	⋮	⋮	⋮	⋮
358	7,134.33	2,413.87	53.51	2,360.36
359	4,773.97	2,413.87	35.80	2,378.07
360	2,395.90	2,413.87	17.97	2,395.90

Students should be able to work through the figures on this table starting from the upper left-hand corner, then working to the left, then down. In this particular example, because n is large (360), use of a computerized spreadsheet will make computations substantially more efficient.

4.11 PERPETUITY MODELS
(Background reading: section 4.9)

As the value of n approaches infinity in the annuity formula, the value of the right-hand side term in the brackets,

$$\frac{1}{(1+k)^n},$$

approaches zero. That is, the cash flows associated with the annuity are paid each year for a period approaching "forever." Therefore, as n approaches infinity, the value of the infinite time horizon annuity approaches

$$PV_A = \frac{CF}{k}[1-0];$$

$$PV_P = \frac{CF}{k}. \tag{4.19}$$

The annuity formula discussed in section 4.9 can be derived intuitively by use of figure 4.1. First, consider a perpetuity as a series of cash flows beginning at time period one (one year from now) and extending indefinitely into perpetuity. Consider a second perpetuity with cash flows beginning in time period n and extending indefinitely into perpetuity. If an investor is to receive an n-year annuity, the second perpetuity represents those cash flows from the first perpetuity that he will not receive. Thus, the

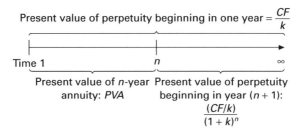

Figure 4.1 Deriving annuity present value from perpetuity present values. The present value of a perpetuity beginning in one year minus the present value of a second perpetuity beginning in year $(n + 1)$ equals the present value of an n-year annuity. Thus, $PVA = CF/k - (CF/k) \div (1 + k)^n = CF/k \cdot [1 - 1/(1 + k)^n]$.

difference between the present values of the first and second perpetuities represents the value of the annuity that he will receive. Note that the second perpetuity is discounted a second time, since its cash flows do not begin until year n:

$$PV_\mathrm{A} = \frac{CF}{k} - \frac{CF/k}{(1+k)^n} = \frac{CF}{k}\left[1 - \frac{1}{(1+k)^n}\right].$$

The perpetuity model is useful in the evaluation of a number of investments. Any investment with an indefinite or perpetual life expectancy can be evaluated with the perpetuity model. For example, the present value of a stock, if its dividend payments are projected to be stable, will be equal to the amount of the annual dividend (cash flow) generated by the stock divided by an appropriate discount rate. In European financial markets, a number of perpetual bonds have been traded for several centuries. In many regions in the United States, ground rents (perpetual leases on land) are traded. The proper evaluation of these and many other investments requires the use of perpetuity models.

The maximum price an investor would be willing to pay for a perpetual bond generating an annual cash flow of $200, each discounted at a rate of 5%, can be determined from equation (4.19):

$$PV_\mathrm{P} = \frac{\$200}{0.05} = \$4,000.$$

4.12   SINGLE-STAGE GROWTH MODELS
(Background reading: sections 4.9 and 4.11)

If the cash flow associated with an investment were expected to grow at a constant annual rate of g, the amount of the cash flow generated by that investment in year t would be

$$CF_t = CF_1(1 + g)^{t-1}, \tag{4.20}$$

where CF_1 is the cash flow generated by the investment in year one. Thus, if a stock paying a dividend of \$100 in year one were expected to increase its dividend payment by 10% each year thereafter, the dividend payment in the fourth year would be \$133.10:

$$CF_4 = CF_1(1 + 0.10)^{4-1}.$$

Similarly, the cash flow generated by the investment in the following year $(t + 1)$ will be

$$CF_{t+1} = CF_1(1 + g)^t.$$

The stock's dividend in the fifth year will be \$146.41:

$$CF_{4+1} = CF_1(1 + 0.10)^4 = \$146.41.$$

If the stock had an infinite life expectancy (as most stocks might be expected to), and its dividend payments were discounted at a rate of 13%, the value of the stock would be determined by

$$PV_{gp} = \frac{\$100}{0.13 - 0.10} = \frac{\$100}{0.03} = \$3,333.33.$$

This expression is often called the Gordon Stock Pricing Model. It assumes that the cash flows (dividends) associated with the stock are known in the first period and will grow at a constant compound rate in subsequent periods. More generally, this growing perpetuity expression can be written as follows:

$$PV_{gp} = \frac{CF_1}{k - g}. \tag{4.21}$$

The growing perpetuity expression simply subtracts the growth rate from the discount rate; the growth in cash flows helps to "cover" the time value of money. This formula for evaluating growing perpetuities can be used only when $k > g$. If $g > K$, either the growth rate or discount rate has probably been calculated improperly. Otherwise, the investment would have an infinite value (even though the formula would generate a negative value).

The formula (4.22) for evaluating growing annuities can be derived intuitively from the growing perpetuity model. In figure 4.2, the difference between the present value of a growing perpetuity with cash flows beginning in time period n is deducted from the present value of a perpetuity with cash flows beginning in year one, resulting in the present value of an n-year growing annuity. Notice that the amount of the cash flow generated by the growing annuity in year $(n + 1)$ is $CF(1 + g)^n$. This is the first of the

Present value of growing perpetuity beginning in one year:

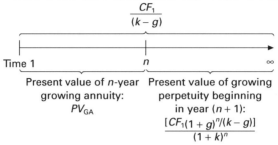

Figure 4.2 Deriving growing annuity present value from growing perpetuity peresent value. The present value of a growing perpetuity beginning in one year minus the present value of a second growing perpetuity beginning in year $(n + 1)$ equals the present value of an n-year growing annuity: $CF_1/(k - g) - [CF_1(1 + g)^n/(k - g)] \div (1 + k)^n$; $PV_{GA} = [CF_1/(k - g)][1 - (1 + g)^n/(1 + k)^n]$.

cash flows not generated by the growing annuity; it is generated after the annuity is sold or terminated. Because the cash flow is growing at the rate g, the initial amount of the cash flow generated by the second perpetuity is exceeded by the initial cash flow of the perpetuity beginning in year one:

$$PV_{GA} = \frac{CF_1}{k - g} \cdot \left[1 - \frac{(1 + g)^n}{(1 + k)^n} \right]. \tag{4.22}$$

Cash flows generated by many investments will grow at the rate of inflation. For example, consider a project undertaken by a corporation whose cash flow in year one is expected to be $10,000. If cash flows were expected to grow at the inflation rate of 6% each year until year six, then terminate, the project's present value would be $48,320.35, assuming a discount rate of 11%:

$$PV_{GA} = \frac{\$10,000}{0.11 - 0.06} \left[1 - \frac{(1 + 0.06)^6}{(1 + 0.11)^6} \right] = \$200,000(1 - 0.7584) = \$48,320.35.$$

Cash flows are generated by this investment through the end of the sixth year. No cash flow was generated in the seventh year. Verify that the amount of cash flow that would have been generated by the investment in the seventh year if it had continued to grow would have been $10,000(1.06)^6 = \$14,185$.

APPLICATION 4.6: STOCK VALUATION MODELS

Consider a stock whose annual dividend next year is projected to be $50. This payment is expected to grow at an annual rate of 5% in subsequent years. An investor has determined that the appropriate discount rate for this stock is 10%. The current value of this stock is $1,000, determined by the growing perpetuity model:

$$PV_{gp} = \frac{\$50}{0.10 - 0.05} = \$1,000.$$

This model is often referred to as the Gordon Stock Pricing Model. It may seem that this model assumes that the stock will be held by the investor forever. But what if the investor intends to sell the stock in five years? Its value would be determined by the sum of the present values of cash flows the investor does expect to receive:

$$PV_{GA} = \frac{DIV_1}{k - g} \cdot \left[1 - \frac{(1 + g)^n}{(1 + k)^n} \right],$$

where P_n is the price the investor expects to receive when he sells the stock in year n; and DIV_1 is the dividend payment the investor expects to receive in year one. The present value of the dividends the investor expects to receive is $207.53:

$$PV_{GA} = \frac{\$50}{0.10 - 0.05} \left[1 - \frac{(1 + 0.05)^5}{(1 + 0.10)^5} \right] = \$207.53.$$

The selling price of the stock in year five will be a function of the dividend payments that the prospective purchaser expects to receive beginning in year six. Thus, in year five, the prospective purchaser will pay $1,276.28 for the stock, based on his initial dividend payment of $63.81, determined by the following equations:

$$DIV_6 = DIV_1(1 + 0.05)^{6-1} = \$63.81,$$

$$\text{stock value in year five} = 63.81/(0.10 - 0.05) = \$1,276.28.$$

The present value of the $1,276.28 that the investor will receive when he sells the stock at the end of the fifth year is $792.47:

$$PV = \frac{\$1,276.28}{(1 + 0.1)^5} = \$792.47.$$

The total stock value will be the sum of the present values of the dividends received by the investor and his cash flows received from the sale of the stock. Thus, the current value of the stock is $207.53 plus $792.47, or $1,000. This is exactly the same sum determined by the growing perpetuity model earlier; therefore, the growing perpetuity model can be used to evaluate a stock even when the investor expects to sell it.

MULTIPLE-STAGE GROWTH MODELS*
(Background reading: section 4.12)

The Gordon Stock Pricing Model may be unrealistic in many scenarios, in that it assumes that one growth rate applies to the firm's cash flows and that this growth rate extends forever. Multiple-stage growth models enable the user to allow for different growth rates in different periods. For example, a growth company might generate cash flows that are expected to grow at a high rate in the short term and then decline as the firm matures. The multistage growth model can accommodate this pattern.

Suppose, for example, that an investor has the opportunity to invest in a stock currently selling for $100 per share. The stock is expected to pay a $3 dividend next year (at the end of year 1). In each subsequent year until the seventh year, the annual dividend is expected to grow at a rate of 20%. Starting in the eighth year, the annual dividend will grow at an annual rate of 3% forever. All cash flows are to be discounted at an annual rate of 10%. Should the stock be purchased at its current price?

The following Two-Stage Growth Model can be used to evaluate this stock:

$$P_0 = DIV_1 \left[\frac{1}{k - g_1} - \frac{(1 + g_1)^n}{(k - g_1)(1 + k)^n} \right] + \frac{DIV_1(1 + g_1)^{n-1}(1 + g_2)}{(k - g_2)(1 + k)^n}. \qquad (4.23)$$

Note that this model begins with an *n*-year annuity at growth rate g_1 and accommodates the new growth rate g_2 in the growing perpetuity that follows. The perpetuity is discounted a second time because it is deferred; it does not commence payments until year *n*. Substituting values from the problem statement yields the following:

$$P_0 = \$3 \left[\frac{1}{0.1 - 0.2} - \frac{(1 + 0.2)^7}{(0.1 - 0.2)(1 + 0.1)^7} \right] + \frac{\$3(1 + 0.2)^{7-1}(1 + 0.03)}{(0.1 - 0.03)(1 + 0.1)^7} = 92.8014519.$$

Since the $100 purchase price of the stock exceeds its 92.8014519 value, the stock should not be purchased.

The following represents a Three-Stage Growth Model which is based on a growing annuity, a deferred growing annuity, and a deferred growing perpetuity:

$$P_0 = DIV_1 \left[\frac{1}{k - g_1} - \frac{(1 + g_1)^{n(1)}}{(k - g_1)(1 + k)^{n(1)}} \right]$$

$$+ DIV_1 \left[\frac{(1 + g_1)^{n(1)-1}(1 + g_2)}{(1 + k)^{n(1)}(k - g_2)} - \frac{(1 + g_1)^{n(1)-1}(1 + g_2)^{n(2)-n(1)+1}}{(k - g_2)(1 + k)^{n(2)}} \right]$$

$$+ \frac{DIV_1(1 + g_1)^{n(1)-1}(1 + g_2)^{n(2)-n(1)}(1 + g_3)}{(k - g_3)(1 + k)^{n(2)}}.$$

There are three stages here, the first ending at time $n(1)$, the second ending at time $n(2)$, and the third extending into perpetuity. It may be a useful exercise to closely examine this expression to determine why it is structured in this manner. Try to determine why the growth rates and discount rates are structured as they are. Be certain to first be comfortable with the Present-Value Growing Annuity and Perpetuity Models and the Two-Stage Growth Model.

EXERCISES

4.1. The Ruth Company borrowed $21,000 at an annual interest rate of 9%. What is the future value of this loan assuming interest is accumulated on a simple basis for eight years?

4.2. The Cobb Company has issued ten million dollars in 10% coupon bonds maturing in five years. Interest payments on these bonds will be made semiannually.

    (a) How much are Cobb's semiannual interest payments?
    (b) What will be the total payment made by Cobb on the bonds in each of the first four years?
    (c) What will be the total payment made by Cobb on the bonds in the fifth year?

4.3. I have the opportunity to deposit $10,000 into my savings account today, which pays interest at an annual rate of 5.5%, compounded daily. What will be the ending balance of my account in five years if I make no additional deposits or withdrawals?

4.4. What would be the future value of the loan in problem 4.1 if interest were compounded:

    (a) annually?
    (b) semiannually?
    (c) monthly?
    (d) daily?
    (e) continuously?

4.5. A consumer has the opportunity to deposit $10,000 into his savings account today, which pays interest at an annual rate of 5.5%, compounded daily. What will be the ending balance of his account in five years if he makes no additional deposits or withdrawals?

4.6. The Speaker Company has the opportunity to purchase a five-year $1,000 certificate of deposit (CD) paying interest at an annual rate of 12%, compounded annually. The company will not withdraw early any of the money in its CD account. Will this account have a greater future value than a five-year $1,000 CD paying an annual interest rate of 10%, compounded daily?

4.7. The Waner Company needs to set aside a sum of money today for the purpose of purchasing, for $10,000, a new machine in three years. Money used to finance this purchase will be placed in a savings account paying interest at a rate of 8%. How much money must be placed in this account now to assure the Waner Company $10,000 in three years if interest is compounded yearly?

4.8. A given savings account pays interest at an annual rate of 3% compounded quarterly. Find the annual percentage yield (*APY*) for this account.

4.9.* Assuming no withdrawals or additional deposits, how much time is required for $1,000 to double if placed in a savings account paying an annual interest rate of 10% if interest were:

   (a) computed on a simple basis?
   (b) compounded annually?
   (c) compounded monthly?
   (d) compounded continuously?

4.10. What is the present value of a security promising to pay $10,000 in five years if its associated discount rate is:

   (a) 20%?
   (b) 10%?
   (c) 1%?
   (d) 0%?

4.11. What is the present value of a security to be discounted at a 10% rate promising to pay $10,000 in:

   (a) 20 years?
   (b) ten years?
   (c) one year?
   (d) six months?
   (e) 73 days?

4.12. The Gehrig Company is considering an investment that will result in a $2,000 cash flow in one year, a $3,000 cash flow in two years, and a $7,000 cash flow in three years. What is the present value of this investment if all cash flows are to be discounted at an 8% rate? Should Gehrig Company management be willing to pay $10,000 for this investment?

4.13. The Cramden Company has the opportunity to pay $30,000 for a security which promises to pay $6,000 in each of the next nine years. Would this be a wise investment if the appropriate discount rate were:

(a) 5%?
(b) 10%?
(c) 20%?

4.14. The Larsen Company is selling preferred stock which is expected to pay a $50 annual dividend per share. What is the present value of dividends associated with each share of stock if the appropriate discount rate were 8% and its life expectancy were infinite?

4.15. The Dinkins Company has purchased a machine whose output will result in a $10,000 cash flow in its first year of operation. This cash flow is projected to grow at the annual 10% rate of inflation over each of the next ten years. What will be the cash flow generated by this machine in:

(a) its second year of operation?
(b) its third year of operation?
(c) its fifth year of operation?
(d) its tenth year of operation?

4.16. The Wagner Company is considering the purchase of an asset that will result in a $5,000 cash flow in its first year of operation. Annual cash flows are projected to grow at the 10% annual rate of inflation in subsequent years. The life expectancy of this asset is seven years, and the appropriate discount rate for all cash flows is 12%. What is the maximum price that Wagner should be willing to pay for this asset?

4.17. What is the present value of a stock whose $100 dividend payment next year is projected to grow at an annual rate of 5%? Assume an infinite life expectancy and a 12% discount rate.

4.18. Which of the following series of cash flows has the highest present value at a 5% discount rate:

(a) $500,000 now?
(b) $100,000 per year for eight years?
(c) $60,000 per year for 20 years?
(d) $30,000 each year forever?

4.19. Which of the cash flow series in problem 4.18 has the highest present value at a 20% discount rate?

4.20. Mr. Sisler has purchased a $200,000 home with $50,000 down and a 20-year mortgage at a 10% interest rate. What will be the periodic payment on this mortgage if they are made:

   (a) annually?
   (b) monthly?

4.21. What discount rate for cash flows in problem 4.13 would render the Cramden Company indifferent regarding its decision to invest $30,000 for the nine-year series of $6,000 cash flows? That is, what discount rate will result in a $30,000 present value for the series?

4.22.* What would be the present value of $10,000 to be received in 20 years if the appropriate discount rate of 10% were compounded:

   (a) annually?
   (b) monthly?
   (c) daily?
   (d) continuously?

4.23. (a) What would be the present value of a 30-year annuity if the $1,000 periodic cash flow were paid monthly? Assume a discount rate of 10% per year.
   (b) Should an investor be willing to pay $100,000 for this annuity?
   (c)* What would be the highest applicable discount rate for an investor to be willing to pay $100,000 for this annuity?

4.24. A firm has purchased a piece of equipment for $10,000, which will be financed by a five-year loan accumulating interest at an annual rate of 10%. The loan will be amortized over the five-year period with equal annual payments. What will be the amount of the annual payment?

4.25.* Demonstrate how to derive an expression to determine the present value of a growing annuity.

4.26.* What would be the present value of a 50-year annuity whose first cash flow of $5,000 is paid in ten years and whose final (50th) cash flow is paid in 59 years? Assume that the appropriate discount rate is 12% for all cash flows.

4.27. Suppose that an investor has the opportunity to invest in a stock currently selling for $100 per share. The stock is expected to pay a $1.80 dividend next year (at the end of year one). In each subsequent year forever, the annual dividend is expected to grow at a rate of 4%. All cash flows are to be discounted at an annual rate of 6%. Should the stock be purchased at its current price?

4.28.   Suppose that an investor has the opportunity to invest in a stock currently selling for $100 per share. The stock is expected to pay a $5 dividend next year (at the end of year one). In each subsequent year until the third year, the annual dividend is expected to grow at a rate of 15%. Starting in the fourth year, the annual dividend will grow at an annual rate of 6% until the sixth year. Starting in the seventh year, dividends will not grow. All cash flows are to be discounted at an annual rate of 8%. Should the stock be purchased at its current price?

APPENDIX 4.A   TIME VALUE SPREADSHEET APPLICATIONS

Spreadsheets are very useful for time value calculations, particularly when there are either a large number of time periods or a large number of potential outcomes. Not only are most time value formulas easy to enter into cells, but the toolbar at the top of the Excel™ screen should have the Paste Function button (f_x) which will direct the user to a variety of time value functions. By left-clicking the Paste Function (f_x), the user will be directed to the Paste Function menu. From the Paste Function menu, one can select the Financial sub-menu. In the Financial sub-menu, scroll down to select the appropriate time value function. Pay close attention to the proper format and arguments for entry. Table 4.A.1 lists a number of time value functions which may be accessed through the Paste Function menu along with the example and notes.

While the formulas entered into table 4.A.1 make use of specialized Paste Functions for Finance, the spreadsheet user can enter his own simple formulas. For example, suppose that the user enters a cash flow in cell A1, a discount rate in cell A2, and a payment or termination period into cell A3. The present value of this cash flow can be found with =A1/(1+A2)^A3 or, in the case of an annuity, with =A1*((1/A2)-(1/(A2*(1+A2)^A3))). Now, enter a deposit amount into cell A1, an interest rate in cell A2 and a payment date or termination date in cell A3. Future values can be found with =A1*(1+A2)^n and =A1*((1/A2)-(1/(A2*(1+A2)^A3)))*(1+A2)^n. These formulas can easily be adjusted for growth, in which case a value for cell A4 may be inserted for the growth rate.

Table 4.A.1 Time value formula entry and paste functions

=Function type from f_x		Format	Entry example	Result	Formula entry
1	Future Value of Single Deposit or Investment	=FV(i, n, CF)	=PV(0.1,5,100)	-1610.51	=-1000*(1+0.1)^5
2	Future Value of Annuity	=FV(i, n, CF)	=PV(0.1,5,100)	-610.51	=100*((1+0.1)^5-1)/0.1
3	Future Value of Annuity with FV	=FV(i, n, CF, FV, Type)	=PV(0.1,5,100,1000,0)	-2221.02	=-100*((1+0.1)^5-1)/0.1-1000*(1+0.1)^5
4	Future Value of Annuity Due with FV	=FV(i, n, CF, FV, Type)	=PV(0.1,5,100,1000,1)	-2282.07	=-100*((1+0.1)^6-(1+0.1))/0.1-1000*(1+0.1)^5
5	Present Value of Future Cash Flow			-620.92	=1000/(1+0.1)^5
6	Net Present Value of Series	=NPV(k, Value 0, Value 1, Value 2, etc.)	=NPV(0.1,-100,110)	0.00	=100/(1+0.1)^0-110/(1+0.1)^1
7	Present Value of Annuity	=PV(k, CF)	=PV(0.1,5,100)	-379.08	=100/0.1*(1-1/(1+0.1)^5)
8	Present Value of Annuity with FV	=PV(k, n, CF, FV, Type)	=PV(0.1,5,100,1000,0)	-1000.00	=100/0.1*(1-1/(1+0.1)^5)-1000/(1+0.1)^5
9	Present Value of Annuity Due with FV	=PV(k, n, CF, FV, Type)	=PV(0.1,5,100,1000,1)	-1037.91	=-100/0.1*(1-1/(1+0.1)^5)*(1+0.1)-1000/(1+0.1)^5
10	Amortized Payment on Loan	=PMT(I, n, PV)	=PMT(0.1,5,1000)	-263.80	=1000*0.1/(1-1/(1+0.1)^5)
11	Amortized Payment on Loan (Due)	=PMT(I, n, PV, 0, Type)	=PMT(0.1,5,1000,1000,1)	-239.82	=(-1000*0.1)/((1-1/(1+0.1)^5)*(1+0.1))

For all the functions above (except 1 and 5), one can either use the f_x format or the Paste Function Menu retrievable from the toolbar above the spreadsheet.

For all the functions, the formula entry method from the right is usable. See notes below on individual function use. Also, notice how the spreadsheet interprets negative and positive cash flows.

1 Just enter Formula from the right to find the future value of a single cash flow. In this example, X = $1,000, i = 10%, and n = 5.

2 The example is for a $100 annuity for 5 years at 10%.

3 The example is for a $100 annuity for 5 years at 10% plus an additional $1,000 deposited at time zero.

4 Same as 3 but with all cash flows at the beginning of the periods.

5 Just enter Formula from the right to find the present value of a single cash flow. In this example, CF = $1,000, k = 10%, and n = 5.

6 Net Present value of a series of cash flows starting at time zero. Just enter the amounts of the cash flows which can vary from year to year.

7 The example is for a $100 annuity for 5 years at 10%.

8 The example is for a $100 annuity for 5 years at 10% plus $1,000 received at time 5.

9 Same as 8 but with beginning-of-year cash flows.

10 Amortized (mortgage) payment on a $1,000 loan at 10% for 5 years.

11 Same as 10 but with beginning-of-year payments.

CHAPTER FIVE
RETURN, RISK, AND CO-MOVEMENT

5.1 RETURN ON INVESTMENT

5.1 RETURN ON INVESTMENT
(Background reading: section 2.8 and application 2.4)

While this chapter is primarily concerned with the measurement and variability of security returns, it is also intended to provide an introduction to certain statistical measures. Investors are most concerned with the economic efficiency and riskiness of their investments, while the statistics branch of mathematics provides us with a variety of important measures of economic efficiency and risk.

Measuring an investment return is intended to enable one to determine the economic efficiency of that investment. An investment's return will express the profits generated by an initial cash outlay relative to the amount of the outlay required to secure that profit. This efficiency measure is, in a sense, the output from an investment relative to the investment's input. There are several methods to determine the return on an investment. The methods presented in this chapter are return on investment and internal rate of return. Holding period, arithmetic mean, and geometric mean rates of return on investment will be discussed along with internal rate of return and bond return measures. These methods differ in their ease of computation and how they account for the timeliness and compounding of cash flows.

Perhaps the easiest method to determine the economic efficiency of an investment is to add all of the investment profits π_t accruing at each time period t and divide this sum by the amount of the initial cash outlay P_0. This measure is called a holding period return:

$$ROI_{\text{H}} = \frac{\displaystyle\sum_{t=1}^{n} \pi_t}{P_0}. \qquad (5.1)$$

A $100 investment that generates $20 profits in each of three years would have a holding period return of 0.60, determined as follows:

$$ROI_H = \frac{\sum_{t=1}^{n} \pi_t}{P_0} = \frac{20+20+20}{100} = \frac{60}{100} = 0.60.$$

To ease comparisons between investments with different life expectancies, one can compute an arithmetic mean return on investment, ROI_A, by dividing the holding period return, ROI_H, by the life expectancy of the investment, n, as follows:

$$ROI_A = \frac{\sum_{t=1}^{n} \pi_t}{P_0} \div n. \qquad (5.2)$$

The subscript A after ROI designates that the return value expressed is an arithmetic mean return and the variable π_t is the profit generated by the investment in year t. Since it is not always clear exactly what the profit on an investment is in a given year, one can compute a return based on periodic cash flows. Therefore, where P_0 is the initial investment, this arithmetic mean rate of return formula can be written as follows:

$$ROI_A = \frac{\sum_{t=1}^{n} CF_t - P_0}{P_0} \div n = \frac{\sum_{t=1}^{n} CF_t - P_0}{nP_0} = \frac{\sum_{t=0}^{n} CF_t}{nP_0}. \qquad (5.3)$$

The numerator in each term represents the investment profits. Notice that the summation in the third expression begins at time zero, ensuring that the initial cash outlay is deducted from the numerator. (The cash flow CF_0 associated with any initial cash outlay or investment will be negative.) The primary advantage of equation (5.3) over equation (5.2) is that a profit level need not be determined each year for the investment; that is, the annual cash flows generated by an investment do not have to be classified as to whether they are profits or merely return of capital. Multiplying P_0 by n in the denominator of equation (5.3) to annualize the return has the same effect as dividing the entire fraction by n as in equation (5.2). In the first two expressions in equation (5.3), the summation begins at time one. The initial outlay is recognized by subtracting P_0 in the numerator. For example, consider a stock whose purchase price three years ago was $100. This stock paid a dividend of $10 in each of the three years and was sold for $130. If time zero is the stock's date of purchase, its arithmetic mean annual return is 20%:

$$ROI_A = \frac{\sum_{t=0}^{n} CF_t}{nP_0} = \frac{-100+10+10+10+130}{3 \cdot 100} = \frac{60}{300} = 0.20.$$

Identically, the stock's annual return is determined by equation (5.4):

$$ROI_A = \frac{\sum_{t=1}^{n} DIV_t}{nP_0} + \frac{P_n - P_0}{nP_0}$$

$$= \frac{10 + 10 + 10}{3 \cdot 100} + \frac{130 - 100}{nP_0} = \frac{30}{300} + \frac{30}{300} = 0.20, \qquad (5.4)$$

where DIV_t is the dividend payment for the stock in time t, P_0 is the purchase price of the stock, and P_n is the selling price of the stock. The difference $P_n - P_0$ is the capital gain realized from the sale of the stock.

Consider a second stock held over the same period whose purchase price was also $100. If this stock paid no dividends and was sold for $160, its annual return would also be 20%:

$$ROI_A = \frac{\sum_{t=1}^{n} DIV_t}{nP_0} + \frac{P_n - P_0}{nP_0} = \frac{0}{3 \cdot 100} + \frac{160 - 100}{nP_0} = \frac{60}{300} = 0.20.$$

Therefore, both the first and second stocks have realized arithmetic mean returns of 20%. The total cash flows generated by each, net of their original $100 investments, is $60. Yet the first stock must be preferred to the second, since its cash flows are realized sooner. The arithmetic mean return (ROI_A) does not account for the timing of these cash flows. Therefore, it evaluates the two stocks identically, even though the first should be preferred to the second. Because this measure of economic efficiency does not account for the timeliness of cash flows, another measure must be developed.

APPLICATION 5.1: FUND PERFORMANCE
(Background reading: sections 2.8 and 5.1 and application 2.4)

This application is concerned with how one might collect price data for a fund and compute returns from that data. Suppose that one is interested in a given publically traded fund for which prices and dividends are reported in standard news sources. First, retrieve fund price and dividend data for each period under consideration. This is easily done with the *Wall Street Journal* or *Barrons*, as well as a variety of online data sources. Calculate periodic holding returns based on the following:

$$r_t = \frac{P_t - P_{t-1} + DIV_t}{P_{t-1}}.$$

Note the similarity of this expression with equation (5.4). The appropriate period to record the dividend is the period during which the fund went "ex-dividend." Suppose that we wished to compute monthly returns for a fund over a period of five months. We collect relevant end-of-month prices along with any dividends. The following table lists prices and dividends collected for a fund from June 30 to November 30. Following the price data are sample return calculations:

Date	t	P_t	P_{t-1}	DIV_t	r_t	Notes
June 30	1	50	–	0	–	First month
July 31	2	55	50	0	0.100	$(55 \div 50) - 1 = 0.10$
August 31	3	50	55	0	−0.091	$(50 \div 55) - 1 = -0.091$
September 30	4	54	50	0	0.080	$(54 \div 50) - 1 = 0.08$
October 31	5	47	54	2	−0.092	ex-$2 dividend; $[(47 + 2) \div 54)] - 1 = -0.092$
November 30	6	51	47	0	0.081	$(51 \div 47) - 1 = 0.081$

Now, five-monthly holding period returns have been computed for the fund. The five-month holding period return might be approximated as the sum of individual monthly returns (although we will discuss some problems with this in section 5.2 and in application 5.2). The holding period and arithmetic mean returns for the fund can be computed with variations of equations (5.1) and (5.2) as follows:

$$ROI_H = \sum_{t=1}^{n} r_t = 0.10 - 0.091 + 0.08 - 0.092 + 0.081 = 0.078,$$

$$ROI_A = \frac{\sum_{t=1}^{n} r_t}{n} = \frac{0.10 - 0.091 + 0.08 - 0.092 + 0.081}{5} = 0.0156.$$

5.2 GEOMETRIC MEAN RETURN ON INVESTMENT
(Background reading: sections 2.10 and 5.1 and application 2.5)

The arithmetic mean return on investment does not account for any difference between dividends (intermediate cash flows) and capital gains (profits realized at the end of the investment holding period). That is, ROI_A does not account for the time value of money or the ability to reinvest cash flows received prior to the end of the investment's life. In reality, if an investor receives profits in the form of dividends, he has the option to reinvest them as they are received. If profits are received in the form of capital gains, the investor must wait until the end of his investment holding period to reinvest them. The difference between these two forms of profits can be accounted for by expressing compounded returns. That is, the geometric mean return on investment will account for the fact that any earnings that are retained by the firm will be automatically reinvested, and thus compounded. The geometric mean return is computed as follows:

$$ROI_g = \sqrt[n]{\prod_{t=1}^{n}(1+r_t)} - 1. \tag{5.5}$$

A \$100 investment that generates \$20 profits in each of three years would have a holding period return equal to 20% in each of those three years. The geometric mean return on this stock would be computed as follows:

$$ROI_g = \sqrt[n]{\prod_{t=1}^{n}(1+r_t)} - 1 = \sqrt[3]{\prod_{t=1}^{3}(1+r_t)} - 1$$

$$= \sqrt[3]{(1+0.2)(1+0.2)(1+0.2)} - 1 = 0.20.$$

Consider a stock that pays no dividends but appreciates from \$100 to \$160 over three years. If each of the end-of-year prices is not given, holding period returns for each of the years may not be determined. However, the three-year geometric return may be computed from the following:

$$ROI_g = \sqrt[n]{P_n \div P_0} - 1. \tag{5.6}$$

Thus, the stock's geometric mean return is determined as follows:

$$ROI_g = \sqrt[n]{P_n \div P_0} - 1 = \sqrt[3]{160 \div 100} - 1 = 0.1696.$$

Notice that both of the stocks in this section generated a total of \$60 in profits. The first stock generated \$20 in each of the three years, while the second stock generated \$60 when the stock is to be sold in the third year. The waiting period for the profits is less for the first stock. Therefore, its geometric mean rate of return is higher.

APPLICATION 5.2: FUND PERFORMANCE, PART II
(Background reading: section 5.2 and application 5.1)

Consider the fund from application 5.1 (we will call it fund A) and compare its monthly returns and prices to a second fund B:

Date	t	Fund A				Fund B			
		P_t	P_{t-1}	DIV_t	r_t	P_t	P_{t-1}	DIV_t	r_t
June 30	1	50	–	0	–	50	–	0	–
July 31	2	55	50	0	0.100	80	50	0	0.60
August 31	3	50	55	0	−0.091	40	80	0	−0.50
September 30	4	54	50	0	0.080	60	40	0	0.50
October 31	5	47	54	2	−0.092	30	60	0	−0.50
November 30	6	51	47	0	0.081	45	30	0	0.50

Recall that the arithmetic mean return on investment for fund A is 0.0156:

$$\overline{ROI}_A = \frac{\sum\limits_{t=1}^{n} r_t}{n} = \frac{0.10 - 0.091 + 0.08 - 0.092 + 0.081}{5} = 0.0156.$$

The arithmetic mean return on investment on fund B might be computed as follows:

$$ROI_A = \frac{\sum\limits_{t=1}^{n} r_t}{n} = \frac{0.60 - 0.50 + 0.50 - 0.50 + 0.50}{5} = 0.12.$$

This computational procedure is obviously quite misleading. Fund B paid no dividends and ended the five-year period worth $5 less than at the beginning of the five-year period. Despite the fact that fund B obviously lost money, its arithmetic mean return was computed to be 0.12 over the five years. Fund A clearly outperformed fund B, yet its arithmetic mean return appears to be lower. Alternatively, one could compute the arithmetic mean rate of return for fund B using the following:

$$ROI_A = \frac{P_n - P_0}{n \cdot P_0} = \frac{45 - 50}{5 \cdot 50} = -0.02.$$

While this seems more intuitively acceptable, the return for fund A cannot be computed in exactly the same way. However, the geometric mean return on investment can be computed for both funds:

$$ROI_g = \sqrt[n]{\prod_{t=1}^{n} (1 + r_t)} - 1 = \sqrt[5]{\prod_{t=1}^{5} (1 + r_t)} - 1,$$

$$ROI_g \text{ for A} = \sqrt[5]{(1 + 0.10)(1 - 0.091)(1 + 0.08)(1 - 0.092)(1 + 0.081)} - 1 = 0.0117,$$

$$ROI_g \text{ for B} = \sqrt[5]{(1 + 0.60)(1 - 0.5)(1 + 0.5)(1 - 0.5)(1 + 0.5)} - 1 = -0.0208.$$

With the geometric mean return computation, changes in the funds' investment bases are accounted for. That is, as the values of the funds change, the amounts on which returns are computed vary. Hence, the geometric mean rate of return can account for compounding and the comparison of fund returns is more meaningful.

5.3 INTERNAL RATE OF RETURN
(Background reading: sections 4.7, 4.8, and 4.9)

The primary strength of the internal rate of return (*IRR*) as a measure of the economic efficiency of an investment is that it accounts for the timeliness of all cash flows generated by that investment. The *IRR* of an investment is calculated by solving for *r* in the present-value series model discussed in section 4.8:

$$NPV = 0 = \sum_{t=0}^{n} \frac{CF_t}{(1+r)^t} = -P_0 + \sum_{t=1}^{n} \frac{CF_t}{(1+r)^t}, \qquad (5.7)$$

where net present value NPV is the present value of the series net of the initial cash outlay, and r is the return or discount rate that sets the investment's NPV equal to zero. The investment's internal rate of return is that value for r that equates NPV with zero.

There exists no general closed-form solution for r in equation (5.7). This means that there is no general equation that enables us to set aside r on one side of equation (5.7) and other terms on the other side. Therefore, we must substitute values for r until we find one that sets NPV equal to zero. Often, this substitution process is very time-consuming, but with experience calculating internal rates of return, one can find short-cuts to solutions in various types of problems. Perhaps the most important shortcut will be to find an easy method for deriving an initial value to substitute for r, resulting in an NPV fairly close to zero. One easy method for generating an initial value to substitute for r is by first calculating the investment's return on investment. Consider again the stock from section 5.1, whose purchase price three years ago was $100, paid a dividend of $10 in each of the three years, and was sold for $130. If an investor wanted to calculate the internal rate of return for this stock, she should substitute for r in the following:

$$0 = NPV = \sum_{t=0}^{n} \frac{CF_t}{(1+r)^t} = \frac{-100}{(1+r)^0} + \frac{10}{(1+r)^1} + \frac{10}{(1+r)^2} + \frac{130+10}{(1+r)^3}.$$

Since we found the arithmetic mean return on investment to be 0.20 in section 5.1, we may try this value as our initial trial solution for r:

$$NPV = \sum_{t=0}^{n} \frac{CF_t}{(1+0.2)^t} = \frac{-100}{(1+0.2)^0} + \frac{10}{(1+0.2)^1} + \frac{10}{(1+0.2)^2} + \frac{140}{(1+0.2)^3} = -3.7.$$

Since this NPV is less than zero, a smaller r value should be substituted. A smaller r value will decrease the right-hand side denominators, increasing the size of the fractions and NPV. Perhaps a feasible value to substitute for r is 10%. The same calculations will be repeated with the new r value of 10%:

$$NPV = \sum_{t=0}^{n} \frac{CF_t}{(1+0.1)^t} = \frac{-100}{(1+0.1)^0} + \frac{10}{(1+0.1)^1} + \frac{10}{(1+0.1)^2} + \frac{140}{(1+0.1)^3} = 22.54.$$

Since this new NPV exceeds zero, the r value of 10% is too small. However, because -3.7 is closer to zero than 22.54, the next value to substitute for r might be closer to 20% than to 10%. Perhaps a better estimate for the IRR will be 18%. Substituting this value for r results in an NPV of 0.86:

$$NPV = \sum_{t=0}^{n} \frac{CF_t}{(1+0.18)^t} = \frac{-100}{(1+0.18)^0} + \frac{10}{(1+0.18)^1} + \frac{10}{(1+0.18)^2} + \frac{140}{(1+0.18)^3} = 0.86.$$

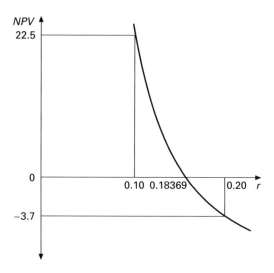

Figure 5.1 The relationship between *NPV* and *r*.

This *NPV* is quite close to zero; in fact, further substitutions will indicate that the true stock internal rate of return is approximately 18.369%. These iterations have a pattern: when *NPV* is less than zero, decrease *r* for the next substitution; when *NPV* exceeds zero, increase *r* for the next substitution. This process of iterations need only be repeated until the desired accuracy of calculations is reached. Figure 5.1 depicts the relationship between *NPV* and *r*.

The primary advantage of the internal rate of return over the return on investment measures is that it accounts for the timeliness of all cash flows generated by that investment. However, *IRR* does have three major weaknesses:

1 As we have seen, *IRR* takes considerably longer to calculate than does *ROI*. Therefore, if ease of calculation is of primary importance in a situation, the investor may prefer to use *ROI* as his measure of efficiency. Of course, calculators, spreadsheets, and other computer programs will compute *IRR* very quickly.
2 Sometimes an investment will generate multiple rates of return; that is, more than one *r* value will equate *NPV* with zero. This will occur when that investment has associated with it more than one negative cash flow. When multiple rates are generated, there is often no method to determine which is the true *IRR*. In fact, none of the rates generated may make any sense. When the *IRR* is infeasible as a method for comparing two investments, and the investor still wishes to consider the time value of money in his calculations, he may simply compare the present values of the investments. This approach and its weaknesses will be discussed in later chapters.
3 The internal rate of return is based on the assumption that cash flows received prior to the expiration of the investment will be reinvested at the internal rate of return. That is, it is assumed that future investment rates are constant and equal to the *IRR*. Obviously, this assumption may not hold in reality.

5.4 BOND YIELDS

By convention, rates of return on bonds are often expressed in terms that are somewhat different from those of other investments. For example, the coupon rate of a bond is the annual interest payment associated with the bond divided by the bond's face value. Thus, a four-year $1,000 corporate bond making $60 annual interest payments has a coupon rate of 6%. However, the coupon rate does not account for the actual purchase price of the bond. Corporate bonds are usually traded at prices that differ from their face values. The bond's current yield accounts for the actual purchase price of the bond:

$$cy = \frac{INT}{P_0}. \tag{5.8}$$

If the 6% bond described above were purchased for $800, its current yield would be 7.5%:

$$cy = \frac{60}{800} = 0.075.$$

The formula for current yield, while easy to work with, does not account for any capital gains (or losses) that may be realized when the bond matures. Furthermore, current yields do not account for the timeliness of cash flows associated with bonds. The bond's yield to maturity, which is essentially its internal rate of return, does account for any capital gains (or losses) that may be realized at maturity in addition to the timeliness of all associated cash flows:

$$NPV = 0 = \sum_{t=0}^{n} \frac{CF_t}{(1+y)^t} = -P_0 + \left[\sum_{t=1}^{n} \frac{INT}{(1+y)^t} \right] + \frac{F}{(1+y)^n}. \tag{5.9}$$

The yield to maturity (y) of the bond described above would be 12.679%. The value of y that sets the bond's NPV equal to zero is the bond's internal rate of return. If the bond makes semiannual interest payments, its yield to maturity can be more accurately expressed as

$$NPV = 0 = -P_0 + \left[\sum_{t=1}^{2n} \frac{INT/2}{\left(1 + \frac{y}{2}\right)^t} \right] + \frac{F}{\left(1 + \frac{y}{2}\right)^{2n}}. \tag{5.10}$$

Here, we are concerned with semiannual interest payments equal to half the annual sum and $2 \cdot n$ six-month time periods, where n is the number of years to the bond's maturity. The yield to maturity of the bond described above making semiannual payments equal to $30 for eight six-month periods would equal 0.125.

5.5 AN INTRODUCTION TO RISK

When individuals and firms invest, they become subjected to at least some level of uncertainty with respect to future cash flows and returns. Investors and firm managers cannot know with certainty what investment payoffs will be. This chapter is concerned with forecasting investment payoffs and returns and the uncertainty associated with these forecasts. We will define expected return in this chapter, focusing on it as a return forecast. This expected return will be expressed as a function of the investment's potential return outcomes and the probabilities associated with these potential outcomes. The riskiness of an investment is simply the potential for deviation from the investment's expected return. The *risk of an investment is defined here as the uncertainty* associated with returns on that investment. Although other definitions for risk, such as the probability of losing money or going bankrupt, can be very useful, they are often less complete or more difficult to measure. Our definition of risk does have some drawbacks as well. For example, an investment which is certain to be a complete loss is not regarded here to be risky, since its return is known to be −100% (although we note that it would not be regarded to be a particularly good investment).

In addition to providing an introduction to investment risk, the remainder of this chapter will provide introductions to important statistical measures of expected value, variability and co-movement. Each of these statistical measures is very important in finance.

5.6 EXPECTED RETURN
(Background reading: sections 2.8 and 5.5)

Consider an economy with three potential states of nature in the next year and stock A, whose return is dependent on these states. If the economy performs well, state one is realized and the stock earns a return of 25%. If the economy performs only satisfactorily, state two is realized and the stock earns a return of 10%. If the economy performs poorly, state three is realized and the stock achieves a return of −10%. Thus, there are three potential return outcomes for the stock; the stock will earn either 25%, 10%, or −10%. Only one of these states may occur and we cannot know in advance which will occur. However, assume that there, is a 20% chance that state one will occur, a 50% chance that state two will occur, and a 30% chance that state three will occur. The expected return on the stock will be 7%, determined by:

$$E[R_A] = \sum_{i=1}^{n} R_{A,i} P_i, \qquad (5.11)$$

$$E[R_A] = (R_{A,1} \cdot P_1) + (R_{A,2} \cdot P_2) + (R_{A,3} \cdot P_3),$$

$$E[R_A] = (0.25 \cdot 0.20) + (0.10 \cdot 0.50) + (-0.10 \cdot 0.30) = 0.07,$$

where $R_{A,i}$ is return outcome i for stock A and P_i is the probability associated with that outcome. Therefore, our forecasted return is 7%. The expected return considers all potential returns and weights more heavily those returns that are more likely to actually occur. Although our forecasted return level is 7%, it is obvious that there is potential for the actual return outcome to deviate from this figure. This potential for deviation (variation) will be measured in the following section.

5.7   VARIANCE AND STANDARD DEVIATION

The statistical concept of variance is a useful measure of risk. Variance accounts for the likelihood that the actual return outcome will vary from its expected value; furthermore, it accounts for the magnitude of the difference between potential return outcomes and the expected return. Variance can be computed with

$$\sigma^2 = \sum_{i=1}^{n} (R_i - E[R])^2 P_i. \qquad (5.12)$$

Table 5.1 lists potential return outcomes for the stock discussed in section 5.5. The variance of stock returns presented in section 5.5 is 0.0156, computed below and in table 5.1:

$$\sigma^2 = (0.25 - 0.07)^2 \cdot 0.2 + (0.10 - 0.07)^2 \cdot 0.5 + (-0.10 - 0.07)^2 \cdot 0.3 = 0.0156.$$

The statistical concept of standard deviation is also a useful measure of risk. The standard deviation of a stock's returns is simply the square root of its variance:

$$\sigma = \sqrt{\sum_{i=1}^{n} (R_i - E[R])^2 P_i}. \qquad (5.13)$$

Thus, the standard deviation of returns on the stock in table 5.1 is 12.49%.

Consider a second security, stock B, whose return outcomes are also dependent on economy outcomes one, two, and three. If outcome one is realized, stock B attains a return of 45%; in outcomes two and three, the stock attains returns of 5% and −15%, respectively. From table 5.2, we see that the expected return on stock B is 7%, the same as for stock A. However, the actual return outcome of stock B is subject to more

Table 5.1 Expected return, variance, and standard deviation of returns for stock A

i	R_i	P_i	$R_i P_i$	$R_i - E[R_a]$	$(R_i - E[R_a])^2$	$(R_i - E[R_a])^2 P_i$
1	0.25	0.20	0.05	0.18	0.0324	0.00648
2	0.10	0.50	0.05	0.03	0.0009	0.00045
3	−0.10	0.30	−0.03	−0.17	0.0289	0.00867
			$E[R_a] = 0.07$			$\sigma_a^2 = 0.01560$
						$\sigma_a = 0.1249$

Table 5.2 Expected return, variance, and standard deviation of returns for stock B

i	R_i	P_i	R_iP_i	$R_i - E[R_b]$	$(R_i - E[R_b])^2$	$(R_i - E[R_b])^2P_i$
1	0.45	0.20	0.09	0.38	0.1444	0.02888
2	0.05	0.50	0.025	0.02	0.0004	0.00020
3	−0.15	0.30	−0.045	0.22	0.0484	0.01452
			$E[R_b] = 0.070$			$\sigma_b^2 = 0.04360$
						$\sigma_b = 0.2088$

uncertainty. Stock B has the potential of receiving either a much higher or much a lower actual return than does stock A. For example, an investment in stock B could lose as much as 15%, whereas an equal investment in stock A cannot lose more than 10%. An investment in stock B also has the potential of attaining a much higher return than an identical investment in stock A. Therefore, returns on stock B are subject to greater variability (or risk) than returns on stock A. The concept of variance (or standard deviation) accounts for this increased variability. The variance of stock B (0.0436) exceeds that of stock A (0.0156), indicating that stock B is riskier than stock A.

Suppose that a stock has a very large or infinite number of potential return outcomes. A function or curve representing a distribution of values may be used to find the probability that the actual return will fall within a specified range. One of the most commonly used probability distributions in finance is the normal distribution. The curve representing the normal distribution is continuous (any fractional value may be selected), symmetric and ranges from −∞ to +∞. The normal curve (representing the normal distribution) is "bell-shaped" (see the z-table on page 266 of appendix B). The normal curve may be used to find the probability that a randomly selected data point from a data set which is approximately normally distributed will fall within a specified range. For example, suppose that we are considering the purchase of a stock whose monthly return is approximately normally distributed with an expected return of 0.01 and a standard deviation of 0.02. We may use the normal curve to find the probability that the stock's return in a given month falls within a given range or exceeds any given value. Suppose that we wish to compute the probability that the stock's return is positive ($\Pr[R_i > 0]$) in a given month. First, we define a normal deviate for outcome i (in this case zero) as follows:

$$z_i = \frac{R_i - E[R]}{\sigma_R},$$

$$z_i = \frac{0 - 0.01}{0.02} = -0.5. \tag{5.14}$$

The normal deviate for a zero return equals −0.5; it is one-half of a standard deviation less than the expected value associated with the distribution. Determining the probability that the stock's return exceeds zero is identical to determining the probability that the normal deviate for the stock's returns exceeds −0.5; $\Pr[R_i > 0] = \Pr[z_i > -0.5]$. Our next step is to find the value on a z-table corresponding to 0.5. By matching the appropriate row and column, we find this to be 0.1915. We actually want the value corresponding with −0.5 (which does not appear on the table), so we take advantage of the symmetry characteristic of the normal curve and associate a value of −0.1915 with our normal deviate of −0.5. We then find the probability that $R_i > 0$ and $z_i > -0.5$ by adding 50% (the area to the right of the mean on the normal curve) to −0.1915. Thus the probability that $z_i > -0.5$ or that the stock return will exceed zero is found to be 0.3085.

Consider another stock with normally distributed returns with an expected level of 7% and a standard deviation of 10%. From the z-table in appendix B, we see that there is a 68% probability that the actual return outcome on this stock will fall between −0.03 and 0.17, one standard deviation less than or greater than the mean value of the distribution:

$$E[R] - 1 \cdot \sigma < R_i < E[R] + 1 \cdot \sigma,$$

$$0.07 - 0.10 < R_i < 0.07 + 0.10.$$

We find in the z-table in appendix B that the z-value corresponding to a normal deviate equal to one is approximately 0.34. Thus, the probability that the stock's return will fall between the mean and one standard deviation greater than the mean equals 0.34. Using the symmetry characteristic of the normal distribution, we find that the probability that the stock's return will be within one standard deviation of its expected value equals two times 0.34, or 68%. A similar analysis indicates a 95% probability that the actual return outcome will fall between −0.13 and 0.27, two standard deviations from the expected value:

$$E[R] - 2 \cdot \sigma < R_i < E[R] + 2 \cdot \sigma,$$

$$0.07 - 0.20 < R_i < 0.07 + 0.20.$$

Obviously, a smaller standard deviation of returns will lead to a narrower range of potential outcomes, given any level of probability. If a security has a standard deviation of returns equal to zero, it has no risk. Such a security is referred to as the risk-free security with a return of r_f. Therefore, the only potential return level of the risk-free security is r_f. No such security exists in reality; however, short-term United States Treasury bills are quite close. The U.S. government has proven to be an extremely reliable debtor. When investors purchase Treasury bills and hold them to maturity, they do receive their expected returns. Therefore, short-term Treasury bills are probably the safest of all securities. For this reason, financial analysts often use the Treasury bill rate (of return) as their estimate for r_f in many important calculations.

5.8 HISTORICAL VARIANCE AND STANDARD DEVIATION

Empirical evidence suggests that historical stock return variances (standard deviations) are excellent indicators of future variances (standard deviations). That is, a stock whose

previous returns have been subject to substantial variability probably will continue
to realize returns of a highly volatile nature. Therefore, past riskiness is often a good
indicator of future riskiness. A stock's historical return variability can be measured with
a historical population variance:

$$\sigma^2 = \sum_{t=1}^{n} (R_t - \bar{R})^2 \frac{1}{n},$$ (5.15)

where R_t is the stock return in time t and R is the historical average return over the n
time periods. The variance of a sample drawn from a population of potential returns
is computed as

$$\sigma^2 = \sum_{t=1}^{n} (R_t - \bar{R})^2 \frac{1}{n-1}.$$ (5.16)

The stock's historical standard deviation of returns is simply the square root of its
variance. If an investor determines that the historical variance is a good indicator of
its future variance, he may need not to calculate potential future returns and their
associated probabilities for risk estimates; he may prefer to simply measure the stock's
riskiness with its historical variance or standard deviation. The historical standard
deviation for a given population (the denominator is the population size) or sample (the
denominator is one less than the sample size) may be computed as follows:

$$\sigma_H = \sqrt{\frac{\sum_{t=1}^{n} (R_i - \bar{R})^2}{n}}, \qquad \sigma_H = \sqrt{\frac{\sum_{t=1}^{n} (R_i - \bar{R})^2}{n-1}}.$$ (5.17)

Table 5.3 demonstrates historical variance and standard deviation computations for
stock D.

Table 5.3   Historical variance and standard deviation of returns of stock D

t	R_t	$R_t - \bar{R}_d$	$(R_t - \bar{R}_d)^2$	$(R_t - \bar{R}_d)^2 \, 1/n$
1	0.10	−0.06	0.0036	0.00072
2	0.15	−0.01	0.0001	0.00002
3	0.20	0.04	0.0016	0.00032
4	0.10	−0.06	0.0036	0.00072
5	0.25	0.09	0.0081	0.00162
	$\bar{R}_d = 0.16$			$\sigma_d^2 = 0.00310$
				$\sigma_d = 0.05568$

5.9   COVARIANCE

Standard deviation and variance provide us with measures of the absolute risk levels of securities. However, in many instances, it is useful to measure the risk of one security relative to the risk of another or relative to the market as a whole. The concept of covariance is integral to the development of relative risk measures. Covariance provides us with a measure of the relationship between the returns of two securities. That is, given that two securities' returns are likely to vary, covariance indicates whether they will vary in the same direction or in opposite directions. The likelihood that two securities will covary in the same direction (or, more accurately, the strength of the relationship between returns on two securities) is measured by

$$\sigma_{k,j} = \sum_{i=1}^{n} (R_{k,i} - E[R_k])(R_{j,i} - E[R_j])P_i, \tag{5.18}$$

where $R_{k,i}$ and $R_{j,i}$ are the return of stocks k and j if outcome i is realized, and P_i is the probability of outcome i. $E[R_k]$ and $E[R_j]$ are simply the expected returns of securities k and j. For example, the covariance between returns of stocks A and B is

$$\text{cov(A,B)} = \{(0.25 - 0.07) \cdot (0.45 - 0.07) \cdot 0.20\}$$
$$+ \{(0.10 - 0.07) \cdot (0.05 - 0.07) \cdot 0.50\}$$
$$+ \{(-0.10 - 0.07) \cdot (-0.15 - 0.07) \cdot 0.30\}$$
$$= \{0.01368\} + \{-0.0003\} + \{0.01122\} = 0.0246.$$

Since this covariance is positive, the relationship between return variability on these two securities is positive. That is, the larger the positive value of covariance, the more likely it is one security will perform well given that the second will perform well. A negative covariance indicates that strong performance by one security implies likely poor performance by the second security. A covariance of zero implies that there is no relationship between returns on the two securities. Table 5.4 details the solution method for this example.

Empirical evidence suggests that historical covariances are strong indicators of future covariance levels. Thus, if an investor is unable to associate probabilities with

Table 5.4   Covariance between returns on stocks A and B

i	R_{ai}	R_{bi}	P_i	$R_{ai} - E[R_a]$	$R_{bi} - E[R_b]$	$(R_{ai} - E[R_a])(R_{bi} - E[R_b])P_i$
1	0.25	0.45	0.20	0.18	0.38	0.01368
2	0.10	0.05	0.50	0.03	−0.02	−0.00030
3	−0.10	−0.15	0.30	−0.17	−0.22	0.01122
					COV(A,B) =	0.0246

Table 5.5 Historical covariance between returns on stocks D and E

t	R_{dt}	R_{et}	$(R_{dt} - \bar{R}_d)$	$(R_{et} - \bar{R}_e)$	$(R_{dt} - \bar{R}_d)(R_{et} - \bar{R}_e)1/n$
1	0.10	0.15	−0.06	−0.05	0.00060
2	0.15	0.18	−0.01	−0.02	0.00004
3	0.20	0.25	0.04	0.05	0.00040
4	0.10	0.20	−0.06	0	0
5	0.25	0.22	0.09	0.02	0.00036
	$\bar{R}_d = 0.16$	$0.20 = \bar{R}_e$			COV(D,E) = 0.00140

potential outcome levels, in many cases he may use historical covariance as his estimate for future covariance. Table 5.5 demonstrates how to determine historical covariance for two hypothetical stocks D and E.

5.10 THE COEFFICIENT OF CORRELATION AND THE COEFFICIENT OF DETERMINATION

The coefficient of correlation provides us with a means of standardizing the covariance between returns on two securities. For example, how large must covariance be to indicate a strong relationship between returns? Covariance will be smaller given low returns on the two securities than given high-security returns. The coefficient of correlation $\rho_{k,j}$ between returns on two securities will always fall between −1 and +1.[1] If security returns are directly related, the correlation coefficient will be positive. If the two security returns always covary in the same direction by the same proportions, the coefficient of correlation will equal one. If the two security returns always covary in opposite directions by the same proportions, $\rho_{k,j}$ will equal −1. The stronger the inverse relationship between returns on the two securities, the closer $\rho_{k,j}$ will be to −1. If $\rho_{k,j}$ equals zero, there is no relationship between returns on the two securities. The coefficient of correlation $\rho_{k,j}$ between returns is simply the covariance between returns on the two securities divided by the product of their standard deviations:

$$\rho_{k,j} = \frac{\text{COV}(k,j)}{\sigma_k \cdot \sigma_j}. \tag{5.19}$$

Equation (5.19) implies that the covariance formula can be rewritten as

$$\text{COV}(k,j) = \sigma_k \sigma_j \rho_{k,j}. \tag{5.20}$$

[1] Many statistics textbooks use the notation $r_{i,j}$ to designate the correlation coefficient between variables i and j. Because the letter r is used in this text to designate return, it will use the lower-case rho, $\rho_{i,j}$ to designate the correlation coefficient.

If an investor can access only raw data pertaining to security returns, he might first find security covariances then divide by the products of their standard deviations to find correlation coefficients. However, if for some reason the investor knows the correlation coefficients between returns on securities, he can use this value along with standard deviations to find covariances.

The coefficient of correlation between returns on stocks A and B is 0.94:

$$\rho_{a,b} = \frac{0.0246}{0.1249 \cdot 0.21} = 0.94.$$

This value can be squared to determine the coefficient of determination between returns of the two securities. The coefficient of determination $\rho_{k,j}^2$ measures the proportion of variability in one security's returns that can be explained by or be associated with variability of returns on the second security. Thus, approximately 88% of the variability of stock A returns can be explained by or associated with variability of stock B returns. The concepts of covariance and correlation are crucial to the development of portfolio risk and relative risk models presented in later chapters.

Historical evidence suggests that covariances and correlations between stock returns remain relatively constant over time. Thus, an investor can use historical covariances and correlations as his forecasted values. However, it is important to realize that these historical relationships apply to standard deviations, variances, covariances, and correlations, but not to the actual returns themselves. That is, we can often forecast future risk levels and relationships on the basis of historical data, but we cannot forecast returns on the basis of historical returns. Thus, last year's return for a given stock implies almost nothing about next year's return for that stock. The historical covariance between returns on securities i and j can be found by solving equation (5.21) for a population or equation (5.22) for a sample:

$$\sigma_{i,j} = \sum_{t=1}^{n} (R_{i,t} - \bar{R}_i)(R_{j,t} - \bar{R}_j)\frac{1}{n}, \tag{5.21}$$

$$\sigma_{i,j} = \sum_{t=1}^{n} (R_{i,t} - \bar{R}_i)(R_{j,t} - \bar{R}_j)\frac{1}{n-2}. \tag{5.22}$$

Historical correlation coefficients may be computed from these covariance results.

EXERCISES

5.1. An investor purchased one share of Mathewson stock for $1,000 in 2002 and sold it exactly one year later for $1,200. Calculate the investor's arithmetic mean return on investment.

5.2. An investor purchased one share of Johnson Company stock in 1976 for $200 and sold it in 1983 for $400. Calculate the following for the investor:

   (a) the arithmetic mean return on investment;
   (b) the geometric mean return on investment;
   (c) the internal rate of return.

5.3. An investor purchased 100 shares of Alexander Company stock for $75 apiece in 1975 and sold each share for $80 exactly six years later. The Alexander Company paid annual dividends of $8 per share in each of the six years the investor held the stock. Calculate the following for the investor:

   (a) the arithmetic mean return on investment;
   (b) the internal rate of return.

5.4. The Young Corporation is considering the purchase of a machine for $100,000, whose output will yield the company $20,000 in annual after-tax cash flows for each of the next five years. At the end of the fifth year, the machine will be sold for its $40,000 salvage value. Calculate the following for the machine that Young is considering purchasing:

   (a) the arithmetic mean return on investment;
   (b) the internal rate of return.

5.5. What is the net present value of an investment whose internal rate of return equals its discount rate?

5.6. An investor purchased 100 shares each of Grove Company stock and Dean Company stock for $10 per share. The Grove Company paid an annual dividend of one dollar per share in each of the eight years during which the investor held the stock. The Dean Company paid an annual dividend of $0.25 per share in each of the eight years during which the investor held the stock. At the end of the eight-year period, the investor sold each of his shares of Grove Company stock for $11 and sold each of his shares of Dean Company stock for $18.

   (a) Calculate the sum of dividends received by the investor from each of the companies.
   (b) Calculate the capital gains realized on the sale of stock of each of the companies.
   (c) Calculate the return on investment for each of the two companies' stock using an arithmetic mean return.
   (d) Calculate the internal rate of return for each of the two stocks.
   (e) Which of the two stocks performed better during their holding periods?

5.7. The Feller Company is considering the purchase of an investment for $100,000 that is expected to pay off $50,000 in two years, $75,000 in four years, and $75,000 in six years. In the third year, Feller must make an additional payment of $50,000 to sustain the investment. Calculate the following for the Feller investment:

(a) Return on investment, using an arithmetic mean return.
(b) The investment internal rate of return.
(c) Describe any complications you encountered in part (b).

5.8. A $1,000 face value bond is currently selling at a premium for $1,200. The coupon rate of this bond is 12% and it matures in three years. Calculate the following for this bond, assuming that its interest payments are made annually:

(a) its annual interest payments;
(b) its current yield;
(c) its yield to maturity.

5.9. Work through each of the calculations in problem 5.8 assuming that interest payments are made semiannually.

5.10* The Radbourne Company invested $100,000 into a small business 20 years ago. Its investment generated a cash flow equal to $3,000 in its first year of operation. Each subsequent year, the business generated a cash flow which was 10% larger than in the prior year; that is, the business generated a cash flow equal to $3,300 in the second year, $3,630 in the third year, and so on for 19 years after the first. The Radbourne Company sold the business for $500,000 after its 20th year of operation. What was the internal rate of return for this investment?

5.11. Megabyte Products management is considering the investment in one of two projects available to the company. The returns on the two projects, A and B, are dependent on the sales outcome of the company. Megabyte management has determined three potential sales outcomes for the company. The highest potential sales outcome for Megabyte is outcome 1 or $800,000. If this sales outcome were realized, project A would realize a return outcome of 30%; project B would realize a return of 20%. If outcome 2 were realized, the company's sales level would be $500,000. In this case, project A would yield 15%, and project B would yield 13%. The worst outcome 3 will result in a sales level of $400,000, and return levels for projects A and B of 1% and 9% respectively. If each sales outcome has an equal probability of occurring, determine the following for the Megabyte Company:

(a) the probabilities of outcomes 1, 2, and 3;
(b) its expected sales level;

(c) the variance associated with potential sales levels;
(d) the expected return of project A;
(e) the variance of potential returns for project A;
(f) the expected return and variance for project B;
(g) standard deviations associated with company sales, returns on project A and returns on project B;
(h) the covariance between company sales and returns on project A;
(i) the coefficient of correlation between company sales and returns on project A;
(j) the coefficient of correlation between company sales and returns on project B;
(k) the coefficient of determination between company sales and returns on project B.

5.12. Which of the projects in problem 5.11 represents the better investment for Megabyte Products?

5.13. The following table provides historical *percentage* returns for the Patterson and Liston Companies along with percentage returns on the market portfolio (index or fund):

Year	Patterson	Liston	Market
1998	4	19	15
1999	7	4	10
2000	11	−4	3
2001	4	21	12
2002	5	13	9

Calculate the following based on the preceding table:

(a) mean historical returns for the two companies and the market portfolio;
(b) variances associated with Patterson Company returns and Liston Company returns along with returns on the market portfolio;
(c) the historical covariance and coefficient of correlation between returns of the two securities;
(d) the historical covariance and coefficient of correlation between returns of the Patterson Company and returns on the market portfolio;

(e)   the historical covariance and coefficient of correlation between returns of the Liston Company and returns on the market portfolio.

5.14.   Project the following for both the Patterson and Liston Companies using your results from problem 5.13:

(a)   the variance and standard deviation of returns;
(b)   the coefficient of correlation between each of the companies' returns and returns on the market portfolio.

5.15.   Windsor Company management projects a return level of 15% for the upcoming year. Management is uncertain as to what the actual sales level will be; therefore, it associates a standard deviation of 10% with this sales level. Managers assume that sales will be normally distributed. What is the probability that the actual return level will:

(a)   fall between 5% and 25%?
(b)   fall between 15% and 25%?
(c)   exceed 25%?
(d)   exceed 30%?

5.16.   What would be each of the probabilities in problem 5.15 if Windsor Company management were certain enough of its forecast to associate a 5% standard deviation with its sales projection?

5.17.   An investor has the opportunity to purchase a risk-free Treasury bill yielding a return of 10%. He also has the opportunity to purchase a stock which will yield either 7% or 17%. Either outcome is equally likely to occur. Compute the following:

(a)   the variance of returns on the stock;
(b)   the coefficient of correlation between returns on the stock and returns on the Treasury bill.

APPENDIX 5.A   RETURN AND RISK SPREADSHEET APPLICATIONS

Table 5.A.1 contains spreadsheet entries for computing stock variances, standard deviations, and covariances. The table lists prices for stocks X, Y, and Z from January 9 to January 20 in cells B3:B14, E3:E14, and H3:H14. From these prices, we compute returns in cells B19:B29, E19:E29, and H19:H29.

Formulas for computing returns are given in rows 19–29 in table 5.A.2. Means, variances, standard deviations, covariances, and correlation coefficients are computed in

Table 5.A.1 Stock prices, returns, risk, and co-movement

	A	B	C	D	E	F	G	H
1	CORP. X			CORP. Y			CORP. Z	
2	DATE	PRICE		DATE	PRICE		DATE	PRICE
3	9-Jan	50.125		9-Jan	20		9-Jan	60.375
4	10-Jan	50.125		10-Jan	20		10-Jan	60.5
5	11-Jan	50.25		11-Jan	20.125		11-Jan	60.25
6	12-Jan	50.25		12-Jan	20.25		12-Jan	60.125
7	13-Jan	50.375		13-Jan	20.375		13-Jan	60
8	14-Jan	50.25		14-Jan	20.375		14-Jan	60.125
9	15-Jan	50.25		15-Jan	21.375		15-Jan	62.625
10	16-Jan	52.375		16-Jan	21.25		16-Jan	69.75
11	17-Jan	52.25		17-Jan	21.375		17-Jan	60.75
12	18-Jan	52.375		18-Jan	21.5		18-Jan	60.875
13	19-Jan	52.5		19-Jan	21.375		19-Jan	60.875
14	20-Jan	52.375		20-Jan	21.5		20-Jan	60.875
15								
16	CORP. X			CORP. Y			CORP. Z	
17	DATE	RETURN		DATE	RETURN		DATE	RETURN
18	9-Jan	N/A		9-Jan	N/A		9-Jan	N/A
19	10-Jan	0		10-Jan	0		10-Jan	0.00207
20	11-Jan	0.002494		11-Jan	0.00625		11-Jan	-0.00413
21	12-Jan	0		12-Jan	0.006211		12-Jan	-0.00207
22	13-Jan	0.002488		13-Jan	0.006173		13-Jan	-0.00208
23	14-Jan	-0.00248		14-Jan	0		14-Jan	0.002083
24	15-Jan	0.039801		15-Jan	0.04908		15-Jan	0.04158
25	16-Jan	0.002392		16-Jan	-0.00585		16-Jan	-0.02994
26	17-Jan	-0.00239		17-Jan	0.005882		17-Jan	0
27	18-Jan	0.002392		18-Jan	0.005848		18-Jan	0.002058
28	19-Jan	0.002387		19-Jan	-0.00581		19-Jan	0
29	20-Jan	-0.00238		20-Jan	0.005848		20-Jan	0
30	Mean	0.004064		Mean	0.006694		Mean	0.00087
31	Variance	0.000145		Variance	0.00022		Variance	0.000266
32	Variance (P)	0.000132		Variance (P)	0.0002		Variance (P)	0.000241
33	St.D.	0.01204		St.D.	0.014842		St.D.	0.016296
34	St.D. (P)	0.011479		St.D. (P)	0.014151		St.D. (P)	0.015538
35		COV(X,Y)=	0.0001494		COV(Y,Z)=	0.000192		
36		COV(X,Z)=	0.000139					
37		CORR(X,Y)=	0.9196541		CORR(Y,Z)=	0.8733657		
38		CORR(X,Z)=	0.7791748					

Table 5.A.2 Stock prices, returns, risk, and co-movement: formula entries

	A	B	C	D	E	F	G	H
16		CORP.X		CORP.Y			CORP.Z	
17	DATE	RETURN		DATE	RETURN		DATE	RETURN
18	9-Jan	N/A		9-Jan	N/A		9-Jan	N/A
19	10-Jan	=B4/B3-1		10-Jan	=E4/E3-1		10-Jan	=H4/H3-1
20	11-Jan	=B5/B4-1		11-Jan	=E5/E4-1		11-Jan	=H5/H4-1
21	12-Jan	=B6/B5-1		12-Jan	=E6/E5-1		12-Jan	=H6/H5-1
22	13-Jan	=B7/B6-1		13-Jan	=E7/E6-1		13-Jan	=H7/H6-1
23	14-Jan	=B8/B7-1		14-Jan	=E8/E7-1		14-Jan	=H8/H7-1
24	15-Jan	=B9/B8-1		15-Jan	=E9/E8-1		15-Jan	=H9/H8-1
25	16-Jan	=B10/B9-1		16-Jan	=E10/E9-1		16-Jan	=H10/H9-1
26	17-Jan	=B11/B10-1		17-Jan	=E11/E10-1		17-Jan	=H11/H10-1
27	18-Jan	=B12/B11-1		18-Jan	=E12/E11-1		18-Jan	=H12/H11-1
28	19-Jan	=B13/B12-1		19-Jan	=E13/E12-1		19-Jan	=H13/H12-1
29	20-Jan	=B14/B13-1		20-Jan	=E14/E13-1		20-Jan	=H14/H13-1
30	Mean	=AVERAGE(B19:B29)		Mean	=AVERAGE(E19:E29)		Mean	=AVERAGE(H19:H29)
31	Variance	=VAR(B19:B29)		Variance	=VAR(E19:E29)		Variance	=VAR(H19:H29)
32	Variance (P)	=VARP(B19:B29)		Variance (P)	=VARP(E19:E29)		Variance (P)	=VARP(H19:H29)
33	St.D.	=STDEV(B19:B29)		St.D.	=STDEV(E19:E29)		St.D.	=STDEV(H19:H29)
34	St.D. (P)	=STDEVP(B19:B29)		St.D. (P)	=STDEVP(E19:E29)		St.D. (P)	=STDEVP(H19:H29)
35			COV(X,Y)=	=COVAR(B19:B29,E19:E29)	COV(Y,Z)=			=COVAR(E19:E29,H19:H29)
36			COV(X,Z)=	=COVAR(B19:B29,H19:H29)				
37			CORR(X,Y)=	=CORREL(B19:B29,E19:E29)	CORR(Y,Z)=			=CORREL(E19:E29,H19:H29)
38			CORR(X,Z)=	=CORREL(B19:B29,H19:H29)				

rows 30–38. Row 30 computes the arithmetic mean return for each of the three stocks. Table 5.A.2 lists formulas associated with the values in cells A30:H30. The =(Average) function may be typed in directly as listed in table 5.A.2, row 30, or obtained from the Paste Function button (f_x) menu under the Statistical sub-menu. Entry instructions are given in the dialogue box obtained when the Average function is selected. The variance formulas in row 31 are based on the Sample formula; the Variance (P) formulas in row 32 are based on the population formula. Standard deviation sample and population results are given in rows 33 and 34. Covariances and correlation coefficients are given in rows 35–38.

CHAPTER SIX
ELEMENTARY PORTFOLIO MATHEMATICS

6.1 AN INTRODUCTION TO PORTFOLIO ANALYSIS
(Background reading: sections 5.1 and 5.5)

An investor's portfolio is the set of all her investments. The investor's wealth and ability to spend is a function of her entire portfolio of investments. Thus, it is reasonable for an investor to be concerned with the performance of individual securities only to the extent that their performance affects overall portfolio performance. Since the returns of individual investments tend to be only somewhat related to one another, the composition of the investor's portfolio is of primary importance. We can demonstrate that investors can more effectively control their investment risk by selecting appropriate securities in appropriate combinations.

The return on an investor's portfolio is a simple weighted average of the component individual security returns. One calculates the expected return of a portfolio based on either a function of potential portfolio returns and their associated probabilities (as computed in chapter 5) or finding the weighted average of expected returns on individual securities. In the vast majority of cases, portfolio returns variance or standard deviation will be less than the weighted average of the individual security return variances or standard deviations. The extent to which overall portfolio risk is less than the weighted average of component asset risk levels will depend on the nature of co-movement between the assets.

6.2 PORTFOLIO RETURN
(Background reading: sections 2.8, 5.5, and 6.1)

In section 5.5, we computed the expected return of a security as a function of potential return outcomes and associated probabilities. The expected return of a portfolio is calculated similarly, using equation (6.1), where the subscript p designates the portfolio and the subscript j is a counter designating a particular outcome out of m potential outcomes:

$$E[R_p] = \sum_{j=1}^{m} R_{p,j} P_j. \tag{6.1}$$

For many portfolio management applications, it is useful to express portfolio return as a function of the returns of the individual securities that comprise the portfolio:

$$E[R_p] = \sum_{i=1}^{n} w_i E[R_i]. \tag{6.2}$$

The subscript i designates a particular security out of n in the portfolio. The weights w_i are the portfolio proportions. Thus, a security weight w_i specifies how much money is invested in security i relative to the total amount invested in the entire portfolio:

$$w_i = \frac{\$ \text{ invested in security } i}{\text{Total } \$ \text{ invested in portfolio p}}.$$

Thus, portfolio return is simply a weighted average of individual security returns.

Consider a portfolio made up of two securities, one and two. The expected return of security one is 10% and the expected return of security two is 20%. If 40% of the dollar value of the portfolio is invested in security one (that is, $[w_1] = 0.40$), and the remainder is invested in security two ($[w_2] = 0.60$), the expected return of the portfolio may be determined as follows by equation (6.2):

$$E[R_p] = (w_1 \cdot E[R_1]) + (w_2 \cdot E[R_2]),$$

$$E[R_p] = (0.4 \cdot 0.10) + (0.6 \cdot 0.20) = 0.16.$$

6.3   PORTFOLIO VARIANCE
(Background reading: sections 2.9, 5.7–5.10, and 6.2)

Portfolio return variance may also be defined as a function of potential portfolio returns and associated probabilities:

$$\sigma_p^2 = \sum_{j=1}^{m} (R_{pj} - E[R_p])^2 P_j. \tag{6.3}$$

Again, it is usually helpful to express portfolio variance as a function of individual security characteristics. However, we stress that the variance of portfolio returns is not simply a weighted average of individual security return variances. We will actually be able to demonstrate that we can combine a set of high-risk assets into a low-risk portfolio. This is due to the important relationship between portfolio risk and return covariances between pairs of securities. The portfolio returns variance can be computed by solving the following function:

$$\sigma_p^2 = \sum_{i=1}^{n}\sum_{j=1}^{n} w_i w_j \sigma_i \sigma_j \rho_{i,j} = \sum_{i=1}^{n}\sum_{j=1}^{n} w_i w_j \sigma_{i,j}. \tag{6.4}$$

Section 2.9 discussed the general process for working with double summations. We would solve equation (6.4) to compute the variance of a two-security portfolio as follows:

$$\sigma_p^2 = w_1 \cdot w_1 \cdot \sigma_1 \cdot \sigma_1 \cdot \rho_{1,1} + w_1 \cdot w_2 \cdot \sigma_1 \cdot \sigma_2 \cdot \rho_{1,2}$$
$$+ w_2 \cdot w_1 \cdot \sigma_2 \cdot \sigma_1 \cdot \rho_{2,1} + w_2 \cdot w_2 \cdot \sigma_2 \cdot \sigma_2 \cdot \rho_{2,2}. \tag{6.5}$$

Notice that we start the summation operations at $i = 1$ and $j = 1$. This means that in the first stage of operation, both i and j refer to security 1. In the second stage, i still refers to security 1 but j refers to security 2. Since n, the number of securities, equals 2, the third stage starts j over again at 1 and i now refers to security 2. In the fourth stage, both i and j refer to security 2. We simplify the result to complete the computational process.

Equation (6.5) can only be used for a two-security portfolio. Equation (6.4) and variations of it to be discussed later may be used to compute portfolio variances when n exceeds 2 (see equation (6.9)). Hence, equation (6.5) is only a special case of equation (6.4).

Consider the portfolio constructed in section 6.2. The weights associated with securities 1 and 2 are 0.4 and 0.6, respectively. Assume that the standard deviations of returns for securities one and two are 0.20 and 0.30, respectively, and that the correlation coefficient $\rho_{i,j}$ between returns on the two securities is 0.5. We should also note that $\rho_{1,2} = \rho_{2,1}$ and that $\rho_{1,1} = \rho_{2,2} = 1$ because the correlation coefficient between anything and itself equals 1. Following equations (6.4) and (6.5), we compute the variance and standard deviation of portfolio returns as follows:

$$\sigma_p^2 = 0.4 \cdot 0.4 \cdot 0.2 \cdot 0.2 \cdot 1 + 0.4 \cdot 0.6 \cdot 0.2 \cdot 0.3 \cdot 0.5$$
$$+ 0.6 \cdot 0.4 \cdot 0.3 \cdot 0.2 \cdot 0.5 + 0.6 \cdot 0.6 \cdot 0.3 \cdot 0.3 \cdot 1 = 0.0532. \tag{6.6}$$

Thus, the standard deviation of portfolio returns would be 0.23, the square root of its 0.0532 variance level. By simplifying the expressions in the first and fourth sets of parentheses, combining the terms in the second and third sets, and rearranging, one can simplify equations (6.5) and (6.6) for two-security portfolios:

$$\sigma_p^2 = w_1^2 \cdot \sigma_1^2 + w_2^2 \cdot \sigma_2^2 + 2(w_1 \cdot w_2 \cdot \sigma_1 \cdot \sigma_2 \cdot \rho_{1,2}),$$
$$\sigma_p^2 = 0.4^2 \cdot 0.2^2 + 0.6^2 \cdot 0.3^2 + 2(0.4 \cdot 0.6 \cdot 0.2 \cdot 0.3 \cdot 0.5) = 0.0504.$$

A careful examination of these expressions will reveal that equation (6.4) can also be rewritten as follows:

$$\sigma_p^2 = \sum_{i=1}^{n} w_i^2 \sigma_i^2 + \sum_{\substack{i=1 \\ i \neq j}}^{n}\sum_{j=1}^{n} w_i w_j \sigma_{i,j}. \tag{6.7}$$

When a portfolio consists of only two securities, its variance can be determined by equation (6.8):

$$\sigma_p^2 = w_1^2 \sigma_1^2 + w_2^2 \sigma_2^2 + 2 w_1 w_2 \sigma_{1,2}. \tag{6.8}$$

Larger portfolios require the use of equations (6.4) or (6.7), accounting for all products of security weights and standard deviations squared and all possible combinations of pair-wise security covariances and weight products. For example, equation (6.8) can be rewritten for a three-security portfolio as

$$\sigma_p^2 = w_1^2 \sigma_1^2 + w_2^2 \sigma_2^2 + w_3^2 \sigma_3^2 + 2 w_1 w_2 \sigma_{1,2} + 2 w_1 w_3 \sigma_{1,3} + 2 w_2 w_3 \sigma_{2,3}. \tag{6.9}$$

Notice that equation (6.9) involves working with three individual security variances (one for each security) and three sets of covariances (between 1 and 2, 1 and 3, and 2 and 3). Also notice the similarities between equation (6.8) for a two-security portfolio and equation (6.9) for a three-security portfolio.

As the number of securities in the portfolio increases, the amount of computational effort increases disproportionately. The number of sets of covariances between nonidentical pairs of securities equals $(n^2 - n)/2$. If 50 securities were to be included in the investor's portfolio, 1,225 sets of covariances would be required to combine with 50 variance terms in order to solve equation (6.7). Obviously, as the number of securities in the portfolio becomes large, computers and computer spreadsheets become quite useful in working through the repetitive calculations. The equations are not difficult to solve; they are merely repetitive and time-consuming.

6.4 DIVERSIFICATION AND EFFICIENCY

The important contribution of the covariance terms in equations (6.4)–(6.9) is that portfolio risk is a function of the extent to which security returns are related to one another. Security risk can be diversified away by constructing portfolios of unrelated assets. The statement "Don't put all your eggs in one basket" has a strong basis in reality. Investment in a variety of different securities with different return structures really does result in portfolio risk reductions. One should expect that portfolio risk levels will be lower than the weighted average security risk levels. Diversification is most effective when the returns of the individual securities are inversely correlated. Lower covariances $\sigma_{i,j}$ result in lower portfolio risk. Portfolio risk is quite dependent on the correlation coefficient of returns $\rho_{i,j}$ between securities included in the portfolio. Lower correlation levels imply lower risk levels. Because the covariance between security returns $\sigma_{i,j}$ equals the product $\sigma_i \sigma_j \rho_{i,j}$, reduced covariances imply reduced correlation coefficients. Thus, lower correlation coefficients between securities imply lower portfolio risk. Portfolio risk should be expected to decline whenever $\rho_{i,j}$ is less than one and diversification increases. We will normally expect any randomly selected pair of securities to have a correlation coefficient less than one. Hence, we should normally expect that adding securities to a randomly selected portfolio will tend to reduce portfolio risk.

In our first example with securities 1 and 2, the weighted average of the standard deviation of returns of the two securities is 26%:

$$Weighted\ Average\ \sigma_i = 0.4 \cdot 0.2 + 0.6 \cdot 0.3 = 0.26.$$

However, recall that the standard deviation of returns of the portfolio that they combine to make is only 23%:

$$\sigma_p = \sqrt{0.4^2 \cdot 0.2^2 + 0.6^2 \cdot 0.3^2 + 2(0.4 \cdot 0.6 \cdot 0.2 \cdot 0.3 \cdot 0.5)} = 0.23.$$

Clearly, some risk has been diversified away by combining the two securities into the portfolio. In fact, the risk of a portfolio will almost always be lower than the weighted average of the standard deviations of the securities that comprise that portfolio. The only two exceptions occur when:

1 The returns correlation coefficient between all pairs of securities equals 1.
2 One of two assets in a two-asset portfolio has a zero standard deviation of returns.

For a more extreme example of the benefits of diversification, consider two securities, 3 and 4, whose potential return outcomes are perfectly inversely related. Data relevant to these securities is listed in table 6.1. If outcome one occurs, security three will realize a return of 30%, and security four will realize a 10% return level. If outcome two is realized, both securities will attain returns of 20%. If outcome three is realized, securities three and four will attain return levels of 10% and 30%, respectively. If each

Table 6.1 A portfolio return with perfectly inversely correlated securities: $w_3 = w_4 = 0.5$

i	R_{3i}	R_{4i}	R_{pi}	P_i
1	0.30	0.10	0.20	0.333
2	0.20	0.20	0.20	0.333
3	0.10	0.30	0.20	0.333

Given:

$$\bar{R}_3 = 0.20, \qquad \bar{R}_4 = 0.20,$$
$$\sigma_3 = 0.08165, \qquad \sigma_4 = 0.08165,$$
$$w_3 = 0.50, \qquad w_4 = 0.50, \qquad \rho_{3,4} = -1.$$

Then:

$$\bar{R}_p = w_3\bar{R}_3 + w_4\bar{R}_4 = (0.5 \cdot 0.20) + (0.5 \cdot 0.20) = 0.20,$$
$$\sigma_p = \sqrt{w_3^2\sigma_3^2 + w_4^2\sigma_4^2 + 2w_3w_4\sigma_3\sigma_4\rho_{3,4}},$$

$$\sigma_p = \sqrt{0.5^2 \cdot 0.0066667 + 0.5^2 \cdot 0.0066667 + 2 \cdot 0.5 \cdot 0.5 \cdot 0.08165 \cdot 0.08165 \cdot (-1)} = 0.$$

outcome is equally likely to occur (P_i is 0.333 for all outcomes), the expected return level of each security is 20%; the standard deviation of returns for each security is 0.08165. The expected return of a portfolio combining the two securities is 20% if each security has equal portfolio weight ($w_3 = w_4 = 0.5$), yet the standard deviation of portfolio returns is zero. Thus, two relatively risky securities have been combined into a portfolio that is virtually risk-free. Application 3.5 in chapter 3 provides a general format for constructing a riskless portfolio in the presence of two perfectly inversely correlated assets.

Notice in the previous paragraph that we first combined securities 3 and 4 into a portfolio and then found that portfolio's return given each outcome. The portfolio's return is 20% regardless of the outcome; thus, it is risk-free. The same result can be obtained with the variances of securities three and four, the correlation coefficient between their returns, and solving for portfolio variance with equation (6.8) as in table 6.1.

The implication of the two examples provided in this chapter is that security risk can be diversified away by combining the individual securities into portfolios. Spreading investments across a variety of securities does result in portfolio risk that is lower than the weighted average risks of the individual securities. This diversification is most effective when the returns of the individual securities are at least somewhat unrelated; or, better still, inversely related, as were securities three and four in the previous example. For example, returns on a retail food company stock and on a furniture company stock are not likely to be perfectly positively correlated; therefore, including both of them in a portfolio may result in a reduction of portfolio risk. From a mathematical perspective, the reduction of portfolio risk is dependent on the correlation coefficient of returns $\rho_{i,j}$ between securities included in the portfolio. Thus, the lower the correlation coefficients between these securities, the lower will be the resultant portfolio risk. In fact, as long as $\rho_{i,j}$ is less than one, which – realistically – is always the case, some reduction in risk can be realized from diversification.

Consider the Portfolio Possibilities Frontier displayed in figure 6.1. This frontier maps out portfolio return and standard deviation combinations as security weights vary. The correlation coefficient between returns of securities C and D is one. Remember that portfolio return is always a weighted average of individual security returns. The standard deviation of returns of any portfolio combining these two securities is a weighted average of the returns of the two securities' standard deviations, but only because the correlation coefficient between returns on these securities equals 1. Thus, both portfolio returns and portfolio standard deviation are linearly related to the proportions invested in each of the two securities. Diversification here yields no benefits. In figure 6.2, the correlation coefficient between returns on securities A and B is 0.5. Portfolios combining these two securities will have standard deviations less than the weighted average of the standard deviations of the two securities. Hence, the portfolio possibilities frontier for these two securities arches toward the vertical axis. Given this lower correlation coefficient, which is more representative of "real-world" correlations, there are clear benefits to diversification. In fact, we can see in figures 6.3 and 6.4 that decreases in correlation coefficients result in increased diversification benefits. Lower correlation coefficients result in lower risk levels at all levels of expected return. The portfolio possibilities frontier will exhibit a more significant arch toward the vertical axis as the correlation coefficient between security returns decreases. Thus, an investor will benefit by constructing his portfolio of securities with low correlation coefficients.

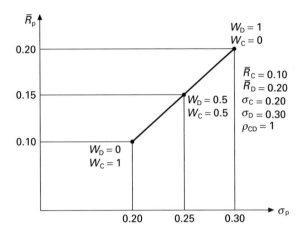

Figure 6.1 The relationship between portfolio return and risk when $\rho_{CD} = 1$.

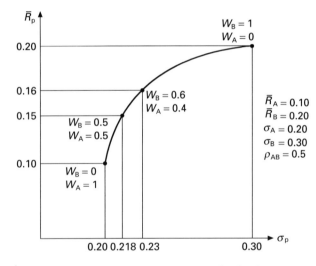

Figure 6.2 The relationship between portfolio return and risk when $\rho_{AB} = 0.5$.

To this point, we have focused on using correlation coefficients to manage the diversification of a portfolio. However, we will also consider a second powerful diversification tool. The risk of a portfolio will tend to decline as n, the number of securities in the portfolio, increases. This result will hold as long as the securities are not perfectly correlated.[1] It is perfectly reasonable to expect that securities will not be perfectly correlated. Thus, two factors govern the level of diversification in a portfolio:

---

[1] This result also requires that as securities are added to the portfolio, their individual variances are not increasing enough to offset the diversification benefits that they provide. If variances among all securities are approximately equal or are randomly distributed with a constant mean, this result will hold. This result will be demonstrated mathematically in application 8.5.

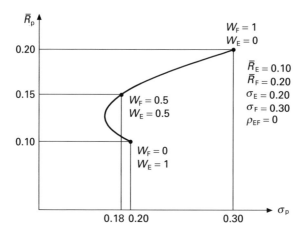

Figure 6.3   The relationship between portfolio return and risk when $\rho_{EF} = 0$.

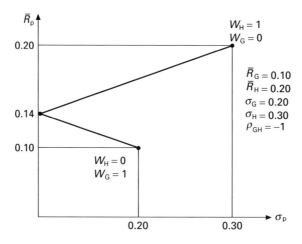

Figure 6.4   The relationship between portfolio return and risk when $\rho_{GH} = -1$.

1   The covariances between pairs of securities in the portfolio. Smaller return covariances of included securities lead to reduced portfolio risk.
2   The number of assets included in the portfolio. Larger numbers of included securities lead to decreased portfolio risk.

6.5   THE MARKET PORTFOLIO AND BETA

The market portfolio is the collective set of all investments that are available to investors. That is, the market portfolio represents the combination or aggregation of all securities (or other assets) that are available for purchase. Investors may wish to consider the performance of this market portfolio to determine the performance of securities in general. Since portfolio return is a weighted average of individual security returns, the return on the market portfolio is the average of returns on securities. Thus, the return on the market portfolio is representative of the return on the "typical" asset. An investor may wish to know the market portfolio return to gauge performance of a particular security or investment portfolio relative to the performance of the market or a "typical" security. The market return is also very useful for constructing additional risk measures such as a security or investment portfolio beta:

$$\beta_i = \frac{\sigma_i}{\sigma_m} \cdot \rho_{i,m} = \frac{\sigma_i \sigma_m \rho_{i,m}}{\sigma_m^2} = \frac{\text{COV}(i,m)}{\sigma_m^2}. \tag{6.10}$$

Consider a stock A whose standard deviation of returns is 0.4 and assume that the market portfolio standard deviation equals 0.2. Further assume that the correlation coefficient between returns on security A and the market equals 0.75. Then the beta (β_A) of security A would be 1.5:

$$\beta_i = \frac{\sigma_i}{\sigma_m} \cdot \rho_{i,m} = \frac{0.4}{0.2} \cdot 0.75 = 1.5.$$

The beta of a stock measures the risk of a stock relative to the risk of the market portfolio. Part of a stock's risk derives from diversifiable sources (firm-specific) and other risks are undiversifiable (market-related). The lower the correlation of a stock with the market, the greater is the risk that can be diversified away. Thus, lower-risk stocks and portfolios will have lower betas. Because beta only accounts for undiversifiable risk, the beta of a portfolio equals the weighted average beta of its component securities.

Determination of the return on the market portfolio requires the calculation of returns on all of the assets available to investors. Because there are hundreds of thousands of assets available to investors (including stocks, bonds, options, bank accounts, real estate, and so on), determining the exact return of the market portfolio may be impossible. Thus, investors generally make use of indices such as the Dow Jones Industrial Average or the Standard and Poor's 500 to gauge the performance of the market portfolio. These indices merely act as surrogates for the market portfolio; we assume that if the indices are increasing, then the market portfolio is performing well. For example, performance of the Dow Jones Industrials Average depends on the performance of the 30 stocks that comprise this index. Thus, if the Dow Jones market index is performing well, the 30 securities, on average, are probably performing well. This strong performance may imply that the market portfolio is performing well. In any case, it is easier to measure the performance of 30 or 500 stocks (for the Standard and Poor's 500) than it is to measure the performance of all of the securities that comprise the market portfolio.

6.6   DERIVING THE PORTFOLIO VARIANCE EXPRESSION
(Background reading: section 6.3)

We first discussed variance as a function of potential squared deviations from expected return outcomes. This is consistent with definitions of variance in most other applications.

For practical purposes, it is normally more useful to define portfolio variance in terms of individual security variances and covariances between pairs of securities. This enables us to characterize risk as a function of portfolio weights. Knowing appropriate portfolio weights enables us to determine appropriate amounts to invest in each security. An understanding of the relationship between the two portfolio risk measures will help us understand more complex concepts concerning portfolio risk.

We will derive the variance of given portfolio p as a function of security variances, covariances, and weights as in equation (6.4). First, we start with the variance expressed as a function of *m* potential portfolio return outcomes *j* and associated probabilities:

$$\sigma_p^2 = \sum_{j=1}^{m} (R_{pj} - E[R_p])^2 P_j. \tag{6.3}$$

For the sake of simplicity, we will work with $n = 2$ securities in our portfolio. It will be easy to generalize this procedure from 2 to *n* securities. Portfolio variance may be rewritten from equation (6.3) as follows:

$$\sigma_p^2 = \sum_{j=1}^{m} (w_1 R_{1j} + w_2 R_{2j} - w_1 E[R_1] - w_2 E[R_2])^2 P_j. \tag{A}$$

The first two terms inside the parentheses in combination refer to returns for securities 1 and 2 given outcome *i*. The last two terms in combination refer to expected returns for securities 1 and 2. Next, we "complete the square" for equation (A) and combine terms multiplied by w_1 and w_2:

$$\sigma_p^2 = \sum_{j=1}^{m} [w_1^2 (R_{1j} - E[R_1])^2 P_j + w_2^2 (R_{2j} - E[R_2])^2 P_j$$

$$+ 2 w_1 w_2 (R_{1j} - E[R_1])(R_{2j} - E[R_2]) P_j]. \tag{B}$$

We next move the summation operation inside the brackets:

$$\sigma_p^2 = w_1^2 \sum_{j=1}^{m} (R_{1j} - E[R_1])^2 P_j + w_2^2 \sum_{j=1}^{m} (R_{2j} - E[R_2])^2 P_j$$

$$+ 2 w_1 w_2 \sum_{j=1}^{m} (R_{1j} - E[R_1])(R_{2j} - E[R_2]) P_j. \tag{C}$$

The derivation is completed by substituting in equation (C) variances and covariances as defined in chapter 5:

$$\sigma_p^2 = w_1^2 \sigma_1^2 + w_2^2 \sigma_2^2 + 2 w_1 w_2 \sigma_{1,2}, \tag{6.8}$$

which is the two-security equivalent for equation (6.4).

EXERCISES

6.1. Seventy-five percent of a portfolio is invested in Honeybell stock and the remaining 25% is invested in MBIB stock. Honeybell stock has an expected return of 6% and an expected standard deviation of returns of 9%. MBIB stock has an expected return of 20% and an expected standard deviation of 30%. The coefficient of correlation between returns of the two securities is expected to be 0.4. Determine the following:

(a) the expected return of the portfolio;
(b) the expected variance of the portfolio;
(c) the expected standard deviation for the portfolio.

6.2. What is the standard deviation of returns for an equally weighted portfolio comprising two securities with return variances equal to 0.09 and a covariance equal to zero?

6.3. Each of the pairs of stock listed below will be combined into two-security portfolios. In each case, the first stock will comprise 60% of the portfolio and the second stock will comprise the remaining 40%. Compute the standard deviation of returns for each portfolio.

(a) $\sigma_1 = 0.60$, $\sigma_2 = 0.60$, $\sigma_{1,2} = 0.36$;
(b) $\sigma_1 = 0.60$, $\sigma_2 = 0.60$, $\sigma_{1,2} = 0.18$;
(c) $\sigma_1 = 0.60$, $\sigma_2 = 0.60$, $\sigma_{1,2} = 0$;
(d) $\sigma_1 = 0.60$, $\sigma_2 = 0.60$, $\sigma_{1,2} = -0.18$;
(e) $\sigma_1 = 0.60$, $\sigma_2 = 0.60$, $\sigma_{1,2} = -0.36$.

6.4. An equally weighted portfolio will consist of shares from AAB Company stock and ZZY Company stock. The expected return and standard deviation levels associated with the AAB Company stock are 5% and 12%, respectively. The expected return and standard deviation levels for ZZY Company stock are 10% and 20%. Find the expected return and standard deviation levels of this portfolio if returns on the two stocks are:

(a) perfectly correlated;
(b) independent; i.e., a zero correlation coefficient;
(c) perfectly inversely correlated.

6.5. How do the coefficient of correlation between returns of securities in a portfolio affect the expected return and risk levels of that portfolio?

6.6. An investor will place one-third of his money into security 1, one-sixth into security 2, and the remainder (one-half) into security 3. Security data is given in the table below:

Security, i	E$[R]$	$\sigma(i)$	COV$(i,1)$	COV$(i,2)$	COV$(i,3)$
1	0.25	0.40	0.16	0.05	0
2	0.15	0.20	0.05	0.04	0
3	0.05	0	0	0	0

Find the expected return and variance of this portfolio.

6.7. The expected variance of returns on my two-security portfolio is 0.08. The variance of my only risky security is 0.10; my other security is riskless and has an expected return of 0.10. The expected return of the risky security is 0.25. What is the expected return of my portfolio?

6.8. There exists a market where all securities have a return standard deviation equal to 0.8. All securities are perceived to have independent return outcomes; that is, returns between pairs of securities are uncorrelated.

(a) What would be the return standard deviation of a two-security portfolio in this market?

(b) What would be the return standard deviation of a four-security portfolio in this market?

(c) What would be the return standard deviation of an eight-security portfolio in this market?

(d) What would be the return standard deviation of a 16-security portfolio in this market?

(e) Suppose that all securities in this market have an expected return equal to 0.10. How do the expected returns of the portfolios in parts (a) through (d) differ?

CHAPTER SEVEN
ELEMENTS OF MATRIX MATHEMATICS

AN INTRODUCTION TO MATRICES

Investors frequently encounter situations involving numerous potential outcomes, many discrete periods of time and large numbers of diverse securities. The process of analyzing such large quantities of inputs and functions can involve extraordinary numbers of repetitive and time-consuming computations. Even the preparation and organization of inputs and data can be enormously complex. Matrices and matrix mathematics are among the tools available to the analyst for the systematizing laborious operations and calculations.

A *matrix* is simply an ordered rectangular array of numbers. A matrix is an entity that enables one to represent a series of numbers as a single object, thereby providing for convenient systematic methods for completing large numbers of repetitive computations. Rules of matrix arithmetic and other matrix operations are often similar to rules of ordinary arithmetic and other operations, but they are not always identical. In this text, matrices will usually be denoted with bold upper-case letters. When the matrix has only one row or one column, bold lower-case letters will be used for identification. The following are examples of matrices:

$$\mathbf{A} = \begin{bmatrix} 4 & 2 & 6 \\ 3 & 7 & 4 \\ 8 & -5 & 9 \end{bmatrix}, \quad \mathbf{B} = \begin{bmatrix} 2 & -3 \\ \frac{3}{4} & -\frac{1}{2} \end{bmatrix}, \quad \mathbf{c} = \begin{bmatrix} 1 \\ 5 \\ 7 \end{bmatrix}, \quad \mathbf{d} = \begin{bmatrix} \frac{3}{5} \end{bmatrix}.$$

The dimensions of a matrix are given by the ordered pair $m \times n$, where m is the number of rows and n is the number of columns in the matrix. The matrix is said to be of *order* $m \times n$ where, by convention, the number of rows is listed first. Thus, $\mathbf{A}$ is 3×3, $\mathbf{B}$ is 2×2, $\mathbf{c}$ is 3×1, and $\mathbf{d}$ is 1×1. Each number in a matrix is referred to as an element. The symbol $a_{i,j}$ denotes the element in row i and column j of matrix $\mathbf{A}$, $b_{i,j}$ denotes the element in row i and column j of matrix $\mathbf{B}$, and so on. Thus, $a_{3,2}$ is -5 and $c_{2,1} = 5$.

There are specific terms denoting various types of matrices. Each of these particular types of matrices has useful applications and unique properties for working with. For example, a *vector* is a matrix with either only one row or one column. Thus, the dimensions of a vector are $1 \times n$ or $m \times 1$. Matrix **c** above is a column vector; it is of order 3×1. A $1 \times n$ matrix is a row vector with n elements. The column vector has one column and the row vector has one row. A *scalar* is a matrix with exactly one element. Matrix **d** is a scalar. A *square matrix* has the same number of rows and columns ($m = n$). Matrix **A** is square and of order 2. The set of elements extending from the upper-leftmost corner to the lower-rightmost corner in a square matrix are said to be in the *principal diagonal*. For each of these elements $i_{i,j}$, $i = j$. The principal diagonal elements of square matrix **A** are $a_{1,1} = 4$, $a_{2,2} = 7$, and $a_{3,3} = 9$. Matrices **B** and **d** are also square matrices.

A *symmetric matrix* is a square matrix where $c_{i,j}$ equals $c_{j,i}$ for all i and j; that is, the ith element in each row equals the jth element in each column. Scalar **d** and matrices **H**, **I**, and **J** below are all symmetric matrices. A *diagonal matrix* is a symmetric matrix whose elements off the principal diagonal are zero, where the *principal diagonal* contains the series of elements for which $i = j$. Scalar **d** and matrices **H** and **I** below are all diagonal matrices. An *identity* or *unit* matrix is a diagonal matrix consisting of ones along the principal diagonal. Both matrices **H** and **I** following are diagonal matrices; **I** is the 3×3 identity matrix:

$$\mathbf{H} = \begin{bmatrix} 13 & 0 & 0 \\ 0 & 11 & 0 \\ 0 & 0 & 10 \end{bmatrix}, \qquad \mathbf{I} = \begin{bmatrix} 1 & 0 & 0 \\ 0 & 1 & 0 \\ 0 & 0 & 1 \end{bmatrix}, \qquad \mathbf{J} = \begin{bmatrix} 1 & 7 & 2 \\ 7 & 5 & 0 \\ 2 & 0 & 4 \end{bmatrix}.$$

APPLICATION 7.1: PORTFOLIO MATHEMATICS
(Background reading: sections 2.9, 6.2, 6.3, and 7.1)

We saw in section 6.3 that computing returns and variances for portfolios with large numbers of securities often involves large numbers of repetitive calculations. The use of matrices provides a means of organizing, systemizing, and generally simplifying these series of calculations. We use standard rules of matrix operations to perform many useful computations. Consider a portfolio comprising three securities with the following characteristics and weights:

$$E[R_1] = 0.12, \qquad \sigma_1 = 0.30, \qquad w_1 = 0.2, \qquad \sigma_{1,2} = 0.01,$$
$$E[R_2] = 0.14, \qquad \sigma_2 = 0.40, \qquad w_2 = 0.5, \qquad \sigma_{1,3} = 0.04,$$
$$E[R_3] = 0.20, \qquad \sigma_3 = 0.80, \qquad w_3 = 0.3, \qquad \sigma_{2,3} = 0.10.$$

We are able to represent the set of security returns with a single vector **r** and the set of portfolio weights with a single vector **w**:

$$\mathbf{r} = \begin{bmatrix} 0.12 \\ 0.14 \\ 0.20 \end{bmatrix}, \qquad \mathbf{w} = \begin{bmatrix} 0.2 \\ 0.5 \\ 0.3 \end{bmatrix}.$$

Bearing in mind that $\sigma_{i,j} = \sigma_{j,i}$ and that $\sigma_i^2 = \sigma_{i,i}$ (because the covariance between anything and itself equals variance), we may represent a covariance matrix for the securities as follows:

$$\mathbf{V} = \begin{bmatrix} 0.09 & 0.01 & 0.04 \\ 0.01 & 0.16 & 0.10 \\ 0.04 & 0.10 & 0.64 \end{bmatrix}.$$

Note that each element $v_{i,j}$ equals the covariance $\sigma_{i,j}$. A portfolio covariance matrix represents the set of security variances and covariances comprising the portfolio. The covariance matrix is always square and symmetric, with elements along the principal diagonal representing security variances. Each covariance between nonidentical securities is represented twice in the matrix. For example, the covariance between returns on security 1 and 2 is the same as the covariance between returns on securities 2 and 1. These covariances are represented by $v_{1,2} = v_{2,1} = 0.01$.

7.2 MATRIX ARITHMETIC

(Background reading: sections 2.9 and 7.1)

Matrix arithmetic provides for standard rules of operation just as conventional arithmetic. Matrices may be added or subtracted if their dimensions are identical. Matrices $\mathbf{A}$ and $\mathbf{B}$ add to $\mathbf{C}$ if $a_{i,j} + b_{i,j} = c_{i,j}$ for all i and j:

$$\begin{bmatrix} a_{1,1} & a_{1,2} & \cdots & a_{1,n} \\ a_{2,1} & a_{2,2} & \cdots & a_{2,n} \\ \vdots & \vdots & \vdots & \vdots \\ a_{m,1} & a_{m,2} & \cdots & a_{m,n} \end{bmatrix} + \begin{bmatrix} b_{1,1} & b_{1,2} & \cdots & b_{1,n} \\ b_{2,1} & b_{2,2} & \cdots & b_{2,n} \\ \vdots & \vdots & \vdots & \vdots \\ b_{m,1} & b_{m,2} & \cdots & b_{m,n} \end{bmatrix} = \begin{bmatrix} c_{1,1} & c_{1,2} & \cdots & c_{1,n} \\ c_{2,1} & c_{2,2} & \cdots & c_{2,n} \\ \vdots & \vdots & \vdots & \vdots \\ c_{m,1} & c_{m,2} & \cdots & c_{m,n} \end{bmatrix}, \quad (7.1)$$

$$\qquad\qquad \mathbf{A} \qquad\qquad + \qquad\qquad \mathbf{B} \qquad\qquad = \qquad\qquad \mathbf{C}.$$

For example,

$$\begin{bmatrix} 2 & 4 & 9 \\ 6 & 4 & 25 \\ 0 & 2 & 11 \end{bmatrix} + \begin{bmatrix} 3 & 0 & 6 \\ 2 & 1 & 3 \\ 7 & 0 & 4 \end{bmatrix} = \begin{bmatrix} 5 & 4 & 15 \\ 8 & 5 & 28 \\ 7 & 2 & 15 \end{bmatrix},$$

$$\qquad \mathbf{A} \qquad + \quad \mathbf{B} \quad = \quad \mathbf{C}.$$

Note that each of the three matrices is of dimension 3×3 and that each of the elements in matrix $\mathbf{C}$ is the sum of corresponding elements in matrices $\mathbf{A}$ and $\mathbf{B}$. The process of subtracting matrices is similar, where $d_{i,j} - e_{i,j} = f_{i,j}$ for $\mathbf{D} - \mathbf{E} = \mathbf{F}$:

$$
\begin{bmatrix} d_{1,1} & d_{1,2} & \cdots & d_{1,n} \\ d_{2,1} & d_{2,2} & \cdots & d_{2,n} \\ \vdots & \vdots & \vdots & \vdots \\ d_{m,1} & d_{m,2} & \cdots & d_{m,n} \end{bmatrix} - \begin{bmatrix} e_{1,1} & e_{1,2} & \cdots & e_{1,n} \\ e_{2,1} & e_{2,2} & \cdots & e_{2,n} \\ \vdots & \vdots & \vdots & \vdots \\ e_{m,1} & e_{m,2} & \cdots & e_{m,n} \end{bmatrix} = \begin{bmatrix} f_{1,1} & f_{1,2} & \cdots & f_{1,n} \\ f_{2,1} & f_{2,2} & \cdots & f_{2,n} \\ \vdots & \vdots & \vdots & \vdots \\ f_{m,1} & f_{m,2} & \cdots & f_{m,n} \end{bmatrix}, \quad (7.2)
$$

$$\mathbf{D} \qquad\qquad - \qquad\qquad \mathbf{E} \qquad\qquad = \qquad\qquad \mathbf{F}.$$

For example,

$$
\begin{bmatrix} 9 & 4 & 9 \\ 6 & 4 & 8 \\ 5 & 2 & 9 \end{bmatrix} - \begin{bmatrix} 5 & 0 & 6 \\ 2 & 1 & 6 \\ 5 & 0 & 9 \end{bmatrix} = \begin{bmatrix} 4 & 4 & 3 \\ 4 & 3 & 2 \\ 0 & 2 & 0 \end{bmatrix},
$$

$$\mathbf{D} \qquad - \qquad \mathbf{E} \qquad = \qquad \mathbf{F}.$$

Now consider a third matrix operation. The *transpose* $\mathbf{A}'$ of matrix $\mathbf{A}$ is obtained by interchanging the rows and columns of matrix $\mathbf{A}$. Each $a_{i,j}$ becomes $a_{j,i}$. The following represent matrix $\mathbf{A}$ and its transpose $\mathbf{A}'$:

$$
\begin{bmatrix} 1 & 8 & 9 \\ 6 & 4 & 25 \\ 3 & 2 & 35 \end{bmatrix} \qquad \begin{bmatrix} 1 & 6 & 3 \\ 8 & 4 & 2 \\ 9 & 25 & 35 \end{bmatrix},
$$

$$\mathbf{A} \qquad\qquad\qquad \mathbf{A}'.$$

The transpose of a column vector is a row vector:

$$
\begin{bmatrix} 9 \\ 6 \\ 3 \\ 7 \end{bmatrix}, \qquad [9 \quad 6 \quad 3 \quad 7],
$$

$$\mathbf{y} \qquad\qquad \mathbf{y}'.$$

Similarly, the transpose of a row vector is a column vector. Note that the transpose $\mathbf{V}'$ of a symmetric matrix $\mathbf{V}$ is $\mathbf{V}$:

$$
\mathbf{V} = \begin{bmatrix} 0.09 & 0.01 & 0.04 \\ 0.01 & 0.16 & 0.10 \\ 0.04 & 0.10 & 0.64 \end{bmatrix}, \qquad \mathbf{V}' = \begin{bmatrix} 0.09 & 0.01 & 0.04 \\ 0.01 & 0.16 & 0.10 \\ 0.04 & 0.10 & 0.64 \end{bmatrix} = \mathbf{V}.
$$

Matrix multiplication is somewhat more complex than matrix addition or subtraction. Furthermore, as we will discuss later, the order of matrices to be multiplied does affect the result. If two matrices may be multiplied, they are said to be *conformable* for multiplication. Any matrix may be multiplied by a scalar. One simply multiplies each of the elements of the matrix by the scalars to obtain the corresponding element of the product; that is, each element $c_{i,j}$ of $\mathbf{C}$ equals $sa_{i,j}$, where $\mathbf{C} = s\mathbf{A}$. More generally, matrices are said to conform for multiplication if the number of rows in the first matrix equals the number of rows in the second to be multiplied. That is, two matrices $\mathbf{A}$ and $\mathbf{B}$ may be multiplied to obtain the product $\mathbf{AB} = \mathbf{C}$ if the number of columns in the first matrix $\mathbf{A}$ equals the number of rows $\mathbf{B}$ in the second. If matrix $\mathbf{A}$ is of dimension $m \times n$ and matrix $\mathbf{B}$ is of dimension $n \times q$, the dimensions of the product matrix $\mathbf{C}$ will be $m \times q$. Each element $c_{i,k}$ of matrix $\mathbf{C}$ is determined by the following sum:

$$c_{i,k} = \sum_{j=1}^{n} a_{i,j} b_{j,k}. \tag{7.3}$$

For example, consider the following product:

$$\begin{bmatrix} 5 & 4 & 9 \\ 6 & 4 & 12 \\ 3 & 2 & 7 \end{bmatrix} \begin{bmatrix} 7 & 6 \\ 5 & 1 \\ 9 & 12 \end{bmatrix} = \begin{bmatrix} 136 & 142 \\ 170 & 184 \\ 94 & 104 \end{bmatrix},$$

$$\mathbf{A} \qquad \cdot \qquad \mathbf{B} \qquad = \qquad \mathbf{C}.$$

Matrix $\mathbf{C}$ in the above is found as follows:

$$\begin{bmatrix} 5 & 4 & 9 \\ 6 & 4 & 12 \\ 3 & 2 & 7 \end{bmatrix} \begin{bmatrix} 7 & 6 \\ 5 & 1 \\ 9 & 12 \end{bmatrix} = \begin{bmatrix} 5\cdot7+4\cdot5+9\cdot9 & 5\cdot6+4\cdot1+9\cdot12 \\ 6\cdot7+4\cdot5+12\cdot9 & 6\cdot6+4\cdot1+12\cdot12 \\ 3\cdot7+2\cdot5+7\cdot9 & 3\cdot6+2\cdot1+7\cdot12 \end{bmatrix},$$

$$\mathbf{A} \qquad \cdot \quad \mathbf{B} \quad = \qquad\qquad\qquad\qquad \mathbf{C}.$$

Notice that the number of columns (3) in matrix $\mathbf{A}$ equals the number of rows in matrix $\mathbf{B}$. Thus matrices $\mathbf{A}$ and $\mathbf{B}$ conform for multiplication. Also note that the number of rows in matrix $\mathbf{C}$ equals the number of rows in matrix $\mathbf{A}$; the number of columns in $\mathbf{C}$ equals the number of columns in matrix $\mathbf{B}$.

Matrix multiplication differs somewhat from ordinary multiplication in that the commutative property does not hold. This means that, in general, $\mathbf{AB} \neq \mathbf{BA}$, and that the order of multiplication does matter. Thus, we should distinguish between *premultiplication* and *postmultiplication*. The first matrix in a product is said to premultiply the second; the second is said to postmultiply the first.

Consider the following system of equations:

$$y_1 = 7x_1 + 4x_2,$$

$$y_2 = 5x_1 + 9x_2.$$

This system can be represented as follows:

$$\begin{bmatrix} y_1 \\ y_2 \end{bmatrix} = \begin{bmatrix} 7 & 4 \\ 5 & 9 \end{bmatrix} \begin{bmatrix} x_1 \\ x_2 \end{bmatrix},$$

$$\mathbf{y} = \mathbf{C} \cdot \mathbf{x}.$$

Notice that **x** with two rows conforms for premultiplication by **C** with two columns. The resultant vector **y** has two rows. When two matrices are multiplied, the order of the resulting matrix will equal the number of rows in the first matrix and the number of columns of the second.

APPLICATION 7.2: PORTFOLIO MATHEMATICS, PART II
(Background reading: application 7.1 and section 7.2)

In application 7.1, we represented the security returns, weights, variances, and covariances with a set of appropriate matrices. We will now perform arithmetic operations on these matrices to determine the expected return and variance of the portfolio. First, we obtain the portfolio's expected return $E[R_p] = \mathbf{w'r}$ as follows:

$$E[R_p] = [0.20 \quad 0.50 \quad 0.30] \begin{bmatrix} 0.12 \\ 0.14 \\ 0.20 \end{bmatrix} = 0.154,$$

$$E[R_p] = \qquad \mathbf{w'} \qquad \mathbf{r} \quad = E[R_p].$$

Note that we transposed the weights vector to make it conform for multiplication with the returns vector (the first matrix to multiply must have the same number of columns as the number of rows in the second matrix to multiply). Since our desired product is a single number (a 1×1 matrix), we want the first matrix to have one row and the second to have one column. This is why we premultiply by the transposed matrix. Next, we find the variance of returns for this portfolio $\sigma_p^2 = \mathbf{w'Vw}$ as follows:

$$\sigma_p^2 = [0.20 \quad 0.50 \quad 0.30] \begin{bmatrix} 0.09 & 0.01 & 0.04 \\ 0.01 & 0.16 & 0.10 \\ 0.04 & 0.10 & 0.64 \end{bmatrix} \begin{bmatrix} 0.20 \\ 0.50 \\ 0.30 \end{bmatrix} = 0.138,$$

$$\sigma_p^2 = \qquad \mathbf{w'} \qquad\qquad \mathbf{V} \qquad\qquad \mathbf{w}.$$

We obtain this product by multiplying from left to right (remember that the commutative property does not hold for multiplication of matrices), starting with $\mathbf{w'V}$:

$$[0.20 \quad 0.50 \quad 0.30] \begin{bmatrix} 0.09 & 0.01 & 0.04 \\ 0.01 & 0.16 & 0.10 \\ 0.04 & 0.10 & 0.64 \end{bmatrix},$$

$$\mathbf{w'} \qquad\qquad\qquad \mathbf{V}$$

$$= [0.018 + 0.005 + 0.012 \quad 0.002 + 0.08 + 0.03 \quad 0.008 + 0.05 + 0.192]$$

$$\mathbf{w'V}$$

$$= [0.035 \quad 0.112 \quad 0.25].$$

$$\mathbf{w'V}$$

We now multiply $\mathbf{w'V}$ by $\mathbf{w}$ to obtain the portfolio variance:

$$[0.035 \quad 0.112 \quad 0.25] \begin{bmatrix} 0.20 \\ 0.50 \\ 0.30 \end{bmatrix} = 0.138,$$

$$\mathbf{w'V} \qquad\qquad \mathbf{w} \quad = \sigma_p^2.$$

Note that the three matrices that we multiplied were of dimension 1×3, 3×3, and 3×1. Our desired result is a single number, or a 1×1 matrix. Therefore, the first matrix in our product should have one row and the last matrix in our product should have one column. To ensure conformability for multiplication, the number of columns in each matrix should be the same as the number of rows in the following matrix. Confirm the following for our three-security portfolio based on the above weights and covariances:

$$\sigma_p^2 = \sum_{i=1}^{n} \sum_{j=1}^{n} w_i w_j \sigma_{i,j} = 0.138 = \mathbf{w'Vw}.$$

This confirmation should verify that our portfolio variance result will be identical to that realized using the simple portfolio equations from chapter 6.

APPLICATION 7.3: PUT–CALL PARITY
(Background reading: section 7.2)

Stock options grant their owners the right (but not the obligation) to purchase or sell shares of specified stock known as the underlying stock at a specified "exercise" price. One type of stock option is a *call*, which grants its owner the right to purchase shares of an underlying stock at the exercise price before the expiration date of the call. The value of a call at its expiration is given by the maximum of either zero or the difference between the stock price at expiration and the exercise price of the call:

$$C_T = \text{MAX}[(S_T - X), 0].$$

Thus, if the call is exercised at its expiration, its value is equal to the value of the underlying stock less the exercise price at which it can be purchased due to the option. If the stock price is lower than the exercise price of the option at its expiration, the call is discarded; its value is zero.

The second type of stock option is a *put*, which grants its owner the right to sell the underlying stock at a specified exercise price on or before its expiration date. The following is the payoff function for the put at expiration:

$$p_T = \text{MAX}[(X - S_T), 0].$$

In this application, we discuss a simple model that expresses the value of a put relative to the value of a call with terms identical to that of the put. First, assume that there exists a European put and a European call (with a value of C_0) written on the same underlying stock, which currently has a value equal to S_T. Both options expire at time T and have an exercise price equal to X. The riskless return rate is r_f. Since the payoff function of the call at expiration is $C_T = \text{MAX}[S_T - X, 0]$ and the payoff function for the put is $p_T = \text{MAX}[X - S_T, 0]$, the following system describes the pricing of a put in terms of the underlying stock, exercise price of options, and the call with the same terms as the put:

$$\begin{bmatrix} p_1 \\ p_2 \\ \vdots \\ p_n \end{bmatrix} = - \begin{bmatrix} S_1 \\ S_2 \\ \vdots \\ S_n \end{bmatrix} + \begin{bmatrix} X \\ X \\ \vdots \\ X \end{bmatrix} + \begin{bmatrix} C_1 \\ C_2 \\ \vdots \\ C_n \end{bmatrix},$$

$$\mathbf{p} = -\mathbf{S} + \mathbf{X} + \mathbf{C},$$

$$\text{MAX}(X - S, 0) = -S + X + \text{MAX}(S - X, 0).$$

This *put–call parity* relation holds regardless of the number of potential outcomes in the state space. The securities need not span the outcome space for the put–call parity relation to hold. Consider the following numerical example where there are three potential stock prices, 60, 100, and 140, and a 105 exercise price for the options:

$$\begin{bmatrix} 0 \\ 5 \\ 45 \end{bmatrix} = - \begin{bmatrix} 140 \\ 100 \\ 60 \end{bmatrix} + \begin{bmatrix} 105 \\ 105 \\ 105 \end{bmatrix} + \begin{bmatrix} 35 \\ 0 \\ 0 \end{bmatrix},$$

$$\mathbf{p} = -\mathbf{S} + \mathbf{X} + \mathbf{C}.$$

Because the put–call parity relation must hold at option expiry regardless of the underlying stock terminal price, the following put–call parity relation must hold at time zero:

$$p_0 = -S_0 + Xe^{-r_f T} + C_0.$$

That is, a put is equivalent in value to a portfolio consisting of a short position in one share of stock (the share is short sold; that is, borrowed and sold with the intent to repurchase at time T) underlying the put, an investment into a riskless asset certain to pay X at time T where X is the exercise price of both options and T is the term to option expiry, and a long position in one call on the stock with the same expiration date and exercise price as the put.

Suppose that the stock whose time T payoff function given above is currently selling for $106. Further assume that a one-year call (let $T = 1$) with an exercise price equal to $105 is currently selling for $18 and the current riskless return rate equals 0.10. A one-year put with an exercise price equal to $105 will be worth $7.0079 according to the put–call parity relation:

$$7.0079 = -106 + 105e^{-0.1 \cdot 1} + 18.$$

7.3   INVERTING MATRICES
(Background reading: sections 3.3 and 7.2)

For any real number $x \neq 0$, there exists a unique number x^{-1} such that $x\,x^{-1} = 1 = x^{-1}x$. The number x^{-1} is said to be the *multiplicative inverse* of x. For example, since $2^{-1} = \frac{1}{2}$, $2 \cdot 2^{-1} = 1$ and 2^{-1} is the inverse of 2. An *inverse* matrix $\mathbf{A}^{-1}$ exists for the square matrix $\mathbf{A}$ if the product $\mathbf{A}^{-1}\mathbf{A}$ or $\mathbf{AA}^{-1}$ equals the identity matrix $\mathbf{I}$. Consider the following product:

$$\begin{bmatrix} 2 & 4 \\ 4 & 2 \end{bmatrix} \begin{bmatrix} -\frac{1}{6} & \frac{1}{3} \\ \frac{1}{3} & -\frac{1}{6} \end{bmatrix} = \begin{bmatrix} 1 & 0 \\ 0 & 1 \end{bmatrix},$$
$$\mathbf{A} \qquad \mathbf{A}^{-1} \quad = \quad \mathbf{I}.$$

If there exists a matrix $\mathbf{A}^{-1}$ which can be used to premultiply or postmultiply $\mathbf{A}$, matrix $\mathbf{A}$ is said to be *invertible*. Only square matrices may have inverses.[1] Those matrices that have inverses are said to be *nonsingular*; matrices that do not have inverses are said to be *singular*.

There are many computational techniques for finding the inverse matrix $\mathbf{A}^{-1}$ for matrix $\mathbf{A}$. The process that we will discuss here is the *Gauss–Jordan method*. There exist many other procedures for inverting matrices, but none are significantly more efficient and applicable generally than the Gauss–Jordan method for matrices of higher order than 3. The Gauss–Jordan method will be performed on matrix $\mathbf{A}$ by first augmenting it with the identity matrix as follows:

$$\begin{bmatrix} 2 & 4 & | & 1 & 0 \\ 4 & 2 & | & 0 & 1 \end{bmatrix}. \tag{A}$$

We will refer to the augmented matrix as matrix $\mathbf{A}$. Next, a series of row operations (see 1, 2, and 3 below) will be performed until the identity matrix appears on the left

[1]   We will ignore left inverses and right inverses, which may exist for matrices that are not square.

side of matrix **A**, replacing the original elements in the left side. Since the same row operations will be performed on the left side, the right side elements will comprise the inverse matrix $\mathbf{A}^{-1}$. Thus, in our final augmented matrix, we will have ones along the principal diagonal on the left side and zeros elsewhere; the right side of the matrix will comprise the inverse of **A**. Allowable row operations include the following:

1   Multiply a given row by any nonzero constant. Each element in the row must be multiplied by the same constant.
2   Add a given row to any other row in the matrix. Each element in a row is added to the corresponding element in the same column of another row.
3   Any combination of the above. For example, a row may be multiplied by a negative constant before it is added to another row.

We will perform a very systematic series of row operations, where we first obtain 1 for element *j* in row *j* and then zeros elsewhere in column *j*. Our first row operation will serve to replace the upper left corner value 2 with 1. We multiply row 1 in **A** (row 1**A**) by 0.5 to obtain the following:

$$\begin{bmatrix} 1 & 2 & \vdots & 0.5 & 0 \\ 4 & 2 & \vdots & 0 & 1 \end{bmatrix}, \qquad 1\mathbf{A} \cdot 0.5 = 1\mathbf{B},$$

where row 1**B** replaces row 1**A**. Now we obtain a zero in the lower left corner by multiplying row 2 in **A** by $\frac{1}{4}$ and subtracting the result from our new row 1 to obtain matrix **B** as follows:

$$\begin{bmatrix} 1 & 2 & \vdots & 0.5 & 0 \\ 0 & 1.5 & \vdots & 0.5 & -\frac{1}{4} \end{bmatrix}, \qquad \begin{array}{l} 1\mathbf{A} \cdot 0.5 = 1\mathbf{B} \\ 1\mathbf{B} - (2\mathbf{A} \cdot \frac{1}{4}) = 2\mathbf{B} \end{array} \tag{B}$$

Next, we move to the second row. We obtain a 1 in the lower right corner of the left side of the matrix by multiplying row 2**B** by $\frac{2}{3}$:

$$\begin{bmatrix} 1 & 2 & \vdots & 0.5 & 0 \\ 0 & 1 & \vdots & \frac{1}{3} & -\frac{1}{6} \end{bmatrix}, \qquad 2\mathbf{B} \cdot (-\frac{2}{3}) = 2\mathbf{C}.$$

Notice that we obtained this lower right corner value of 1 without affecting the 1 or 0 that we previously obtained in matrix **B**. We obtain a zero in the upper right corner of the left side matrix by multiplying row 2 above by 2 and subtracting from row 1 in matrix **B**:

$$\begin{bmatrix} 1 & 0 & \vdots & -\frac{1}{6} & \frac{1}{3} \\ 0 & 1 & \vdots & \frac{1}{3} & -\frac{1}{6} \end{bmatrix}, \qquad \begin{array}{l} 1\mathbf{B} - (2\mathbf{C} \cdot 2) = 1\mathbf{C} \\ 2\mathbf{B} \cdot (-\frac{2}{3}) = 2\mathbf{C} \end{array} \tag{C}$$

The left side of augmented matrix **C** is the identity matrix and the right side of **C** is $\mathbf{A}^{-1}$, the inverse of matrix **A**.

Matrices cannot be divided as numbers can be in arithmetic. However, since one can invert a matrix, this inverted matrix can be premultiplied by another matrix to obtain a result analogous to a quotient in dividing. This process of inverting matrices is most useful for solving many types of linear equations.

7.4 SOLVING SYSTEMS OF LINEAR EQUATIONS

(Background reading: sections 1.3, 3.3, and 7.3)

Matrices are very useful for arranging systems of equations for repetitive calculations. Solving systems of linear equations simultaneously for variables is a particularly useful application for matrix inverses. For example, consider the following system:

$$0.1x_1 + 0.24x_2 = 0.1,$$

$$0.2x_1 + 0.6x_2 = 0.16.$$

In matrix format, this system is represented as follows:

$$\begin{bmatrix} 0.1 & 0.24 \\ 0.2 & 0.6 \end{bmatrix} \begin{bmatrix} x_1 \\ x_2 \end{bmatrix} = \begin{bmatrix} 0.1 \\ 0.16 \end{bmatrix},$$

$$\mathbf{C} \qquad \mathbf{x} = \qquad \mathbf{s}.$$

We are not able to divide $\mathbf{s}$ by $\mathbf{C}$ to obtain $\mathbf{x}$; instead, we invert $\mathbf{C}$ to obtain $\mathbf{C}^{-1}$ and postmultiply it by $\mathbf{s}$ to obtain $\mathbf{x}$:

$$\mathbf{C}^{-1}\mathbf{s} = \mathbf{x}.$$

Therefore, to solve for vector $\mathbf{x}$, we first invert $\mathbf{C}$ by augmenting it with the identity matrix:

$$\begin{bmatrix} 0.1 & 0.24 & \bigm| & 1 & 0 \\ 0.2 & 0.6 & \bigm| & 0 & 1 \end{bmatrix}. \tag{A}$$

We then perform a series of row operations to invert matrix $\mathbf{C}$ as follows:

$$\begin{bmatrix} 1 & 2.4 & \bigm| & 10 & 0 \\ 0 & 0.6 & \bigm| & -10 & 5 \end{bmatrix}, \qquad \begin{array}{l} \text{row } 1\mathbf{B} = 1\mathbf{A} \cdot 10 \\ \text{row } 2\mathbf{B} = (5 \cdot 2\mathbf{A}) - 1\mathbf{B} \end{array}; \tag{B}$$

$$\begin{bmatrix} 1 & 0 & \bigm| & 50 & -20 \\ 0 & 1 & \bigm| & -\frac{50}{3} & \frac{25}{3} \end{bmatrix}, \qquad \begin{array}{l} \text{row } 1\mathbf{C} = 1\mathbf{B} - (2.4 \cdot 2\mathbf{C}) \\ \text{row } 2\mathbf{C} = 2\mathbf{B} \cdot \frac{5}{3} \end{array}; \tag{C}$$

$$\mathbf{I} \qquad\qquad \mathbf{C}^{-1}.$$

Thus, we obtain vector **x** with the following product:

$$\begin{bmatrix} 50 & -20 \\ -\frac{50}{3} & \frac{25}{3} \end{bmatrix} \begin{bmatrix} 0.1 \\ 0.16 \end{bmatrix} = \begin{bmatrix} x_1 \\ x_2 \end{bmatrix} = \begin{bmatrix} 1.8 \\ -\frac{1}{3} \end{bmatrix}$$

(D)

$$\mathbf{C}^{-1} \quad \cdot \quad \mathbf{s} \quad = \quad \mathbf{x} \quad = \quad \mathbf{x}.$$

Thus, we find that $x_1 = 1.8$ and $x_2 = -\frac{1}{3}$.

APPLICATION 7.4: EXTERNAL FUNDING REQUIREMENTS
(Background reading: section 7.5 and application 3.7)

Recall the Albert Company whose financial statements are given in tables 3.1 and 3.2, in application 3.7. The firm's Earnings Before Interest and Tax (*EBIT*) level was projected to be $300,000 next year. The firm had previously borrowed $600,000, requiring $50,000 in interest payments. Management expected the firm to remain in the 40% corporate income tax bracket ($\tau = 0.4$) and pay out one third of its after-tax earnings in dividends ($\delta = 0.333$). Since the firm's production level is expected to increase next year, management has determined that each asset account must also increase by 40%. Assets currently total $1,000,000 and will increase to $1,400,000. Current liabilities will also increase from its present level of $150,000 by 40%; $\Delta CL = \$60,000$. The firm pays no interest on its current liabilities. Managers have already decided to sell bonds at an interest rate of 10% to provide any external capital necessary to finance the asset level increase. Management's problem is to determine how much additional capital to raise through this 10% bond issue. Based on this information, we should be able to determine the Albert Company's external financing needs (*EFN*) for next year.

Since management has determined that it must change its asset total by $\Delta Assets = \$400,000$, it must determine how these assets will be financed. That is, management must determine the total sum of capital required to support the change in the total asset level. Some of this necessary capital can be derived from internal sources such as retained earnings (*RE*) or changes in current liabilities (ΔCL). These sources are likely to change simultaneously with the firm's production level and provide capital directly from the increase in the firm's level of operation. For example, an increase in the firm's sales level may result directly in an increase in the firm's level of retained earnings, since revenues, variable costs, and profits can be expected to increase. Furthermore, as the firm's sales level increases, it may be reasonable to anticipate an increase in the firm's number of employees, further resulting in an increase in the firm's accrued wages level. Other current liability levels are likely to increase in a similar manner. The remaining funds must be obtained through some external source such as the sale of long-term bonds or equity. In summary, the amount of money the firm must raise from external sources is determined by the following equation:

$$EFN = \Delta Assets - \Delta CL - RE = \$400,000 - \$60,000 - RE = \$340,000 - RE,$$

where

$$RE = (EBIT - INT) \cdot (1 - \tau) \cdot (1 - \delta)$$
$$= (\$300{,}000 - \$50{,}000 - i \cdot EFN) \cdot (1 - 0.4) \cdot (1 - 0.333),$$

which can be simplified as follows:

$$RE = (\$250{,}000 \cdot 0.4) - 0.04 \cdot EFN = \$100{,}000 - 0.04 \cdot EFN.$$

Our EFN and RE functions above can be rewritten as

$$\$100{,}000 = RE + 0.04 \cdot EFN,$$
$$\$340{,}000 = RE + EFN.$$

We now have two equations with two variables to solve. This problem is structured in matrix format as follows:

$$\begin{bmatrix} 1 & 0.04 \\ 1 & 1 \end{bmatrix} \begin{bmatrix} RE \\ EFN \end{bmatrix} = \begin{bmatrix} 100{,}000 \\ 340{,}000 \end{bmatrix},$$

$$\mathbf{C} \qquad \cdot \quad \mathbf{x} \quad = \qquad \mathbf{s}.$$

Performing a series of row operations to obtain matrix $\mathbf{C}^{-1}$ yields the following:

$$\begin{bmatrix} 1.041667 & -0.04167 \\ -1.04167 & 1.041667 \end{bmatrix} \begin{bmatrix} 100{,}000 \\ 340{,}000 \end{bmatrix} = \begin{bmatrix} 90{,}000 \\ 250{,}000 \end{bmatrix} = \begin{bmatrix} RE \\ EFN \end{bmatrix},$$

$$\mathbf{C}^{-1} \qquad\qquad \cdot \quad \mathbf{s} \quad = \quad \mathbf{x} \quad = \quad \mathbf{x}.$$

Thus, $RE = \$90{,}000$ and $EFN = \$250{,}000$. More generally, the following equation may be used to solve simultaneously for RE and EFN:

$$\begin{bmatrix} 1 & [i \cdot (1 - \tau) \cdot (1 - \delta)] \\ 1 & 1 \end{bmatrix} \begin{bmatrix} RE \\ EFN \end{bmatrix} = \begin{bmatrix} [(EBIT - INT_{EX}) \cdot (1 - \tau) \cdot (1 - \delta)] \\ (\Delta Assets - \Delta CL) \end{bmatrix},$$

$$\mathbf{C} \qquad\qquad \cdot \quad \mathbf{x} \quad = \qquad\qquad \mathbf{s}.$$

where INT_{EX} represents the interest payments on existing debt and i represents the interest rate on new debt. If equity rather than debt is to finance the asset increase, zero may be substituted for i and the system solves rather easily. In any case, solving this system requires substituting values in for variables, inverting matrix $\mathbf{C}$, and solving for vector $\mathbf{x}$.

APPLICATION 7.5: COUPON BONDS AND DERIVING YIELD CURVES
(Background reading: sections 4.8, 4.9, and 7.4 and applications 2.6 and 4.4)

The *spot rate* is the yield at present prevailing for zero coupon bonds of a given maturity. The t-year yield $y_{0,t}$ of a zero coupon bond is determined as follows:

$$y_{0,t} = \sqrt[t]{\frac{F}{P_0}} - 1,$$

where F is the face value or principal of the bond, P_0 is the purchase price of the bond, and t is the zero coupon bond's term to maturity. The t-year spot rate is denoted here by $y_{0,t}$, which represents an implied spot rate on a loan to be made at time zero and repaid in its entirety at time t. Spot rates may be estimated from bonds with known future cash flows and their current prices. We are able to obtain spot rates from yields implied from series of bonds when we assume that the Law of One Price holds. Recall that the Law of One Price maintains that securities generating identical cash flows must sell for the same price.

The yield curve represents yields or spot rates of bonds with varying terms to maturity. For example, at a given moment in time, the yield or spot rate for one-year bonds may be 4% ($y_{0,1} = 0.04$), while the yield for five-year bonds may be 6% ($y_{0,5} = 0.06$). This section is concerned with how interest rates or yields vary with maturities of bonds. The simplest bonds to work with from an arithmetic perspective are *pure discount notes*, also known as zero coupon notes, which make no interest payments. Such notes make only one payment at one point in time – on the maturity date of the note. Determining the relationship between yield and term to maturity for these bonds is quite trivial. The return that one obtains from a pure discount note is strictly a function of capital gains; that is, the difference between the face value F of the note and its purchase price P_0. Short-term U.S. Treasury bills are an example of pure discount (or zero coupon) notes. Coupon bonds are somewhat more difficult to work with from an arithmetic perspective because they make payments to bondholders at a variety of different periods. Since they make multiple payments, coupon bonds are analogous to portfolios of pure discount bonds.

A coupon bond may be treated as a portfolio of pure discount notes, with each coupon being treated as a separate note maturing on the date the coupon is paid. Using coupon bonds slightly complicates the process for determining yields, but is necessary when there aren't pure discount notes maturing in key time periods. Consider an example involving three bonds whose terms and prices are given in table 7.1. The three bonds are trading at known prices with a total of eight annual coupon payments among them (two for bond A and three each for bonds B and C). Bond yields or spot rates must be determined simultaneously to avoid associating contradictory rates for the annual coupons on each of the three bills.

Table 7.1 Coupon bonds A, B, and C

Bond	Current price	Face value	Coupon rate	Years to maturity
A	947.376	1,000	0.06	2
B	904.438	1,000	0.08	3
C	980.999	1,000	0.10	3

Let D_t be the discount function for time t; that is, $D_t = 1/(1 + y_{0,t})^t$. Since $y_{0,t}$ is the spot rate or discount rate that equates the present value of a bond with its current price, the following equations may be solved for discount functions then spot rates:

$$947.376 = 50D_1 + 1{,}050D_2,$$

$$904.438 = 60D_1 + 60D_2 + 1{,}060D_3,$$

$$980.999 = 90D_1 + 90D_2 + 1{,}090D_3.$$

This system of equations may be represented by the following system of matrices:

$$\begin{bmatrix} 50 & 1{,}050 & 0 \\ 60 & 60 & 1{,}060 \\ 90 & 90 & 1{,}090 \end{bmatrix} \begin{bmatrix} D_1 \\ D_2 \\ D_3 \end{bmatrix} = \begin{bmatrix} 947.376 \\ 904.438 \\ 980.999 \end{bmatrix},$$

$$\mathbf{CF} \qquad \cdot \quad \mathbf{d} \ = \qquad \mathbf{P}_0.$$

To solve this system we first invert matrix $\mathbf{CF}$ to obtain $\mathbf{CF}^{-1}$. We then use this inverse matrix to premultiply vector $\mathbf{P}_0$ to obtain vector $\mathbf{d}$:

$$\begin{bmatrix} -0.001 & -0.03815 & 0.0371 \\ 0.001 & 0.001817 & -0.00177 \\ 0 & 0.003 & -0.002 \end{bmatrix} \begin{bmatrix} 947.376 \\ 904.438 \\ 980.999 \end{bmatrix} = \begin{bmatrix} D_1 \\ D_2 \\ D_3 \end{bmatrix} = \begin{bmatrix} 0.943396 \\ 0.857339 \\ 0.751315 \end{bmatrix},$$

$$\mathbf{CF}^{-1} \qquad\qquad \cdot \quad \mathbf{P}_0 \ = \ \mathbf{d}.$$

Thus, we find from solving this system for vector $\mathbf{d}$ that $D_1 = 0.943396$, $D_2 = 0.857339$, and $D_3 = 0.751315$. Since $D_t = 1/(1 + y_{0,t})^t$, $1/D_t = (1 + y_{0,t})^t$, and $y_{0,t} = 1/D^{1/t} - 1$, spot rates are determined as follows:

$$\frac{1}{D_1} - 1 = \frac{1}{0.943396} - 1 = 0.06,$$

$$\frac{1}{D_2^{1/2}} - 1 = \frac{1}{0.857339^{1/2}} - 1 = 0.08,$$

$$\frac{1}{D_3^{1/3}} - 1 = \frac{1}{0.751315^{1/3}} - 1 = 0.10.$$

In this example, there exists a different spot rate (or discount rate) for each term to maturity. However, the spot rates for all cash flows generated by all bonds at a given period of time are the same. This consistency is necessary for the market to avoid arbitrage opportunities. Thus, $y_{0,t}$ will vary over terms to maturity, but all bonds in the market will be subject to this single yield for a given time period.

APPLICATION 7.6: ARBITRAGE WITH RISKLESS BONDS
(Background reading: application 7.5)

Arbitrage was defined in section 1.4 as the simultaneous purchase and sale of assets or portfolios yielding identical cash flows. Assets generating identical cash flows (certain or risky cash flows) should be worth the same amount. This is known as the Law of One Price. If assets generating identical cash flows sell at different prices, opportunities exist to create a profit by buying the cheaper asset or combination and selling the more expensive asset or combination. The ability to realize a profit from this type of transaction is known as an arbitrage opportunity. Solutions for multiple variables in systems of equations are most useful in the application of the Law of One Price and for those seeking arbitrage opportunities.

The example given in application 7.5 above consisted of three default risk-free bonds. The result defined spot rates for all three relevant years. The cash flow structure of any one-, two-, or three-year bond that might be added to this market can be replicated by some portfolio of bonds A, B, and C. Consider for example, Bond D, a three-year issue that can be replicated by a portfolio of bonds A, B, and C. Assume for this example that there now exists Bond D, a three-year, 12% coupon issue selling in this market for $1,040. This bond will make payments of $120 in years 1 and 2 followed by a $1,120 payment in year 3. A portfolio of bonds A, B, and C can be comprised to exactly replicate this cash flow series. Thus, we will determine exactly how much to invest in each of our bonds A, B, and C to replicate Bond D. Portfolio combinations to replicate Bond D will be determined by the following system of equations or matrices:

$$120 = \quad 50b_A + \quad 60b_B + \quad 90b_C,$$
$$120 = 1{,}050b_A + \quad 60b_B + \quad 90b_C,$$
$$1{,}120 = \quad 0b_A + 1{,}060b_B + 1{,}090b_C;$$

$$\begin{bmatrix} 50 & 60 & 90 \\ 1{,}050 & 60 & 90 \\ 0 & 1{,}060 & 1{,}090 \end{bmatrix} \begin{bmatrix} b_A \\ b_B \\ b_C \end{bmatrix} = \begin{bmatrix} 120 \\ 120 \\ 1{,}120 \end{bmatrix},$$

$$\mathbf{CF} \qquad\qquad \cdot \ \mathbf{b} \ = \ \mathbf{cf}_D.$$

To solve this system, we first invert matrix **CF**, then use it to premultiply vector $\mathbf{cf}_D$ to obtain vector **b**:

$$\begin{bmatrix} -0.001 & 0.001 & 0 \\ -0.03815 & 0.001817 & 0.003 \\ 0.0371 & -0.00177 & -0.002 \end{bmatrix} \begin{bmatrix} 120 \\ 120 \\ 1{,}120 \end{bmatrix} = \begin{bmatrix} b_A \\ b_B \\ b_C \end{bmatrix} = \begin{bmatrix} 0 \\ -1 \\ 2 \end{bmatrix},$$

$$\mathbf{CF}^{-1} \qquad\qquad\qquad \cdot \ \ \mathbf{cf}_D \ = \ \mathbf{b}.$$

Thus, we find from this system that $b_A = 0$, $b_B = -1$, and $b_C = 2$. We determine the value of the portfolio replicating bond D by weighting the current market prices of bonds B and C from application 7.5: $(-1 \cdot \$904.438) + (2 \cdot \$980.999) = \$1,057.56$. This means that we short sell (borrow and then sell) one bond B and purchase two of bond C.[2] Cash flows in years one, two, and three are given as follows:

Year	Bond B	Bond C	Portfolio	Bond D
1	−60	180	120	120
2	−60	180	120	120
3	−1,060	2,180	1,120	1,120

Thus, the cash flows from the portfolio exactly match the cash flows generated by bond D. Thus, by the Law of One Price, bond D should sell for the same price as the portfolio. Based on the portfolio's price, the value of bond D was calculated to be $1,057.56, although its actual current market price is $1,040. Thus, one gains an arbitrage profit from the purchase of this bond for $1,040 financed by the sale of the portfolio containing the short position in bond B (one B is now purchased since the portfolio is to be sold) and two bonds C for a total price of $1,057.56 for the portfolio. Here, we simply swap a portfolio comprised of bonds B and C for bond D. Our cash flows in years 1, 2, and 3 will be zero, although we receive a positive cash flow at time zero of $17.56 ($-\$904.438 + 2 \cdot \$980.999 - \$1,040$). This is a clear arbitrage profit. Again, to realize this $17.56 arbitrage profit, the arbitrageur purchases one bond B, sells two bonds C, and buys one bond D. This arbitrage opportunity will persist until the value of the portfolio equals the value of bond D.

APPLICATION 7.7: FIXED INCOME PORTFOLIO DEDICATION
(Background reading: application 7.6)

A fixed income portfolio is concerned with assuring the provision of a relatively stable income over a period of time. Typically, a fixed income fund is expected to provide a fixed series of payments to its creditors, clients, or owners for a given period. For example, a pension fund is often expected to make a series of fixed payments to pension fund participants. Such funds must invest their assets to ensure that their liabilities are paid. In many cases, fixed income funds will purchase assets such that their cash inflows exactly match the liability payments that they are required to make. This exact matching strategy is referred to as portfolio dedication; that is, cash flows generated by assets are dedicated to assuring payments required by creditors or other stakeholders. Portfolio dedication is intended to minimize the risk of the fund. The process of dedication is quite similar to the arbitrage swaps discussed in application 7.6 above. The fund manager determines the cash flows associated with his liability structure and replicates the cash flow structure with a series of default risk-free bonds. For example, assume

---

[2]   Short selling a bond occurs when one borrows a bond from another investor and sells it on his own account. The short-seller needs to replace the interest payments in the lender's account as well as the principal when the borrowed bond matures. One short sells to satisfy a hedging or portfolio strategy or when the bond's price is expected to drop.

Table 7.2   Coupon bonds E, F, and G

Bond	Current price	Face value	Coupon rate	Years to maturity
E	1,000	1,000	0.10	2
F	1,035	1,000	0.12	2
G	980	1,000	0.10	3

that a pension fund manager needs to make payments to pension plan participants of $10,000,000 in one year, $20,000,000 in two years, and $30,000,000 in three years. She needs to match these cash flows with a portfolio of bonds E, F, and G, whose characteristics are given in table 7.2. These three bonds must be used to match the cash flows associated with the fund's liability structure. For example, in year 1, bond E will pay $100, F will pay $120, and G will pay $100. These payments must be combined to total $10,000,000. Cash flows must be matched in years 2 and 3 as well. Only one matching strategy exists for this scenario. The following system may be solved for **b** to determine exactly how many of each of the bonds are required to satisfy the fund's cash flow requirements:

$$
\begin{bmatrix} 100 & 120 & 100 \\ 1,100 & 1,120 & 100 \\ 0 & 0 & 1,100 \end{bmatrix}
\begin{bmatrix} b_E \\ b_F \\ b_G \end{bmatrix}
=
\begin{bmatrix} 10,000,000 \\ 20,000,000 \\ 30,000,000 \end{bmatrix},
$$

$$
\mathbf{CF} \qquad\qquad \cdot\ \mathbf{b}\ = \qquad \mathbf{L}.
$$

Inverting matrix **CF** and multiplying by vector **L** yields the following system:

$$
\begin{bmatrix} -0.056 & 0.006 & 0.00454545 \\ 0.055 & -0.005 & -0.00454545 \\ 0 & 0 & 0.000909091 \end{bmatrix}
\begin{bmatrix} 10,000,000 \\ 20,000,000 \\ 30,000,000 \end{bmatrix}
=
\begin{bmatrix} -303,636.36 \\ 313,636.36 \\ 27,272.72 \end{bmatrix},
$$

$$
\mathbf{CF}^{-1} \qquad\qquad \cdot \qquad \mathbf{L} \qquad = \qquad \mathbf{b}.
$$

Thus, we find that the sale of 303,636.36 bonds E, and the purchase of 313,636.36 bonds F and 27,272.72 bonds G satisfies the manager's exact matching requirements. The fund's time zero payment for these bonds totals $47,704,545 at their current market prices.

APPLICATION 7.8: BINOMIAL OPTION PRICING
(Background reading: section 7.4 and application 7.3)

Consider a one-time-period, two-potential-outcome framework where there exists company X stock currently selling for $100 per share and a riskless $100 face-value T-bill currently selling for $90. Suppose that company Q faces uncertainty, such that it will pay its owner either $60 or $140 in one year. The T-bill will certainly pay its owner $100 in one year. Further assume that a call with an exercise price of $110 exists on one share of Q stock. This call will be worth either $0 or $30 when it expires, based on the value of the underlying stock. More generally, the value of the call at expiration is the larger of either zero or the difference between the value of its underlying security and the call exercise price. In this example, if the stock is worth $60, the call is worthless; if the stock is worth $140, the call is worth $30. The payoff vectors for stock q, the T-bill (**b**), and the call (**c**) are given as follows:

$$\mathbf{x} = \begin{bmatrix} 60 \\ 140 \end{bmatrix}, \quad \mathbf{b} = \begin{bmatrix} 100 \\ 100 \end{bmatrix}, \quad \mathbf{c} = \begin{bmatrix} 0 \\ 30 \end{bmatrix}.$$

The payoff structure for the call can be replicated by a portfolio consisting of shares of the underlying stock and T-bills as follows:

$$\begin{bmatrix} 60 & 100 \\ 140 & 100 \end{bmatrix} \begin{bmatrix} \#x \\ \#b \end{bmatrix} = \begin{bmatrix} 0 \\ 30 \end{bmatrix}.$$

To determine the number of shares and T-bills needed to replicate the call, we invert the payoffs matrix, to obtain:

$$\begin{bmatrix} -0.0125 & 0.0125 \\ 0.0175 & -0.0075 \end{bmatrix} \begin{bmatrix} 0 \\ 30 \end{bmatrix} = \begin{bmatrix} 0.375 \\ -0.225 \end{bmatrix}.$$

We find that $\#x = 0.375$ and $\#b = -0.225$. This implies that the payoff structure of a single call can be replicated with a portfolio comprising 0.375 shares of X company stock for a total of $0.375 \cdot \$100 = \$37.50$ and short-selling 0.225 T-bills (in effect, borrowing $0.225 \cdot \$90 = \$20.25$ at the T-bill rate). This portfolio requires a net investment of $\$37.50 - \$20.25 = \$17.00$. Since the call on X company stock has the same payoff structure as this portfolio, its current value must be $17.

7.5 SPANNING THE STATE SPACE

(Background reading: sections 7.3 and 7.4)

A vector is a matrix with either only one row or one column. Any column vector **v** consisting of n real elements is said to be within the set $\mathbb{R}^n$, which represents the n-dimensional *vector space*. $\mathbb{R}^n$ is defined as the set of all vectors with n real-valued elements or coordinates. The following represent vectors in three-dimensional space:

$$\mathbf{a} = \begin{bmatrix} 4 \\ 2 \\ 9 \end{bmatrix}, \quad \mathbf{b} = \begin{bmatrix} -5 \\ 14 \\ 22 \end{bmatrix}, \quad \mathbf{c} = \begin{bmatrix} 10 \\ 10 \\ -3 \end{bmatrix}; \quad \mathbf{a}, \mathbf{b}, \mathbf{c} \in \mathbb{R}^3.$$

Vectors **a**, **b**, and **c** are all elements of the three-dimensional space $\mathbb{R}^3$ because each of the vectors contains three elements. Each of the n elements of a vector **v** might be regarded as a coordinate of a point in n-dimensional space or an n-dimensional hyperplane. All of the vectors falling within this hyperplane are said to exist in set $\mathbb{R}^n$.

Each of these three vectors might be said to represent cash flows for a security over a three-year time period, as in applications 7.5–7.7 above. Alternatively, the three elements in any one of these vectors might represent cash flows contingent on potential outcomes of an uncertain scenario, as in applications 7.3 and 7.8 above. Hence, each of the dimensions in an n-dimensional vector space might represent cash flows over n periods or potential cash flows contingent on n possible outcomes. Cash flow vectors might also be structured to represent the combination of all potential cash flow outcomes in each of many time periods.

Vector addition and scalar multiplication are allowable vector operations. *Linear combinations* of given vectors are applications of these two vector operations. A linear combination of vectors may be executed by performing any one or combination of the following:

1 Multiplication of any vector by a scalar.
2 Addition of any combination of vectors either before or after multiplication by scalars.

If a vector in a given n-dimensional space can be expressed as a linear combination of a set of other vectors in the same space, we say that the given vector is *linearly dependent* on that set of vectors. Similarly, if a set of vectors {**x**} can be multiplied by a series of scalars α (where at least one of the scalars is nonzero) and combined to obtain a vector of zeros, we say that linear dependence exists among the set of vectors {**x**}:

$$\alpha_1 \mathbf{x}_1 + \alpha_2 \mathbf{x}_2 + \alpha_3 \mathbf{x}_3 + \ldots + \alpha_n \mathbf{x}_n = [0]. \tag{7.4}$$

If at least one of the scalars α_i above has a nonzero value, this set of n vectors **x** is said to be linearly dependent. *Linear independence* within a set of vectors {**x**} exists where the only set of scalars that satisfies this equality consists only of zeros. When linear independence exists for a set {**x**} of vectors, no vector in the set can be expressed as a linear combination of other vectors in the set.

Linear dependence exists within vector sets (A) and (B) below because equation (7.4) can be satisfied with scalars such that at least one $\alpha \neq 0$. Furthermore, within each set of vectors, any one vector may be described as a linear combination of the other two.

$$\begin{bmatrix} 9 \\ 4 \\ 1 \end{bmatrix} \quad \begin{bmatrix} 0 \\ 5 \\ 10 \end{bmatrix} \quad \begin{bmatrix} 0 \\ 1 \\ 2 \end{bmatrix} \qquad \begin{aligned} 0\mathbf{x}_1 + 0.2\mathbf{x}_2 - 1\mathbf{x}_3 &= [0], \\ 0\mathbf{x}_1 + 0.2\mathbf{x}_2 &= \mathbf{x}_3; \end{aligned} \qquad \text{(A)}$$

$$\qquad \mathbf{x}_1 \qquad \mathbf{x}_2 \qquad \mathbf{x}_3$$

$$\begin{bmatrix} 6 \\ 3 \\ 9 \end{bmatrix} \quad \begin{bmatrix} 2 \\ 4 \\ 6 \end{bmatrix} \quad \begin{bmatrix} 10 \\ 11 \\ 21 \end{bmatrix}$$

$$1\mathbf{x}_1 + 2\mathbf{x}_2 - 1\mathbf{x}_3 = [0],$$

$$1\mathbf{x}_1 + 2\mathbf{x}_2 = \mathbf{x}_3. \qquad \text{(B)}$$

$$\mathbf{x}_1 \qquad \mathbf{x}_2 \qquad \mathbf{x}_3$$

We determine that vector set (A) is linearly dependent by demonstrating that there exists a set of values for α satisfying

$$9\alpha_1 + 0\alpha_2 + 0\alpha_3 = 0,$$

$$4\alpha_1 + 5\alpha_2 + 1\alpha_3 = 0,$$

$$1\alpha_1 + 10\alpha_2 + 2\alpha_3 = 0.$$

It is obvious from the first equation that α_1 equals zero. Using α_1 equal to zero in the second and third equations, we find that any value for α_2 will satisfy the equality as long as α_3 equals $-5\alpha_2$. Since at least one of the scalars α may be nonzero when satisfying the three equations, this set of three vectors is linearly dependent. If it had been true that three nonzero scalars could not be found to satisfy the equations, linear independence would have existed within the set.

Each of vector sets (C) and (D) below are linearly independent because the set of scalars satisfying equation (7.4) for each set will all have zero values. For example, in vector set (C), α_1, α_2, and α_3 must all equal zero for a vector of zeros to be a linear combination of the three vectors. Furthermore, no vector in set (C) can be defined as a linear combination of the other vectors in set (C) and no vector in set (D) can be defined as a linear combination of the other vectors in set (E).

$$\begin{bmatrix} 1 \\ 0 \\ 0 \end{bmatrix} \quad \begin{bmatrix} 0 \\ 1 \\ 0 \end{bmatrix} \quad \begin{bmatrix} 0 \\ 0 \\ 1 \end{bmatrix} \qquad \text{Linearly independent set of vectors,} \qquad \text{(C)}$$

$$\begin{bmatrix} 20 \\ 20 \\ 1{,}020 \end{bmatrix} \quad \begin{bmatrix} 45 \\ 45 \\ 1{,}045 \end{bmatrix} \quad \begin{bmatrix} 100 \\ 1{,}100 \\ 0 \end{bmatrix} \qquad \text{Linearly independent set of vectors.} \qquad \text{(D)}$$

We will discuss how to verify whether linear independence exists shortly.

A set of n vectors is said to *span* the n-dimensional vector space if that set of n vectors is linearly independent. A set of n vectors consisting of n elements each, which do not span a vector space, is not linearly independent. Vector sets (A) and (B) do not span the three-dimensional vector space; vector sets (C) and (D) do span the three-dimensional vector space.

When a set of n vectors spans the n-dimensional vector space, this set of n vectors is known as the *basis* for the n-dimensional space. Any n-dimensional vector outside of this basis can be expressed as a linear combination of vectors in this basis. The basis for $\mathbb{R}^n$ is said to *span* the n-dimensional space. For example, any three-dimensional vector (such as $[1,2,3]'$, which equals $1\mathbf{x}_1 + 2\mathbf{x}_2 + 3\mathbf{x}_3$) can be expressed as a linear combination of the three vectors in set (C) above, since the three vectors in set (C) each have three elements and are linearly independent. This set of three vectors is a basis for $\mathbb{R}^3$; these three vectors span $\mathbb{R}^3$. The same can be said for vector set (D); this set represents a basis for and spans $\mathbb{R}^3$.

In a sense, when one vector is linearly dependent on another $n-1$ vectors, the information in the other $n-1$ vectors can be used to replicate the information in the nth vector. In a financial sense, where elements within a vector represent payoffs of a given security contingent on outcomes or associated with a points in time, the payoff structure of the nth security can be replicated with a portfolio comprising the other $n-1$ securities on which its payoff vector is linearly dependent. When a set of n payoff vectors span the n potential outcome or time space, the payoff structure for any other security or portfolio in the same outcome or time space can be replicated with the payoff vectors of the n securities forming the basis for the n-dimensional payoff space. Securities or portfolios whose payoff vectors can be replicated by portfolios of other securities must sell for the same price as those portfolios; otherwise, the Law of One Price is violated.

Consider application 7.6 above examining arbitrage opportunities in bond markets. An arbitrage opportunity will exist when the payoff vector of a given bond can be replicated by a linear combination of payoff vectors for other bonds, yet sell for a price different from the portfolio which replicates it. Thus, an arbitrage opportunity exists. In the absence of arbitrage opportunities, if that bond's payoff vector is linearly dependent on the payoff vectors of the $n-1$ bonds in the portfolio, the bond cannot sell for a price different from that of the portfolio. Application 7.7 concerning portfolio dedication also requires that the liability structure be dependent on the payoff vectors of bonds. In application 7.5, spot rates are implied based on the assumption that arbitrage opportunities do not exist among the bonds used to construct the yield curve. If one wishes to compute n spot rates, a minimum of n bonds forming the basis for the n-dimensional time space are required.

APPLICATION 7.9: USING OPTIONS TO SPAN THE STATE SPACE
(Background reading: section 7.5 and application 7.8)

If a set of payoff vectors form the basis for the n-dimensional state space for an economy, any security that exists in that economy can be priced as a linear combination of those payoff vectors. This means that any security in an economy can be priced if n other securities with linearly independent payoff vectors are priced. In an actual setting, the difficulty with pricing securities with this methodology is locating securities whose payoff vectors can be exactly specified outcome-by-outcome. For example, how does one determine the exact element to place in the third row of payoff vectors for three unrelated stocks? Can we really identify what the payoff for each of these three stocks is in the third outcome?

Since derivative securities have payoff vectors that are contingent on the payoff vectors for other securities, one can define the outcome space relative to the payoff vector for the underlying security. One can create unlimited numbers of derivative securities such as options on stocks or other existing assets. Payoff vectors for these options can be linearly independent. The state space can be spanned with the underlying security and the options written on that security. Thus, the underlying security and options written on that security can form the basis for the n-potential outcome economy. Consider a stock that will pay either 20, 40, or 60. Two calls are written on that stock, one with an exercise price of 30 and a second with an exercise price of 50:

$$\begin{bmatrix} 20 \\ 40 \\ 60 \end{bmatrix} \quad \begin{bmatrix} 0 \\ 10 \\ 30 \end{bmatrix} \quad \begin{bmatrix} 0 \\ 0 \\ 10 \end{bmatrix},$$

Stock $X = 30$ $X = 50$.

These three securities form the basis for the three-dimensional state space. Any other security with a defined payoff vector in this three-potential outcome economy can be valued as a linear combination of these three securities. For example, consider a call option with an exercise price of 40. This option with a payoff vector of $[0, 0, 20]'$ can be replicated with a portfolio of payoff vectors forming the basis as follows:

$$\begin{bmatrix} 20 & 0 & 0 \\ 40 & 10 & 0 \\ 60 & 30 & 10 \end{bmatrix}^{-1} \begin{bmatrix} 0 \\ 0 \\ 20 \end{bmatrix} = \begin{bmatrix} \#S \\ \#c_{X=30} \\ \#c_{X=50} \end{bmatrix}.$$

   Thus, this call can be priced as a linear combination of the prices of the three securities forming the basis. One should always be able to form a basis for an n-state economy with a stock and $n - 1$ priced options written on that stock. Any other security (usually other options on that stock) whose payoff vectors can be defined for that economy can be priced as a linear combination of the prices of the securities forming the basis of payoff vectors for that economy.

EXERCISES

7.1.   Add the following matrices:

(a) $\begin{bmatrix} 4 \\ 6 \\ 5 \end{bmatrix} + \begin{bmatrix} 3 \\ -6 \\ 5 \end{bmatrix} = $;   (b) $\begin{bmatrix} 4 & 6 \\ 5 & 2 \end{bmatrix} + \begin{bmatrix} 3 & -6 \\ 5 & 0.5 \end{bmatrix} = $.

7.2.   Transpose the following matrices:

(a) $\begin{bmatrix} 4 \\ 6 \\ 5 \end{bmatrix}$;   (b) $\begin{bmatrix} 4 & 5 \\ 6 & 2 \end{bmatrix}$.

7.3.   Sampson Company stock is currently selling for $50 per share. One-year put and call options are selling on this stock with exercise prices equal to $40 per share. Sampson Company stock may increase or decrease by either 20% or 40% per share over the next year. Thus, there are four possible outcomes for this stock. The riskless return rate is 10%. The call is currently selling for $18.

   (a) Write out the payoff vectors for the put, stock, riskless asset (face value of $40) and the call.
   (b) What is the current value of the put?

7.4.   Multiply the following matrices:

   (a) $\begin{bmatrix} 2 & 4 \\ 3 & 4 \end{bmatrix}\begin{bmatrix} -2 & 1 \\ \frac{3}{2} & -\frac{1}{2} \end{bmatrix} = $;   (b) $\begin{bmatrix} 1 & 0 \\ 0 & 1 \end{bmatrix}\begin{bmatrix} -2 & 1 \\ \frac{3}{2} & -\frac{1}{2} \end{bmatrix} = $;

   (c) $\begin{bmatrix} 0.04 & 0.04 \\ 0.04 & 0.16 \end{bmatrix}\begin{bmatrix} 33.3333 & -8.3333 \\ -8.3333 & 8.3333 \end{bmatrix} = $;

   (d) $[0.02 \quad 0.16 \quad 0.10]\begin{bmatrix} 0.02 \\ 0.16 \\ 0.10 \end{bmatrix} = $;   (e) $\begin{bmatrix} 4 \\ 5 \\ 6 \end{bmatrix}[4 \quad 5 \quad 6] = $.

7.5.   An investor has invested into three funds, fund A, fund B, and fund C. Each of these funds is comprised of three stocks, stock 1, stock 2, and stock 3. The portfolio weights for each of the stocks in each of the funds and the stock returns are given in the following tables:

	w_1	w_2	w_3		Stock	Return
Fund A	0.15	0.25	0.60		1	0.12
Fund B	0.40	0.30	0.30		2	0.18
Fund C	0.30	0.25	0.45		3	0.24

   (a) Construct a single matrix of portfolio weights for the funds. Fund A will be represented in the first row, fund B in the second row, and fund C will be represented in the third row.
   (b) Construct a column vector of stock returns.
   (c) Multiply the weights matrix by the returns vector to obtain a column vector for returns on the two funds.
   (d) Using matrix notation, demonstrate how one would find the return on the investor's overall portfolio if it were equally invested in the three funds.

7.6.   The expected returns for three stocks in portfolio P are 0.07 for stock X, 0.09 for stock Y, and 0.13 for stock Z. The variance of returns for stock X is 0.04, 0.16 for stock Y, and 0.36 for stock Z. The covariance between returns on stocks X and Y is 0.01, 0.02 between stocks X and Z, and 0.08 between stocks Y and Z. Stock X comprises 30% of the portfolio, Y comprises 50% of the portfolio, and Z comprises 20%.

(a) Write an expected returns vector for the three stocks.
(b) Write the covariance matrix for the three stocks.
(c) Write the weights vector for the portfolio.
(d) What are the dimensions for the three matrices written for parts (a), (b), and (c)?
(e) Find the expected return of the portfolio using matrices written for parts (a), (b), and (c).
(f) Find the variance of returns for the portfolio using matrices written for parts (a), (b), and (c).

7.7. Invert the following matrices:

(a) $[8]$;   (b) $\begin{bmatrix} 1 & 0 \\ 0 & 1 \end{bmatrix}$;   (c) $\begin{bmatrix} 4 & 0 \\ 0 & \frac{1}{2} \end{bmatrix}$;   (d) $\begin{bmatrix} 1 & 2 \\ 3 & 4 \end{bmatrix}$;

(e) $\begin{bmatrix} 0.02 & 0.04 \\ 0.06 & 0.08 \end{bmatrix}$;   (f) $\begin{bmatrix} -2 & 1 \\ 1.5 & -0.5 \end{bmatrix}$;

(g) $\begin{bmatrix} 33.\overline{33} & -8.\overline{33} \\ -8.\overline{33} & 8.\overline{33} \end{bmatrix}$;   (h) $\begin{bmatrix} 2 & 0 & 0 \\ 2 & 4 & 0 \\ 4 & 8 & 20 \end{bmatrix}$.

7.8. Solve the following for **x**:

$$\begin{bmatrix} 33.\overline{3} & -8.\overline{3} \\ -8.\overline{3} & 8.\overline{3} \end{bmatrix} \begin{bmatrix} x_1 \\ x_2 \end{bmatrix} = \begin{bmatrix} 0.01 \\ 0.11 \end{bmatrix},$$

$$\mathbf{C} \qquad \cdot \ \mathbf{x} \ = \quad \mathbf{s}.$$

7.9. Solve the following for **x**:

$$\begin{bmatrix} 0.08 & 0.08 & 0.1 & 1 \\ 0.08 & 0.32 & 0.2 & 1 \\ 0.1 & 0.2 & 0 & 0 \\ 1 & 1 & 0 & 0 \end{bmatrix} \begin{bmatrix} x_1 \\ x_2 \\ x_3 \\ x_4 \end{bmatrix} = \begin{bmatrix} 0.1 \\ 0.1 \\ 0.1 \\ 0.1 \end{bmatrix},$$

$$\mathbf{C} \qquad\qquad \cdot \ \mathbf{x} \ = \quad \mathbf{s}.$$

7.10. The Victoria Company's financial statements are given below. Management is forecasting an increase in the company's sales level by 50% to $1,125,000. Managers predict that this 50% sales increase will increase the firm's Cost of Goods Sold level by 50% to $450,000. Fixed costs will remain constant at $150,000. The firm will continue to make the $50,000 interest payments necessary to sustain its current $600,000 in bonds outstanding. Management expects the firm to remain in the 40% corporate income tax bracket and pay out one third of its earnings in dividends. In order to sustain this 50% increase in sales, management has determined that each asset account must also increase by 50%; that is, the total must increase by $500,000. Current Liabilities will also increase by 50%. The firm pays no interest on its Current Liabilities. Managers have already decided to sell bonds at an interest rate of 10% to provide any external capital necessary to finance the asset level increase. Management's problem is to determine how much additional capital to raise through this 10% bond issue. Based on this information and the company's financial statements given below, determine the Victoria Company's 2001 external funding needs (*EFN*).

VICTORIA COMPANY FINANCIAL STATEMENTS

Income statement, 2000

Sales (*TR*)	$750,000
Cost of Goods Sold	300,000
Gross Margin	450,000
Fixed Costs	150,000
EBIT	300,000
Interest Payments	50,000
Earnings Before Taxes	250,000
Taxes (@ 40%)	100,000
Net Income After Tax	150,000
Dividends (@ 33%)	50,000
Retained Earnings	100,000

Pro-forma income statement, 2001

Sales (*TR*)	$1,125,000
Cost of Goods Sold	450,000
Gross Margin	675,000
Fixed Costs	150,000
EBIT	525,000
Interest Payments	_____
Earnings Before Taxes	
Taxes (@ 40%)	_____
Net Income After Taxes	
Dividends (@ 33%)	_____
Retained Earnings	

Balance sheet, December 31, 2000

ASSETS		LIABILITIES AND EQUITY	
Cash	$100,000	Accounts Payable	$100,000
Accounts Receivable	100,000	Accrued Wages	50,000
Inventory	100,000	Current Liabilities	150,000
Current Assets	300,000	Bonds Payable	600,000
Plant and Equipment	700,000	Equity	250,000
Total Assets	1,000,000	Total Capital	1,000,000

Pro-forma balance sheet, December 31, 2001

ASSETS		LIABILITIES AND EQUITY	
Cash	$150,000	Accounts Payable	$150,000
Accounts Receivable	150,000	Accrued Wages	75,000
Inventory	150,000	Current Liabilities	225,000
Current Assets	450,000	Bonds Payable	_____
Plant and Equipment	1,050,000	Equity	_____
Total Assets	1,500,000	Total Capital	1,500,000

7.11. The following table reflects riskless bond prices, coupon rates and terms to maturity for a given economy:

Bond	Price	Coupon rate (%)	Years to maturity
A	1,000	10	1
B	980	10	2
C	960	10	3
D	940	10	4

Assuming the bonds make annual coupon payments at year end, answer the following questions based on the above information:

(a) What are spot rates for years one through four?
(b) What is the two-year forward rate for a loan originated in one year?

7.12. Consider two three-year bonds with $1,000 face values. The coupon rate of bond X is 5% and 8% for bond Y. Now consider a third bond Z with coupon rate of 11% and a maturity of two years. Bond Z's face value is also $1,000. The current market prices of bonds X, Y, and Z are $878.9172, $955.4787, and $1,055.419, respectively.

(a) What are the spot rates implied by these bonds?
(b) Find a portfolio of bonds X, Y, and Z which would replicate the cash flow structure of bond Q, which has a face value of $1,000, a maturity of three years, and a coupon rate of 15%.

7.13. A pension fund expects to make payments of $80,000,000 in one year, $100,000,000 in two years, $120,000,000 in three years, and $140,000,000 in four years to shareholders in the fund. These anticipated cash flows are to be matched with a portfolio of the following $1,000 face value bonds:

Bond	Current price	Coupon rate	Years to maturity
1	1,000	0.10	1
2	980	0.10	2
3	1,000	0.11	3
4	1,000	0.12	4

How many of each of the four bonds should the fund purchase to exactly match its anticipated payments to shareholders?

7.14. Bond A, a two-year, 12% coupon issue can be purchased for $957.9920. Bond B, a two-year, 5% coupon issue can be purchased for $840.2471.

(a) What is the one-year spot rate of interest ($y_{0,1}$)?

(b) What is the two-year spot rate of interest ($y_{0,2}$)?

(c) What would be the value of a $1,000 face value pure discount bond maturing in two years?

(d) The two-year pure discount bond in part (c) can be replicated with a portfolio comprised of bonds A and B. What should the portfolio weights of these bonds be? (Short selling is permitted.)

(e) I need to raise $15,000 at the end of year one and $12,000 at the end of year two to repay some debts. How much should I buy (sell) of each of bonds A and B to exactly match my debt payments? (Fractional purchases and sales of bonds are permitted.)

7.15. Buford Company stock currently sells for $24 per share and is expected to be worth either $20 or $32 in one year. The current riskless return rate is 0.125. What would be the value of a one-year call with an exercise price of $16?

7.16. Robinson Company stock currently sells for $20 per share and will pay off either $15 or $25 in one year. A one-year call with an exercise price equal to $18 has been written on this stock. This call sells for $3.5.

(a) What is the value of a one-year call with an exercise price equal to $22?

(b) What is the riskless return rate for this economy?

(c) What is the value of a one-year put that can be exercised for $40?

APPENDIX 7.A MATRIX MATHEMATICS ON A SPREADSHEET

(Background reading: sections 7.3, 7.4, and 7.5 and appendix 3.A)

Solving equations with matrices of higher order by hand or with a calculator can be an extremely time-consuming and frustrating process. However, spreadsheets can be used quite effectively to multiply and invert matrices. Suppose that we wished to solve the following for **x** using an Excel™ spreadsheet:

$$\begin{bmatrix} 8 & 4 \\ 2 & 6 \end{bmatrix} \begin{bmatrix} x_1 \\ x_2 \end{bmatrix} = \begin{bmatrix} 10 \\ 20 \end{bmatrix},$$

$$\mathbf{C} \quad \cdot \quad \mathbf{x} \ = \ \mathbf{s}.$$

We may start to solve this system by insert the coefficients from matrix **C** in the spreadsheet as follows:

	A	B	C	D	E
1	8	4			
2	2	6			
3					
4					
5					

To solve the system, we will first invert matrix **C** in cells A1:B2. First, use the mouse to highlight cells A4 to B5, where we will insert the inverse of matrix **C**. We then select from the toolbar at the top of the screen the Paste Function button (f_x). From the Paste Function menu, we select the MATH & TRIG sub-menu. In the MATH & TRIG sub-menu, we scroll down to select MINVERSE, the function, which inverts the matrix. The MINVERSE function will prompt for an array; we enter the location of the matrix to be inverted: A1:B2. To fill all four cells A4 to B5, we simultaneously hit the Ctrl, Shift, and Enter keys. This is important. The spreadsheet should then appear as follows:

	A	B	C	D	E
1	8	4			
2	2	6			
3					
4	0.15	-0.1			
5	-0.05	0.2			

The matrix in cells A4:B5 is $\mathbf{C}^{-1}$. Now, we enter into cells C4 and C5 the equation solution vector **s** containing elements 10 and 20. Then highlight cells D4 and D5 to solve for vector **x**, left click again the Paste Function key in the Toolbar and select the MATH & TRIG menu. Then scroll down to and select the MMULT function, which will enable us to premultiply our solutions vector **s** by matrix $\mathbf{C}^{-1}$. The dialog box will prompt for two arrays. The first will be matrix $\mathbf{C}^{-1}$ in cells A4:B5. Then hit the Tab key and enter the cells for the second array C4:C5. Then hit the Ctrl, Shift, and Enter keys simultaneously to fill cells D4 and D5. The result will be vector **x** with elements -0.5 and 3.5. Thus, $x_1 = -0.5$ and $x_2 = 3.5$. The final spreadsheet will appear as follows:

	A	B	C	D	E
1	8	4			
2	2	6			
3					
4	0.15	-0.1	10	-0.5	
5	-0.05	0.2	20	3.5	

The process of expanding this solution procedure to larger matrices is quite simple. First, be certain that each equation in the system is linear (no exponents other than 0 or 1 on the variables) and that the coefficient matrix is square. In many cases, the systems cannot be solved. Among these are the following: the coefficients matrix is not square; matrices do not conform for multiplication; or the coefficients matrix is singular. Consider the following fourth order system:

$$\begin{bmatrix} 8 & 4 & 2 & 10 \\ 2 & 4 & 1 & 12 \\ 0 & 4 & 2 & 16 \\ 5 & 6 & 8 & 20 \end{bmatrix} \begin{bmatrix} x_1 \\ x_2 \\ x_3 \\ x_4 \end{bmatrix} = \begin{bmatrix} 10 \\ 20 \\ 30 \\ 40 \end{bmatrix},$$

$$\mathbf{C} \qquad \cdot \mathbf{x} = \mathbf{s}.$$

Now, examine the following spreadsheet, which is used to solve the system:

	A	B	C	D	E	F	G
1	8	4	2	10			
2	2	4	1	12			
3	0	4	2	16			
4	5	6	8	20			
5							
6	0.235294	-0.29412	0.147059	-0.05882	10	-1.470588	
7	-0.52941	1.578431	-1.12255	0.215686	20	1.2254902	
8	-0.11765	-0.01961	-0.15686	0.196078	30	1.5686275	
9	0.147059	-0.39216	0.362745	-0.07843	40	1.372549	

Thus, $x_1 = -1.470588$, $x_2 = 1.2254902$, $x_3 = 1.5686275$, and $x_4 = 1.372549$.

CHAPTER EIGHT
DIFFERENTIAL CALCULUS

8.1 FUNCTIONS AND LIMITS
(Background reading: sections 2.2 and 3.5)

Most of this book is concerned with the relationships among mathematical variables and numbers. The natures of these relationships are defined by *functions*. A function is a rule that assigns to each number in a set a unique second number. Functions are generally represented by equations, graphs, and tables. The following example is a "generic" functional relationship in equation form: $y = f(x)$, which reads "y is a function of x." For each value of x, the function assigns a unique value for y. If y increases as x increases, we say that y is a direct, or increasing, function of x. The following are examples where y is an increasing function of x:

(a) $y = 10x$;   (b) $y = 2x + 1$;
(c) $y = \frac{1}{2}x$;   (d) $y = 3e^x$;
(e) $y = 5x^2 + 3x + 1$ (when $x > -0.3$);   (f) $y = 9x^3 + 3x^2 + 2x + 1$.

Functions (a), (b), and (c) are linear; graphs depicting the relationships between x and y would be represented by lines. Equation (d) represents an exponential function. Equation (e) is a quadratic function (it is a polynomial of order 2) and equation (f) is a cubic function (it is a polynomial of order 3). If y decreases as x increases, we say that y is a decreasing, or inverse, function of x. The following are examples where y is a decreasing function of x:

$$y = \frac{1}{x} \quad (\text{where } x > 0), \qquad\qquad y = -x + 5,$$

$$y = -2x^2 - 4x \quad (\text{where } x > -1), \qquad y = 2e^{-x},$$

$$y = \frac{2}{5x} \quad (\text{where } x > 0), \qquad\qquad y = -5(x^2).$$

Now consider a function $y = f(x)$. As x approaches (gets closer to) some value a (without actually equaling a), causing y to approach L, we say that the *limit* of $f(x)$ as x approaches a equals L. The limit is expressed as follows:

$$\lim_{x \to a} f(x) = L. \tag{8.1}$$

The limit of $f(x)$ as x approaches a is L. Consider the following examples of limits:

(a) $\displaystyle\lim_{x \to \infty} \left(\frac{1}{x} \right) = 0;$ 　　　　　(b) $\displaystyle\lim_{n \to \infty} \sum_{t=1}^{n} \left(\frac{1}{(1+k)^t} \right) = \frac{1}{k};$

(c) $\displaystyle\lim_{x \to \infty} \left(\frac{3x}{5x^2} \right) = 0;$ 　　　　(d) $\displaystyle\lim_{m \to \infty} \left(1 + \frac{1}{m} \right)^m = e \approx 2.71828;$

(e) $\displaystyle\lim_{m \to \infty} \left(1 + \frac{i}{m} \right)^{m \cdot n} = e^{i \cdot n};$ 　　(f) $\displaystyle\lim_{h \to \infty} \frac{2(x+h) - 2x}{h} = 2.$

Thus, the limits of functions (a) and (c) are 0; the limit of function (b) is $1/k$, the limit of function (d) is e; the limit of function (e) is e^{in}; and the limit of function (f) is 2.

APPLICATION 8.1: THE NATURAL LOG
(Background reading: sections 2.5, 2.11, 4.4, 4.5, and 8.1 and application 2.7)

The number e is most useful for growth, time value, and probability-based models in finance. This number e is defined as a limit as follows:

$$\lim_{m \to \infty} \left(1 + \frac{1}{m} \right)^m = e \approx 2.71828.$$

Thus, as m approaches infinity, the value of function $(1 + 1/m)^m$ approaches number e, which is approximated at 2.71828. Notice the likeness of the above limit to a standard compounded interest formula from section 4.4. The number e can also be derived as follows:

$$\lim_{n \to \infty} \sum_{i=0}^{n} \frac{1}{i!} = \left(\frac{1}{0!} + \frac{1}{1!} + \frac{1}{2!} + \frac{1}{3!} + \frac{1}{4!} + \ldots \right) = e.$$

As n approaches infinity, the value of this function approaches the number e.

8.2 SLOPES, DERIVATIVES, MAXIMA, AND MINIMA
(Background reading: section 8.1)

Among the most useful financial applications of differential calculus are finding rates of change and growth and determining maximum and minimum values for functions. Let y be a function of x; that is, $y = f(x)$. A change in x may affect a change in y. For example, if $y = 3x$, a change in x by one will result in a change in y by 3. Therefore, the slope of this function is 3. Because the slope of this function does not change as x changes, this function is said to be linear. Thus, y is a linear function of x. The slope m of any line is defined as follows:

$$m = \frac{y_1 - y_0}{x_1 - x_0} = \frac{\Delta y}{\Delta x}, \tag{8.2}$$

where $x_1 - x_0 = \Delta x$ does not equal zero. In our example where $y = 3x$, if $x_0 = 2$ and $x_1 = 4$, then $y_0 = 6$ and $y_1 = 12$. We find that $\Delta x = 2$ and $\Delta y = 6$. Clearly, $\Delta y \div \Delta x = 3$, the slope of the function. This slope or rate of change in y is constant with respect to x. Thus, this function can be represented by a line.

Consider a second function: $y = 3x^2$, which is represented by figure 8.1. Clearly, the slope of the function y in figure 8.1 changes as x changes. Because the slope of function y is not constant, equation (8.2) cannot be used to determine its slope over a finite range, except where the change in x approaches zero. Now, we will define h as Δx as Δx approaches zero. Thus, h is defined as the limit of Δx as Δx approaches zero.

We can use the calculus concept of a derivative to measure rates of change in functions or slopes in graphs. When functions have slopes that are continuously changing, the derivative is used to find an instantaneous rate of change. That is, the derivative provides the change in y induced by an infinitesimal change in x. Let y be given as a function of x. If x were to increase by a small (infinitesimal – that is,

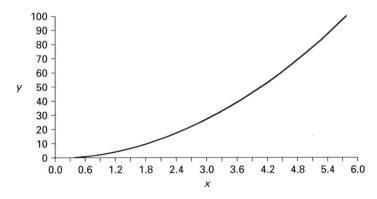

Figure 8.1   Changing slope: $y = 3x^2$.

approaching though never equaling zero) amount h, how much would we expect y to change? This rate of change is given by the derivative of y with respect to x, which is defined using the limit function as follows:

$$\frac{dy}{dx} = f'(x) = \lim_{h \to 0} \frac{f(x+h) - f(x)}{h}. \tag{8.3}$$

Thus, if an infinitesimal value h (that is, a value approaching zero) were to be added to x, y would change by the derivative of y with respect to x multiplied by the amount of change in x:

$$dy = \left[\frac{dy}{dx}\right] \cdot dx.$$

Now, consider a second function $y = f(x)$. The derivative of this function with respect to x, $dy/dx = f'(x)$, is itself a function of x. The slope of the curve representing the function is positive whenever the derivative is positive. Whenever this derivative is positive, an infinitesimal increase in x will lead to an increase in y by $f'(x) \cdot \Delta x$. The slope of the function represented by figure 8.1 is positive throughout (since $x > 0$ at all points in the figure). In figure 8.2, the slope is positive to the right of the minimum point and negative to the left. In figure 8.3, the slope is positive to the left of the maximum point and negative to the right. Whenever the derivative is negative, an infinitesimal increase in x will lead to a decrease in y. A zero derivative implies that an infinitesimal change in x will lead to no change in y. A zero derivative *may* imply a minimum or maximum value for y, as is the case in figures 8.2 and 8.3. One may frequently find the minimum or maximum points in a function by determining when its derivative is equal to zero.

The function $f'(x)$ representing the derivative (or first derivative) indicates the slope of the original function $f(x)$. The function representing the derivative of the derivative $f''(x)$ (the second derivative) indicates the slope of the first derivative function and the

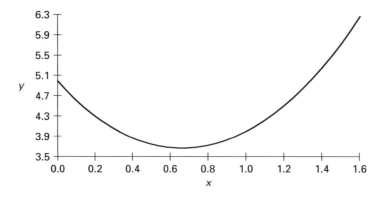

Figure 8.2   Concave up function: $y = 3x^2 - 4x + 5$.

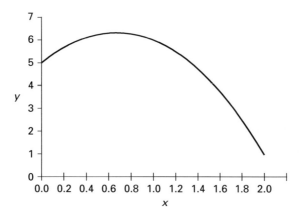

Figure 8.3   Concave down function: $y = -3x^2 + 4x + 5$.

concavity (change in the slope) of the original function $f(x)$. Notice that the slopes in figures 8.1 through 8.3 change as x changes. The rate of change in a slope is determined by the second derivative:

$$\frac{d^2y}{dx^2} = f''(x) = \lim_{h \to 0} \frac{f'(x+h) - f'(x)}{h}. \tag{8.4}$$

The second derivative $f''(x)$ of a function is simply the derivative of the first derivative. The function represented in figure 8.1 has a positive second derivative when $x > 0$, as suggested by the fact that it appears concave up, indicating that its slope increases as x increases. Note that the first derivative of this function is always positive. The function represented in figure 8.2 has a positive second derivative, as indicated by its upwards concavity. Thus, the slope of this function is increasing as x increases. The slope of this function is negative when x is small, is zero when the function is minimized, and becomes positive when x rises above that level which minimizes y. The function represented in figure 8.3 has a negative second derivative, consistent with the downward concavity in figure 8.3. Thus, the slope of this function decreases as x increases. Its slope is positive when x is small, is zero when the function is maximized, and becomes negative when x rises above that level which maximizes y.

8.3   DERIVATIVES OF POLYNOMIALS
(Background reading: section 8.2)

The polynomial function is among the most commonly used in financial modeling. The polynomial function specifies variable y in terms of a coefficient c (or series of coefficients c_j), variable x (or series of variables x_j), and an exponent n (or series of exponents n_j). While all the exponents in a polynomial equation will be nonnegative integers, the rules that we discuss here will still apply when the exponents assume negative or noninteger values. Where there exists a single coefficient, variable, and exponent, the polynomial function is represented as follows:

$$y = c \cdot x^n. \tag{8.5}$$

For example, let $c = 3$ and $n = 2$. Our polynomial function is written as follows: $y = 3x^2$. The derivative of y with respect to x in equation (8.5) is the following function:[1]

$$\frac{dy}{dx} = c \cdot n \cdot x^{n-1}. \tag{8.6}$$

The derivative of y with respect to x is for this polynomial is found by multiplying the original coefficient c by the original exponent n and subtracting 1 from the original exponent. Taking the derivative of y with respect to x in our example, we obtain $dy/dx = 3 \cdot 2 \cdot x^{2-1} = 6x$. Note that this particular derivative is always positive when $x > 0$, implying that the slope of this curve is always positive when $x > 0$. Consider a second polynomial with more than one term (m terms in total). In this second case, there will be one variable x, m coefficients (c_j), and m exponents (n_j):

$$y = \sum_{j=1}^{m} c_j \cdot x^{n_j}. \tag{8.7}$$

The derivative of such a function y with respect to x is given by

$$\frac{dy}{dx} = \sum_{j=1}^{m} c_j \cdot n_j \cdot x^{n_j-1}. \tag{8.8}$$

That is, the derivative of equation (8.7) is found by simply taking the derivative of each term in y with respect to x and then summing these derivatives. Consider a second example, a second order (the largest exponent is 2) polynomial function given by $y = 3x^2 - 4x + 5$. The derivative of this function with respect to x is $dy/dx = 6x - 4$. This function is plotted in figure 8.2. Note that the function is maximized when $x = \frac{2}{3}$. Also note that when $x = \frac{2}{3}$, the slope of the curve equals zero. We can demonstrate that the derivative equals zero as follows:

$$6x - 4 = 0,$$

$$6x = 4,$$

$$x = \tfrac{2}{3}.$$

[1]   This rule is derived in appendix 8.A.

This derivative is positive when $x > \frac{2}{3}$, zero when $x = \frac{2}{3}$, and negative when $x < \frac{2}{3}$. Thus, when $dy/dx > 0$, y increases as x increases; when $dy/dx < 0$, y decreases as x increases; and when $dy/dx = 0$, y may be either minimized or maximized. The slopes in figure 8.2 are consistent with these derivatives. When $x = \frac{2}{3}$, $dy/dx = 0$ and the value of $y = f(x)$ is minimized at $3\frac{2}{3}$.

In many instances, derivatives can be used to find minimum and maximum values of functions. To ensure that we have found a minimum (rather than a maximum), we determine the second derivative. The second derivative of a function indicates its concavity. A positive second derivative indicates upward concavity, which indicates that the function $f(x)$ either increases in x at an increasing rate or decreases in x at a decreasing rate. The function depicted in figure 8.2 exhibits positive concavity. A negative second derivative indicates downward concavity, which indicates that the function $f(x)$ either increases in x at a decreasing rate or increases in x at a decreasing rate.

The second derivative is found by taking the derivative of the first derivative. If the first derivative equals zero and the second derivative is greater than zero, we have a minimum value for y (the function is concave up). If the first derivative is zero and the second derivative is less than zero, we have a maximum (the function is concave down). If the second derivative is zero, we have neither a minimum nor a maximum. The second derivative in the above example is given by $d^2y/dx^2 = 6$, also written $f''(x) = 6$. Since the second derivative 10 is greater than zero, the function $f(x)$ is concave up and we have found a minimum value for y. In many cases, more than one "local" minimum or maximum value will exist.

Consider a third example where $y = -3x^2 + 4x + 5$. The first derivative is $dy/dx = -6x + 4$. Setting the first derivative equal to zero, we find our maximum as follows:

$$-6x + 4 = 0,$$

$$-6x = -4,$$

$$x = \tfrac{2}{3}.$$

We check second order conditions (the second derivative) to ensure that this is a maximum. The second derivative is $d^2y/dx^2 = -6$. Since -6 is less than zero, the function $f(x)$ is concave up and we have a maximum at $\frac{2}{3}$.

APPLICATION 8.2: MARGINAL UTILITY
(Background reading: section 8.3 and application 3.9)

In application 3.9, we defined a utility of wealth function for a particular individual as follows:

$$U = f(W).$$

Now, let us consider the following more specific utility function:

$$U = 1{,}000W - 0.002W^2 \qquad \text{for } 0 \le W < 250{,}000.$$

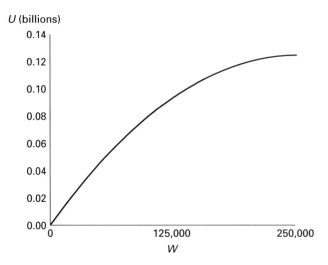

U (billions)

Figure 8.4   Utility of wealth and risk aversion. Utility-of-wealth function for risk-averse individual: $f'(W) > 0$; $f''(W) < 0$. For example, $U_w = 1{,}000W - 0.002W^2$ for $0 < W < 250{,}000$.

The curve for this function is plotted in figure 8.4. In the range from $W = 0$ to $W = 250{,}000$, utility increases as wealth increases. For example, when wealth equals 40,000, utility equals 36,800,000; when wealth equals 50,000, utility equals 45,000,000. Using the polynomial rule, we find the first derivative with respect to W of the utility function as follows:

$$f'(W) = 1{,}000 - 0.004W > 0 \qquad \text{for } 0 \le W < 250{,}000.$$

This derivative is positive, indicating that utility increases as wealth increases – as long as wealth remains within the specified range. When wealth equals 40,000, the derivative of utility with respect to wealth equals 840. This derivative is positive as long as wealth is between 0 and 250,000.

The second derivative of the utility function is found:

$$f''(W) = -0.004 < 0.$$

Thus, this utility function is concave down, indicating diminishing marginal utility with respect to wealth. This implies that rates of increase in utility resulting from increases in wealth become smaller as investors grow wealthier. That is, an individual derives smaller increases in utility when wealthier than when with less wealth. Each additional unit of wealth decreases the level of utility increase resulting from additional wealth by 0.004.

Downward concavity of a utility of wealth function indicates risk aversion. This is because potential wealth increases associated with actuarially fair gambles result in smaller utility changes than potential wealth decreases. This means that a gamble that results in zero change in expected wealth reduces expected utility, because potential lost utility from losing a given amount of wealth exceeds potential the utility gain from an identical increase in wealth. Investors are risk averse because the "pain" derived from a possible wealth loss exceeds the satisfaction derived from an equal possible wealth gain. Consider a gamble in which the investor assumes a risk where his $40,000 wealth level may either increase to $50,000 or decrease to $30,000. Recall that the investor's utility level before the gamble is 36,800,000. Potential utility levels associated with the gamble are obtained as follows:

$$U = 1,000 \cdot 50,000 - 0.002 \cdot (50,000)^2 = 45,000,000,$$

$$U = 1,000 \cdot 30,000 - 0.002 \cdot (30,000)^2 = 28,200,000.$$

The utility gain associated with the potential wealth gain of $50,000 − $40,000 = $10,000 is 45,000,000 − 36,800,000 = 8,200,000. The utility loss associated with the potential wealth loss of $40,000 − $30,000 = $10,000 is 36,800,000 − 28,200,000 = 8,400,000. Note that the potential utility loss exceeds the potential utility gain.

APPLICATION 8.3: DURATION AND IMMUNIZATION
(Background reading: sections 4.8, 4.9, 5.4, and 8.3 and application 4.4)

United States Treasury bonds, notes, and bills are generally regarded to be free of default risk and to have very low liquidity risk. However, these bonds, particularly those with longer terms to maturity, are still subject to price fluctuations when they are traded in secondary markets. The primary sources of these fluctuations are changes in interest rates offered on new issues. Such interest rate changes frequently have some element of unpredictability. One should expect that as interest rates on newly issued bonds increase, values of existing bonds will decrease. Similarly, interest rate decreases affecting new bond issues will increase the values of bonds which are already outstanding. The duration model is intends to measure the proportional change in the value of an existing bond induced by a change in interest rates or yields of new issues.

The simple present-value model is most useful for the valuation of bonds and other fixed-income instruments. Yields to maturity of priced issues are frequently used as discount rates to value new issues and to value other issues with comparable terms. It is important for analysts to know how changes in new-issue interest rates or yields will affect values of other fixed-income instruments. Bond *duration* measures the proportional price sensitivity of a bond to changes in the market rate of interest (or yields at which comparable bonds are selling). Consider a two-year 8% coupon Treasury issue that is currently selling for $982.41. The yield to maturity y of this bond is 9%. Since default risk and liquidity risk are presumed to be insignificant, interest rate risk is of primary concern. Assume that this bond's yield or discount rate is consistent with market yields of comparable Treasury issues. Further assume that bonds of all terms to maturity have the same yield and that the market prices all bonds at their present values. Thus, discount rates k for all bonds equal their yields to maturity y and these yields are invariant with respect to bond terms to maturity. If market interest rates and yields were to rise for new Treasury issues, then the yield of this bond would rise accordingly. However, since the contractual terms of this bond will not change, the bond's market price must drop to accommodate a yield consistent with the market. More generally, the value of an n-year bond paying interest at a rate of c on face value F is determined by a present-value model with the yield y of comparable issues serving as the discount rate k:

$$PV = \sum_{t=1}^{n} \frac{cF}{(1+y)^t} + \frac{F}{(1+y)^n}. \tag{8.9}$$

Assume that the terms of the bond contract, n, F, and c, are constant. We want to measure the proportional change in the price of a bond induced by a proportional change in market interest rates (actually, a proportional change in $[1+y]$). This proportional change or elasticity may be approximated by the bond's Macaulay Simple Duration Formula, as follows:

$$\frac{\Delta PV}{PV} \div \frac{\Delta(1+y)}{1+y} \approx Dur = \frac{dPV}{PV} \div \frac{d(1+y)}{1+y} = \frac{dPV}{d(1+y)} \cdot \frac{1+y}{PV}. \tag{8.10}$$

Equation (8.10) generally provides a reasonably good approximation of the proportional change in the value of a bond in a market meeting the assumptions described above, induced by an infinitesimal proportional change in $1+y$. To compute the bond's sensitivity, we first rewrite equation (8.9) in polynomial form (to take derivatives later) and substitute y for k (since they are assumed to be equal):

$$PV = \sum_{t=1}^{n} \frac{cF_t}{(1+y)^t} + \frac{F}{(1+y)^n} = \sum_{t=1}^{n} cF(1+y)^{-t} + F(1+y)^{-n}. \tag{8.11}$$

We find the derivative of PV with respect to $(1+y)$:

$$\frac{dPV}{d(1+y)} = \sum_{t=1}^{n} -tcF(1+y)^{-t-1} - nF(1+y)^{-n-1}. \tag{8.12}$$

Equation (8.12) is rewritten

$$\frac{dPV}{d(1+y)} = \frac{\sum_{t=1}^{n} -tcF(1+y)^{-t} - nF(1+y)^{-n}}{1+y}. \tag{8.13}$$

Since the market rate of interest is assumed to equal the bond yield to maturity, the bond's price will equal its present value. We multiply both sides of equation (8.14) by $(1+y) \div P_0$ to maintain consistency with equation (8.10), and obtain the duration formula as follows:

$$Dur = \frac{dPV}{d(1+y)} \cdot \frac{1+y}{P_0} = \frac{\sum_{t=1}^{n} -tcF(1+y)^{-t} - nF(1+y)^{-n}}{P_0}. \qquad (8.14)$$

Thus, duration is defined as the proportional price change of a bond induced by an infinitesimal proportional change in $(1 + y)$ or 1 plus the market rate of interest:

$$Dur = \frac{dPV}{d(1+y)} \cdot \frac{1+y}{P_0} = \frac{\sum_{t=1}^{n} \frac{-tcF}{(1+y)^t} + \frac{-nF}{(1+y)^n}}{P_0}. \qquad (8.15)$$

Since the market rate of interest will likely determine the yield to maturity of any bond, the duration of the bond described above is determined as follows from equation (8.15):

$$Dur = \frac{\frac{-1 \cdot 0.08 \cdot 1,000}{1+0.09} + \frac{-2 \cdot 0.08 \cdot 1,000}{(1+0.09)^2} + \frac{-2 \cdot 1,000}{(1+0.09)^2}}{982.41} = -1.925.$$

This duration level of -1.925 suggests that the proportional decrease in the value of this bond would equal 1.925 times the proportional increase in market interest rates. This duration level also implies that this bond has exactly the same interest rate sensitivity as a *pure discount bond* (a bond making no coupon payments, also known as a zero coupon bond) which matures in 1.925 years.

Application of the Simple Macaulay Duration model does require several important assumptions, some of which were described above. The accuracy of the model will be impaired by violations in these assumptions. First, the model assumes that yields are invariant with respect to maturities of bonds; that is, the yield curve is flat. Second, the model assumes that the investor's reinvestment rate for coupon payments will be identical to the bond's yield to maturity. Finally, any change in interest rates will be infinitesimal and will also be invariant with respect to time.

In chapter 7, we discussed bond portfolio dedication, which is concerned with exactly matching payouts required to satisfy liabilities with cash flows to be derived from bond portfolios. This process assumes that the portfolio is not adjusted by adding or selling bonds over time and that cash flows associated with liabilities will remain as originally anticipated. With shifting interest rates over time, these assumptions will not hold for many institutions. Alternatively, one may hedge fixed income portfolio risk by using *immunization* strategies, which are concerned with matching the present values of asset portfolios with the present values of cash flows associated with future liabilities. In particular, immunization strategies are primarily concerned with matching the duration of the asset side of the institution with the duration of the liability side of the portfolio. If institutional asset and liability durations are matched, it is expected that the net fund value (the fund's equity or surplus) will not be affected by a shift in interest rates. Thus, overall fund risk is minimized as fund asset and liability value changes offset each other. This simple immunization strategy requires the same assumptions as the Simple Duration Model:

1   Changes in $1 + y$ are infinitesimal.
2   The yield curve is flat (yields do not vary over terms to maturity).
3   All yields change by the same amount, regardless of term to maturity.
4   Only interest rate risk is significant.

APPLICATION 8.4: PORTFOLIO RISK AND DIVERSIFICATION
(Background reading: sections 6.1, 6.4, 6.5 and 8.2)

Differential calculus can be used to demonstrate that the risk of a portfolio decreases as the number of securities in the portfolio increases. First, in section 6.1, we defined portfolio variance as follows:

$$\sigma_p^2 = \sum_{i=1}^{n} \sum_{j=1}^{n} w_i w_j \sigma_i \sigma_j \rho_{i,j} = \sum_{i=1}^{n} \sum_{j=1}^{n} w_i w_j \sigma_{i,j}$$

$$= \sum_{\substack{i=1 \\ i \neq j}}^{n} \sum_{j=1}^{n} w_i w_j \sigma_{i,j} + \sum_{i=1}^{n} w_i^2 \sigma_i^2. \tag{A}$$

We will argue here that, as n increases, σ_p^2 decreases. For the sake of simplicity, we will assume the following:

1   The portfolio is equally weighted in n securities; that is, $w_i = w_j = 1/n$ for each security.
2   All securities have the same variance, σ_i^2.
3   Each security has the same covariance $\sigma_{i,j}$ with every other security. This covariance will be equal to the average covariance between pairs of securities.
4   Returns on component securities are not perfectly correlated.

Now we rewrite equation (A), substituting $1/n$ for w_i and w_j:

$$\sigma_p^2 = \sum_{\substack{i=1 \\ i \neq j}}^{n} \sum_{j=1}^{n} \frac{1}{n}\frac{1}{n} \sigma_{i,j} + \sum_{i=1}^{n} \frac{1}{n^2} \sigma_i^2. \tag{B}$$

By definition, $\sum_{i=1}^{n}(1/n)\sigma_i^2$ is the mean of the security variances. Thus, the right-side term following the "+" is the mean security variance divided by n. There will be a total of $n(n-1)$ covariance terms. The average covariance between pairs of securities is written

$$\bar{\sigma}_{1,j} = \sum_{j=1}^{n} \frac{1}{n} \sigma_{i,j}. \tag{C}$$

Since the average covariance term will be added $n-1$ times, we rewrite portfolio variance as follows:

$$\sigma_p^2 = \sum_{j=1}^{n-1} \frac{1}{n}\overline{\sigma}_{i,j} + \frac{1}{n}\overline{\sigma}_i^2 = \frac{(n-1)}{n}\overline{\sigma}_{i,j} + \frac{1}{n}\overline{\sigma}_i^2 = \overline{\sigma}_{i,j} - \frac{1}{n}\overline{\sigma}_{i,j} + \frac{1}{n}\overline{\sigma}_i^2$$

$$= \overline{\sigma}_{i,j} - n^{-1}\overline{\sigma}_{i,j} + n^{-1}\overline{\sigma}_i^2 = \overline{\sigma}_{i,j} + n^{-1}(\overline{\sigma}_i^2 - \overline{\sigma}_{i,j}). \tag{D}$$

To demonstrate that portfolio variance decreases as n (the number of securities) increases, we simply show that the derivative of σ_p^2 with respect to n is negative:

$$\frac{d\sigma_p^2}{dn} = -n^{-2}(\overline{\sigma}_i^2 - \overline{\sigma}_{i,j}) < 0, \tag{E}$$

which will be true whenever the average security variance exceeds the average covariance between different securities. This must hold whenever the correlation coefficient between security returns is less than one.

We can see from the final part of equation (D) that as the number of securities in the portfolio approaches infinity, the portfolio's risk approaches the average covariance between pairs of securities. Individual security variances are insignificant except to the extent that they affect covariances. Thus, only covariance is significant for large, well-diversified portfolios. If security returns are entirely independent ($\sigma_{i,j} = 0$), portfolio risk approaches zero as the number of securities included in the portfolio approaches infinity.

8.4 PARTIAL AND TOTAL DERIVATIVES
(Background reading: section 8.3)

Thus far, we have focused on univariate functions, where a dependent variable y is expressed as a function of a single independent variable x. A multivariate function is expressed as a dependent variable y and a series of independent variables (e.g., $y = f[x_1, x_2]$). The partial derivative (e.g., $\partial y/\partial x_1$) of a function expresses the rate of change in the dependent variable induced by change in one of its independent variables, while holding other variables constant. The following represents a multivariate function and its relevant partial derivatives:

$$y = 10x_1^4 + 3x_2^3 + 2x_1^2x_2,$$

$$\frac{\partial y}{\partial x_1} = 40x_1^3 + 4x_1x_2,$$

$$\frac{\partial y}{\partial x_2} = 9x_2^2 + 2x_1^2.$$

Finance practitioners frequently deal with changes in the dependent variable induced by simultaneous changes in independent variables. One may use the total derivative dy to indicate changes in the dependent variable y induced by changes in one or more of n independent variables x_i:

$$dy = \sum_{i=1}^{n} \frac{\partial y}{\partial x_i} dx_i.$$

In the above example, the total derivative would be determined as follows:

$$dy = \frac{\partial y}{\partial x_1}dx_1 + \frac{\partial y}{\partial x_2}dx_2 = (40x_1^3 + 4x_1x_2)dx_1 + (9x_2^2 + 2x_1^2)dx_2.$$

This total derivative dy is expressed as a function of derivatives of y with respect to each of the independent variables x_i and infinitesimal changes in each of these independent variables.

8.5 THE CHAIN RULE, PRODUCT RULE, AND QUOTIENT RULE

(Background reading: sections 8.3 and 8.4)

Each of the functions discussed in section 8.3 are written in polynomial form. Many functions are not or cannot be written in this manner. Other rules must be derived to find derivatives for these functions. The chain rule may be used to find derivatives for some of them. For example, consider the following function:

$$y = 7(5 + 3x)^2.$$

Although this function can be written in polynomial form ($y = 63x^2 + 210x + 175$; its derivative using the polynomial rule is $126x + 210$), we will apply the chain rule to find its derivative. The first step here in applying the chain rule is to define a function u such that $u = (5 + 3x)$. Now we write y as $y = 7u^2$. Also note that $du/dx = 3$ and $dy/du = 14u$. The chain rule is quite simple, although it does have useful and powerful implications:

$$\frac{dy}{dx} = \frac{dy}{du} \cdot \frac{du}{dx}. \tag{8.16}$$

That is, if y can be written as a function of function u, which itself is a function x, then the derivative of y with respect to x equals the derivative of y with respect to function u multiplied by the derivative of function u with respect to x. In our example, we find the derivative of y with respect to x as follows:

$$\frac{\partial y}{\partial x} = 7 \cdot 2 \cdot (5 + 3x)^{\,1} \quad \cdot \; 3 = 14(5 + 3x) \cdot 3 = 210 + 126x,$$

$$c \quad n \qquad u \quad n-1 \quad \frac{\partial u}{\partial x}.$$

In the calculations above, $c \cdot n \cdot u^{n-1} = dy/du$ and 3 is du/dx.

Another highly useful tool from calculus is the product rule, which may be applied to a function such as $y = u \cdot v$. Consider the function $(3x + 5)(7x + 4)$, where function u is $3x + 5$ and function v is $7x + 4$. The product rule, defined as follows, may be applied to find the derivative of function y, where function y equals function u times function v ($y = u \cdot v$):

$$\frac{\partial y}{\partial x} = \frac{\partial u}{\partial x} v + \frac{\partial v}{\partial x} u. \tag{8.17}$$

In our example, the derivative of y with respect to x may be found as follows:

$$\frac{\partial y}{\partial x} = 3(7x + 4) + 7(3x + 5) = 42x + 47,$$

$$\frac{\partial u}{\partial x} \quad v \quad \frac{\partial v}{\partial x} \quad u.$$

Another highly useful tool from calculus is the quotient rule, which may be applied to a function such as $y = u \div v$. Consider the function $y = (3x + 5)/(7x + 4)$. Again, define a function u (the numerator) as $3x + 5$ and a function v (the denominator) as $7x + 4$. The quotient rule, defined as follows, may be applied to find the derivative of function y:

$$\frac{\partial y}{\partial x} = \left[\frac{\partial u}{\partial x} v - \frac{\partial v}{\partial x} u \right] \div v^2. \tag{8.18}$$

The quotient rule states that the derivative of y with respect to x equals the derivative of the numerator with respect to x times the denominator minus the derivative of the denominator with respect to x times the numerator all divided by the denominator squared. Thus, the derivative of y with respect to x is found as follows:

$$\frac{dy}{dx} = \left[\frac{3(7x + 4) - 7(3x + 5)}{(7x + 4)^2} \right] = \left[\frac{-1}{49x^2 + 56x + 16} \right].$$

APPLICATION 8.5: PLOTTING THE CAPITAL MARKET LINE
(Background reading: sections 6.4, 7.4, and 8.5)

In section 6.4, we discussed the addition of securities with varying correlation coefficients to a portfolio and the impact of these additional securities on the risk and efficiency of that portfolio. More efficient combinations of securities can reduce portfolio risk without decreasing expected portfolio returns. As we add securities to a portfolio, the fact that they are not perfectly correlated with other securities in that portfolio will lead to reductions in portfolio risk and increases in portfolio efficiency.

Portfolio efficiency improves when portfolio risk is reduced without corresponding reductions in portfolio expected return. In this application, we are concerned with obtaining portfolio weights for the most efficient combinations of assets available in the economy. We will map out the most efficient combinations of securities at varying expected return levels. These most efficient portfolio combinations will be those which have the lowest risk of any potential portfolio with the same expected return. The set of portfolios which have the lowest levels of risk given their expected return levels have risk/expected returns lying on the Efficient Frontier. The Efficient Frontier represents the risk–return combinations (in standard deviation–expected-return space) of this set of most efficient portfolios available in the market. It contains the risk–return coordinates of each portfolio that minimizes risk given an expected portfolio return level. Similarly, the Efficient Frontier contains the risk–return coordinates of each portfolio that maximizes return given a risk level.

In any market with more than one security, there are infinitely many ways to combine those securities into portfolios. While investors cannot affect the characteristics (return, risk, and covariances) of the individual securities in which they invest, they are able to control portfolio weights. Investors should select securities and assign them weights in their personal portfolios such that the portfolios are as efficient as possible.

Each investor in the market intends to minimize risk by selecting each of the securities available in the market with the most appropriate portfolio weightings. Each security is considered for each investor's portfolio, with weights greater than zero (the security is purchased), equal to zero (the security is left out of the portfolio), or less than zero (the security is sold short).

Suppose that an investor is able to invest in some combination of risky assets (stocks) and a riskless asset (bond). Any portfolio consisting of a portfolio of risky assets and a risk-free asset will have an expected return and standard deviation combination lying on a line as in figure 8.5. This line represents the portfolio possibilities frontier

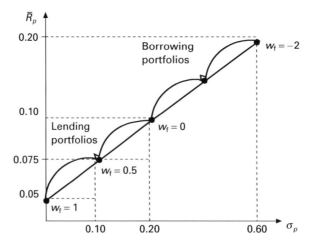

Figure 8.5   Combining a portfolio of risky assets with the riskless asset.

for the combination of risky assets and the riskless asset. Consider a portfolio of risky assets with an expected return equal to 0.10 and a standard deviation of returns equal to 0.20. Suppose that this portfolio of risky assets is to be combined with a riskless asset with a return of 5%. The expected return and standard deviation combination of this resultant portfolio will be determined by the portfolio weights that the investor associates with the portfolio of risky assets (w_R) and the riskless asset (w_f) :

$$E[R_p] = w_R \cdot 0.10 + w_f \cdot 0.05, \tag{A}$$

$$\sigma_p = \sqrt{w_R^2 \cdot 0.20^2 + w_f^2 \cdot 0^2 + 2(w_R \cdot w_f \cdot 0.1 \cdot 0 \cdot 0)}, \tag{B}$$

$$\sigma_p = \sqrt{w_R^2 \cdot \sigma_R^2 + 0 + 0}, \tag{C}$$

$$\sigma_p = w_R \cdot \sigma_R. \tag{D}$$

By rewriting equation (D) as $w_R = \sigma_p \div \sigma_R$, and substituting it into equation (A) for w_R, we find that the expected return of a portfolio combining risky assets and the riskless asset is a linear function of the return standard deviation of the portfolio of risky assets as follows:

$$E[R_p] = \frac{\sigma_p}{\sigma_R} \cdot 0.10 + w_f \cdot 0.05, \tag{E}$$

$$E[R_p] = \frac{\sigma_p}{\sigma_R} \cdot 0.10 + \left(1 - \frac{\sigma_p}{\sigma_R}\right) \cdot 0.05, \tag{F}$$

$$E[R_p] = 0.05 + \frac{\sigma_p}{\sigma_R} \cdot (0.10 - 0.05). \tag{G}$$

More generally, equation (G) can be written as follows:

$$E[R_p] = r_f + \frac{\sigma_p}{\sigma_R} \cdot (E[R_p] - r_f). \tag{8.19}$$

Defining Θ_p as $\{E[R_p] - r_f\} \div \sigma_R$, we obtain the linear relationship between portfolio expected return and standard deviation as follows:

$$E[R_p] = r_f + \frac{E[R_p] - r_f}{\sigma_R} \cdot \sigma_p = r_f + \Theta_p \cdot \sigma_p.$$

Theta (Θ_p) is the slope of the portfolio possibilities frontier depicted in figure 8.5. If there is a riskless asset in the economy, all of the most efficient portfolios will have a risk–return combination lying on a portfolio possibilities frontier known as the Capital

Market Line. The Capital Market Line is the portfolio possibilities frontier with the greatest slope. The investor's objective is to choose that portfolio of risky assets enabling him to maximize the slope of this line; that is, the investor should pick that portfolio with the largest possible Θ_p as defined by:

$$\Theta_p = \frac{E[R_p] - r_f}{\sigma_p}. \tag{8.20}$$

Consider an investor who has the opportunity to combine any one of an infinity of portfolios with the riskless asset. However, only one of these portfolios (if none are perfectly correlated) can be used to comprise the Capital Market Line. Hence, the investor's portfolio objective is to select portfolio weights w_i such that Θ_p is maximized:

$$\Theta_p = \frac{E[R_p] - r_f}{\sigma_p} = \frac{\sum\limits_{i=1}^{n} w_i(E[R_i] - r_f)}{\sqrt{\sum\limits_{\substack{i=1 \\ i \neq j}}^{n}\sum\limits_{j=1}^{n} (w_i w_j \sigma_{i,j})}}.$$

This portfolio that maximizes Θ_p is known as the market portfolio of risky assets. Any combination of the market portfolio and the riskless asset will lie on the Capital Market Line and will dominate (be more efficient than) any other asset or portfolio with equal expected return. Thus, any investor should invest in some combination of this dominant portfolio of risky assets (stocks) and the riskless asset (bonds). The investor's first problem is to select the portfolio weights which comprise the market portfolio of stocks.

Suppose that the investor can invest in any combination of two risky securities 1 and 2. The expected returns, standard deviations, and covariance are given as follows:

$$E[R_1] = 0.11, \qquad \sigma_1 = 0.20,$$

$$E[R_2] = 0.15, \qquad \sigma_2 = 0.40, \qquad \sigma_{1,2} = -0.01.$$

The Treasury bill (riskless) rate in this economy is 0.06. We will now derive the set of equations that the investor needs to find his optimal portfolio of riskless assets.

Since the investor's objective is to select a portfolio of the two risky assets such that the slope of the Capital Market Line is maximized, we will select stock portfolio weights such that Θ_p is maximized. To accomplish this, we will find partial derivatives of Θ_p with respect to weights of each of each of the two stocks, set the partial derivatives equal to zero and solve for the weight values w_1 and w_2. First, we write Θ_p for the simple two-stock portfolio as follows:

$$\Theta_p = \frac{E[R_p] - r_f}{\sigma_p} = \frac{w_1(E[R_1] - r_f) + w_2(E[R_2] - r_f)}{(w_1^2 \sigma_1^2 + w_2^2 \sigma_2^2 + 2w_1 w_2 \sigma_{1,2})^{1/2}}. \tag{A}$$

Next, we use the quotient rule to begin the process of finding the partial derivatives of Θ_p with respect to w_1 and w_2:

$$\frac{\partial\Theta_p}{\partial w_1} = \frac{\dfrac{\partial(E[R_p]-r_f)}{\partial w_1}\sigma_p - \dfrac{\partial\sigma_p}{\partial w_1}(E[R_p]-r_f)}{\sigma_p^2} = 0, \tag{B1}$$

$$\frac{\partial\Theta_p}{\partial w_2} = \frac{\dfrac{\partial(E[R_p]-r_f)}{\partial w_2}\sigma_p - \dfrac{\partial\sigma_p}{\partial w_2}(E[R_p]-r_f)}{\sigma_p^2} = 0. \tag{B2}$$

Before completing this process, we use the chain rule to find the partial derivatives $\partial\sigma_p/\partial w_1$ and $\partial\sigma_p/\partial w_1$ (from the denominator of equation (A)):

$$\frac{\partial\sigma_p}{\partial w_1} = \tfrac{1}{2}(\sigma_p^2)^{-1/2}(2w_1\sigma_1^2 + 2w_2\sigma_{1,2}) = \frac{w_1\sigma_1^2 + w_2\sigma_{1,2}}{\sigma_p}, \tag{C1}$$

$$\frac{\partial\sigma_p}{\partial w_2} = \tfrac{1}{2}(\sigma_p^2)^{-1/2}(2w_2\sigma_2^2 + 2w_1\sigma_{1,2}) = \frac{w_2\sigma_2^2 + w_1\sigma_{1,2}}{\sigma_p}. \tag{C2}$$

We can find from equation (A) that the derivative of $(E[R_p]-r_f)$ with respect to w_i equals $(E[R_i]-r_f)$. Next, we substitute our results of equations (C1) and (C2) into equations (B1) and (B2), to obtain:

$$\frac{\partial\Theta_p}{\partial w_1} = \frac{(E[R_1]-r_f)\sigma_p - (E[R_p]-r_f)(w_1\sigma_1^2 + w_2\sigma_{1,2})/\sigma_p}{\sigma_p^2} = 0, \tag{D1}$$

$$\frac{\partial\Theta_p}{\partial w_2} = \frac{(E[R_2]-r_f)\sigma_p - (E[R_p]-r_f)(w_2\sigma_2^2 + w_1\sigma_{1,2})/\sigma_p}{\sigma_p^2} = 0. \tag{D2}$$

Because the derivatives from equations (D1) and (D2) are both set equal to zero, we may multiply the numerator of each by σ_p and maintain the equalities. Next, we rewrite the equations as follows:

$$E[R_1]-r_f = \frac{(E[R_p]-r_f)(w_1\sigma_1^2 + w_2\sigma_{1,2})}{\sigma_p^2}, \tag{E1}$$

$$E[R_2]-r_f = \frac{(E[R_p]-r_f)(w_1\sigma_{1,2} + w_2\sigma_2^2)}{\sigma_p^2}. \tag{E2}$$

To continue the process of simplification, define the variable z_i to be $w_i(E[R_p]-r_f)/\sigma_p^2$ and rewrite equations (E1) and (E2) as follows:

$$E[R_1] - r_f = z_1\sigma_1^2 + z_2\sigma_{1,2},$$
$$E[R_2] - r_f = z_1\sigma_{2,1} + z_2\sigma_2^2.$$

Substituting numerical values from our example, we have

$$0.11 - 0.06 = 0.2^2 z_1 - 0.01z_2,$$
$$0.15 - 0.06 = 0.01z_1 + 0.4^2 z_2,$$

or

$$0.05 = 0.04z_1 - 0.01z_2,$$
$$0.09 = -0.01z_1 + 0.16z_2.$$

Solving the above simultaneously yields $z_1 = 1.41$ and $z_2 = 0.65$. Since $E[R_p]$, r_f, and σ_p are the same for both z_1 and z_2, the ratio between w_1 and w_2 must be the same as the ratio between z_1 and z_2. Therefore, portfolio weights w_1 and w_2 are determined as follows:

$$w_1 = z_1 \div (z_1 + z_2) = 0.68,$$
$$w_2 = z_2 \div (z_1 + z_2) = 0.32.$$

Thus, 68% and 32% of this investor's wealth will be invested in securities 1 and 2. This represents the market portfolio (m) to the investor and is the most efficient combination of risky assets given the prevailing riskless rate of return at 6%. The return and risk levels of the portfolio (m) with two risky stocks are simply

$$E[R_m] = 0.68 \cdot 0.11 + 0.32 \cdot 0.15 = 0.12,$$
$$\sigma_m = [0.68^2 \cdot 0.04 + 0.32^2 \cdot 0.16 + 2 \cdot 0.68 \cdot 0.32 \cdot (-0.01)]^{0.5} = 0.17.$$

The equation for the Capital Market Line is as follows:

$$E[R_p] = r_f + \frac{E[R_m] - r_f}{\sigma_m} \cdot \sigma_p$$
$$= 0.06 + \frac{0.12 - 0.06}{0.17} \cdot \sigma_p = 0.06 + 0.35\sigma_p.$$

These results enable the investor to determine weightings for his optimal portfolio of risky assets (stocks). The investor allocates funds to this most efficient portfolio of risky assets and bonds based on his own attitudes toward return and risk. Finally, this derivation can easily be extended to include as many securities as exist in the market. Matrix mathematics such as the methodologies discussed in section 7.4 may simplify computations of larger systems.

8.6   LOGARITHMIC AND EXPONENTIAL FUNCTIONS
(Background reading: sections 2.5, 2.6, 8.1, and 8.2)

Logarithmic and exponential functions and derivatives of these functions are most useful in finance for modeling growth. Consider the following function:

$$f(x) = e^{tx}.$$

The derivative with respect to x of this exponential function is found as follows:

$$f'(x) = \lim_{h \to 0} \frac{e^{t(x+h)} - e^{tx}}{h} = e^{tx} \lim_{h \to 0} \frac{e^{th} - 1}{h}.$$

It is easy to demonstrate (or verify on a hand calculator) that as h approaches zero, $(e^{th} - 1)/h$ will approach t. Thus, the derivative of the exponential function is found as follows:

$$\frac{de^{tx}}{dx} = te^{tx}. \tag{8.21}$$

Thus, the derivative of $e^{0.05x}$ with respect to x is simply $0.05e^{0.05x}$. If we accept the special case of equation (8.21) that $de^x/dx = e^x$, the following more general expression for the derivative of an exponential function can be verified using the chain rule:

$$\frac{de^{g(x)}}{dx} = g'(x)e^{g(x)}. \tag{8.22}$$

From equation (8.22), we can derive a function for the derivative of a logarithmic function $y = \ln(x)$. First, by definition, $e^{\ln(x)} = x$, implying that $de^{\ln(x)}/dx = 1$. Now, consider the following special case of equation (8.22):

$$\frac{de^{\ln(x)}}{dx} = \frac{d\ln(x)}{dx} e^{\ln(x)}.$$

This equation is written

$$1 = \frac{d\ln(x)}{dx} \cdot x,$$

which implies

$$\frac{d\ln(x)}{dx} = \frac{1}{x}. \tag{8.23}$$

8.7   TAYLOR SERIES EXPANSIONS
(Background reading: sections 2.11 and 8.3)

The derivative was used in section 8.3 to determine the rate of change in $f(x)$ induced by a change in x. Unfortunately, when $f(x)$ is not linear in x, the estimates of change based on this derivative is normally accurate only for infinitesimal changes in x. The Taylor series approximation or expansion may be used for finite changes in x. Taylor series expansions are frequently used to evaluate a function $f(x)$ at a point x_1 that differs from a starting point x_0 at which $f(x_0)$ has already been evaluated. That is, the Taylor series may be used to approximate a rate of change in $f(x)$ induced by a change in x. An nth order Taylor series is defined as follows for a function $f(x)$ that is differentiable n times:

$$f(x_0 + \Delta x) \approx f(x_0) + f'(x_0) \cdot \Delta x + \frac{1}{2!} \cdot f''(x_0) \cdot (\Delta x)^2$$

$$+ \frac{1}{3!} \cdot f'''(x_0) \cdot (\Delta x)^3 + \ldots + \frac{1}{n!} \cdot f^n(x_0) \cdot (\Delta x)^n. \qquad (8.24)$$

For example, consider the function $y = 10x^3$. Let $x_0 = 2$, such that we have $f(x_0) = 80$, $f'(x_0) = 30x_0^2 = 120, f''(x_0) = 60x_0 = 120$, and $f'''(x_0) = 60$, and all higher order derivatives are equal to zero. Now, suppose that we wish to increase x by $\Delta x = 3$ to $x_1 = 5$. The Taylor series expansion may be used to evaluate x_1 as follows:

$$f(2 + 3) = f(2) + f'(2) \cdot 3 + \frac{1}{2!} \cdot f''(2) \cdot 3^2 + \frac{1}{3!} \cdot f'''(2) \cdot 3^3$$

$$= 80 + 120 \cdot 3 + \tfrac{1}{2} \cdot 120 \cdot 9 + \tfrac{1}{6} \cdot 60 \cdot 27 = 80 + 360 + 540 + 270 = 1{,}250.$$

This third order expansion provided an exact solution for $f(5) = 1{,}250$. This third order expansion provided an exact solution for $f(x)$ because $f(x)$ was differentiable only three times (fourth and higher derivatives equal zero) and our approximation used all three nonzero derivatives. In many cases, we will be able to obtain reasonable approximations, although not precise solutions, where not all nonzero derivatives are used. In this example, first order approximation results in $f(5) \approx 440$ and the second order approximation results in $f(5) \approx 980$:

$$f(2 + 3) \approx f(2) + f'(2) \cdot 3 = 80 + 120 \cdot 3 = 80 + 360 = 440,$$

$$f(2 + 3) \approx f(2) + f'(2) \cdot 3 + \frac{1}{2!} \cdot f''(2) \cdot 3^2$$

$$= 80 + 120 \cdot 3 + \tfrac{1}{2} \cdot 120 \cdot 9 = 80 + 360 + 540 = 980.$$

Note that the second order approximation based on first and second derivatives is superior to the first order approximation based only on the first derivative. Generally,

Taylor series approximations will improve as order of the approximating equation increases (as n increases). If the equation is differentiable n or fewer times, the Taylor series approximation of the nth order will be precise.

APPLICATION 8.6: CONVEXITY AND IMMUNIZATION
(Background reading: section 8.7 and application 8.4)

The duration model in application 8.4 was used to approximate the change in a bond's value resulting from a change in interest rates $1 + y$. However, the accuracy of the duration model is reduced when interest rates change by finite amounts. This is important because interest rate changes can be quite sudden and quite large. Duration may be regarded as yielding a first order approximation (it only uses the first derivative) of the change in the value of a bond resulting from a change in interest rates. As we saw above, a second order approximation will probably yield superior estimates to the first order approximation. *Convexity* is determined by the second derivative of the bond's value with respect to $1 + y$. Recall that the first derivative of the bond's price with respect to $1 + y$ is

$$\frac{\partial P_0}{\partial (1 + y)} = \sum_{t=1}^{n} -tcF(1 + y)^{-t-1} - nF(1 + y)^{-n-1}. \tag{8.25}$$

We find the second derivative by solving for the derivative of equation (8.25) as follows:

$$\frac{\partial^2 P_0}{\partial (1 + y)^2} = \left[\sum_{t=1}^{n} -t(-t - 1)cF(1 + y)^{-t-2} \right] - [n(-n - 1)F(1 + y)^{-n-2}]$$

$$= \left[\sum_{t=1}^{n} \frac{(t^2 + t)cF}{(1 + y)^{t+2}} \right] + \left[\frac{(n^2 + n)F}{(1 + y)^{n+2}} \right]. \tag{8.26}$$

This second derivative divided by the bond's price as defined as the bond's convexity. Thus, convexity is the second derivative of P_0 with respect to $1 + y$ divided by P_0. The two derivatives given by equations (8.25) and (8.26) may be used in a Taylor series expansion to approximate new bond prices affected by changes in interest rates:

$$P_1 \approx P_0 + f(1 + y_0) \cdot [\Delta(1 + y)] + \frac{1}{2!} \cdot f''(1 + y_0) \cdot [\Delta(1 + y)]^2,$$

$$P_1 \approx P_0 + \left[\sum_{t=1}^{n} \frac{-tcF_t}{(1 + y_0)^{t+1}} - \frac{nF}{(1 + y_0)^{n+1}} \right] \cdot [\Delta y]$$

$$+ \frac{1}{2} \left[\sum_{t=1}^{n} \frac{(t^2 + t) \cdot cF_t}{(1 + y_0)^{t+2}} + \frac{(n^2 + n) \cdot F}{(1 + y_0)^{n+2}} \right] \cdot [\Delta y]^2. \tag{8.27}$$

Consider an example involving a three-year 6% $1,000-face-value coupon bond currently selling at par (face value). The yield to maturity of this bond is computed to be $y_0 = 0.06$. The first derivative of the bond's market value with respect to $1 + y$ at $y_0 = 0.06$ is found by equation (8.25) to be $-3,003.39$ (duration is $-3.00339 \cdot 1.06 \div 1,000 = -2.83339$); the second derivative is found from equation (8.26) to be 9,891.03 (convexity is $9,891.03 \div 1,000 = 9.89103$). If yields on comparable bonds were to increase from 0.06 to 0.09, the actual value of this bond would decrease to 924.06, as determined from a standard present-value model. If we were to use a first order series (the duration model) to estimate the new value of the bond, our approximation is 919.81. This approximation is not likely to be acceptable for most purposes. If we use the second order series (the convexity model), our approximation is 924.26:

$$924.26 = 1,000 - 2,83339 \cdot 0.03 \cdot \frac{1,000}{1+0.06} + \tfrac{1}{2} \cdot 1,000 \cdot 9.89103 \cdot 0.03^2. \quad (8.28)$$

While the estimate provided by this second order approximation is not precise, it does yield a new bond value that is closer to the bond's actual new value as determined by the present-value model. Therefore, the duration and immunization (application 8.4 above) applications can be substantially improved by using second order approximations of bond prices. Although duration and convexity provide only approximations of bond prices after interest rate shifts, their real value is in their application in bond risk management. The fixed income manager intending to hedge portfolio risk should match the convexities of fund assets and liabilities as well as the durations of fund assets and liabilities. This combination provides for a superior hedge.

8.8   THE METHOD OF LAGRANGE MULTIPLIERS
(Background reading: sections 7.4 and 8.4)

Differential calculus is particularly useful for determining minimums or maximums of functions of many types. Many optimization problems require constraints or limitations on functions to be minimized or maximized. For example, a portfolio manager may structure security weights in a portfolio so as to minimize portfolio risk. The most efficient portfolio minimizes risk at a given expected return level. The method of Lagrange multipliers enables function optimization subject to constraints. This method of Lagrange multipliers supplements the original function to be optimized by adding one term for each constraint to be considered. This extra term for each constraint is the product of a function of the constraint and a Lagrange multiplier λ. The method of Lagrange multipliers is most useful for nonlinear functions with more than one independent variable. For example, suppose that we wish to minimize the function $y = 5x^2 + 12z^2 + 6xz$ subject to the constraint that $3x + 2z = 50$. This problem may be written as follows:

$$OBJ: Min\ y = 5x^2 + 12z^2 + 6xz$$

$$s.t.:\ 3x + 2z = 50.$$

This problem statement reads. "Objective function: Minimize $y = 5x^2 + 12z^2 + 6xz$ subject to $3x + 2z = 50$." The Lagrange function combines the original function and the constraints as follows:

$$L = 5x^2 + 12z^2 + 6xz + \lambda(50 - 3x - 2z).$$

Notice that we have added a second function to the original function to be minimized. This second function is the product of a Lagrange multiplier λ and the constraint. This product will have a numerical value equal to zero. The Lagrange multiplier by itself may be interpreted as the change in y that will be induced by a change in the constraint numerical value (in this case, 50); that is, λ is a sensitivity variable. If the constraint is not binding, λ will equal zero. If the constraint is binding in this example, $3x + 2z$ will equal 50. Since either the contents within the parentheses or the Lagrange multiplier will equal zero, the numerical value of the function that we have added to our original function to be optimized will be zero. Although the numerical value of our original function is unchanged by the supplement representing the constraint, its derivatives will be affected by the constraint.

We solve our optimization problem by setting partial derivatives equal to zero. That is, we set partial derivatives of function L with respect to each of our variables x, z, and λ equal to zero. This process is known as finding first order conditions:

$$\frac{\partial L}{\partial x} = 10x + 6z - 3\lambda = 0,$$

$$\frac{\partial L}{\partial z} = 24z + 6x - 2\lambda = 0,$$

$$\frac{\partial L}{\partial \lambda} = 50 - 3x - 2z = 0.$$

We rewrite this system as follows:

$$10x + 6z - 3\lambda = 0,$$

$$6x + 24z - 2\lambda = 0,$$

$$-3x - 2z + 0\lambda = -50.$$

This system is solved in matrix format as follows:

$$\begin{bmatrix} 10 & 6 & -3 \\ 6 & 24 & -2 \\ -3 & -2 & 0 \end{bmatrix} \begin{bmatrix} x \\ z \\ \lambda \end{bmatrix} = \begin{bmatrix} 0 \\ 0 \\ -50 \end{bmatrix},$$

$$\mathbf{C} \qquad \cdot \mathbf{x} = \mathbf{s}.$$

We find the inverse for the coefficients matrix then solve for security weights and our Lagrange multiplier as follows:

$$
\begin{bmatrix}
0.021739 & -0.03261 & -0.32609 \\
-0.03261 & 0.048913 & -0.01087 \\
-0.32609 & -0.01087 & -1.1087
\end{bmatrix}
\begin{bmatrix} 0 \\ 0 \\ -50 \end{bmatrix}
=
\begin{bmatrix} x \\ z \\ \lambda \end{bmatrix},
$$

$$ \mathbf{C}^{-1} \qquad\qquad \cdot \ \mathbf{s} \ = \mathbf{x}. $$

We find that $x = 16.30435$, $z = 0.543478$, and $\lambda = 55.43478$. Thus, the minimum value for y subject to the constraint is $1{,}279.537$. This constraint is binding since λ is nonzero. Note that $3x + 2z = 50$.

The term λ may be considered to be a sensitivity coefficient. This sensitivity coefficient indicates the change in y that would result from a change in the constraint on $3x + 2z$. If, for example, we were to increase the constraint by 1 from 50 to 51, the value of y would increase by approximately 55.43478, since this is the value of λ. The accuracy of this approximation declines as the change in the constraint increases.

APPLICATION 8.7: OPTIMAL PORTFOLIO SELECTION
(Background reading: sections 6.3, 6.4, and 8.7)

One important application of Lagrange optimization in finance is in specifying weights of most efficient portfolios. Suppose that an investor has the opportunity to construct a portfolio consisting of three assets whose characteristics are specified as follows:

Asset	E[R]	σ
A	0.06	0.20
B	0.09	0.30
C	0.12	0.40
$\rho_{A,B} = \rho_{A,C} = \rho_{B,C} = 0.4$		

Suppose that the investor intends to invest \$1,000,000 into a portfolio that enables him to minimize his risk level. The investor requires an expected portfolio return of at least 10% and the weights of his portfolio should sum to 1. We need to determine how much the investor should place into each of the three securities. First, we use the data given above to compute relevant variances and covariances for the individual securities and pairs. The portfolio objective function and constraints are given as follows:

$$ OBJ:\ Min\ \sigma_p^2 = 0.04w_A^2 + 0.09w_B^2 + 0.16w_C^2 + 0.048w_A w_B + 0.064w_A w_C + 0.096w_B w_C $$

$$ s.t.:\ 0.06w_A + 0.09w_B + 0.12w_C = 0.10, $$

$$ w_A + w_B + w_C = 1. $$

The Lagrange function is constructed as follows:

$$L = 0.04w_A^2 + 0.09w_B^2 + 0.16w_C^2 + 0.048w_Aw_B + 0.064w_Aw_C + 0.096w_Bw_C$$
$$+ \lambda_1(0.10 - 0.06w_A - 0.09w_B - 0.12w_C) + \lambda_2(1 - w_A - w_B - w_C).$$

Our first order conditions are given by the following:

$$\frac{\delta L}{\delta w_A} = 0.08w_A + 0.048w_B + 0.064w_C - 0.06\lambda_1 - \lambda_2 = 0,$$

$$\frac{\delta L}{\delta w_B} = 0.18w_B + 0.048w_A + 0.096w_C - 0.09\lambda_1 - \lambda_2 = 0,$$

$$\frac{\delta L}{\delta w_C} = 0.32w_C + 0.064w_A + 0.096w_B - 0.12\lambda_1 - \lambda_2 = 0,$$

$$\frac{\delta L}{\delta \lambda_1} = 0.10 - 0.06w_A - 0.09w_B - 0.12w_C = 0,$$

$$\frac{\delta L}{\delta \lambda_2} = 1 - 1w_A - 1w_B - 1w_C = 0.$$

This system is written in matrix format as follows:

$$
\begin{bmatrix}
0.08 & 0.048 & 0.064 & -0.06 & -1 \\
0.048 & 0.18 & 0.096 & -0.09 & -1 \\
0.064 & 0.096 & 0.32 & -0.12 & -1 \\
-0.06 & -0.09 & -0.12 & 0 & 0 \\
-1 & -1 & -1 & 0 & 0
\end{bmatrix}
\begin{bmatrix}
w_A \\ w_B \\ w_C \\ \lambda_1 \\ \lambda_2
\end{bmatrix}
=
\begin{bmatrix}
0 \\ 0 \\ 0 \\ -0.10 \\ -1
\end{bmatrix},
$$

$$\mathbf{C} \qquad\qquad \cdot \quad \mathbf{x} \ = \quad \mathbf{S}.$$

We now invert matrix $\mathbf{C}$ and then solve for vector $\mathbf{x}$:

$$
\begin{bmatrix}
1.488095 & -2.97619 & 1.488095 & 20.2381 & -2.14286 \\
-2.97619 & 5.952381 & -2.97619 & -7.14286 & 0.285714 \\
1.488095 & -2.97619 & 1.488095 & -13.0952 & 0.875143 \\
20.2381 & -7.14286 & -13.0952 & -66.9841 & 4.457143 \\
-2.14286 & 0.285714 & 0.857143 & 4.457143 & -0.37029
\end{bmatrix}
\begin{bmatrix}
0 \\ 0 \\ 0 \\ -0.10 \\ -1
\end{bmatrix}
=
\begin{bmatrix}
w_A \\ w_B \\ w_C \\ \lambda_1 \\ \lambda_2
\end{bmatrix}.
$$

We determine the following weights: $w_A = 0.119$, $w_B = 0.429$, and $w_C = 0.452$. The two Lagrange multipliers are $\lambda_1 = 2.24$ and $\lambda_2 = -0.075$. The expected portfolio return and standard deviation are 0.10 and 0.273, respectively. The portfolio variance is 0.074. Since the first Lagrange multiplier is 2.24, an increase by 0.01 in the return constraint would change portfolio weights, leading to an increase in portfolio variance of approximately 0.0224. We would find the actual new portfolio variance by inserting 0.11 into the return constraint of the Lagrange function. In this case, we see that the actual revised portfolio variance increases to 0.100.

EXERCISES

8.1. Solve the following for y':

$$y' = \lim_{h \to 0} \frac{7(x+h)^2 - 7x^2}{h}.$$

8.2. Find derivatives of y with respect to x for each of the following:

(a) $y = 5$;
(b) $y = 7x^3$;
(c) $y = 2x^4 + 5x^3$;
(d) $y = 10x^{0.5} - 11x^3$;
(e) $y = 5x^{1/5}$;
(f) $y = 2/x^2 + 2/3x^{1/2} + 3x^{-1/5} + 1/x$.

8.3. Find second derivatives of y with respect to x for each function in problem 8.2.

8.4. Identify those functions that have finite maximum values for y. For these functions, what values for x maximize y?

(a) $y = 15x^2 + 12$;
(b) $y = 20x$;
(c) $y = -3x^2 + 6x$;
(d) $y = 2x^3 - 6x^2 + x - 12$;
(e) $y = 12x^3$;
(f) $y = 3 + x^2 + 10x$.

8.5. Identify those functions that have finite minimum values for y. For these functions, what values for x minimize y?

(a) $y = 15x^2 + 12$;
(b) $y = 6x$;
(c) $y = 3x^2 + 6x$;
(d) $y = x^3 - 3x^2 + 2x - 21$;
(e) $y = 12x^3$;
(f) $y = 13 - x^2 + 8x$.

8.6. Find the durations for the following pure discount (zero coupon) bonds:

(a) A $1,000-face-value bond maturing in one year. The bond is currently selling for $900.
(b) A $1,000-face-value bond maturing in two years. The bond is currently selling for $800.
(c) A $2,000-face-value bond maturing in three years. The bond is currently selling for $1,400.

(d) A portfolio consisting of one of each of the three bonds listed in parts (a), (b), and (c) of this problem.
(e) A portfolio consisting of $100,800 in each of the three bonds listed in parts (a), (b), and (c) of this problem.

8.7. Find the duration of each of the following $1,000-face-value coupon bonds assuming that coupon payments are made annually:

(a) a-three year 7% bond currently selling for $950;
(b) a-three year 12% bond currently selling for $1,040;
(c) a-four year 10% bond currently selling for $900;
(d) a-four year 10% bond currently selling for $800.

8.8. Based on duration computations, what would happen to the prices of each of the bonds in problem 8.7 if market interest rates ($r = ytm$) were to increase by 1%?

8.9. What is the duration of a portfolio containing one of each of the bonds listed in problem 8.7?

8.10. Consider each of the following functions:

(a) $y = 5x$;
(b) $y = 5x^2 + 10z$;
(c) $y = 2x^7 + 8q^5$;
(d) $y = 5x^3 + 10z^2 + 7xz$;
(e) $y = 12x^3z^5 + 3xz^2$;
(f) $y = \sum_{i=1}^{n} nx^i z^2$.

(i) For each of the functions (a)–(f) above, find partial derivatives for y with respect to x.
(ii) For each of the functions (a)–(f) above, find partial derivatives for y with respect to z.

8.11. Find derivatives for y with respect to x for each of the following:

(a) $y = (4x + 2)^3$;
(b) $y = (3x^2 + 8)^{1/2}$;
(c) $y = 6x(4x^3 + 5x^2 + 3)$;
(d) $y = (1.5x - 4)^3(2.5x - 3.5)^4$;
(e) $y = 25/x^2$;
(f) $y = (6x - 16) \div (10x - 14)$.

8.12. Investors have the opportunity to invest in any combination of the 5% risk-less asset and the two risky securities given in the table below:

i	$E[R_i]$	σ_i	$\sigma_{1,i}$	$\sigma_{2,i}$	$\sigma_{3,i}$
1	0.15	0.50	0.25	0.05	0
2	0.08	0.40	0.05	0.16	0

(a) What are the security weights for the optimal (market) portfolio of risky assets?

(b) What are the market portfolio expected return and standard deviation levels?

8.13. Investors have the opportunity to invest in any combination of the 5% risk-less asset and the three risky securities given in the table below:

i	$E[R_i]$	σ_i	$\sigma_{1,i}$	$\sigma_{2,i}$	$\sigma_{3,i}$
1	0.15	0.50	0.25	0.05	0.04
2	0.08	0.40	0.05	0.16	0.03
3	0.06	0.30	0.04	0.16	0.09

(a) What are the security weights for the optimal (market) portfolio of risky assets?

(b) What are the market portfolio expected return and standard deviation levels?

8.14.* An investor has the opportunity to invest in a portfolio combining the following two risky stocks:

Security	Expected return	Standard deviation	
A	0.08	0.30	COV(A,B) = 0
B	0.12	0.60	

The investor can borrow money at a rate of 6%, lend money at 4%, and has $5,000,000 to invest. The investor intends to minimize the risk of her portfolio, but requires an expected return of 18%. How much money should she borrow or lend? How much should she invest in each of the two stocks?

8.15. Differentiate each of the following with respect to x:

(a) $y = e^{0.05x}$;   (c) $y = 5 \ln(x)$;
(b) $y = (e^x)/x$;   (d) $y = e^x \ln(x)$.

8.16. Find durations and convexities for each of the following bonds:

(a) a 6% three-year bond selling for $1,020;
(b) a 9% four-year bond selling for $1,100.

8.17. For each of the bonds listed in problem 8.16 above, complete the following, assuming that all interest rates (yields) change to 8%:

(a) Use the duration (first order) approximation models to estimate bond value changes induced by changes in interest rates (yields) to 8%.
(b) Use the convexity (second order) approximation models to estimate bond value changes induced by changes in interest rates (yields) to 8%.
(c) Find the present values of each of the bonds after yields (cash flow discount rates) change to 8%.

8.18. Our objective is to find the value for x that enables us to maximize the function $y = 50x^2 - 10x$ subject to the constraint that $0.1x = 100$. Set up and solve a Lagrange function for this problem.

8.19. Solve the following: MAX $y = 25 + 3x + 10x^2$ s.t.: $5x = 10$.

8.20. An investor intends to create a portfolio of two assets with the following expected return and standard deviation levels:

Asset	E[R]	σ
A	0.10	0.20
B	0.20	0.40
		$\sigma_{AB} = 0.04$

Determine the following:

(a) Optimal portfolio weights given each of the following expected return constraints:

(i) $E(R_p) = 0.15$;
(ii) $E(R_p) = 0.12$;
(iii) $E(R_p) = 0.18$.

(b) Optimal portfolio weights given each of the same expected return constraints in part (a) above, securities A and B from above and assuming the existence of a riskless asset with a 9% expected return. Use the Lagrange optimization procedure.

8.21. Securities A, B, and C have expected standard deviations of returns equal to 0, 0.50, and 0.90, respectively. Securities A, B, and C have expected returns equal to 0.05, 0.07, and 0.11, respectively. The covariance between returns on B and C is zero. What are the security weights of the optimal portfolio with an expected return of 0.10?

APPENDIX 8.A   DERIVATIVES OF POLYNOMIALS
(Background reading: sections 2.12 and 8.3)

The derivative of the polynomial $y = cx^n$ with respect to x is determined by

$$f'(x) = \lim_{h \to 0} \frac{c(x+h)^n - cx^n}{h}$$

$$= \lim_{h \to 0} \frac{cx^n + cnx^{n-1}h + c\binom{n}{1}x^{n-2}h^2 + \ldots + cnxh^{n-1} + ch^n - cx^n}{h}. \qquad (8.A.1)$$

The binomial theorem enables us to obtain the second part of equation (8.A.1) from the first. Recall from section 2.3 that the term $\binom{n}{1}$ reads "n choose one". Generally, the function $\binom{n}{j}$ can be used to determine the number of ways in which a subset of size j can be taken from a set of size n. Its value is determined as follows:

$$\binom{n}{j} = \frac{n!}{j!(n-j)!} = \frac{n(n-1)(n-2)\cdot\ldots\cdot2\cdot1}{j(j-1)(j-2)\cdot\ldots\cdot1(n-j)(n-j-1)\cdot\ldots\cdot1}. \qquad (8.A.2)$$

For example, $\binom{5}{2}$ reads "5 choose 2" and has a value equal to $5! \div [2!(5-2)!] = 120 \div [2(3 \cdot 2)] = 10$. Thus, there are 10 subsets of 2 outcomes from a set of 5.

To simplify the right-hand side of equation (8.A.1), we first note that the cx^n terms cancel out. Next, we note that h is divided into each of the remaining terms, leaving us with

$$f'(x) = \lim_{h \to 0}\left[cnx^{n-1} + c\binom{n}{1}x^{n-2}h + \ldots + cnxh^{n-2} + ch^{n-1} \right]. \qquad (8.A.3)$$

As h approaches zero, all terms multiplied by h, or by h raised to any positive integer power, will approach zero. This leaves us with

$$f'(x) = \lim_{h \to 0} [cnx^{n-1}] = cnx^{n-1}. \qquad (8.A.4)$$

Thus, the derivative of cx^n with respect to x is cnx^{n-1}. If we were to have a polynomial of the form

$$y = \sum_{j=1}^{m} c_j \cdot x^{n_j}, \qquad (8.A.5)$$

the derivative of such a function y with respect to x would be given by

$$\frac{dy}{dx} = \sum_{j=1}^{m} c_j \cdot n_j \cdot x^{n_j - 1}. \qquad (8.A.6)$$

APPENDIX 8.B A TABLE OF RULES FOR FINDING DERIVATIVES

Function	Derivative	Example	Derivative
$f(x) = c$	$f'(x) = 0$	$f(x) = 3$	$f'(x) = 0$
$f(x) = cx$	$f'(x) = c$	$f(x) = 3x$	$f'(x) = 3$
$f(x) = cx^n$	$f'(x) = cnx^{n-1}$	$f(x) = 3x^5$	$f'(x) = 15x^4$
$f(x) = g(x) + h(x)$	$f'(x) = g'(x) + h'(x)$	$f(x) = 3x^5 + 3x$	$f'(x) = 15x^4 + 3$
$f(x) = g(x) \cdot h(x)$	$f'(x) = g'(x) \cdot h(x) + h'(x) \cdot g(x)$	$f(x) = (2 + 7x)(3x^4 + 11x)$	$f'(x) = 7(3x^4 + 11x) + (12x^3 + 11) \cdot 7$
$f(x) = g(x) \div h(x)$	$f'(x) = [g'(x) \cdot h(x) - h'(x) \cdot g(x)]/[h(x)]^2$	$f(x) = (2 + 7x) \div (3x^4 + 11x)$	$f'(x) = [7(3x^4 + 11x) - 7(12x^3 + 11)]/(3x^4 + 11x)^2$
$f(x) = g(h(x))$	$f'(x) = g'(h(x)) \cdot h'(x)$	$f(x) = (10 + 4x^2)^7$	$f'(x) = 7 \cdot 4 \cdot 2(10 + 4x^2)^6$
$f(x) = \ln(x)$	$f'(x) = 1/x$	$f(x) = \ln(x)$	$f'(x) = 1/x$
$f(x) = e^x$	$f'(x) = e^x$	$f(x) = e^x$	$f'(x) = e^x$
$f(x) = e^{g(x)}$	$f'(x) = g'(x) \cdot e^{g(x)}$	$f(x) = e^{0.1x}$	$f'(x) = 0.1e^{0.1x}$
$f(x) = c^x$	$f'(x) = c^x \ln(c)$	$f(x) = 3^x$	$f'(x) = 3^x \ln(3)$

APPENDIX 8.C   PORTFOLIO RISK MINIMIZATION
ON A SPREADSHEET
(Background reading: section 8.8, application 8.8,
and appendix 7.C)

This appendix employs the Lagrange optimization routine (application 8.8) on an Excel™ spreadsheet to determine optimal portfolio weights. The routine minimizes portfolio standard deviation subject to an expected portfolio return. Consider an investor who intends to select weights for an n-security portfolio whose characteristics may be inferred from the following system:

$$
\begin{bmatrix}
2\sigma_1^2 & 2\sigma_{1,2} & \cdots & 2\sigma_{1,n} & -E[R_1] & -1 \\
2\sigma_{2,1} & 2\sigma_2^2 & \cdots & 2\sigma_{2,n} & -E[R_2] & -1 \\
\vdots & \vdots & \vdots & \vdots & \vdots & \vdots \\
2\sigma_{n,1} & 2\sigma_{n,2} & \cdots & 2\sigma_n^2 & -E[R_n] & -1 \\
-E[R_1] & E[R_2] & \cdots & E[R_n] & 0 & 0 \\
-1 & -1 & \cdots & -1 & 0 & 0
\end{bmatrix}
\begin{bmatrix}
w_1 \\
w_2 \\
\vdots \\
w_n \\
\lambda_1 \\
\lambda_2
\end{bmatrix}
=
\begin{bmatrix}
0 \\
0 \\
\vdots \\
0 \\
-r_p \\
-1
\end{bmatrix}.
$$

This system may be applied regardless of the size of the portfolio. Where the number of securities under consideration for the portfolio equals n, the square coefficients matrix will have $n + 2$ rows and $n + 2$ columns.

This system may be input to a spreadsheet to solve for the system of n weights and two Lagrange multipliers. Table 8.C.1 represents an Excel™ spreadsheet printout of a system used to solve for optimal weights in a two-security portfolio. The target return for this portfolio is 0.07 and the expected security returns are 0.05 for security A and 0.15 for security B. Security standard deviations are expected to be 0.1 for A and 0.5 for B. The covariance between returns on A and B is expected to be -0.025. These optimization inputs are represented in the first two rows of the spreadsheet.

The left part of the table represents numerical values displayed by the spreadsheet; the right part represents actual cell entries. Rows 1 and 2 are numerical inputs for the file from the problem to be solved; Rows 4–7 are the rows of the coefficients matrix to be inverted. See appendix 7.A for details on how to invert this matrix. We then multiply the solutions vector in range E9:E12 by the inverse of the coefficients matrix in range A9:D12, using the procedure discussed in appendix 7.A. The solutions to the problem are given in range A14:A17. This procedure is easily extended to accommodate as many securities as is necessary.

Table 8.C.1 Portfolio optimization problem (spreadsheet routine). Problem: minimize the portfolio variance given the inputs in cells A1:B2, D1:D2, and E1:F1

	A	B	C	D	E	F
1	0.1	-0.03		0.05	0.07	1
2	-0.03	0.5		0.15		
3						
4	0.02	-0.05	-0.05	-1		
5	-0.05	0.5	-0.15	-1		
6	-0.05	-0.15	0	0		
7	-1	-1	0	0		
8						
9	0	0	10	-1.5	0	
10	0	0	-10	0.5	0	
11	10	-10	-62	3.8	-0.07	
12	-1.5	0.5	3.8	-0.245	-1	
13						
14	0.8					
15	0.2					
16	0.54					
17	-0.02					
18						
19						

	A	B	C	D	E	F
1	σA	σA.B		E[RA]	rp	1
2	+b1	σB		E[RB]		
3						
4	=2*a1^2	=2*b1	=-D1	=-F1		
5	=2*b1	=2*b2^2	=-D2	=-F1		
6	=-D1	=-D2	0	0		
7	=-F1	=-F1	0	0		
8						
9	Cell range A9:D12 is the inverted				0	
10	coefficients matrix. Highlight this range,				0	
11	and use the MINVERSE function under				=-E1	
12	the Paste function. Don't forget to enter				=-F1	
13	by pressing Ctrl., Shft & Enter together.					
14	A14 is wA	Cell range A14:A17 represents the				
15	A15 is wB	final solutions. This range is obtained by				
16	A16 is λ1	multiplying range A9:D12 by E9:E12				
17	A17 is λ2	using MMULT under the Paste function (fx).				
18						
19						

9.1 ANTIDIFFERENTIATION AND THE INDEFINITE INTEGRAL
(Background reading: section 8.3)

The derivative and the integral are the two most essential concepts from calculus. One might interpret the derivative, $f'(x)$, of a function $f(x)$ to be the slope of the curve plotted by that function. An analogous interpretation of the integral $\int f(x)dx$ is the area $F(x)$ under a curve plotting the function $f(x)$. Thus, integrals are most useful for finding areas under curves. Similarly, they are useful for determining expected values and variances based on continuous probability distributions. As the Σ operator is used for summing countable numbers of objects, integrals are used for performing summations of uncountably infinite objects.

Integral calculus is also useful for analyzing the behavior of variables (such as cash flows) over time. A function $f(x)$ known as a differential equation might describe the rate of change of variable $f(x)$ over time; the solution to this differential equation, $F(x)$, describes the path itself over time. For example, $f(x)$ might describe the change in value or profit of an investment over time, while $F(x)$ provides its actual value.

Integrals of many functions can be determined by using the process of *antidifferentiation*, which is the inverse process of differentiation. If $F(x)$ is a function of x whose derivative equals $f(x)$, then $F(x)$ is said to be the antiderivative, or integral, of $f(x)$, written as follows:

$$F(x) = \int f(x)dx. \qquad (9.1)$$

The integral sign, $\int$, is used to denote the antiderivative of the *integrand* $f(x)$; the *indefinite integral* is denoted by $\int f(x)dx$. The following is implied by equation (9.1):

$$\frac{dF(x)}{dx} = f(x). \qquad (9.2)$$

Consider the following function: $f(x) = 4x^3$. The function for which $f(x)$ is the derivative is $F(x)$, the antiderivative of $f(x)$. The antiderivative of $f(x) = 4x^3$ is $F(x) = x^4 + k$. Therefore, $f(x) = 4x^3$ is the derivative of $F(x) = x^4 + k$, where k is simply any real-valued constant:

$$\frac{dF(x)}{dx} = \frac{d(x^4 + k)}{dx} = 4x^3.$$

Thus, the derivative of the function $F(x)$ is the original function $f(x)$, implying that $F(x)$ is the antiderivative of $f(x)$. The constant of integration k must be included in the antiderivative. Thus, all of the following could be antiderivatives of $4x^3$: $F(x) = x^4 + 77$, $F(x) = x^4 + 6$, and $F(x) = x^4 + 1.25$. It is important for the antiderivative computation to be able to accommodate any of these possible constant values k.

The following are a few of the rules that apply to the computation of indefinite integrals (where k is a real-valued constant).

Let $f(x) = x^n$:

$$\int f(x)dx = \frac{x^{n+1}}{n+1} + k \qquad \text{for } n \neq -1. \tag{9.3}$$

Equation (9.3) is the polynomial (power) rule for finding antiderivatives.

$$\int Kf(x)dx = K \int f(x)dx, \tag{9.4}$$

where K is a constant.

$$\int [f(x) + g(x)]dx = \int f(x)dx + \int g(x)dx; \tag{9.5}$$

$$\int \frac{1}{x}dx = \ln x + k. \tag{9.6}$$

The rule given by equation (9.6) is useful for many growth models. The following rule is particularly important for time value and valuation models:

$$\int e^{nx}dx = \frac{1}{n}e^{nx} + k \qquad \text{for } n \neq 0. \tag{9.7}$$

Other rules are provided in appendix 9.A.

9.2 RIEMANN SUMS
(Background reading: section 9.1)

Consider a function $y = f(x)$. Suppose that we wish to find the area under a curve represented by this function over the range from $x = a$ to $x = b$. The lower limit of integration is said to be a; the upper limit of integration is said to be b. We will first show

how to find the area under a curve by demonstrating a method similar to one suggested by the Greek mathematician Archimedes in the third century B.C.E. This method was formalized by Bernhard Riemann in the mid-1800s and is now particularly useful for computer-based evaluations of integrals. The Riemann sum is also most useful for evaluating integrals of functions for which antiderivatives do not exist.

Consider the function $f(x) = 10x(1 - 0.1x)$. Suppose that we wish to find the area under the curve represented by this function over the range from $x = 0$ to $x = 1$. The method of Riemann sums divides the area under the curve into a number of rectangles, as in figure 9.1. Data for figure 9.1 are given in table 9.1. This curve has been divided into ten segments of width $x_i - x_{i-1} = 1/10$. The height of each rectangle is $y_i = f(x_i)$.

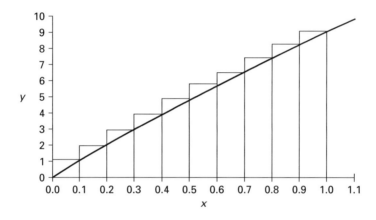

Figure 9.1   Finding the area under a curve using Riemann sums: $y = 10x(1 - 0.1x)$. When $x_i - x_{i-1} = 0.1$, the sum of the areas of the ten rectangles equals 5.115. As the number of rectangles approaches infinity, and their widths approach zero, the sum of their areas will approach $4\frac{2}{3}$.

Table 9.1   The area under the curve represented by $y = 10x(1 - 0.1x^2)$

Data point i	y_i	x_i	$x_i - x_{i-1}$	$y_i \cdot (x_i - x_{i-1})$
1	0.99	0.1	0.1	0.099
2	1.96	0.2	0.1	0.196
3	2.91	0.3	0.1	0.291
4	3.84	0.4	0.1	0.384
5	4.75	0.5	0.1	0.475
6	5.64	0.6	0.1	0.564
7	6.51	0.6	0.1	0.651
8	7.36	0.8	0.1	0.736
9	8.19	0.9	0.1	0.819
10	9.00	1.0	0.1	0.900
			$\sum[y_i \cdot (x_i - x_{i-1})] =$	5.115

Thus, the area of each rectangle is $f(x_i)(x_i - x_{i-1})$. The Riemann approximation for the area in the range from $x = 0$ to $x = 1$ based on ten rectangles is

$$\int_0^1 10x(1 - 0.1x)\mathrm{d}x \approx \sum_{i=1}^{10} f(x_i)(x_i - x_{i-1}) = \sum_{i=1}^{10} 0.1 \cdot 10x_i(1 - 0.1x_i) = 5.115.$$

Notice that the areas of rectangles in figure 9.1 do not correspond exactly with the areas of the curve that they are intended to simulate. Finer estimates of the area under the curve may be obtained by increasing the numbers of rectangles while decreasing their widths. We will continue to do this until the number of rectangles is sufficiently large to produce the desired level of accuracy. Generally, more rectangles of narrower widths lead to more accurate integral estimation.

The method of Riemann sums requires that we find the area of each of n rectangles. Each of these rectangles, which are arranged sequentially, will have a width of $x_i - x_{i-1}$. The rectangle width $x_i - x_{i-1} = 1/n$ will approach zero as the number of rectangles approaches infinity. The rectangle height will be $f(x^*)$, where x^* is some value between x_i and x_{i-1} (here we assume $x^* = x_i$).

To obtain increasingly finer area estimates, the number of these rectangles under the curve will approach infinity, and the width of each of these rectangles will approach (though not quite equal) zero. The area of each of these rectangles (where the product is nonnegative) is simply the product of its height and width:

$$\lim_{(x_i - x_{i-1}) \to 1/n} f(x^*) \cdot (x_i - x_{i-1}). \tag{9.8}$$

Thus, the area of a region extending from $x = a$ to $x = b$ under a curve can be found with the use of the definite integral over the interval from $x = a$ to $x = b$ as follows:

$$\int_a^b f(x)\mathrm{d}x = \lim_{\substack{n \to \infty \\ x_i - x_{i-1} \to 1/n}} \sum_{i=1}^n f(x^*)(x_i - x_{i-1}). \tag{9.9}$$

The right-hand side of equation (9.9) is the *Riemann sum*. The width of each rectangle equals $x_i - x_{i-1} = (b - a)/n \to 0$ and the height of each rectangle equals $f(x^*)$. We can use the Riemann sum to find the area under the curve in the example presented above as follows:

$$\int_0^1 10x(1 - 0.1x)\mathrm{d}x = \lim_{\substack{n \to \infty \\ x_i - x_{i-1} \to 1/n}} \sum_{i=1}^n 10x^*(1 - 0.1x^*)(x_i - x_{i-1}). \tag{A}$$

Since $b - a$ equals 1, each $x_i - x_{i-1}$ will equal $1/n$, and we obtain

$$\int_0^1 10x(1 - 0.1x)\mathrm{d}x = \lim_{n \to \infty} \sum_{i=1}^n \frac{10x_i(1 - 0.1x_i)}{n}. \tag{B}$$

Next, we note that our initial x_i value equals zero and that each x_i value equals i/n, since our units of increase are $1/n$. The counter i represents the number of increases accounted for at some point i in the summation. This enables us to obtain

$$\int_0^1 10x(1-0.1x)dx = 0 + 10 \cdot \lim_{n\to\infty} \sum_{i=1}^n \frac{\frac{i}{n}\cdot\left(1-0.1\frac{i}{n}\right)}{n}$$

$$= 10 \cdot \lim_{n\to\infty} \sum_{i=1}^n \frac{i}{n^2}\left(1-0.1\frac{i}{n}\right) = 10 \cdot \lim_{n\to\infty} \sum_{i=1}^n \left(\frac{i}{n^2}-0.1\frac{i^2}{n^3}\right). \qquad (C)$$

The results of the series in equation (C) are well known and may be verified by induction:

$$\sum_{i=1}^n \frac{i}{n^2} = \frac{n(n+1)/2}{n^2}, \qquad \sum_{i=1}^n \frac{i^2}{n^3} = \frac{n(n+1)(2n+1)/6}{n^3}.$$

The results of these series are used to simplify equation (C):

$$\int_0^1 10x(1-0.1x)dx = 10 \cdot \left(\lim_{n\to\infty} \sum_{i=1}^n \frac{i}{n^2} - 0.1 \cdot \lim_{n\to\infty} \sum_{i=1}^n \frac{i^2}{n^3}\right)$$

$$= 10 \cdot \left(\lim_{n\to\infty} \frac{n(n+1)/2}{n^2} - 0.1 \cdot \lim_{n\to\infty} \frac{n(n+1)(2n+1)/6}{n^3}\right)$$

$$= 5 \cdot \lim_{n\to\infty}\left(1+\frac{1}{n}\right) - \frac{10\cdot 0.1}{6}\cdot\lim_{n\to\infty}\left(2+\frac{1}{n^2}+\frac{3}{n}\right) = 5 - \tfrac{2}{6} = 4\tfrac{2}{3}. \qquad (D)$$

Thus, as n approaches ∞, it is easy to see that the area under the curve extending from $x=0$ to $x=1$ approaches $4\tfrac{2}{3}$.

The use of Riemann sums to determine the precise area under a curve within a defined region involves the summation of areas of an infinite number of rectangles of infinitesimal width which lie within this area. We have calculated the area under our curve here and were able to do so precisely because we were able to easily simplify two infinite series. However, this process can be quite time-consuming, or must serve as only a finite approximation, when the series cannot be simplified. On the other hand, sums to reasonably large finite numbers can often provide an acceptable level of accuracy and can be a most useful means to obtain numerical values for integrals. This is particularly true when the integral to be evaluated has no antiderivative. We will discuss spreadsheet evaluations of integrals in appendix 9.B. Reading through this appendix may be quite helpful in understading the application of Riemann sums.

9.3   DEFINITE INTEGRALS AND AREAS
(Background reading: sections 9.1 and 9.2)

Another, more elegant method for integration makes use of the Fundamental Theorem of Integral Calculus, based on a brilliant insight by Sir Isaac Barrow. This theorem is stated as follows:

If $f(x)$ is a continuous function within the range from $x = a$ to $x = b$, and $F(x)$ is the antiderivative of $f(x)$, the following must hold:

$$\int_a^b f(x)dx = F(b) - F(a) = F(x)\Big|_a^b. \tag{9.10}$$

Thus, we may use the Fundamental Theorem of Integral Calculus to find the area under the function $f(x) = 10x(1 - 0.1x)$ by using antiderivatives as follows:

$$\int_0^1 10x(1 - 0.1x)dx = \int_0^1 10x - x^2$$

$$= F(1) - F(0) = (5x^2 - \tfrac{1}{3}x^3)\Big|_0^1$$

$$= (5 \cdot 1^2 - \tfrac{1}{3} \cdot 1^3 + k) - (5 \cdot 0^2 - \tfrac{1}{3} \cdot 0^3 + k)$$

$$= 5 - \tfrac{1}{3} = 4\tfrac{2}{3}. \tag{E}$$

Notice that the constants of integration k canceled out. Essentially, we found the antiderivative of our function at a (or 0), then subtracted this antiderivative from the antiderivative of our function at b (or 1).

Consider a second function, $y = -3x^2 + 4x + 8$, represented by figure 9.2. Suppose that we wished to find the area between this curve and the horizontal axis within the range from $x = 0$ to $x = 3$. Again, we may use the Fundamental Theorem of Integral Calculus to find the area under the curve by using antiderivatives as follows:

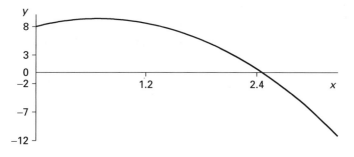

Figure 9.2   The area between the curve and the horizontal axis: $y = -3x^2 + 4x + 8$.

$$\int_0^3 (-3x^2 + 4x + 8)dx = (-x^3 + 2x^2 + 8x)\Big|_0^3$$

$$= (-3^3 + 2 \cdot 3^2 + 8 \cdot 3 + k) - (-0^3 + 2 \cdot 0^2 + 8 \cdot 0 + k)$$

$$= -27 + 18 + 24 = 15. \tag{A}$$

The area between this curve and the horizontal axis net of the area under the curve but above the horizontal axis within the range $x = 0$ to $x = 3$ equals 15.

APPLICATION 9.1: CUMULATIVE DENSITIES
(Background reading: sections 2.4 and 9.3)

A probability density function is a theoretical model for a frequency distribution. The (density at x^*) $\cdot$ dx might be regarded as the probability that a continuous random variable x lies between x^* and $x^* + $ dx as d$x \to 0$.[1] Thus, in a sense, the density function may be used to determine the probability $p(x_i)$ that a continuous random variable x_i will be exactly equal to a constant x^*. However, it is important to note that because the continuous random variable x_i may assume any one of an infinity of potential values, the probability that the function assumes any particular exact value x^* approaches zero ($p(x_i)$d$x \to 0$). A continuous probability distribution P(x) may be used to determine the probability that a randomly distributed variable will fall within a given range or below a given value. Among the continuous probability distributions used by statisticians are the normal distribution, the uniform distribution, and the gamma distribution. A density function $p(x)$ can be computed based on a differentiable distribution function P(x) as follows:

$$p(x) = \frac{\text{dP}(x)}{\text{d}x} = \text{P}'(x). \tag{9.11}$$

This implies that the distribution function P(x) may be found from the density function:

$$\text{P}(x) = \int p(x)\text{d}x. \tag{9.12}$$

Consider a very simple density function $\{p(x) = 6(x - x^2)$ for $0 \le x \le 1$ and 0 elsewhere$\}$ for a particular randomly distributed variable x_i. From this density function, we can obtain a distribution function by integrating as follows:

$$\text{P}(x) = \int p(x)\text{d}x = \int 6[x - x^2]\text{d}x = 6[\tfrac{1}{2}x^2 - \tfrac{1}{3}x^3]. \tag{A}$$

---

[1]   The function $p(x)$ is a continuous version of P_i, which was used for the probability associated with a particular outcome i drawn from a discrete set of potential outcomes. See sections 5.5 and 5.6.

Notice that P(0) = 0 and P(1) = 1 and that $0 \leq p(x)$ for all x, as one would expect for any density function ranging from zero to one. Now, suppose that the potential or random return r_i for a given stock is expected to range from 0 to 25%. Further suppose that potential returns track the random continuously distributed variable x_i whose probability distribution function is given by equation (A) ranging from 0 to 1. More specifically, the return on the stock is $r_i = f(x_i) = 0.25x_i$, or 25% of the value of this randomly distributed variable. The stock's return will always be 25% of the level of the random variable. We can use a definite integral to determine the probability that the random variable x_i is less than some constant x^*; this probability will be the same as for r_i being less than $0.25x^*$. The distribution function for the random variable is simply the cumulative density function. For example, we determine the probability that x_i will be less than 0.5 and that r_i will be less than 0.125 as follows:

$$P(x_i < 0.5) = P(r_i < 0.125) = \int_0^{0.5} p(x)dx = \int_0^{0.5} 6[x - x^2]dx$$

$$= 6[\tfrac{1}{2}x^2 - \tfrac{1}{3}x^3]\Big|_0^{0.5} = 6[\tfrac{1}{2}(0.5^2) - \tfrac{1}{3}(0.5^3)] - 6[\tfrac{1}{2}(0^2) - \tfrac{1}{3}(0^3)]$$

$$= 0.5 - 0 = 0.5. \tag{B}$$

Note that the lower limit of integration is zero because the density function is nonzero only over the interval from zero to one. Thus, there is a 50% probability that x_i will be less than 0.5 and that r_i will be less than 0.25.

We can also use definite integrals to determine the probability that the random variable will fall within a specified range. For example, we can integrate the density function $p(x)$ over the interval from 0.2 to 0.5 to determine the probability that x_i will fall between 0.2 and 0.5 (and that r_i will range between 0.05 and 0.125):

$$P(0.2 < x_i < 0.5) = P(0.05 < r_i < 0.125) = \int_{0.2}^{0.5} p(x)dx = \int_{0.2}^{0.5} 6[x - x^2]dx$$

$$= 6[\tfrac{1}{2}x^2 - \tfrac{1}{3}x^3]\Big|_{0.2}^{0.5} = 6[\tfrac{1}{2}(0.5^2) - \tfrac{1}{3}(0.5^3)] - 6[\tfrac{1}{2}(0.2^2) - \tfrac{1}{3}(0.2^3)]$$

$$= 0.5 - 0.104 = 0.396. \tag{C}$$

The probability that the return will range between 0.05 and 0.125 is also equal to 0.396. We can just as easily determine that the probability that x_i will fall between 0.4 and 0.6 (and the probability that r_i will fall between 0.04 and 0.06):

$$P(0.4 < x_i < 0.6) = P(0.10 < r_i < 0.15) = \int_{0.4}^{0.6} p(x)dx = \int_{0.4}^{0.6} 6[x - x^2]dx$$

$$= 6[\tfrac{1}{2}x^2 - \tfrac{1}{3}x^3]\Big|_{0.4}^{0.6} = 6[\tfrac{1}{2}(0.6)^2 - \tfrac{1}{3}(0.6^3)] - 6[\tfrac{1}{2}(0.4^2) - \tfrac{1}{3}(0.4^3)]$$

$$= 0.648 - 0.352 = 0.296. \tag{D}$$

The normal density function is the most useful density function in finance:

$$p(x) = \frac{1}{\sigma\sqrt{2\pi}} e^{\frac{-(x-\mu)^2}{2\sigma^2}},$$

where μ and σ are parameters representing the mean and standard deviation of random variable x. Unfortunately, no closed-form solution exists for the following integral (see appendix 9.A):

$$P(x) = N(x) = \int_{-\infty}^{x^*} \frac{1}{\sigma\sqrt{2\pi}} e^{\frac{-(x-\mu)^2}{2\sigma^2}} \, dy.$$

Riemann sums and polynomials are often constructed to evaluate these integrals (see appendix 9.B).

APPLICATION 9.2: EXPECTED VALUE AND VARIANCE (Background reading: sections 5.6, 5.7, and 9.2 and application 9.1)

Expected values and variances are very useful in characterizing probability distributions, random variables, and functions based on random variables. For our example, we will continue to use the density function from application 9.1: $p(x) = 6(x - x^2)$ for $0 \leq x \leq 1$ and 0 elsewhere. We will evaluate integrals of this density function to generate an expected value and a variance for our randomly distributed variable and the stock whose return tracks that random variable. To find the expected return, use the density function to weight each random return r_i:

$$
\begin{aligned}
E[r_i] &= \int_0^1 f(x_i)p(x_i)dx = \int_0^1 0.25(x_i)p(x_i) \\
&= \int_0^1 0.25(x_i) \cdot 6(x_i - x_i^2) = \int_0^1 1.5(x_i^2 - x_i^3)
\end{aligned}
\tag{A}
$$

for $0 \leq x \leq 1$ and 0 elsewhere. Notice the similarity between $E[r_i] = \int f(x_i)p(x_i)dx$ for continuous functions and $E[r_i] = \sum r_i p(i)$, that we used earlier for discrete probability functions. Assuming that the constant of integration equals zero, the indefinite integral of this density function for r is determined as follows:

$$\int f(x)p(x)dx = 1.5[\tfrac{1}{3}x^3 - \tfrac{1}{4}x^4]dx.\tag{B}$$

The expected value of this random variable r is determined as follows:

$$E[r] = \int_0^1 f(x)p(x)dx = 1.5[\tfrac{1}{3}x^3 - \tfrac{1}{4}x^4]\Big|_0^1$$

$$= 1.5[\tfrac{1}{3} \cdot 1^3 - \tfrac{1}{4} \cdot 1^4] - 1.5[\tfrac{1}{3} \cdot 0^3 - \tfrac{1}{4} \cdot 0^4]$$

$$= 1.5[\tfrac{1}{3} - \tfrac{1}{4}] - 0 = 0.125. \tag{C}$$

Thus, the expected return for this security equals 0.125.

The variance of returns for a stock may be determined using the following:

$$\sigma^2 = E[r_i - E[r]]^2 = E[r_i^2] - E[r]^2$$

$$= \left[\int_0^1 [f(x)]^2 p(x)dx \right] - \left[\int_0^1 f(x)p(x)dx \right]^2. \tag{D}$$

Again, notice the similarity of the top line of equation (D) to discrete variance formulas. The variance of returns for the stock in our example is determined as follows:

$$\sigma^2 = \int_0^1 0.25^2 x^2 \cdot 6[x - x^2]dx - 0.125^2 = \int_0^1 0.4[x^3 - x^4]dx - 0.125^2$$

$$= 0.4[\tfrac{1}{4}x^4 - \tfrac{1}{5}x^5]\Big|_0^1 - 0.125^2 = 0.4[\tfrac{1}{4} - \tfrac{1}{5}] - 0 - 0.125^2$$

$$= 0.02 - 0.015625 = 0.004375; \qquad \sigma = 0.066144. \tag{E}$$

Thus, the variance of returns in this distribution is 0.004375 and the standard deviation of returns is 0.066144.

APPLICATION 9.3: VALUING CONTINUOUS DIVIDEND PAYMENTS
(Background reading: sections 4.5, 4.8, 9.2, and 9.3)

Many companies make dividend payments on a quarterly basis. However, payment calendars vary from firm to firm. An index simulating a portfolio of a large number of stocks paying dividends will probably reflect dividend payments scattered throughout the year. For example, a portfolio of securities intended to match the S&P 500 Index would probably receive dividends from companies on practically a daily or continuous basis (500 stocks, each receiving up to four dividend payments per 365-day year). It may be practical to model the dividend payment structure into such a portfolio as though the dividends were received continuously.

Suppose that we wished to value the dividend stream received by a fund over a five-year period. The fund contains a large number of stocks paying dividends staggered throughout the year. We will assume that this fund receives dividends on a continuous basis at a rate of $100,000 per year, starting at time $t = 0$. The same dividend amount is received by the fund each day; the dividend stream is continuous. Further assume that these dividends will be discounted at a continuously compounded rate of $k = 5\%$

per year. The present value of all dividends received in any infinitesimal interval $[t,t+dt]$ is as follows:

$$PV[t,t+dt] = PV[0,t+dt] - PV[0,t],\qquad(9.12)$$

where $PV[t,t+dt]$ equals the present value of dividends received during the interval $[t,t+dt]$. Equation (9.12) implies that dividends received increase the value of the fund. Equation (9.12) describes the rate of change in the fund due to dividends received. The amount of dividend payment to be received at any infinitesimal time interval dt equals $f(t)dt = 100,000dt$. The present value of this sum equals $f(t)e^{-kt}dt = 100,000e^{-0.05t}dt$. Thus, the present value of dividends received over the infinitesimal interval dt is

$$PV[t,t+dt] = PV[0,t+dt] - PV[0,t] = f(t)e^{-kt}dt = 100,000e^{-0.05t}dt.\qquad(A)$$

To find the present value of a sum received over a finite interval beginning with $t=0$, one may apply the definite integral as follows:

$$PV[0,T] = \int_0^T f(t)e^{-kt}dt.\qquad(9.13)$$

While equations (9.12) and (A) represent the rate of change or direction of the dividend stream value, equations (9.13) and (B) following represent the path or cumulative value. In our numerical example, one may find the present value of dividends to be paid to the fund from time 0 for five years as follows:

$$PV[0,5] = \int_0^5 100,000e^{-0.05t}dt = 100,000\left[-\frac{e^{-0.05t}}{0.05}\right]\Bigg|_0^5$$

$$= \frac{100,000}{0.05}(1 - e^{-0.25}) = \$442,398.\qquad(B)$$

A useful application of this methodology is to the valuation of index contracts that are not dividend protected. Many indices reflect component stock prices but not dividends paid by component stocks. Since stock prices decline to reflect the value of dividends paid, the funds that include the stocks will decline in value to reflect the value of dividends paid. Investors taking positions in options and futures contracts in such funds will find that the fund values will decline as dividends are paid by component securities and must structure valuation models to account for dividends. For example, suppose that one can take a position on a contract to purchase a fund at time T. Any dividends to be received by the fund will be paid immediately to current fund investors as they are received.

Suppose that the fund described above is currently worth $2,000,000 to current investors and pays to its investors any dividends as they are received. Assume that a call option contract enabling the investor to purchase shares of the fund in five years will not enable the investor to obtain any dividends paid by the fund over the next five years. The portion of the fund's current value attributable to dividends to be paid over the next five years should be deducted from its overall value, since the investor exercising the option will not have a right to receive these dividends. The investor with the option contract to purchase the fund in five years may value the fund after dividends at $2,000,000 - $442,398 = $1,557,602 based on the present value of dividends that he will not be able to receive should he exercise his call option.

APPLICATION 9.4: EXPECTED OPTION VALUES
(Background reading: section 9.3 and application 7.8)

The expected future value of a European call is equal to its expected value if it is exercised, $E[(S_n - X)|S_n - X]$, multiplied by the probability that it will be exercised, $P[S_n > X]$. If the range of potential stock prices is continuous, this might be written as follows:

$$E[c_n] = \int_X^\infty (S_n - X)p(S_n)dS_n, \tag{9.14}$$

where $p(S_n)$ is the density function for the stock's price. Note that the call's value is zero when $S_n < X$. The probability that the call will be exercised equals

$$P[S_n > X] = \int_X^\infty p(S_n)dS_n. \tag{9.15}$$

The expected value of the call conditioned on it being exercised is

$$E[c_n|S_n > X] = \frac{\int_X^\infty (S_n - X)p(x)dS_n}{\int_X^\infty p(S_n)dS_n}. \tag{9.16}$$

The expected value of the call (9.14) is simply the product of equations (9.15) and (9.16).

9.4 DIFFERENTIAL EQUATIONS

Financial economists and practitioners are often concerned with the development or change of a variable or asset over time. A *differential equation* might be structured to model the change (evolution or direction) of an asset over time. From this equation, a second equation (*solution*) might be derived to describe the asset's value (state or path) at a given point in time. A differential equation is defined as a function for which one or more derivatives exist. The solution of a differential equation is a function that, when substituted for the dependent variable in the differential equation, leads to an identity. The following is a simple differential equation and its solution involving dependent variable x and independent variable t:

$$\frac{dx}{dt} = t, \tag{A}$$

$$x = \tfrac{1}{2}t^2 + k. \tag{B}$$

We verify the solution to differential equation (A) by noting that it represents the derivative of x with respect to t in its solution (B). Equation (A) represents the change in variable x over time ($dx = tdt$). Note that this rate of change increases as t increases. Equation (B) represents the state or value of x at a given point in time t.

A differential equation is said to be *separable* if it can be rewritten in the form $g(x)dx = f(t)dt$. A separable differential equation written in this form can be solved by the following:

$$\int g(x)dx = \int f(t)dt. \tag{9.17}$$

The following is an example of a separable differential equation:

$$\frac{dx}{dt} = 0.05x.$$

In this equation, $f(t) = 0.05$ and $g(x) = 1/x$. To solve this equation, we first separate the variables as follows:

$$\frac{1}{x} \quad dx = 0.05 \quad dt,$$

$$g(x) \quad dx = f(t) \quad dt.$$

Next, we integrate both sides and to obtain a *general solution* for x:

$$\int \frac{dx}{x} = \int 0.05dt,$$

$$\int \frac{1}{x}dx = \int 0.05dt,$$

$$\ln x + k_1 = 0.05t + k_2,$$

$$\ln x = 0.05t - k_1 + k_2,$$

$$e^{\ln x} = e^{0.05t} \cdot e^{-k_1+k_2},$$

$$x = Ke^{0.05t} \quad \text{where } e^{-k_1+k_2} = K.$$

The constant K can assume any value. Thus, the general solution for our differential equation could assume any of an infinity of values. A *particular solution* results when K assumes a specific value. In this case, one particular solution for x could be $x = x_0 e^{0.05t}$, where x_0 is the value of x when $t = 0$. This type of differential equation typical of those used for modeling growth.

APPLICATION 9.5: SECURITY RETURNS IN CONTINUOUS TIME
(Background reading: section 9.4 and application 9.3)

Many valuation models are based on continuous time and continuous space. This means that the securities that they value evolve continuously over time (their prices can be observed at every instant) and their prices can take on any real number value. Suppose that the evolution of a stock's price could be described by the following separable differential equation:

$$\frac{dS_t}{dt} = \mu S_t. \tag{9.18}$$

The term μ represents the security's drift or mean instantaneous rate of return. Thus, the security's price change per infinitesimal unit of time equals μdt. This differential equation can be separated as follows:

$$\frac{dS_t}{S_t} = \mu dt. \tag{9.19}$$

The solution to this differential equation gives the security's price at a moment in time t. The solution to differential equation (9.18) can be obtained with the following integrals:

$$\int \frac{dS_t}{S_t} = \int \mu dt.$$

These integrals can be solved as follows:

$$\ln(S_t) + k_1 = \mu t + k_2.$$

We let $K = k_2 - k_1$ and write the anti-logs of the results of both sides, as

$$e^{\ln(S_t)} = e^{\mu t + K},$$

$$S_t = e^{\mu t} \cdot e^K. \tag{9.20}$$

Equation (9.20) represents a general solution to our differential equation (9.18). If we set e^K equal to the stock's price S_0 at time zero, the particular solution to equation (9.18) would be:

$$S_t = S_0 e^{\mu t}. \tag{9.21}$$

Differential equations such as (9.18) are very useful in the modeling of security prices and are adaptable to the modeling of stochastic (random) return processes.

Now, consider a security with value S_t in time t, generating returns on a continuous basis such that the security were to double in value every seven years. Suppose that the value of this security after ten years were $100. What would have been the initial value S_0 of this security? We will use equation (9.18) as the security's return generating process:

$$\frac{dS_t}{S_t} = \mu dt.$$

The solution to this equation is given by equation (9.20):

$$S_7 = S_0 e^{7\mu} = 2S_0.$$

Thus, $\mu = \ln(2) \div 7 = 0.09902$. With this result, we can easily solve for the security's initial value:

$$S_0 = S_{10} e^{-10 \cdot 0.09902} = \$100 e^{-10 \cdot 0.09902} = \$37.15.$$

APPLICATION 9.6: ANNUITIES AND GROWING ANNUITIES
(Background reading: section 9.4 and application 9.5)

Consider an investor who continuously collects dividends from his brokerage account at a rate of $100,000 per year. The dividends are collected in equal installments during each interval of time (day or smaller time period dt) during the year such that the installments can be modeled as being continuous. If dividend payments are to be discounted at an annual rate of 5%, what would be the present value of the dividend payment stream over a one-year period?

The amount of dividend payment to be received by the investor during any infinitesimal interval dt equals $f(t)dt = \$100,000dt$. The present value of this sum received at time t equals $f(t)e^{-kt}dt = \$100,000e^{-0.05t}dt$. To find the present value of the entire sum received over a finite interval beginning with $t = 0$, solve the following definite integral:

$$PV[0,T] = \int_0^T f(t)e^{-kt}dt,$$

$$PV[0,1] = \int_0^1 \$100,000e^{-0.05t}dt = \$100,000\left[-\frac{e^{-0.05t}}{0.05}\right]_0^1$$

$$= \frac{\$100,000}{0.05}(1 - e^{-0.05}) = \$97,541.15.$$

Now, consider a growing series of cash flows. We will derive a growing annuity for-mula with continuous cash flow streams. First, we structure and combine the growth and discount functions to be integrated over time:

$$PV[t, t + dt] = CF_0 e^{gt} e^{-kt} dt = CF_0 e^{(g-k)t} dt,$$

$$PV[0, T] = \int_0^n CF_t e^{(g-k)t} dt.$$

Integrating and canceling constants of integration, we obtain the following annuity function:

$$PV[0, n] = \int_0^n CF_0 e^{(g-k)t} dt = CF_0 \left[-\frac{e^{(g-k)t}}{k - g} \right]_0^n$$

$$= \frac{CF_0}{k - g} (1 - e^{(g-k)n}). \tag{9.22}$$

Note the similarity between the continuous growing annuity formula above and the discrete cash flow version below:

$$PV[0, n] = \sum_{t=0}^n CF_0 \frac{(1 + g)^t}{(1 + k)^t} = \frac{CF_0}{k - g} \left[1 - \frac{(1 + g)^n}{(1 + k)^n} \right].$$

Now, suppose that the dividend stream in the example presented above were grow-ing at a continuously compounded rate of 2% per year. Assume that its initial annual rate were $100,000. The present value of this stream over its first year is evaluated as follows:

$$PV[0, 1] = \frac{100,000}{0.05 - 0.02} (1 - e^{(0.02 - 0.05) \cdot 1}) = 98,514.89.$$

EXERCISES

9.1. Integrate each of the following functions over x:

(a) $f(x) = 0$;
(b) $f(x) = 5$;
(c) $f(x) = 15x^2$;
(d) $f(x) = 15x^2 + 5$;
(e) $f(x) = e^x$;
(f) $f(x) = 0.5e^{0.5x}$;

(g) $f(x) = 5^x \ln(5)$;

(h) $f(x) = 1/x$.

9.2.   Solve each of the following definite integrals:

(a) $\displaystyle\int_0^1 x dx$;

(b) $\displaystyle\int_2^4 (x + 5)dx$;

(c) $\displaystyle\int_0^{20} 100{,}000e^{0.10t}dt$.

9.3.   Calculate Riemann sums for each of the three functions in problem 9.2. Let $n = 5$ (five boxes) for each part.

9.4.   Assume that the density function $\{p(x_i) = P'(x_i)\}$ for a randomly distributed variable x is given by the following: $p(x) = 1.5x^2 + x$ for $0 \leq x \leq 1$ and 0 elsewhere.

(a) Find the distribution function $P(x)$ based on $p(x)$.

(b) Find the expected value of x in the range 0.2 to 1.

(c) Find the expected value of x in the range 0 to 0.2.

(d) Find the expected value of x in the range 0 to 1.

(e) Find the variance of x in the range 0 to 1.

9.5.   A stock's terminal value S has a uniform distribution; that is, it is equally likely to assume any value in the range (0–100) and will not assume any value outside of this range. The random variable x on which this stock's value is based has a density function $p(x) = 1$ for $0 \leq x \leq 1$ and 0 elsewhere. The stock's random terminal value is $f(x) = 100x$.

(a) Find the distribution function $P(x)$ for $p(x)$.

(b) Find the expected value of the stock's terminal S value assuming that it will fall within the range 50–100.

(c) Find the expected value of the stock's terminal S value assuming that it will fall within the range 0–50.

(d) Find the expected value of S in the range 0–100.

(e) Find the variance of S in the range 0–100.

(f) What would be the expected future cash flow (contingent on its exercise) of a call option written on this stock if its exercise price were $50? That is, what is the expected cash flow of the option conditional on its exercise?

(g)   What would be the expected cash flow of a call option written on this stock if its exercise price were $50? That is, what is the unconditional expected cash flow associated with this option?

(h)   If the appropriate continuously compounded discount rate for all assets equals 0.10 and the cash flows described in parts (a) through (g) were to be paid in one year, what would be the present value of the call option?

9.6.   Assume that the density function p_f for a randomly distributed variable is given by $p_f(x) = 4x^3$ for $0 \leq x \leq 1$ and 0 elsewhere. A second density function p_g for a randomly distributed variable is given by $p_g(x) = (3x^4 + 0.8x)$ for $0 \leq x \leq 1$ and 0 elsewhere. Find $P_f(x)$ and $P_g(x)$.

9.7.   A pension fund collects $3,000,000 in dividends per year from its various securities. The dividends are received in equal installments during each interval (day or dt) during the year such that they can be modeled as being continuous. If dividends are to be discounted at an annual rate of 6%, what would be the present value of the dividend stream over the next ten years?

9.8.   A dividend stream with an initial annual rate of $10,000 will grow at a continuously compounded rate of 3% per year. Cash flows are discounted at 5%. Find the present value of this stream over its first two years.

9.9.   An individual wishes to retire with $1,000,000 invested at an annual interest rate of 6%. She will withdraw $75,000 per year for living expenses. Assume that she will make withdrawals continuously throughout the year.

(a)   Let PV designate the present value of the account, let FV_t designate the value of the account at time t, let PMT designate the payment made from the account during each year, and let i designate the interest rate. Devise an appropriate differential equation describing the rate of change in the retiree's account during any given time period.

(b)   Solve the differential equation to find the balance of the account at any time T.

(c)   Based on the solution to the relevant differential equation and the numbers given in the example, how much money would the retiree have in his account after ten years?

(d)   If the retiree continues to spend $100,000 per year, at what point (how many years) will she run out of money?

9.10. Work through each of the parts of exercise 9.9 assuming that the investor wished for her payments to start at an annual rate of $75,000 but increase at an annual rate of 2% to cover anticipated inflation.

APPENDIX 9.A   RULES FOR FINDING INTEGRALS

Let $f(x) = x^n$:

$$\int x^n \mathrm{d}x = \frac{x^{n+1}}{n+1} + k \qquad \text{for } n \neq -1;$$

$$\int Kf(x)\mathrm{d}x = K \int f(x)\mathrm{d}x;$$

$$\int [f(x) + g(x)]\mathrm{d}x = \int f(x)\mathrm{d}x + \int g(x)\mathrm{d}x;$$

$$\int \frac{1}{x}\mathrm{d}x = \ln|x| + k;$$

$$\int e^{nx}\mathrm{d}x = \frac{1}{n}e^{nx} + k \qquad \text{for } n \neq 0;$$

$$\int a^x \mathrm{d}x = \frac{1}{\ln a}a^x + k \qquad \text{for } a > 0, a \neq 1;$$

$$\int_{-\infty}^{\infty} f(x)\mathrm{d}x = \lim_{\substack{a \to -\infty \\ b \to +\infty}} \int_{a}^{b} f(x)\mathrm{d}x;$$

$$\int f(x)g'(x)\mathrm{d}x = f(x)g(x) - \int f'(x)g(x)\mathrm{d}x \text{ (integration by parts)};$$

$$\int f(x)\mathrm{d}x = \int f[g(t)]g'(t)\mathrm{d}t \text{ (change of variable of integration)}.$$

The following integrals have no closed-form solutions and are often estimated using Riemann sums or polynomial approximations:

$$\int e^{x^2}\mathrm{d}x,$$

$$\int e^{-x^2}\mathrm{d}x,$$

$$\int \frac{e^x}{x}\mathrm{d}x,$$

$$\int \frac{1}{\ln x}\mathrm{d}x.$$

APPENDIX 9.B RIEMANN SUMS ON A SPREADSHEET
(Background reading: section 9.2)

The Riemann sum was introduced in section 9.2 as a means of integrating a function without the need to find an antiderivative. This tool can be particularly useful for spreadsheet files that require the computation of an integral. An approximation using a Riemann sum of a finite number of rectangles with finite widths may be obtained fairly efficiently on a spreadsheet. As n gets larger, computational accuracy will tend to increase, although computational time will increase.

Suppose that we wish to evaluate the function $F(x) = \int_0^1 3(x - x^2)dx$ using a Riemann approximation. The lower limit of integration is 0; the upper limit of integration is 1. We will start by dividing the area under the curve into 20 rectangles. Data for these rectangles are given in table 9.B.1. Each of these rectangles, which are numbered sequentially, will have a width of $x_i - x_{i-1} = 1/20 = 0.05$ and a height of $f(x^*) = 3(x - x^2)$. We see that the area of each of these rectangles is simply the product of its height and width:

$$\text{area} = f(x_i^*) \cdot (x_i - x_{i-1}) = f(x_i^*) \cdot 0.05. \tag{9.B.1}$$

Thus, the area of a region extending from $x = a$ to $x = b$ under this curve can be approximated with the following Riemann sum of 20 rectangle areas:

$$\text{area} = \sum_{i=1}^{n} f(x_i^*) \cdot (x_i - x_{i-1}) = \sum_{i=1}^{20} 3 \cdot (0.05i - (0.05i)^2) \cdot 0.05. \tag{9.B.2}$$

For example, the first rectangle (as all the others) has a width equal to 0.05. Its height is $3(0.05 - 0.05^2) = 0.1425$. Hence its area is $0.05 \cdot 0.1425 = 0.007125$. The second box has a height equal to $3(0.1 - 0.01) = 0.27$, giving it an area of 0.0135. We continue this process until $i = 20$ and sum the rectangle areas. This provides us with a total area approximation equal to 0.49875, slightly less than the exact area of 0.5 found by antidifferentiating. The accuracy of our estimate is improved by increasing n, which increases the number of rectangles while decreasing the width of each.

An important application of Riemann sums is to the evaluation of integrals for which no antiderivatives exist (see appendix 9.A). For example, consider the normal curve:

$$F(Y) = N(Y) = \int_{-\infty}^{Y} \frac{1}{\sigma\sqrt{2\pi}} e^{\frac{-(y-\mu)^2}{2\sigma^2}} dy.$$

No antiderivative exists for this function. However, we can use Riemann sums quite easily to approximate this integral, as in table 9.B.2. Suppose that we wished to find the area under the normal curve extending from 0 to 2. The lower limit of integration will be 0 and the upper limit will be 1. Let us assume that our normal curve has a mean of 0 and a standard deviation equal to 1. Again, we will divide the area between 0 and

Table 9.B.1 Riemann approximation for $F(x) = \int_0^1 3(x - x^2)\,dx$

	A	B	C	D	E	F	G
1	$F(x) = \int_0^1 3(x - x^2)\,dx$	Entries	X(i)	X(i)-X(i-1)	f(X(i))	f(x(i))(X(i)-X(i-1))	SUM[f(x(i))(X(i)-X(i-1))]
2	Enter Function Here (In Cell B2):	0	0	N/A	0	N/A	N/A
3	Enter Lower Limit of Integration:	0	0.05	0.05	0.1425	0.007125	0.007125
4	Enter Upper Limit of Integration:	1	0.1	0.05	0.27	0.0135	0.020625
5	Enter Number of Boxes Under Curve:	20	0.15	0.05	0.3825	0.019125	0.03975
6			0.2	0.05	0.48	0.024	0.06375
7	Upper Minus Lower Limit of Integration:	1	0.25	0.05	0.5625	0.028125	0.091875
8	Width of Each Box:	0.05	0.3	0.05	0.63	0.0315	0.123375
9			0.35	0.05	0.6825	0.034125	0.1575
10	Directions:		0.4	0.05	0.72	0.036	0.1935
11	1. Enter Function to integrate in Cell B2.		0.45	0.05	0.7425	0.037125	0.230625
12	2. Type the same function in Cell E2.		0.5	0.05	0.75	0.0375	0.268125
13	3. Copy down the function in E2.		0.55	0.05	0.7425	0.037125	0.30525
14	4. Enter values for B3, B4 and B5.		0.6	0.05	0.72	0.036	0.34125
15	5. Definite integral estimate corresponds		0.65	0.05	0.6825	0.034125	0.375375
16	to the cell in Column C holding the		0.7	0.05	0.63	0.0315	0.406875
17	upper limit of integration. The integral		0.75	0.05	0.5625	0.028125	0.435
18	is located in Column G in the cell		0.8	0.05	0.48	0.024	0.459
19	corresponding to the upper limit of		0.85	0.05	0.3825	0.019125	0.478125
20	integration in column C. In this		0.9	0.05	0.27	0.0135	0.491625
21	example, see Cell G22.		0.95	0.05	0.1425	0.007125	0.49875
22	Note: Cell A1 may be entered if desired, but		1	0.05	-7E-16	-3.33067E-17	0.49875
23	it serves no computational role.						

Table 9.B.2   Riemann approximation for the area under the normal curve

	A	B	C	D	E	F	G
1	f(x) = (1/(sigma * 2 * pi)^.5 * e^-((x-u)^2)/2)f	Entries	X(i)	X(i)-X(i-1)	f(X(i))	f(x(i))(X(i)-X(i-1))	SUM[f(x(i))(X(i)-X(i-1))]
2	Enter Mean Here	0	0	N/A	0.3989	N/A	N/A
3	Enter Lower Limit of Integration:	0	0.1	0.1	0.397	0.039695335	0.039695335
4	Enter Upper Limit of Integration:	2	0.2	0.1	0.391	0.039104348	0.078799683
5	Enter Number of Boxes Under Curve:	20	0.3	0.1	0.3814	0.038138858	0.116938541
6	Enter Standard Deviation Here:	1	0.4	0.1	0.3683	0.036827088	0.153765629
7	Upper Minus Lower Limit of Integration:	2	0.5	0.1	0.3521	0.035206604	0.188972233
8	Width of Each Box:	0.1	0.6	0.1	0.3332	0.033322527	0.222294761
9			0.7	0.1	0.3123	0.031225456	0.253520217
10	Directions:		0.8	0.1	0.2897	0.028969214	0.282489431
11	1. Enter Mean in B2 and Standard Deviation		0.9	0.1	0.2661	0.026608579	0.309098009
12	in B6.		1	0.1	0.242	0.024197121	0.333295131
13	2. Enter the other values for Cells B3 to B5.		1.1	0.1	0.2179	0.021785262	0.355080392
14	3. Definite integral estimate corresponds		1.2	0.1	0.1942	0.019418645	0.374499037
15	to the cell in Column C holding the		1.3	0.1	0.1714	0.017136894	0.391635931
16	upper limit of integration. The integral		1.4	0.1	0.1497	0.014972777	0.406608708
17	is located in Column G in the cell		1.5	0.1	0.1295	0.012951786	0.419560494
18	corresponding to the upper limit of		1.6	0.1	0.1109	0.011092106	0.4306526
19	integration in column C. Here, the area is		1.7	0.1	0.094	0.009404927	0.440057526
20	Cell G22.		1.8	0.1	0.079	0.007895032	0.447952558
21	Riemann Sum for the Cumulative Normal		1.9	0.1	0.0656	0.006561595	0.454514153
22	Density Function		2	0.1	0.054	0.005399108	0.459913261
23							

2 under the normal curve into 20 rectangles. The width of each rectangle equals 0.1. The height of each equals:

$$f(x^*) = \frac{1}{\sigma\sqrt{2\pi}} e^{\frac{-(f(x^*)-\mu)^2}{2\sigma^2}} = \frac{1}{\sqrt{2\pi}} e^{\frac{-(f(x^*))^2}{2}}.$$

We find areas just as in the previous example and sum them. Our area estimate is given in cell G22 as 0.459913261 in table 9.B.2. Hence, approximately 46% of the area under the normal curve lies between the mean and two standard deviations to the right of the mean. An alternative estimate of 0.47725 is obtained with the NORMDIST function in the Statistical submenu of the Paste Function f_x and subtracting 0.5. While both are estimates, the accuracy of the Riemann sum can be improved substantially by using n equal to 1,000 or a much larger value.

ELEMENTS OF OPTIONS MATHEMATICS

10.1 AN INTRODUCTION TO STOCK OPTIONS

A *stock option* is a legal contract that grants its owner the right (though, not obligation) to either buy or sell a given stock. There are two types of stock options: puts and calls. A *call* grants its owner to purchase stock (called underlying shares) for a specified exercise price (also known as a striking price or exercise price) on or before the expiration date of the contract. In a sense, a call is similar to a coupon that one might find in a newspaper enabling its owner to, for example, purchase a roll of paper towels for one dollar. If the coupon seems to be a bargain, it will be exercised and the consumer will purchase the paper towels. If the coupon is not worth exercising, it will simply be allowed to expire. The value of the coupon when exercised would be the amount by which value of the paper towels exceeds one dollar (or zero if the paper towels are worth less than one dollar). Similarly, the value of a call option at exercise equals the difference between the underlying market price of the stock and the exercise price of the call.

Suppose, for example, that a call option with an exercise price of $90 currently exists on one share of stock. The option expires in one year. This share of stock is expected to be worth either $80 or $120 in one year, but we do not know which at the present time. If the stock were to be worth $80 when the call expires, its owner should decline to exercise the call. It would simply not be practical to use the call to purchase stock for $90 (the exercise price) when it can be purchased in the market for $80. The call would expire worthless in this case. If, instead, the stock were to be worth $120 when the call expires, its owner should exercise the call. Its owner would then be able to pay $90 for a share which has a market value of $120, representing a $30 profit. In this case, the call would be worth $30 when it expires. Let T designate the options term to expiry, let S_T be the stock value at option expiry, and let c_T be the value of the call option at expiry. The value of this call at expiry is determined as follows:

$$c_T = \mathrm{MAX}[0, S_T - X];$$

$$\text{when} \quad S_T = 80, \ c_T = \mathrm{MAX}[0, 80 - 90] = 0,$$

$$\text{when} \quad S_T = 120, \ c_T = \mathrm{MAX}[0, 120 - 90] = 30. \tag{10.1}$$

A *put* grants its owner the right to sell the underlying stock at a specified exercise price on or before its expiration date. A put contract is similar to an insurance contract. For example, an owner of stock may purchase a put contract ensuring that he can sell his stock for the exercise price given by the put contract. The value of the put when exercised is equal to the amount by which the put exercise price exceeds the underlying stock price (or zero if the put is never exercised).

To continue the above example, suppose that a put option with an exercise price of $90 currently exists on one share of stock. The put option expires in one year. Again, this share of stock is expected to be worth either $80 or $120 in one year, but we do not know which at the present time. If the stock were to be worth $80 when the put expires, its owner should exercise the put. In this case, its owner could use the put to sell stock for $90 (the exercise price) when it can be purchased in the market for $80. The put would be worth $10 in this case. If, instead, the stock were to be worth $120 when the put expires, its owner should not exercise the put. Its owner should sell for $90 for a share which has a market value of $120. In this case, the call would be worth nothing when it expires. Let p_T be the value of the put option at expiry. The value of this put at expiry is determined as follows:

$$p_T = \text{MAX}[0, X - S_T];$$

$$\text{when} \quad S_T = 80, \ p_T = \text{MAX}[0, 90 - 80] = 10,$$

$$\text{when} \quad S_T = 120, \ p_T = \text{MAX}[0, 90 - 120] = 0. \tag{10.2}$$

The owner of the option contract may exercise his right to buy or sell; however, he is not obligated to do so. Stock options can simply be contracts between two investors issued with the aid of a clearing corporation, exchange, and broker which ensure that investors honor their obligations to each other. For each owner of an option contract, there is a seller or "writer" who creates the contract, sells it to a buyer, and must satisfy an obligation to the owner of the option contract. The option writer sells (in the case of a call exercise) or buys (in the case of a put exercise) the stock when the option owner exercises. The owner of a call is likely to profit if the stock underlying the option increases in value over the exercise price of the option (he can buy the stock for less than its market value); the owner of a put is likely to profit if the underlying stock declines in value below the exercise price (he can sell stock for more than its market value). Since the option owner's right to exercise represents an obligation to the option writer, the option owner's profits are equal to the option writer's losses. Therefore, an option must be purchased from the option writer; the option writer receives a "premium" from the option purchaser for assuming the risk of loss associated with enabling the option owner to exercise.

Options may be classified into either the European variety or the American variety. European options may be exercised only at the time of their expiration; American options may be exercised any time before and including the date of expiration. Most option contracts traded in the United States (and Europe as well) are of the American variety. We will demonstrate in the next section that American options can never be worth less than their otherwise identical European counterparts.

10.2 BINOMIAL OPTION PRICING: ONE TIME PERIOD
(Background reading: section 10.1 and application 7.8)

The binomial option pricing model is based on the assumption that the underlying stock follows a binomial return generating process. This means that for any period during the life of the option, the stock's value will change by one of two potential constant values. For example, the stock's value will be either u (multiplicative upward movement) times its current value or d (multiplicative downward movement) times its current value. Thus, in an upcoming period, there are two potential outcomes, which we might name u and d.

Consider a stock currently selling for 100 and assume for this stock that u equals 1.2 and d equals 0.8. The stock's value in the forthcoming period will be either 120 (if outcome u is realized) or 80 (if outcome d is realized). Suppose that there exists a European call trading on this particular stock during this one-time-period model, with an exercise price of 90. The call expires at the end of this period when the stock value is either 120 or 80. Thus, if the stock were to increase to 120, the call would be worth 30 ($c_u = 30$), since one could exercise the call by paying 90 for a stock which is worth 120. If the stock value were to decrease to 80, the value of the call would be zero ($c_d = 0$), since no one would wish to exercise by paying 90 for shares which are worth only 80. Furthermore, suppose that the current riskless return rate is 0.10. Based on this information, we should be able to determine the value of the call based on the methodology presented in application 7.8 and restated below.

Notice that we have not specified probabilities of a stock price increase or decrease during the period prior to option expiration. Nor have we specified a discount rate for the option or made inferences regarding investor risk preferences. We will not determine *ex ante* expected option values, nor will we employ a risk-adjusted discount rate to value the option. We will value this call based on the fact that, during this single time period, we can construct a riskless hedge portfolio consisting of a position in a single call and offsetting positions in α shares of stock. This means that by purchasing a single call and by selling α shares of stock, we can create a portfolio whose value is the same regardless of whether the underlying stock price increases or decreases. Let us first define the following terms for our numerical example:

$S_0 = 100 = $ initial stock value

$u = 1.2 = $ multiplicative upward stock price movement

$d = 0.8 = $ multiplicative downward stock price movement

$c_u = 30 = \text{MAX}[0, uS_0 - X]$; value of call if stock price increases

$c_d = 0 = \text{MAX}[0, dS_0 - X]$; value of call if stock price decreases

$\alpha = $ hedge ratio

$r_f = 0.10 = $ riskless return rate

Our first step in determining the value of the call might be to determine α, the hedge ratio. The hedge ratio defines the number of shares of stock that must be sold (or short sold) in order to maintain a riskless portfolio.[1] This riskless portfolio will be comprised of one call option along with a short position in α shares of stock. In this case, the riskless hedge portfolio made up of one call option and $-\alpha$ shares of stock will have the same value whether the stock price increases to uS_0 or decreases to dS_0. If we were to purchase one call and sell α shares of stock, our riskless hedge condition would be given as follows:

$$c_u - \alpha uS_0 = c_d - \alpha dS_0,$$
$$30 + \alpha \cdot 120 = 0 - \alpha \cdot 80. \tag{10.3}$$

We defined α to be the number of shares to sell for every call purchased. This value is known as a hedge ratio; by maintaining this hedge ratio, we maintain our hedged portfolio. Solve for the hedge ratio α as follows:

$$\alpha = \frac{c_u - c_d}{S_0(u - d)}, \qquad \alpha = \frac{30 - 0}{100(1.2 - 0.8)} = 0.75. \tag{10.4}$$

In our example, $\alpha = 0.75$, meaning that the investor should sell 0.75 shares of underlying stock for each call option that he purchases to maintain a riskless portfolio. Since this hedge portfolio is riskless, it must earn the riskless rate of return, otherwise arbitrage opportunities will exist:

$$c_u - \alpha uS_0 = c_d - \alpha dS_0 = (c_0 - \alpha S_0)(1 + r_f). \tag{10.5}$$

From here, we can work equally well with either with outcome u or outcome d; since it makes no difference, we will work with outcome d. Note that the time-zero option value c_0 can be solved for by rearranging equation (10.5). Again, if equation (10.5) does not hold, or if the current price of the option is inconsistent with equation (10.5), a riskless arbitrage opportunity will exist. Thus, we will rewrite equation (10.5) to solve for the zero *NPV* condition that eliminates positive profit arbitrage opportunities:

$$c_0 - \alpha S_0 - \frac{c_d - \alpha dS_0}{1 + r_f} = 0. \tag{10.6}$$

It is now quite simple to solve for the call value c_0 by rewriting equation (10.6):

$$c_0 = \frac{(1 + r_f)\alpha S_0 + c_d - \alpha dS_0}{1 + r_f},$$
$$c_0 = \frac{(1 + 0.10) \cdot 0.75 \cdot 100 + 0 - 0.75 \cdot 0.8 \cdot 100}{1 + 0.10} = 20.4545. \tag{10.7}$$

---

[1] Shorting stock is the same as selling stock. If we do not already own shares, we can short sell the stock. For practical purposes, this means that we can borrow the stock and sell it with the obligation of re-purchasing it at a later date.

10.3   BINOMIAL OPTION PRICING: MULTIPLE TIME PERIODS
(Background reading: section 10.2)

Equation (10.7) is quite appropriate for evaluating a European call in a one-time-period framework. That is, in the model presented thus far, share prices can either increase or decrease once by a pre-specified percentage. Thus, there are only two potential prices that the stock can assume at the expiration of the stock. This binomial option pricing model can easily be extended to cover as many potential outcomes and time periods as necessary for a particular scenario. Our next step in the development of a more real-istic model is to extend the framework to two time periods. One complication is that the hedge ratio only holds for the beginning of the first time period. After this period, the hedge ratio must be updated to reflect price changes and movement through time. Thus, our first step in extending the model to two time periods is to substitute for the hedge ratio based on equation (10.4):

$$c_0 = \frac{(1 + r_f)\left(\dfrac{c_u - C_d}{S_0(u - d)}\right)S_0 + c_d - \left(\dfrac{c_u - C_d}{S_0(u - d)}\right)dS_0}{1 + r_f}. \tag{10.8}$$

The next two steps of our development are to simplify equation (10.8):

$$c_0 = \frac{\left(\dfrac{(1 + r_f)(c_u - c_d) + c_d(u - d) - d(c_u - c_d)}{u - d}\right)}{1 + r_f}, \tag{10.9}$$

$$c_0 = \frac{c_u\left(\dfrac{(1 + r_f) - d}{u - d}\right) + c_d\left(\dfrac{u - (1 + r_f)}{u - d}\right)}{1 + r_f}. \tag{10.10}$$

This expression (10.10) is quite convenient because of the arrangement of potential cash flows in its numerator. Assume for the moment that investors will discount cash flows derived from the call based on the riskless rate r_f. This assumption is reasonable if investors investing in options behave as though they are risk neutral; in fact, they will evaluate options as though they are risk neutral because they can eliminate risk by setting appropriate hedge ratios. Their extent of risk aversion will already be reflected in the prices that they associate with underlying stock. Note that equation (10.10) defines the current call value in terms of the two potential call prices c_u and c_d and this riskless return rate. Since it is reasonable to assume that investors behave toward options as though they are risk neutral, the numerator of equation (10.10) may be regarded as an expected cash flow. Hence, the terms that c_u and c_d are multiplied by might be regarded as probabilities. Define π to be the probability that the risk-neutral investor associates with the stock price changing to uS_0 and $1 - \pi$ as the probability that the stock price changes to dS_0:

$$\pi = \frac{(1 + r_f) - d}{u - d}, \qquad 1 - \pi = \frac{u - (1 + r_f)}{u - d}. \tag{10.11}$$

We simplify equation (10.10) by substituting in equation (10.11):

$$c_0 = \frac{c_u \pi + c_d (1 - \pi)}{1 + r_f}. \tag{10.12}$$

Equation (10.12) represents a slightly simplified version of the one-time-period option pricing model. However, it is easily extended to a two-period model. Let c_u^2 be the call's expiration value after two time periods, assuming that the stock's price has risen twice; c_d^2 is the value of the call assuming the stock price declined twice during the two periods, and c_{ud} is the value of the call assuming the stock price increased once and decreased once during this period. Thus, our two-time-period model becomes:

$$c_0 = \frac{c_u^2 \pi^2 + 2\pi(1 - \pi)c_{ud} + (1 - \pi)^2 c_d^2}{(1 + r_f)^2}. \tag{10.13}$$

Using the binomial distribution function, this model is easily extended to n time periods as follows:

$$c_0 = \frac{\sum_{j=0}^{n} \frac{n!}{j!(n - j)!} \pi^j (1 - \pi)^{n-j} \text{MAX}[0, (u^j d^{n-j} S_0) - X]}{(1 + r_f)^n}. \tag{10.14}$$

The number of computational steps required to solve equation (10.14) is reduced if we eliminate from consideration all of those outcomes where the option's expiration date price is zero. The first step in estimating the probability that the call will be exercised is to determine the minimum number of price increases j needed for S_n to exceed X:

$$S_n = u^j d^{n-j} S_0 > X. \tag{10.15}$$

We solve this inequality for the minimum nonnegative integer value for j such that $u^j d^{n-j} S_0 > X$. Take logs of both sides, to obtain

$$j \cdot \ln(u) + n \cdot \ln(d) - j \cdot \ln(d) + \ln(S_0) > \ln(X),$$

$$j \cdot \ln\left(\frac{u}{d}\right) > \ln(X) - n \cdot \ln(d) - \ln(S_0). \tag{10.16}$$

Next, divide both sides by $\log(u/d)$ and simplify. Thus, we shall define a to be the smallest nonnegative integer for j, where $S_n > X$:

$$a = \text{MAX}\left[\frac{\ln\left(\frac{X}{S_0 d^n}\right)}{\ln\left(\frac{u}{d}\right)}, 0\right]. \tag{10.17}$$

The call option is exercised whenever $j > a$. The probability that this will occur is given by the following binomial distribution:

$$P[j > a] = \sum_{j=a}^{n} \frac{n!}{j!(n-j)!} \pi^j (1-\pi)^{n-j},$$ (10.18)

where π is the probability that an increase in the stock's price will occur in a given trial. We do assume that π does not vary over trials. Finally, we substitute equation (10.17) into equation (10.14) to obtain the binomial option pricing model:

$$c_0 = \frac{\sum_{j=a}^{n} \frac{n!}{j!(n-j)!} \pi^j (1-\pi)^{n-j} [u^j d^{n-j} S_0 - X]}{(1 + r_f)^n},$$ (10.19)

or

$$c_0 = S_0 \left[\sum_{j=a}^{n} \frac{n!}{j!(n-j)!} \cdot \frac{(\pi u)^j [(1-\pi)d]^{n-j}}{(1+r_f)^n} \right] - \left(\frac{X}{(1+r_f)^n} \right) \left[\sum_{j=a}^{n} \frac{n!}{j!(n-j)!} \cdot (\pi^j (1-\pi)^{n-j}) \right],$$ (10.20)

or, in shorthand form,

$$C = S_0 B[a,n,\pi'] - X(1 + r_f)^{-n} B[a,n,\pi],$$ (10.21)

where $\pi' = \pi u/(1 + r_f)$. Two points regarding equation (10.21) are worth further discussion. First, assuming that investors behave as though they are risk neutral, $B[\alpha,n,\pi]$ may be interpreted as the probability that the stock price will be sufficiently high at the expiration date of the option to warrant its exercise. Second, $B[\alpha,n,\pi']$ may be interpreted as a hedge ratio, although it must be updated at every period.

One apparent difficulty in applying the binomial model as it is presented above is in obtaining estimates for u and d that are required for π; all other inputs are normally quite easily obtained. However, if we assume that stock returns are to follow a binomial distribution, we can relate u and d to standard deviation estimates as follows:

$$u = e^{\sigma\sqrt{1/n}},$$

$$d = 1/u.$$ (10.22)

In the model presented here, σ might be regarded as a standard deviation of annual historical returns, r_f as the annual riskless return rate, and n as the number of jumps or trials over the period. This model may be regarded as appropriate for discrete time, discrete jump processes where $n < \infty$. Appropriate adjustments to a specific problem should be made if years are not the standard unit of measure for time. The Black–Scholes model presented in the following section is more appropriate when it is necessary to assume continuous time and continuous stock price movement. It may also be computation-ally more simple, since it is not necessary to work through large summations.

(10.4)   THE BLACK–SCHOLES OPTION PRICING MODEL
(Background reading: section 10.3)

As the number of trials in a binomial distribution approaches infinity ($n \to \infty$), the binomial distribution approaches the normal distribution. Black and Scholes provide a derivation for an option pricing model based on the assumption that the natural log of stock price relatives will be normally distributed.[2] The assumptions on which the Black–Scholes options pricing model and its derivation are based are as follows:

1   There exist no restrictions on short sales of stock or writing of call options.
2   There are no taxes or transactions costs.
3   There exists continuous trading of stocks and options.
4   There exists a constant riskless borrowing and lending rate.
5   The range of potential stock prices is continuous.
6   The underlying stock will pay no dividends during the life of the option.
7   The option can be exercised only on its expiration date; that is, it is a European option.
8   Shares of stock and option contracts are infinitely divisible.
9   Stock prices follow an Îto process; that is, they follow a continuous time random walk in two-dimensional continuous space.

We shall also assume that investors behave as though they are risk neutral. That is, investors price options as though they are risk neutral because they can always con-struct riskless hedges comprising options and their underlying securities. From an applica-tions perspective, one of the most useful aspects of the Black–Scholes model is that it only requires five inputs. With the exception of the variance of underlying stock returns, all of these inputs are normally quite easily obtained:

1   The current stock price (S_0). Use the most recent quote.
2   The variance of returns on the stock (σ^2). Several methods will be discussed later.
3   The exercise price of the option (X). This is given by the contract.
4   The time to maturity of the option (T). This is given by the contract.
5   The risk-free return rate (r_f). Use a treasury issue rate with an appropriate term to maturity.

It is important to note that the following less easily obtained factors are not required as model inputs:

1   The expected or required return on the stock or option.
2   Investor attitudes toward risk.

---

[2]   The stock price relative for a given period t is defined as $(P_t - P_{t-1}) \div P_{t-1}$. Thus, the log of the stock price relative is defined as $\ln[(P_t - P_{t-1}) \div P_{t-1}]$.

If the assumptions given above hold, the Black–Scholes model holds that the value of a call option is determined by

$$c_0 = S_0 N(d_1) - \frac{X}{e^{r_f T}} N(d_2) = c_0[S_0, T, r_f, \sigma, X], \qquad (10.23)$$

where

$$d_1 = \frac{\ln\left(\dfrac{S_0}{X}\right) + (r_f + \tfrac{1}{2}\sigma^2)T}{\sigma\sqrt{T}}, \qquad (10.24)$$

$$d_2 = d_1 - \sigma\sqrt{T}, \qquad (10.25)$$

and $N(d^*)$ is the cumulative normal distribution function for (d^*). This is a function that is frequently referred to in a statistics setting as the z-value for d^*. From a computational perspective, one would first work through equation (10.24) and then equation (10.25), before valuing the call with equation (10.23).

$N(d_1)$ and $N(d_2)$ are areas under the standard normal distribution curves (z-values). Simply locate the z-value corresponding to the $N(d_1)$ and $N(d_2)$ values on the z-table on page 266 in appendix B. From a computational perspective, it is useful to generate an equation to determine normal density functions (z-values) rather than rely on z-tables. This is especially true when one computes option values with the assistance of a computer. Riemann sums from section 9.2 and appendix 9.B, or the following fifth order polynomial, may be used for estimating density functions $N(d[Y])$:

$$N(Y) \approx 1 - (1/\sqrt{2\pi})e^{-z^2/2}(b_1 k + b_2 k^2 + b_3 k^3 + b_4 k^4 + b_5 k^5), \qquad (10.26)$$

where

$$k = 1/(1 + aY), \qquad a = 0.2316419,$$
$$b_1 = 0.319381530, \qquad b_2 = -0.356563782,$$
$$b_3 = 1.781477937, \qquad b_4 = -1.821255978,$$
$$b_5 = 1.330274429.$$

Note that Y equals d_1 or d_2 in the Black–Scholes setting. In an Excel™ spreadsheet setting, either Riemann sums, the fifth order polynomial above, or the =NORMDIST function from the Paste Function (f_x) menu any be used to find z-values.

Consider the following example of a Black–Scholes model application where an investor may purchase a six-month call option for $7.00 on a stock which is currently selling for $75. The exercise price of the call is $80 and the current riskless rate of return is 10% per annum. The variance of annual returns on the underlying stock is 16%. At its current price of $7.00, does this option represent a good investment? We will note the model inputs in symbolic form:

$$T = 0.5, \qquad r_f = 0.10, \qquad e \approx 2.71828.$$

$$X = 80, \qquad \sigma^2 = 0.16,$$

$$\sigma = 0.4, \qquad S_0 = 75,$$

Our first step in solving for the call value is to find d_1 and d_2:

$$d_1 = \frac{\ln\left(\dfrac{75}{80}\right) + (0.10 + \frac{1}{2}\cdot 0.16)\cdot 0.5}{0.4\sqrt{0.5}} = \frac{\ln(0.9375) + 0.09}{0.2828} = 0.09,$$

$$d_2 = 0.09 - 0.4\sqrt{0.5} = 0.09 - 0.2828 = -0.1928.$$

Next, by using the polynomial estimating function above, or with the z-table on page 266 in appendix B, we find cumulative normal density functions for d_1 and d_2:

$$N(d_1) = N(0.09) = 0.535864,$$

$$N(d_2) = N(-0.1928) = 0.423558.$$

Finally, we use $N(d_1)$ and $N(d_2)$ to value the call:

$$c_0 = 75\cdot 0.536 - \frac{80}{e^{0.10\cdot 0.5}}\cdot 0.42 = 7.958.$$

Since the 7.958 value of the call exceeds its 7.00 market price, the call represents a good purchase.

10.5 PUTS AND VALUATION

(Background reading: sections 10.1 and 10.4 and application 7.9)

A put was defined in section 10.1 as an option that grants its owner the right to sell the underlying stock at a specified exercise price on or before its expiration date. Put values are closely related to call values. In application 7.9, we used the state preference theory framework to value puts relative to calls with identical exercise terms. This framework, generalized here, results from *put–call parity*. Assume that there exists a European put (with a current value of p_0) and a European call (with a value of c_0) written on the same underlying stock, which currently has a value equal to X. Both options expire at time T and the riskless return rate is r_f. The basic put–call parity formula is as follows:

$$c_0 + Xe^{-r_f T} = S_0 + p_0. \qquad (10.27)$$

Table 10.1 Put–call parity

Outcome	If $S_T \le X$	If $S_T > X$
Ending stock price, S_T	S_T	S_T
Ending put price, p_T: MAX[0, $X - S_T$]	$X - S_T$	0
Ending call price, c_T: MAX[$S_T - X$]	0	$S_T - X$
Ending Treasury bill value, X	X	X
Ending value for portfolio A: $c_T + X$	X	S_T
Ending value for portfolio B: $p_T + S_T$	X	S_T

That is, a portfolio consisting of one call with an exercise price equal to X and a pure discount riskless note (zero coupon riskless bond) with a face value equal to X must have the same value as a second portfolio consisting of a put with exercise price equal to X and one share of the stock underlying both options. This relation is proven by first assuming the existence of a portfolio A consisting of one call with an exercise price equal to X and a pure discount riskless note with a face value equal to X. We also assume portfolio B, which consists of a put with exercise price equal to X and one share of the stock underlying both options (see table 10.1). Regardless of the final stock price, portfolio A will have the same terminal value as portfolio B at time 1. Therefore, at time 0, the two portfolios must have equal value. This is put–call parity.

There are a number of useful implications of the put–call parity relation. One is that we can easily derive the price of a put given a stock price, call price, exercise price, and riskless return:

$$p_0 = C_0 + Xe^{-r_fT} - S_0. \tag{10.28}$$

Thus, we can value a put in a Black–Scholes environment by first valuing the call with identical terms or value the put in the binomial environment by first valuing the call.

10.6 BLACK–SCHOLES MODEL SENSITIVITIES
(Background reading: sections 8.4, 8.5, and 10.4)

Option traders find it very useful to know how values of option positions change as factors used in the pricing model vary. Sensitivity calculations (sometimes called Greeks) are particularly useful to investors holding portfolios of options and underlying shares. For example, we mentioned above that the sensitivity of the call's value to the stock's price is given by *delta*:

$$\frac{\partial C}{\partial S} = N(d_1) > 0 \qquad \text{delta, } \Delta. \tag{10.29}$$

Thus, a small increase in the value of the underlying stock would lead to approximately $N(d_1)$ times the amount of that increase in the price of the call option. A call investor may hedge his portfolio risk associated with infinitesimal share price changes by short-ing $N(d_1)$ shares of underlying stock for each purchased call option. However, because this delta is based on a partial derivative with respect to the share price, it holds exactly only for an infinitesimal change in the share price; it holds only approximately for finite changes in the share price. This delta only approximates the change in the call value resulting from a change in the share price, because any change in the price of the underlying shares would lead to a change in the delta itself:

$$\frac{\partial^2 C}{\partial S^2} = \frac{\partial \Delta}{\partial S} = \frac{\partial N(d_1)}{\partial S} = \frac{e^{-d_1^2/2}}{\sqrt{2\pi} \cdot S\sigma\sqrt{T}} > 0 \qquad \text{gamma, } \Gamma. \qquad (10.30)$$

This change in delta resulting from a change in the share price is known as *gamma*. Since gamma is positive, an increase in the share price will lead to an increase in delta. However, again, this change in delta resulting from a finite share price change is only approximate. Each time the share price changes, the investor must update his port-folio. Gamma indicates the number of additional shares that must be purchased or sold given a change in the stock's price.

Since call options have a date of expiration, they are said to amortize over time. As the date of expiration draws nearer, the value of the European call option might be expected to decline, as indicated by a positive *theta*:

$$\frac{\partial C}{\partial T} = r_f X e^{-r_f T} N(d_2) + S \frac{\sigma}{\sqrt{T}} \frac{e^{-d_1^2/2}}{2\sqrt{2\pi}} > 0 \qquad \text{theta, } \theta. \qquad (10.31)$$

Vega measures the sensitivity of the option price to the underlying stock's standard deviation of returns. One might expect the call option price to be directly related to the underlying stock's standard deviation:

$$\frac{\partial C}{\partial \sigma} = S\sqrt{T} \frac{e^{-d_1^2/2}}{\sqrt{2\pi}} > 0 \qquad \text{vega, } v. \qquad (10.32)$$

In addition, one would expect that the value of the call would be directly related to the riskless return rate and inversely related to the call exercise price:

$$\frac{\partial C}{\partial e^{r_f}} = T X e^{-r_f T} N(d_2) > 0 \qquad \text{rho, } \rho; \qquad (10.33)$$

$$\frac{\partial C}{\partial X} = -e^{-r_f T} N(d_2) < 0. \qquad (10.34)$$

Put sensitivities are given in table 10.2. Sensitivities for the call option given in the example in section 10.4 are computed as follows:

Table 10.2 Black–Scholes option sensitivities

Sensitivity	Call	Put
Δ	$N(d_1)$	$1 - N(d_1)$
θ	$-r_f Xe^{-r_f T}N(d_2) - S\dfrac{\sigma}{\sqrt{T}}\dfrac{e^{-d_1^2/2}}{2\sqrt{2\pi}}$	$r_f Xe^{-r_f T}N(d_2) - S\dfrac{\sigma}{\sqrt{T}}\dfrac{e^{-d_1^2/2}}{2\sqrt{2\pi}}$
v	$S\sqrt{T}\dfrac{e^{-d_1^2/2}}{\sqrt{2\pi}}$	$S\sqrt{T}\dfrac{e^{-d_1^2/2}}{\sqrt{2\pi}}$
ρ	$TXe^{-r_f T}N(d_2)$	$-TXe^{-r_f T}N(-d_2)$
$\dfrac{\partial C}{\partial X}$	$-e^{-r_f T}N(d_2)$	$-e^{-r_f T}N(d_2) + e^{-r_f T}$
Γ	$\dfrac{e^{-d_1^2/2}}{\sqrt{2\pi}\cdot S\sigma\sqrt{T}}$	$\dfrac{e^{-d_1^2/2}}{\sqrt{2\pi}\cdot S\sigma\sqrt{T}}$

$$\frac{\partial C}{\partial S} = N(d_1) = \Delta = 0.536,$$

$$\frac{\partial^2 C}{\partial S^2} = \frac{\partial \Delta}{\partial S} = \frac{\partial N(d_1)}{\partial S} = \frac{e^{-d_1^2/2}}{\sqrt{2\pi}\cdot S\sigma\sqrt{T}} = \Gamma = 0.0187,$$

$$\frac{\partial C}{\partial T} = -r_f Xe^{-r_f T}N(d_2) - S\frac{\sigma}{\sqrt{T}}\frac{e^{-d_1^2/2}}{2\sqrt{2\pi}} = \theta = -0.032 \text{ (per day)},$$

$$\frac{\partial C}{\partial \sigma} = S\sqrt{T}\frac{e^{-d_1^2/2}}{\sqrt{2\pi}} = v = 21.06,$$

$$\frac{\partial C}{\partial e^{r_f}} = TXe^{-r_f T}N(d_2) = \rho = 16.1156,$$

$$\frac{\partial C}{\partial X} = -e^{-r_f T}N(d_2) = -0.4028.$$

10.7 ESTIMATING IMPLIED VOLATILITIES
(Background reading: sections 8.6 and 10.6)

Analysts often employ historical return variances to estimate the volatility of securities. However, one cannot always assume that variances will be constant over time or that historical data properly reflects current conditions. An alternative procedure to estimate security variances is based on the assumption that investors price options based on consideration of the underlying stock risk. If the price of the option is taken to be correct, and if the Black–Scholes option pricing model is appropriate for valuing options, then one can infer the underlying stock standard deviation based on the known market price of the option and the option pricing model. Consider the following example pertaining to a six-month call currently trading for $8.20 and its underlying stock currently trading for $75:

$$T = 0.5, \qquad r_f = 0.10, \qquad c_0 = 8.20.$$

$$X = 80, \qquad S_0 = 75,$$

If investors have used the Black–Scholes options pricing model to evaluate this call, the following must hold:

$$8.20 = 75 \cdot \mathrm{N}(d_1) - 80 \cdot e^{-0.1 \cdot 0.5} \cdot \mathrm{N}(d_2),$$

$$d_1 = \{\ln(75/80) + (0.1 + 0.5\sigma^2) \cdot 0.5\} \div \sigma\sqrt{0.5},$$

$$d_2 = d_1 - \sigma\sqrt{0.5}.$$

Thus, we wish to solve the above system of equations for σ. This is equivalent to solving for the root of

$$f(\sigma^*) = 0 = 75 \cdot \mathrm{N}(d_1) - 80 \cdot e^{-0.1 \cdot 0.5} \cdot \mathrm{N}(d_2) - 8.20.$$

There is no closed-form solution for $f(\sigma^*)$. That is, we cannot algebraically solve for σ^*. Thus, we will substitute values for σ^* into $f(\sigma^*)$ until we find one that satisfies the equality. While this may seem cumbersome at first, there are a number of "tricks" that will make the process much more efficient. When systemizing a procedure to find implied volatilities, attempt the following:

1 Have a model that generates a good initial trial value. Many analysts use historical variances, Parkinson extreme value estimators, or Brenner–Subrahmanyam estimators. (We will discuss the latter two later.)
2 Remember that an increase in the volatility (variance or standard deviation) will increase the value of the call; a decrease in volatility decreases call value.
3 Use an efficient numerical technique to iterate for improved trial solutions. Interpolation, the method of bisection, Newton–Raphson, and finite difference methods are frequently used by professional analysts. We will focus on Newton–Raphson here.

First, we need to obtain an initial trial estimate for σ^*. In our example, we could compute a historical volatility if we had relevant historical data. Unfortunately, such data is not always available (for new stocks, for example) and computations can be very time-consuming. We can save substantial time using the extreme value indicators (based on security high and low prices) such as that derived by Parkinson (1980). It is most useful for reducing the amount of data required for statistically significant standard deviation estimates:

$$\sigma_p \approx 0.601 \cdot \ln\left(\frac{HI}{LO}\right), \tag{10.36}$$

where HI designates the stock's high price for a given period and LO designates the low price over the same period.

If there are no historical returns from which to obtain an initial trial value, or if risk circumstances are substantially different today, we may work with an estimate from a variation of the Black–Scholes formula. Brenner and Subrahmanyam (1988) provide a simple formula to estimate an implied standard deviation (or variance) from the value c_0 of a call option whose striking price equals the current market price S_0 of the underlying asset:

$$\sigma_{BS}^2 \approx \frac{2\pi c_0^2}{TS_0^2}, \tag{10.37}$$

where T is the number of time periods prior to the expiration of the option. As the market price differs more from the option striking price, the estimation accuracy of this formula will worsen. For the option in our example, we may obtain a trial value for volatility as follows:

$$\sigma_{BS}^2 \approx \frac{2\pi c_0^2}{TS_0^2} \approx \frac{2 \cdot 3.141 \cdot 8.20^2}{0.5 \cdot 75^2} = \frac{422.40}{2{,}812.5} = 0.15, \quad \sigma_{BS} = 0.387.$$

Now, we use the method of Newton–Raphson to iterate for an improved volatility estimate, as in table 10.3. By the Newton–Raphson method, we first select an initial trial solution x_0. We have selected 0.387 as our initial trial value. We substitute this trial value for σ^* into equation (10.35), to obtain $f(\sigma^*) = -0.515551$ as in the first row of table 10.3. Then we iterate for an improved trial value based on a first order Taylor approximation from section 8.6 to solve for x_1 as follows:

$$f(x_0) + (x_1 - x_0)f'(x_0) = -0.515551 + (x_1 - 0.387) \cdot f'(x_0). \tag{10.38}$$

Here, we use -0.515551 as $f(\sigma^*)$ and we use equation (10.32) from section 10.6 to obtain $f'(x_0) = 21.831$:

$$v = \frac{\partial C}{\partial \sigma} = S\sqrt{t}\frac{e^{-d_1^2/2}}{\sqrt{6.282}} = 75 \cdot \sqrt{0.5} \cdot \frac{2.71828^{-0.0836971^2/2}}{\sqrt{6.282}} = 21.831, \tag{10.39}$$

Table 10.3 The Newton–Raphson method and implied volatilities. Initial equation: $SN(d_1) - Xe^{-rt}N(d_2)$. $r_f = 0.1$, $S_0 = 75$, $X = 80$, $c_0 = 8.20$, $T = 0.5$, $\sigma_0 = 0.387$

n	σ_n	$f'(\sigma_n)$	$d_1(\sigma_n)$	$d_2(\sigma_n)$	$N(|d_1|)$	$N(|d_2|)$	$N(d_1)$	$N(d_2)$	$f(\sigma_n)$
1	0.387	21.083134	0.0836971	-0.18995326	0.533351425	0.4246701	0.5333514	0.4246729	-0.515551
2	0.4114532	21.06085	0.0955001	-0.19544131	0.538041247	0.4225208	0.5380412	0.4225238	-0.000269
3	0.411466	21.060837	0.0955061	-0.19544427	0.538043654	0.4225196	0.5380437	0.4225226	-5E-10
4	0.411466	21.060837	0.0955061	-0.19544427	0.538043654	0.4225196	0.5380437	0.4225226	-3.91E-14
5	0.411466	21.060837	0.0955061	-0.19544427	0.538043654	0.4225196	0.5380437	0.4225226	4.619E-14
6	0.411466	21.060837	0.0955061	-0.19544427	0.538043654	0.4225196	0.5380437	0.4225226	-3.91E-14

where σ in our vega estimate equals 0.387. Thus, we have the following for x_1:

$$x_1 \approx x_0 - \frac{f(x_0)}{f'(x_0)} = 0.387 - \frac{-0.515551}{21.831} = 0.4114532. \qquad (10.40)$$

We now have a second trial value for σ. We substitute 0.4114532 into equations (10.38)–(10.40) and continue the process until we have reached a desired level of accuracy. In most instances, two or three iterations will suffice, as demonstrated in table 10.3.

EXERCISES

10.1. Company X exists in a one-time-period, two-potential-outcome framework. Its stock is currently selling for $50 per share and the riskless return rate is 0.11111. Suppose that company X stock will be worth either $30 or $70 in one year. A call with an exercise price of $55 exists on company X stock.

   (a) What are the two potential values that the call might have at its expiration?
   (b) What is the hedge ratio for this call option? That is, how many shares of stock should be shorted for each call option purchased in order to maintain a perfectly hedged portfolio?
   (c) What is the current value of this option?

10.2. Arkin Company stock currently sells for $12 per share and is expected to be worth either $10 or $16 in one year. The current riskless return rate is 0.125. What would be the value of a one-year call with an exercise price of $8?

10.3. A stock currently selling for $50 has a variance of returns equal to 0.36. The riskless return rate equals 0.08. Under the binomial framework, what would be the value of nine-month (0.75 year) European calls and European puts with striking prices equal to $80 if the number of tree steps (n) were:

   (a) 2?
   (b) 3?
   (c) 8?

10.4. Ibis Company stock is currently selling for $50 per share, and has a multiplicative upward movement equal to 1.2776 and a multiplicative downward movement equal to 0.7828. What is the value of a nine-month (0.75 year) European call and a European put with striking prices equal to $60 if the number of tree steps were 2?

10.5. Kestrel Company stock is currently selling for $40 per share. Its historical standard deviation of returns is 0.5. The one-year Treasury bill rate is currently 5%. Assume that all of the standard Black–Scholes option pricing model assumptions hold.

   (a) What is the value of a put on this stock if it has an exercise price of $35 and expires in one year?
   (b) What is the implied probability that the value of the stock will be less than $30 in one year?

10.6. The following series of four European calls and four European puts exist on the same stock with the following terms:

Option 1	Option 2	Option 3	Option 4
$T = 1$	$T = 1$	$T = 1$	$T = 2$
$S = 30$	$S = 30$	$S = 30$	$S = 30$
$\sigma = 0.3$	$\sigma = 0.3$	$\sigma = 0.5$	$\sigma = 0.3$
$r = 0.06$	$r = 0.06$	$r = 0.06$	$r = 0.06$
$X = 25$	$X = 35$	$X = 35$	$X = 35$

Evaluate each of these four calls and each of these four puts.

10.7. The following series of European options on Kiwi Company stock can be traded. Prices for each of the options are listed in the table. Determine whether each of the options in the series should be purchased or sold at the given market prices. The current market price of Kiwi stock is 60; the March options expire in 45 days, April options in 76 days and May options in 106 days. The stock return standard deviations prior to expirations are projected to be 0.40. The Treasury bill rate is projected to be 0.05 for each of the three periods prior to expiration. Do not forget to convert the number of days given to fractions of 365-day years (e.g., 45 days is 0.123288 years).

Calls

X	March	April	May
50	9.900	11.500	11.625
55	6.625	7.000	8.125
60	3.250	4.875	5.355
65	1.250	2.125	3.335
70	0.931	1.750	1.955

X	March	April	May
		Puts	
50	0.021	0.500	1.250
55	0.975	1.500	2.250
60	2.688	6.500	4.250
65	6.625	7.000	7.375
70	11.625	10.500	11.000

Exercise prices for 15 calls and 15 puts are given in the left columns. Expiration dates are given in column headings and current market prices are given in the table interiors. What are the values of these calls and puts? Which should be purchased? Which should be sold?

10.8. Emu Company stock currently trades for $50 per share. The current riskless return rate is 0.06. Under the Black–Scholes framework, what would be the standard deviations implied by six-month (0.5 year) European calls with current market values based on each of the following striking prices:

    (a) $X = 40$, $c_0 = 11.50$?
    (b) $X = 45$, $c_0 = 8.25$?
    (c) $X = 50$, $c_0 = 4.75$?
    (d) $X = 55$, $c_0 = 2.50$?
    (e) $X = 60$, $c_0 = 1.25$?

REFERENCES

Bodie, Zvi, Kane, Alex, and Marcus, Alan J. 1999: *Investments*, 4th edn., Boston: Irwin McGraw-Hill.

Black, Fischer and Scholes, Myron 1972: The valuation of options contracts and a test of market efficiency. *Journal of Finance*, 27, 399–417.

Black, Fischer and Scholes, Myron 1973: The pricing of options and corporate liabilities. *Journal of Political Economy*, 81, 637–54.

Brealey, Richard A. and Myers, Stewart C. 2000: *Principles of Corporate Finance*, 6th edn., New York: McGraw-Hill.

Brealey, Richard A., Myers, Stewart C., and Marcus, Alan J. 1995: *Fundamentals of Corporate Finance*. New York: McGraw-Hill.

Brenner, Menachem and Subrahmanyam, Marti 1988: A simple formula to compute the implied standard deviation. *Financial Analysts Journal*, 44, 80–3.

Copeland, Thomas E. and Weston, J. Fred 1988: *Financial Theory and Corporate Policy*, 3rd edn., New York: Addison-Wesley.

Elton, Edwin and Gruber, Martin 1995: *Modern Portfolio Theory and Investment Analysis*, 5th edn., New York: John Wiley.

Hull, John C. 2001: *Options, Futures and Other Derivatives*, 4th edn., Upper Saddle River, New Jersey: Prentice-Hall.

Jarrow, Robert A. and Rudd, Andrew 1983: *Option Pricing*. Homewood, Illinois: Dow Jones – Irwin.

Jarrow, Robert A. and Turnbull, Stuart 1996: *Derivative Securities*. Cincinnati, Ohio: South-Western College Publishing.

Macauley, Frederick R. 1938: *The Movements of Interest Rates, Bond Yields and Stock Prices in the United States Since 1856*. New York: National Bureau of Economic Research.

Markowitz, Harry 1952: Portfolio selection. *Journal of Finance*, 7, 77–91.

Markowitz, Harry 1959: *Portfolio Selection*. New Haven, Connecticut: Yale University Press.

Neftci, Salih N. 1996: *An Introduction to the Mathematics of Financial Derivatives*. San Diego, California: Academic Press.

Parkinson, M. 1980: The extreme value method for estimating the variance of the rate of return. *Journal of Business*, 57, 61–5.

Pliska, Stanley R. 1997: *Introduction to Mathematical Finance*. Oxford: Blackwell.

Ross, Stephan A., Westerfield, Randolph W., and Jordan, Bradford D. 2001: *Essentials of Corporate Finance*, 3rd edn., Boston: McGraw-Hill Irwin.

Teall, John L. 1999: *Financial Market Analytics*. Westport, Connecticut: Quorum Books.

Vasicek, Oldrich A. 1977: An equilibrium characterization of the term structure. *Journal of Financial Economics*, 5, 177–88.

APPENDIX A
SOLUTIONS TO EXERCISES

CHAPTER 2

2.1. (a) 25;   (e) 0.04;   (i) 2.2360;   (m) 11.1803;
     (b) 125;   (f) 0.008;   (j) 1.7099;   (n) 0.5848;
     (c) 625;   (g) 0.0016;   (k) 1.4953;   (o) 3.3437;
     (d) 625;   (h) 0.0016;   (l) 5;   (p) 11.1803.

2.2. (a) 1;   (e) add the exponents, $5^2 = 25$;
     (b) 1;   (f) add the exponents, $5^{-8/3} = 0.0136798$;
     (c) 1;   (g) add the exponents, $5^1 = 5$;
     (d) 1;   (h) add the exponents, $25^1 = 25$.

2.3. $FV = 50(1 + 0.3)^4 = 50(1.3)^4 = 50 \cdot 2.8561 = 142.805$.

2.4. $PV = 180(1 + 0.2)^{-0.5} = 180(1.2)^{-0.5} = 180 \cdot 0.9128709 = 164.31677$.

2.5. (a) $y = 24x^3(12x) = 288x^4$;
     (b) $y = 7(-3x^2 + 3x) + 4x = -21x^2 + 21x + 4x = -21x^2 + 25x$;
     (c) $y = 25 + \{2x[3x + 4(x + 5)(x + 5) \cdot 6] - 5\} - 7x^2$
$$= 25 + \{2x[3x + 4(x^2 + 10x + 25) \cdot 6] - 5\} - 7x^2$$
$$= 25 + \{2x[3x + 24x^2 + 240x + 600] - 5\} - 7x^2$$
$$= 25 + \{6x^2 + 48x^3 + 480x^2 + 1{,}200x - 5\} - 7x^2 = 48x^3 + 479x^2 + 1{,}200x + 20.$$

2.6. (a) $y = 9(4(7 + 9)^2)^{0.5} + 216 \cdot 5(9) = 9(4(16)^2)^{0.5} + 9{,}720$
$$= 9(4 \cdot 256)^{0.5} + 9{,}720 = 9 \cdot 1{,}024^{0.5} + 9{,}720 = 9 \cdot 32 + 9{,}720 = 10{,}008;$$
     (b) $y = ((7 + 16)(27 \cdot 16 + 2)^3)^{-0.5} = (23(432 + 2)^3)^{-0.5} = (23 \cdot 434^3)^{-0.5}$
$$= (23 \cdot 81{,}746{,}504)^{-0.5} = 1{,}880{,}169{,}600^{-0.5} = 0.000023.$$

2.7. Simplify as follows:

$$PVA = \$250 \cdot \left[\frac{1}{0.08} - \frac{1}{0.08 \cdot (1 + 0.08)^7} \right] = \$250 \cdot \left[\frac{1}{0.08} - \frac{1}{0.08 \cdot (1.08)^7} \right]$$

$$= \$250 \cdot \left[\frac{1}{0.08} - \frac{1}{0.08 \cdot 1.7138243} \right] = \$250 \cdot \left[\frac{1}{0.08} - \frac{1}{0.1371059} \right]$$

$$= \$250 \cdot \left[\frac{1}{0.08} - 7.29363 \right] = \$250 \cdot [12.5 - 7.29363]$$

$$= \$250 \cdot 5.20637 = \$1,301.59.$$

2.8. (a) −13.8155; (c) 0; (e) 0.99325; (g) 1.0986; (i) 4.60517;
(b) −0.693147; (d) 0.09531; (f) 0.99989; (h) 2.3025; (j) 6.90775.

2.9. Assume for each of the accounts that the initial deposit is 1 for each account and its future value is 2. Then, the general procedure for each account is to solve the following for n given each interest rate i:

$$2 = 1(1 + i)^n,$$

$$\ln(2) = \ln(1) + n \cdot \ln(1 + i),$$

$$n = \frac{\ln(2) - \ln(1)}{\ln(1 + i)} = \frac{0.69314718 - 0}{\ln(1 + i)}.$$

(a) $0.69314718 \div \ln(1.03) = 23.44977$ years;
(b) $0.69314718 \div \ln(1.05) = 14.20699$ years;
(c) $0.69314718 \div \ln(1.07) = 10.24476$ years;
(d) $0.69314718 \div \ln(1.10) = 7.27254$ years;
(e) $0.69314718 \div \ln(1.12) = 6.11625$ years;
(f) $0.69314718 \div \ln(1.15) = 4.95948$ years.

2.10. (a) $72 \div 3 = 24$ years;
(b) $72 \div 5 = 14.4$ years;
(c) $72 \div 7 = 10.286$ years;
(d) $72 \div 10 = 7.2$ years;
(e) $72 \div 12 = 6$ years;
(f) $72 \div 15 = 4.8$ years.

2.11. First, for the sake of simplicity, assume PV to be 1 and FV_n to be 2:

$$2 = 1 \cdot e^{rn} = e^{rn}.$$

Now, find the natural logs of both sides:

$$\ln(2) = rn,$$

$$\ln(2) \approx 0.693 \approx 0.72 \approx rn,$$

$$\frac{0.72}{r} \approx n.$$

Thus, for example, if the interest rate equals 0.10, it will take approximately 7.2 years for an account to double.

2.12. Our demonstration is as follows:

$$FV_n = PV \cdot e^{rn} = 1 \cdot e^{0.1 \cdot 10} = e.$$

2.13. (a) $X_1 = 15, X_2 = 25, X_3 = 35, X_4 = 45$;
(b) $15 + 25 + 35 + 45 = 120$;
(c) $3 \cdot 15 + 3 \cdot 25 + 3 \cdot 35 + 3 \cdot 45 = 3 \cdot 120 = 360$;
(d) $3 \cdot 15^2 + 3 \cdot 25^2 + 3 \cdot 35^2 + 3 \cdot 45^2 = 3 \cdot 225 + 3 \cdot 625 + 3 \cdot 1225 + 3 \cdot 2025$
$= 12,300$;

(e) $\prod_{t=1}^{4} 3X_t^2 = (3 \cdot 15^2) \cdot (3 \cdot 25^2) \cdot (3 \cdot 35^2) \cdot (3 \cdot 45^2)$
$= (3 \cdot 225) \cdot (3 \cdot 625) \cdot (3 \cdot 1225) \cdot (3 \cdot 2025) \approx 2.8255869 \cdot 10^{13}$
$= 28,255,869,000,000;$

(f) $\sum_{t=1}^{4} X_t/n = (15 + 25 + 35 + 45)/4 = 120/4 = 30;$

(g) $(\prod_{t=1}^{4} X_t)^{1/n} = (15 \cdot 25 \cdot 35 \cdot 45)^{1/4} = 27.722217.$

2.14. (a) $\sum_{i=1}^{3} w_i = 0.4 + 0.5 + 0.1 = 1;$

(b) $\sum_{i=1}^{3}\sum_{j=1}^{3} w_i w_j x_{i,j} = [0.4 \cdot 0.4 \cdot 7] + [0.4 \cdot 0.5 \cdot 4] + [0.4 \cdot 0.1 \cdot 9] + [0.5 \cdot 0.4 \cdot 6]$
$+ [0.5 \cdot 0.5 \cdot 4] + [0.5 \cdot 0.1 \cdot 12] + [0.1 \cdot 0.4 \cdot 3] + [0.1 \cdot 0.5 \cdot 2] + [0.1 \cdot 0.1 \cdot 17]$
$= 1.12 + 0.8 + 0.36 + 0.12 + 1 + 0.6 + 1.2 + 0.1 + 0.17 = 5.47.$

2.15. The three-year rate is based on a geometric mean of the short-term spot rates as follows:

$$y_{0,n} = \sqrt[n]{\prod_{t=1}^{n} (1 + y_{t-1,t})} - 1 = \sqrt[3]{(1 + y_{0,1})(1 + y_{1,2})(1 + y_{2,3})} - 1$$

$$= \sqrt[3]{(1 + 0.05)(1 + 0.06)(1 + 0.07)} - 1 = 0.05997.$$

2.16. $FV = \sum_{t=1}^{4} 25(1 + 0.10)^t = 25(1.1)^1 + 25(1.1)^2 + 25(1.1)^3 + 25(1.1)^4$
$= 25(1.1) + 25(1.21) + 25(1.331) + 25(1.4641) = 127.6275.$

2.17. (a) $x = 8! = 8 \cdot 7 \cdot 6 \cdot 5 \cdot 4 \cdot 3 \cdot 2 \cdot 1 = 40,320;$

(b) $x = 9! = 9 \cdot 8! = 9 \cdot 8 \cdot 7 \cdot 6 \cdot 5 \cdot 4 \cdot 3 \cdot 2 \cdot 1 = 362,880;$

(c) $x = 0! = 1.$

2.18. (a) $(6 \cdot 5 \cdot 4 \cdot 3) = 360;$ (d) $(6 \cdot 5)/(2 \cdot 1) = 15;$

(b) $(4 \cdot 3 \cdot 2 \cdot 1) = 24;$ (e) $1;$

(c) $(8 \cdot 7) = 56;$ (f) $(8 \cdot 7)/(2 \cdot 1) = 28.$

Chapter 3

3.1. (a) $90 = 5x, 90/5 = x = 18;$

(b) $-2,500 = -2x, (-2,500)/(-2) = 1,250;$

(c) $85 = 8x, 85/8 = x = 10.625;$

(d) $50 = 60 + 5x, -10 = 5x, -10/5 = x = -2;$

(e) $20 - 10 - 25 = -15/x, -15 = -15/x, x = 1;$

(f) $25 - 100 = 3x - 2x + 5x, -75 = 6x, -75/6 = x = -12.5.$

3.2. (a) $100 \div 90 = (1 + x)^2, 1.1111111 = (1 + x)^2, (1.1111111)^{1/2} = 1 + x,$
$1.05409 = 1 + x, x = 0.05409;$

(b) $100 \div 90 = (1 + x)^3, 1.1111111 = (1 + x)^3, (1.1111111)^{1/3} = 1 + x,$
$1.03574 = 1 + x, x = 0.03574;$

(c) $100 \div 90 = (1 + x)^{-2}, 1.1111111 = (1 + x)^{-2}, (1.1111111)^{-1/2} = 1 + x,$
$0.94868 = 1 + x, x = -0.051316;$

(d) $90 \div 100 = (1 + x)^{-2}, 0.9 = (1 + x)^{-2}, 0.9^{-1/2} = 1 + x, 1.05409 = 1 + x, x = 0.05409.$

3.3. (a) The value of \$1 is equal to the value of £0.6. Thus, the value of £1 must be \$1/0.6 = \$1.6667. Since the value of \$1 is ¥108, the value of £1 must be $1.6667 \cdot ¥108 = ¥180$. Thus, we could have solved as follows: £1 = (\$1 ÷ 0.6) · ¥108 = ¥180.

(b) The value of \$1 is equal to the value of ¥108. Thus, the value of ¥1 must be \$1/¥108 = \$0.0092593. Since the value of £1 is \$1.6667, the value of ¥1 must be $1 \div (1.6667 \cdot ¥108) = £0.0055556$. Thus, we could have solved as follows: $¥1 = $1 \div (1/0.6 \cdot ¥108) = £0.0055556$.

(c) $300 = £0.6 \cdot 300 = £180. $300 = ¥108 \cdot 300 = ¥32,400$.

3.4. The firm's break-even production level is determined by solving for Q when profits π equal zero:

$$0 = 80Q - (500,000 + 50 \cdot Q).$$

First, we will add 500,000 to both sides:

$$500,000 = 80Q - 50Q.$$

Next, note that $80Q - 50Q = 30Q$, so that we will divide both sides of the above equation by 30 to obtain:

$$500,000 \div 30 = Q^* = 16,666.67,$$

where Q^* is the break-even production level (the asterisk does not represent a product symbol here). Thus, the firm must produce 16,666.67 units to recover its fixed costs in order to break even.

3.5. The three-year rate is based on a geometric mean of the short-term spot rates as follows:

$$(1 + y_{0,3})^3 = \prod_{t=1}^{3}(1 + y_{t-1,t}) = (1 + 0.05)(1 + 0.06)(1 + 0.07) = 1.19091,$$

$$y_{0,3} = [(1 + 0.05)(1 + 0.06)(1 + 0.07)]^{1/3} - 1 = \sqrt[3]{1.19091} - 1 = 0.0599686.$$

3.6. The three-year rate is based on a geometric mean of the short-term spot rates as follows:

$$(1 + y_{0,3})^3 = (1.07)^3 = 1.22504 = \prod_{t=1}^{3}(1 + y_{t-1,t}) = (1 + 0.05)(1 + 0.07)(1 + y_{2,3}).$$

We solve for $y_{2,3}$ as follows:

$$1.22504 \div [(1 + 0.05)(1 + 0.07)] - 1 = y_{2,3} = 0.07.$$

3.7. (a) The firm's profit function, total revenues minus total costs, is

$$\pi = 50Q - 0.00002Q^2 - (500,000 + 20Q + 0.00001Q^2),$$

which simplifies to

$$\pi = -0.00003Q^2 + 30Q - 500,000.$$

(b) Note that the terms are arranged in descending order of exponents for Q. Our coefficients for this quadratic equation are $a = -0.00003$, $b = 30$, and $c = -500,000$. We can solve for the break-even production level by setting π equal to zero, using the quadratic formula as follows:

$$Q = \frac{-30 \pm \sqrt{30^2 - 4 \cdot (-0.00003) \cdot (-500,000)}}{2 \cdot (-0.00003)} = \frac{-30 \pm \sqrt{900 - (60)}}{-0.00006}$$

$$= \frac{-30 \pm \sqrt{840}}{-0.00006} = \frac{-30 \pm 28.982753}{-0.00006} = \frac{-1.0172466}{-0.00006} \text{ and } \frac{-58.982753}{-0.00006}$$

$$= 16,954.11 \text{ and } 983,045.88 \text{ units.}$$

Either of the above production levels will enable the firm to break even with a profit level equal to zero.

3.8.   We need to solve this equation for w_1 using the quadratic formula. This is accomplished as follows:

$$w_1 = \frac{-b + \sqrt{b^2 - 4ac}}{2a}, \qquad \text{where } a = 0.25, \, b = -0.3, \text{ and } c = 0.09.$$

We fill in our coefficients' values to determine the proportion of the investor's money to be invested in stock 1:

$$w_1 = \frac{0.3 \pm \sqrt{(-0.3)^2 - 4 \cdot 0.25 \cdot 0.09}}{2 \cdot 0.25} = \frac{0.3 \pm \sqrt{0}}{0.5} = 0.6.$$

The value under the square root sign (the radical) will be zero. Hence, there will be only one value for $w_1 = 0.6$. Therefore, we find that the portfolio is riskless when $w_1 = 0.6$. Thus, 60% of the riskless portfolio should be invested in stock 1 and 40% of the portfolio should be invested in stock 2.

3.9.   First, number the equations as follows:

$$0.04x_1 + 0.04x_2 = 0.01, \tag{A1}$$

$$0.04x_1 + 0.16x_2 = 0.11. \tag{A2}$$

Now, write equation (A1) in terms of x_1:

$$0.04x_1 = 0.01 - 0.04x_2,$$

$$x_1 = 0.01/0.04 - 0.04x_2/0.04,$$

$$x_1 = 0.25 - 1x_2.$$

Next, we substitute our revised version of x_1 back into equation (A2) to obtain the following:

$$0.11 = 0.04(0.25 - 1x_2) + 0.16x_2,$$

which simplifies to

$$0.10 = -0.12x_2. \tag{B2}$$

Thus, $x_2 = 0.83333$. Substitute x_2 back into either equation (A1) or equation (A2) and we find that $x_1 = -0.58333$.

3.10.

$$20x - 5\lambda \quad = -3 \tag{1a}$$
$$-5x - 0\lambda \quad = -100 \tag{2a}$$

$$x = 20 \tag{1b) = (2a) $\div$ -5}$$
$$20 \cdot 20 - 5\lambda = -3 \tag{2b) = (1a)}$$

$$-5\lambda = -403$$
$$\lambda = 403/5 = 80\tfrac{3}{5}, \; x = 20.$$

3.11.   First, number the equations as follows:

$$962 = 100x_1 + 100x_2 + 1{,}100x_3, \tag{A1}$$

$$1{,}010.4 = 120x_1 + 120x_2 + 1{,}120x_3, \tag{A2}$$

$$970 = 100x_1 + 1{,}100x_2. \tag{A3}$$

Now, write equation (A3) in terms of x_1:

$$100x_1 = 970 - 1,100x_2,$$

$$x_1 = 970/100 - 1,100x_2/100,$$

$$x_1 = 9.7 - 11x_2.$$

Next, we plug our revised version of x_1 back into equations (A1) and (A2) to obtain the following:

$$962 = 100(9.7 - 11x_2) + 100x_2 + 1,100x_3,$$

$$1,010.4 = 120(9.7 - 11x_2) + 120x_2 + 1,120x_3,$$

which simplifies to

$$-8 = -1,000x_2 + 1,100x_3, \qquad \qquad \text{(B1)}$$

$$-153.6 = -1,200x_2 + 1,120x_3. \qquad \qquad \text{(B2)}$$

Now solve equations (B1) and (B2) for x_3 by multiplying equation (B1) by 1.2 and subtracting the result from equation (B2):

$$
\begin{array}{lr}
-153.6 = -1,200x_2 + 1,120x_3 & \text{(B2)} \\
\underline{(-9.6 = -1,200x_2 + 1,320x_3)} & \text{(B1)} \cdot 1.2 \\
-144 = \qquad\qquad -200x_3 &
\end{array}
$$

Thus, $x_3 = 0.72$. Plug x_3 back into either equation (B1) or equation (B2) and we find that $x_2 = 0.8$. Now, substitute $x_3 = 0.72$ and $x_2 = 0.8$ back into any of equations (A1), (A2), or (A3) and we find that $x_1 = 0.9$. Thus, we obtain $x_1 = 0.9$, $x_2 = 0.8$, and $x_3 = 0.72$.

3.12. (a) $16.80 = 4 \cdot GNP + 80 \cdot i,$
$9.00 = 2 \cdot GNP + 50 \cdot i;$
(b) $16.80 = 4 \cdot GNP + 80 \cdot i,$
$9.00 = 2 \cdot GNP + 50 \cdot i.$

$$
\begin{array}{l}
16.80 = 4 \cdot GNP + 80 \cdot i \\
\underline{18.00 = 4 \cdot GNP + 100 \cdot i} \\
-1.20 = \qquad\qquad -20i;
\end{array}
$$

$$i = 0.06, \ GNP = 3.$$

3.13. Our first problem is to complete a pro-forma income statement for 2001. However, we don't know what the company's interest expenditure in 2001 will be until we know how much money it will borrow (*EFN*). At the same time, we cannot determine how much money the firm needs to borrow until we know its interest expenditure (so we can solve for retained earnings). Therefore, we must solve simultaneously for *EFN* and interest expenditure. We know that *EFN* can be found as follows:

$$EFN = \Delta Assets - \Delta CL - RE,$$

$$EFN = \$400,000 - \$60,000 - RE.$$

Retained earnings (*RE*) can be found using the following pro-forma income statement for 2001:

Pro-forma Income Statement, 2001	
Sales (*TR*)	$1,050,000
Cost of Goods Sold.........................	450,000
Gross Margin..................................	600,000
Fixed Costs	150,000
EBIT	450,000
Interest Payments.........................	$50,000 + (0.10 \cdot EFN)$
Earnings Before Tax.......................	$400,000 - (0.10 \cdot EFN)$
Taxes (@ 40%)	$160,000 - (0.04 \cdot EFN)$
Net Income After Tax	$240,000 - (0.06 \cdot EFN)$
Dividends (@ 33%).........................	$80,000 - (0.02 \cdot EFN)$
Retained Earnings..........................	$160,000 - (0.04 \cdot EFN)$

Now, rewrite the *EFN* expression, substituting in for *RE*:

$$EFN = \$400,000 - \$60,000 - (\$160,000 - (0.04 \cdot EFN)),$$

$$EFN = \$180,000 + 0.04 \cdot EFN,$$

$$0.96 \cdot EFN = \$180,000,$$

$$EFN = \$187,500.$$

Our *EFN* problem is complete. We now know that the firm must borrow $187,500. Thus, the firm's total interest payments for 2001 must be $50,000 plus 10% of $187,500, or $68,750.

3.14.
$$1,200 = 100(1 + x + x^2 + x^3 + \ldots + x^9),$$

$$1,200x = 100(x + x^2 + x^3 + \ldots + x^{10}),$$

$$1,200x - 1,200 = 100(x + x^2 + x^3 + \ldots + x^{10} - 1 - x - x^2 - x^3 - \ldots - x^9),$$

$$1,200(x - 1) = 100(x^{10} - 1),$$

$$12 = (x^{10} - 1)/(x - 1).$$

Substitute for *x*:

$$x = 1.0398905.$$

3.15. The expansion is performed as follows:

$$\Delta Y = \Delta \bar{C} + Y(c + c^2 + c^3 + \ldots + c^\infty), \tag{B}$$

$$c\Delta Y = c\Delta \bar{C} + Y(c^2 + c^3 + c^4 + \ldots + c^{\infty+1}), \tag{C}$$

$$(1 - c)\Delta Y = (1 - c)\Delta \bar{C} + Y(c - c^{\infty+1}) \qquad \text{where } 0 < c \leq 1, \tag{D}$$

$$\Delta Y = \Delta \bar{C} + Y[c \div (1 - c)] \qquad \text{where } c^{\infty+1} = 0. \tag{E}$$

Thus, the income multiplier equals $c/(1 - c) = c/s$, where *s* represents the proportion of marginal income saved by individuals.

3.16. Plot several points for *x* and *y* for the functions, one function at a time. When enough points have been plotted to determine the shape of the curve, map out the graph. Functions (a) and (b) will plot similarly to the two functions in figure 3.2 in section 3.5. Functions (c) and (d) will plot similarly to the two functions in figure 3.1 in section 3.5.

CHAPTER 4

4.1. $FV_8 = 21{,}000(1 + 8 \cdot 0.09) = 21{,}000 \cdot 1.72 = 36{,}120.$

4.2.   (a) $[10\% \cdot \$10{,}000{,}000]/2 = \$500{,}000;$
       (b) $10\% \cdot \$10{,}000{,}000 = 2 \cdot \$500{,}000 = \$1{,}000{,}000;$
       (c) $\$10{,}000{,}000 + \$1{,}000{,}000 = \text{principal} + \text{interest in year five} = \$11{,}000{,}000.$

4.3. $\$10{,}000(1 + 0.055/365)^{5 \cdot 365} = \$13{,}165.03.$

4.4.   (a) $FV_8 = 10{,}500(1 + 0.09)^8 = 10{,}500 \cdot 1.99256 = 20{,}921.908;$

       (b) $FV_8 = 10{,}500\left(1 + \dfrac{0.09}{2}\right)^{2 \cdot 8} = 10{,}500 \cdot 2.0223702 = 21{,}234.887;$

       (c) $FV_8 = 10{,}500\left(1 + \dfrac{0.09}{12}\right)^{12 \cdot 8} = 10{,}500 \cdot 2.0489212 = 21{,}513.673;$

       (d) $FV_8 = 10{,}500\left(1 + \dfrac{0.09}{365}\right)^{365 \cdot 8} = 10{,}500 \cdot 2.0542506 = 21{,}569.632;$

       (e) $FV_8 = 10{,}500e^{0.09 \cdot 8} = 10{,}500 \cdot 2.0544332 = 21{,}571.549.$

4.5. $\$10{,}000(1 + 0.055/365)^{5 \cdot 365} = \$13{,}165.03.$

4.6.   For example, let $X_0 = \$1{,}000$ in each case:

       for CD_1, $FV_5 = 1{,}000(1 + 0.12)^5 = 1{,}762.3417;$

       for CD_2, $FV_5 = 1{,}000\left(1 + \dfrac{0.10}{365}\right)^{365 \cdot 5} = 1{,}648.6005.$

4.7.   Solve for X_0:

$$X_0 = \frac{FV_n}{(1 + i)^n} = \frac{10{,}000}{(1 + 0.08)^3} = 7{,}938.322.$$

4.8   Solve the following for *APY*:

$$APY = \left(1 + \frac{i}{m}\right)^m - 1 = \left(1 + \frac{0.03}{4}\right)^4 - 1 = 0.0303391.$$

4.9.   In all cases here, $FV_n = 2X_0$. Thus, let $FV_n = 2{,}000$ and $X_0 = 1{,}000$:

       (a) $2{,}000 = 1{,}000(1 + n \cdot 0.1),\ 2 = (1 + n \cdot 0.1),\ 1 = 0.1n,\ n = 10$ years.
       (b) $2{,}000 = 1{,}000(1.1)^n$. Using logs:

$$\log 2{,}000 = (\log 1{,}000) + n \cdot \log(1.1),$$

$$3.30103 = 3 + n \cdot (0.04139),$$

$$0.30103 = n(0.04139), \qquad n = 7.2725 \text{ years.}$$

       (c) $2{,}000 = 1{,}000\left(1 + \dfrac{0.10}{12}\right)^{12n}:$

$$\log 2{,}000 = (\log 1{,}000) + 12n \cdot \log(1.008333),$$

$$n = 6.96059 \text{ years.}$$

(d) $2{,}000 = 1{,}000e^{0.1 \cdot n}$. Use natural logs:

$$\ln 2{,}000 = (\ln 1{,}000) + 0.1n, \qquad n = 6.93148 \text{ years.}$$

4.10. (a) $PV = \dfrac{CF_n}{(1+k)^n} = \dfrac{10{,}000}{(1+0.20)^5} = \dfrac{10{,}000}{1.2^5} = \dfrac{10{,}000}{2.48832} = 4{,}018.775;$

(b) $PV = \dfrac{10{,}000}{1.10^5} = \dfrac{10{,}000}{1.61051} = 6{,}209.213;$

(c) $PV = \dfrac{10{,}000}{1.01^5} = \dfrac{10{,}000}{1.0510101} = 9{,}514.656;$

(d) $PV = \dfrac{10{,}000}{1.0^5} = \dfrac{10{,}000}{1} = 10{,}000.$

4.11. (a) $PV = \dfrac{10{,}000}{1.1^{20}} = \dfrac{10{,}000}{6.7275} = 1{,}486.436;$

(b) $PV = \dfrac{10{,}000}{1.1^{10}} = \dfrac{10{,}000}{2.5937425} = 3{,}855.432;$

(c) $PV = \dfrac{10{,}000}{1.1^1} = \dfrac{10{,}000}{1.1} = 9{,}090.909;$

(d) $PV = \dfrac{10{,}000}{1.1^{0.5}} = \dfrac{10{,}000}{1.1^{0.5}} = \dfrac{10{,}000}{1.0488088} = 9{,}534.625$

(note that six months is 0.5 of one year);

(e) $PV = \dfrac{10{,}000}{1.1^{0.2}} = \dfrac{10{,}000}{1.0192449} = 9{,}811.184$

(note that 73 days is 0.2 of one year).

4.12. $PV = \displaystyle\sum_{t=1}^{n} \dfrac{CF_t}{(1+k)^t} = \dfrac{2{,}000}{1.08^1} + \dfrac{3{,}000}{1.08^2} + \dfrac{7{,}000}{1.08^3};$

$$PV = 1{,}851.85 + 2{,}572.02 = 5{,}556.83 = 9{,}980.70;$$

$$10{,}000 > 9{,}980.70.$$

Since $P_0 > PV$, the investment should not be purchased.

4.13. $PV_n = CF\left[\dfrac{1}{k} - \dfrac{1}{k(1+k)^n}\right]:$

(a) $PV_A = 2{,}000\left[\dfrac{1}{0.05} - \dfrac{1}{0.05(1.05)^9}\right] = 6{,}000(20 - 12.892178) = 42{,}646.93;$

(b) $PV_A = 2{,}000\left[\dfrac{1}{0.10} - \dfrac{1}{0.10(1.10)^9}\right] = 6{,}000(10 - 4.2409762) = 34{,}554.14;$

(c) $PV_A = \left[\dfrac{1}{0.2} - \dfrac{1}{0.2(1.2)^9}\right] = 6{,}000(5 - 0.9690335) = 24{,}185.80.$

4.14. $PV_p = \dfrac{CF}{K} = \dfrac{50}{0.08} = 625.$

4.15. $CF_n = CF_1(1 + g)^{n-1}$:

    (a) $CF_2 = 10,000(1 + 0.1)^{2-1} = 10,000(1 + 0.1) = 10,000 \cdot 1.1 = 11,000;$

    (b) $CF_3 = 10,000(1 + 0.1)^{3-1} = 10,000 \cdot 1.21 = 12,100;$

    (c) $CF_5 = 10,000(1 + 0.1)^{5-1} = 10,000 \cdot 1.4641 = 14,641;$

    (d) $CF_{10} = 10,000(1 + 0.1)^{10-1} = 10,000 \cdot 2.3579477 = 23,579.477.$

4.16. $PV_{ga} = CF_1 \cdot \left[\dfrac{1}{k - g} - \dfrac{(1 + g)}{(k - g)(1 + k)^n} \right]$

$$= 5,000 \cdot \left[\dfrac{1}{0.02} - \dfrac{(1 + 0.10)^7}{(0.12 - 0.10)(1 + 0.12)^7} \right];$$

$PV_{ga} = 5,000 \cdot [50 - 44.075033] = 29,624.837.$

4.17. $PV_{gp} = \dfrac{CF_1}{k - g} = \dfrac{100}{0.12 - 0.05} = 1,428.5714.$

4.18. $60,000 per year for 20 years:

    (a) $PV = 500,000;$

    (b) $PV = 100,000 \left[\dfrac{1}{0.05} - \dfrac{1}{0.05(1.05)^8} \right] = 646,321.27;$

    (c) $PV = 60,000 \left[\dfrac{1}{0.05} - \dfrac{1}{0.05(1.05)^{20}} \right] = 747,732.62;$

    (d) $PV = \dfrac{30,000}{0.05} = 600,000.$

Series (c) has the highest present value.

4.19. $500,000 now:

    (a) $PV = 500,000;$

    (b) $PV = 100,000 \left[\dfrac{1}{0.2} - \dfrac{1}{0.2(1.2)^8} \right] = 383,715.98;$

    (c) $PV = 60,000 \left[\dfrac{1}{0.2} - \dfrac{1}{0.2(1.2)^{20}} \right] = 292,174.78;$

    (d) $PV = \dfrac{30,000}{0.2} = 150,000.$

4.20. $\mathrm{Pay} = \mathrm{Principal} \left/ \left[\dfrac{1}{i} - \dfrac{1}{i(1 + i)^n} \right] \right. ;$

$\mathrm{Principal} = 200,000 - 50,000 = 150,000:$

(a) $\text{Pay} = 150{,}000 \Big/ \left[\dfrac{1}{0.1} - \dfrac{1}{0.1(1+0.1)^{20}} \right]$

$\qquad = 150{,}000/8.5135637 = 17{,}618.944;$

(b) $\text{Pay} = 150{,}000 \Big/ \left[\dfrac{1}{0.008333} - \dfrac{1}{0.008333(1.008333)^{240}} \right]$

$\qquad = 150{,}000/103.62442 = 1{,}447.5352$

(note that $10\%/12 = 0.008333$; $20 \cdot 12 = 240$.

4.21.   Substitute discount rates into the present-value annuity function until you find one that sets *PV* equal to the purchase price:

$$\begin{array}{ll}
\text{try } 15\%, & PV = 9{,}543.1685 < 10{,}000; \\
\text{try } 13\%, & PV = 10{,}803.31 > 10{,}000; \\
\text{try } 14\%, & PV = 9{,}892.8294 < 10{,}000; \\
\text{try } 13.7\%, & PV = 10{,}001.638 > 10{,}000; \\
\text{try } 13.71\%, & PV = 9{,}997.977 < 10{,}000; \\
\text{try } 13.704\%, & PV = 10{,}000.174 > 10{,}000.
\end{array}$$

Thus, *K* is approximately 13.704%.

4.22.   (a) $PV = \dfrac{10{,}000}{1.1^{20}} = \dfrac{10{,}000}{6.7275} = 1{,}486.436;$

(b) $PV = \dfrac{10{,}000}{(1+0.1/12)^{12 \cdot 20}} = \dfrac{10{,}000}{7.328074} = 1{,}364.615;$

(c) $PV = \dfrac{10{,}000}{(1+0.1/365)^{365 \cdot 20}} = \dfrac{10{,}000}{7.3870321} = 1{,}353.7236;$

(d) $PV = 10{,}000 \cdot e^{-0.1 \cdot 20} = 1{,}353.3528.$

4.23.   (a)   First, the monthly discount rate is $0.1 \div 12 = 0.008333$:

$$PV = 1{,}000 \cdot \left[\dfrac{1}{0.008333} - \dfrac{1}{0.008333(1+0.008333)^{360}} \right]$$

$$= 1{,}000 \cdot 113.95082 = \$113{,}950.82.$$

(b)   Yes, since the *PV* exceeds the $100,000 price.

(c) $100{,}000 = 1{,}000 \cdot \left[\dfrac{1}{(k/12)} - \dfrac{1}{(k/12) \cdot (1+k/12)^{360}} \right].$

Solve for *k*; by a process of substitution, we find that $k = 0.11627$.

4.24.   Use the present-value annuity function to amortize the loan. The payment is $2,637.97.

4.25. $PV_{ga} = CF \left[\dfrac{(1+g)^0}{(1+k)^1} + \dfrac{(1+g)^1}{(1+k)^2} + \dots + \dfrac{(1+g)^{n-1}}{(1+k)^n} \right];$

$PV_{ga} \cdot \dfrac{(1+k)}{(1+g)} = CF \left[\dfrac{(1+g)^{-1}}{(1+k)^0} + \dfrac{(1+g)^0}{(1+k)^1} + \dots + \dfrac{(1+g)^{n-2}}{(1+k)^{n-1}} \right];$

$$PV_{ga} \cdot \frac{(1+k)}{(1+g)} - PV_{ga} = CF\left[\frac{(1+g)^{-1}}{(1+k)^0} - \frac{(1+g)^{n-1}}{(1+k)^n}\right];$$

$$PV_{ga} \cdot \frac{(1+k)-(1+g)}{(1+g)} = PV_{ga}\frac{(k-g)}{(1+g)} = CF\left[\frac{(1+g)^{-1}}{(1+k)^0} - \frac{(1+g)^{n-1}}{(1+k)^n}\right];$$

$$PV_{ga} = CF\left[\frac{1}{k-g} - \frac{(1+g)^n}{(k-g)(1+k)^n}\right].$$

4.26. This problem can be solved with either of the following:

$$PV = \$5,000 \cdot \frac{\dfrac{1}{0.12} - \dfrac{1}{0.12(1+0.12)^{50}}}{(1+0.12)^9} = \$14,973.42;$$

$$PV = \$5,000 \cdot \left(\frac{1}{0.12} - \frac{1}{0.12(1+0.12)^{59}}\right) - \$5,000 \cdot \left(\frac{1}{0.12} - \frac{1}{(1+0.12)^9}\right) = \$14,973.42.$$

4.27. The following Single-Stage Growth Model can be used to evaluate this stock:

$$p_0 = \frac{DIV_1}{k-g},$$

$$p_0 = \frac{\$1.80}{0.06-0.04} = \$90.$$

Since the \$100 purchase price of the stock is less than its \$90 model value, the stock should not be purchased.

4.28. The following Three-Stage Growth Model can be used to evaluate this stock:

$$p_0 = DIV_1\left[\frac{1}{k-g_1} - \frac{(1+g_1)^{n(1)}}{(k-g_1)(1+k)^{n(1)}}\right]$$

$$+ DIV_1\left[\frac{(1+g_1)^{n(1)-1}(1+g_2)}{(1+k)^{n(1)}(k-g_2)} - \frac{(1+g_1)^{n(1)-1}(1+g_2)^{n(2)-n(1)+1}}{(k-g_2)(1+k)^{n(2)}}\right]$$

$$+ \frac{DIV_1(1+g_1)^{n(1)-1}(1+g_2)^{n(2)-n(1)}(1+g_3)}{(k-g_3)(1+k)^{n(2)}},$$

$$p_0 = \$5\left[\frac{1}{0.08-0.15} - \frac{(1+0.15)^3}{(0.08-0.15)(1+0.08)^3}\right]$$

$$+ \$5\left[\frac{(1+0.15)^{3-1}(1+0.06)}{(1+0.08)^3(0.08-0.06)} - \frac{(1+0.15)^{3-1}(1+0.06)^{6-3+1}}{(0.08-0.06)(1+0.08)^6}\right]$$

$$+ \frac{\$5(1+0.15)^{3-1}(1+0.06)^{6-3}(1+0)}{(0.08-0)(1+0.08)^6} = 92.0171078.$$

Since the \$100 purchase price of the stock exceeds its \$92.0171 value, the stock should not be purchased.

Chapter 5

5.1. $ROI = \sum_{t=0}^{n} CF_t \div nP_0$

$= 200/(1(1,000)) = 0.20$, or 20%.

5.2. (a) $ROI = (400 - 200)/(7(200)) = 0.1428$, or 14.28%;
(b) $ROI = (400/200)^{1/7} - 1 = (2)^{1/7} - 1 = 0.1041$, or 10.41%;
(c) $IRR = 10.41\%$ (note that $ROI_{AG} = IRR$ when there is only capital gain profit).

5.3. (a) $ROI = (500 + 4,800)/6(7,500) = 0.1178$, or 11.78%;
(b) $IRR = 11.499\%$.

5.4. (a) $ROI = (-100,000 + 20,000 + 20,000 + 20,000 + 20,000 + 60,000)/5(100,000)$
$= 40,000/500,000$
$= 0.08$, or 8%;
(b) $IRR = 10.21\%$.

5.5. $NPV = 0$, by the definition of IRR.

5.6. (a) Dividends:

Grove = $800,

Dean = $200.

(b) Capital gains:

Grove = $1,100 - $1,000 = $100,

Dean = $1,800 - $1,000 = $800.

(c) Arithmetic mean capital gain return:

Grove = $(100 + 800)/8(1,000)$

$= 0.1125$, or 11.25%;

Dean = $(800 + 200)/8(1,000)$

$= 0.125$, or 12.5%.

(d) IRR:

Grove = 11.08477%,

Dean = 9.598%.

Summary of results

Company	Dividends	Capital gains	ROI_a	IRR
Grove	800	100	11.25%	10.0%
Dean	200	800	12.50%	9.5%

(e) Under ROI_a = Dean,
under IRR = Grove.

The performance evaluation depends on the measure used. This depends on the investor's time value of money. A higher time value indicates that *IRR* is more useful.

5.7.   (a) $ROI_A = \sum_{t=0}^{n} CF_t \div nP_0$

$= (-100{,}000 + 50{,}000 - 50{,}000 + 75{,}000 + 75{,}000)/6(100{,}000)$

$= 0.083$, or 8.3%.

$100{,}000 = 50{,}000/(1 + r)^2 - 50{,}000/(1 + r)^3 + 75{,}000/(1 + r)^4 + 75{,}000/(1 + r)^6$,

$IRR = 9.32487405\%$, $IRR = -227.776188859\%$.

(c)   There are actually two internal rates of return for this problem. However, 9.32487% seems to be a reasonable rate.

5.8.   (a)   Its annual interest payments:

$$i_y = Int/F_0,$$

$$Int = i_y(F_0)$$

$$= (0.12) \cdot (1{,}000)$$

$$= \$120.$$

(b)   Its current yield:

$$cy = Int/P_0$$

$$= 120/1{,}200$$

$$= 0.10.$$

(c)   With equation (4.8), yield to maturity is found to be 0.04697429, or 4.697429%.

5.9.   (a)   Its annual interest payments: $120, or $60 every six months.
(b) $120 \div 1{,}200 =$ its current yield $= 0.10$, or 10%.
(c)   Its yield to maturity:

$-1{,}200 + 60/[1 + (r/2)]^1 + 60/[1 + (r/2)]^2 + \ldots + 60/[1 + (r/2)]^5 + 1{,}060/[1 + (r/2)]^6$,

$r = 0.0476634.$

5.10. $PV_{ga} = CF_1 \cdot \left[\dfrac{1}{r - g} - \dfrac{(1 + g)^n}{(r - g) \cdot (1 + r)^n} \right] + \dfrac{CF_n}{(1 + r)^n};$

$CF_1 = \$3{,}000,$ $n = 20,$ $g = 0.10.$

Solve for *r* above to obtain $IRR = 0.11794166365$.

5.11.   (a)   Each outcome has a one-third or 0.333 probability of being realized, since the probabilities are equal and must sum to one.
(b) $E[SALES] = (800{,}000 \cdot 0.333) + (500{,}000 \cdot 0.333) + (400{,}000 \cdot 0.333)$,
$E[SALES] = 566{,}667$.
(c)   Compute as follows:

$VAR[Sales] = [(800{,}000 - 566{,}667)^2 \cdot 0.333 + (500{,}000 - 566{,}667)^2 \cdot 0.333$

$(400{,}000 - 566{,}667) \cdot 0.333] = 28{,}888{,}000{,}000 = \sigma_{sales}^2.$

(d) Expected return of project A:

$$(0.3 \cdot 0.333) + (0.15 \cdot 0.333) + (0.01 \cdot 0.333) = 0.15333.$$

(e) Variance of A's returns:

$$[(0.3 - 0.1533)^2 \cdot 0.333 + (0.15 - 0.1533)^2 \cdot 0.333$$
$$+ (0.01 - 0.1533)^2 \cdot 0.333] = 0.0140222 = \sigma_A^2.$$

(f) Expected return of project B:

$$(0.2 \cdot 0.333) + (0.13 \cdot 0.333) + (0.09 \cdot 0.333) = 0.14.$$

Variance of B's returns:

$$[(0.2 - 0.14)^2 \cdot 0.333 + (0.13 - 0.14)^2 \cdot 0.333$$
$$+ (0.09 - 0.14)^2 \cdot 0.333] = 0.0020666 = \sigma_B^2.$$

(g) Standard deviations are square roots of variances:

$$\sigma_{sales} = 169,964,$$
$$\sigma_A = 0.1184154,$$
$$\sigma_B = 0.0454606.$$

(h) Compute as follows:

$$\mathrm{COV}[Sales] = \sum_{i=1}^{n} (Sales_i - \mathrm{E}[Sales]) \cdot (R_{Ai} - \mathrm{E}[R_A]) \cdot P_i,$$

$$\mathrm{COV}[Sales, A] = (800,000 - 566,667) \cdot (0.3 - 0.1533) \cdot 0.333$$
$$+ (500,000 - 566,667) \cdot (0.15 - 0.1533) \cdot 0.333$$
$$+ (400,000 - 566,667) \cdot (0.01 - 0.1533) \cdot 0.333$$
$$= 19,444 = \sigma_{sales,A}.$$

(i) $\rho_{s,A} = \dfrac{\sigma_{sales,A}}{\sigma_{sales} \cdot \sigma_A} = \dfrac{19,444}{169,964 \cdot 0.118} = 0.97.$

(j) First, find the covariance between sales and returns on B:

$$\mathrm{COV}[Sales, B] = (800,000 - 566,667) \cdot (0.20 - 0.14) \cdot 0.333$$
$$+ (500,000 - 566,667) \cdot (0.13 - 0.14) \cdot 0.333$$
$$+ (400,000 - 566,667) \cdot (0.09 - 0.14) \cdot 0.333$$
$$= 7,666.67 = \sigma_{sales,B};$$

$$\rho_{sales,B} = \dfrac{\sigma_{sales,B}}{\sigma_{sales} \cdot \sigma_B} = \dfrac{7,666}{169,964 \cdot 0.0454} = 0.993.$$

(k) The coefficient of determination is the correlation coefficient squared: $0.993^2 = 0.986.$

5.12. Project A has a higher expected return; however, it is riskier. Therefore, it does not clearly dominate project B. Similarly, B does not dominate A. Therefore, we have insufficient evidence to determine which of the projects is better.

5.13. (a) $\bar{R}_P = 0.062,$
$\bar{R}_L = 0.106,$
$\bar{R}_M = 0.098.$

(b) $\sigma_P^2 = 0.000696$

(remember to convert returns to percentages),

$$\sigma_L^2 = 0.008824,$$

$$\sigma_M^2 = 0.001576.$$

(c) $COV[L,Y] = [(0.04 - 0.062) \cdot (0.19 - 0.106) + (0.07 - 0.062) \cdot (0.04 - 0.106)$

$$+ (0.11 - 0.062) \cdot (-0.04 - 0.106) + (0.04 - 0.062) \cdot (0.21 - 0.106)$$

$$+ (0.05 - 0.062) \cdot (0.13 - 0.106)]/5 = -0.002392,$$

$$\rho_{P,L} = \frac{COV[L,Y]}{\sigma_P \sigma_L} = \frac{-0.002392}{0.0264 \cdot 0.094} = -0.96521.$$

(d) $COV[L,M] = [(0.04 - 0.062) \cdot (0.15 - 0.098) + (0.07 - 0.062) \cdot (0.10 - 0.098)$

$$+ (0.11 - 0.062) \cdot (0.03 - 0.098) + (0.04 - 0.062) \cdot (0.12 - 0.098)$$

$$+ (0.05 - 0.062) \cdot (0.09 - 0.098)] \div 5 = -0.000956,$$

$$\rho_{P,M} = \frac{COV[L,M]}{\sigma_P \sigma_M} = \frac{-0.000956}{0.0264 \cdot 0.039} = -0.912.$$

(e) $COV[M,Y] = [(0.15 - 0.098) \cdot (0.19 - 0.106) + (0.10 - 0.098) \cdot (0.04 - 0.106)$

$$+ (0.03 - 0.098) \cdot (-0.04 - 0.106) + (0.12 - 0.098) \cdot (0.21 - 0.106)$$

$$+ (0.09 - 0.098) \cdot (0.13 - 0.106)] \div 5 = 0.003252,$$

$$\rho_{M,L} = \frac{COV[M,Y]}{\sigma_M \sigma_Y} = \frac{0.003252}{0.039 \cdot 0.094} = 0.872.$$

5.14. Assuming variance and correlation stability, the forecasted values would be the same as the historical values in problem 5.13.

5.15. Standardize returns by standard deviations and consult "z" tables: $(R_i - E[R]) \div \sigma_i = z_i$. Only use positive values for z.

(a) $(0.05 - 0.15) \div 0.10 = z(\text{low}) = -1$, $(0.25 - 0.15) \div 0.10 = z(\text{high}) = 1$.
From the z-table in appendix B, we see that the probability that the security's return will fall between 0.05 and 0.15 is 0.34. 0.34 is also the probability that the security's return will fall between 0.15 and 0.25. Therefore, the probability that the security's return will fall between 0.05 and 0.25 is 0.68.

(b) From part (a), we see that the probability is 0.34.

(c) 0.16.

(d) 0.0668.

5.16. Simply reduce the standard deviations in the z-scores in problem 5.15 to 0.05:

(a) 0.95;

(b) 0.47;

(c) 0.0228;

(d) 0.0013.

5.17. (a) VAR = 0.0025.

(b) 0. The coefficient of correlation between returns on any asset and returns on a riskless asset must be zero. Riskless asset returns do not vary.

Chapter 6

6.1. (a) $\bar{R}_p = (w_M \cdot \bar{R}_M) = (w_H \cdot \bar{R}_H) = (0.25 \cdot 0.20) + (0.75 \cdot 0.06) = 0.09$;

(b) $\sigma_p^2 = w_H^2 \cdot \sigma_H^2 + w_M^2 \cdot \sigma_M^2 + 2 \cdot w_H \cdot w_M \cdot \sigma_H \cdot \sigma_M \cdot \rho_{H,M}$;

$\sigma_p^2 = 0.75^2 \cdot 0.09^2 + 0.25^2 \cdot 0.30^2 + 2 \cdot 0.75 \cdot 0.25 \cdot 0.09 \cdot 0.30 \cdot 0.4 = 0.05068$;

(c) $\sigma_p = \sqrt{0.05068} = 0.2251$,

since the standard deviation is the square root of the variance.

6.2. $\sigma_p = [0.5^2 \cdot 0.09 + 0.5^2 \cdot 0.09 + 2(0.5 \cdot 0.5 \cdot 0)]^{1/2} = [0.0225 + 0.0225]^{1/2} = 0.2121$.

6.3. The following equation will be used for each part of this problem:

$$\sigma_p^2 = w_1^2 \cdot \sigma_1^2 + w_2^2 \cdot \sigma_2^2 + 2(w_1 \cdot w_2 \cdot \sigma_1 \cdot \sigma_2 \cdot \rho_{1,2}).$$

(a) $0.36 = (0.6^2 \cdot 0.6^2) + (0.4^2 \cdot 0.6^2) + 2(0.6 \cdot 0.4 \cdot 0.36)$, $\sigma_p = 0.6$;

(b) $0.2736 = (0.6^2 \cdot 0.6^2) + (0.4^2 \cdot 0.6^2) + 2(0.6 \cdot 0.4 \cdot 0.36)$, $\sigma_p = 0.523$;

(c) $0.1872 = (0.6^2 \cdot 0.6^2) + (0.4^2 \cdot 0.6^2) + 2(0.6 \cdot 0.4)$, $\sigma_p = 0.433$;

(d) $0.1008 = (0.6^2 \cdot 0.6^2) + (0.4^2 \cdot 0.6^2) + 2[0.6 \cdot 0.4 \cdot (-0.18)]$, $\sigma_p = 0.3175$;

(e) $0.0144 = (0.6^2 \cdot 0.6^2) + (0.4^2 \cdot 0.6^2) + 2[0.6 \cdot 0.4 \cdot (-0.36)]$, $\sigma_p = 0.12$.

6.4. (a) $\bar{R}_p = 0.075$, $\sigma_p = 0.16$;

(b) $\bar{R}_p = 0.075$, $\sigma_p = 0.116619$;

(c) $\bar{R}_p = 0.075$, $\sigma_p = 0.04$.

6.5. The correlation coefficients have no effect on the expected return of the portfolio. However, a decrease in the correlation coefficients between security returns will decrease the variance or risk of the portfolio.

6.6. $E[R_p] = 0.33333 \cdot 0.25 + 0.16667 \cdot 0.15 + 0.5 \cdot 0.05 = 0.13333$;

$\sigma_p^2 = w_1^2 \cdot \sigma_1^2 + w_2^2 \cdot \sigma_2^2 + w_3^2 \cdot \sigma_3^2 + 2w_1 \cdot w_2 \cdot \sigma_{1,2} + 2w_1 \cdot w_3 \cdot \sigma_{1,3} + 2w_2 \cdot w_3 \cdot \sigma_{2,3}$;

$0.02444 = 0.33333^2 \cdot 0.40^2 + 0.16667^2 \cdot 0.20^2 + 0.5^2 \cdot 0^2$
$+ 2 \cdot 0.16667 \cdot 0.33333 \cdot 0.05 + 2 \cdot 0.16667 \cdot 0.5 \cdot 0 + 2 \cdot 0.33333 \cdot 0.5 \cdot 0$;

$\sigma_p^2 = 0.02444$, $\sigma_p = 0.15635$.

6.7. $0.08 = w_{risky}^2 \cdot 0.10 + w_{riskless}^2 \cdot 0$, $w_{risky} = 0.8944$;

$E[R_p] = 0.8944 \cdot 0.25 + 0.1056 \cdot 0.10 = 0.2342$.

6.8. (a) Recall that correlation coefficients (and covariances) equal zero:

$\sigma_p^2 = w_1^2 \cdot \sigma_1^2 + w_2^2 \cdot \sigma_2^2 = 0.5^2 \cdot 0.8^2 + 0.5^2 \cdot 0.8^2 = 0.32$, $\sigma_p = 0.565685$.

(b) $\sigma_p^2 = w_1^2 \cdot \sigma_1^2 + w_2^2 \cdot \sigma_2^2 + w_3^2 \cdot \sigma_3^2 + w_4^2 \cdot \sigma_4^2 = 0.25^2 \cdot 0.8^2 + 0.25^2 \cdot 0.8^2$
$+ 0.25^2 \cdot 0.8^2 + 0.25^2 \cdot 0.8^2 = 0.16$, $\sigma_p = 0.4$.

(c) $\sigma_p^2 = 0.125^2 \cdot 0.8^2 + 0.125^2 \cdot 0.8^2 + 0.125^2 \cdot 0.8^2 + 0.125^2 \cdot 0.8^2 + 0.125^2 \cdot 0.8^2$
$+ 0.125^2 \cdot 0.8^2 + 0.125^2 \cdot 0.8^2 + 0.125^2 \cdot 0.8^2 = 0.08$, $\sigma_p = 0.282843$.

(d) $\sigma_p^2 = 0.0625^2 \cdot 0.8^2 + 0.0625^2 \cdot 0.8^2 + 0.0625^2 \cdot 0.8^2 + 0.0625^2 \cdot 0.8^2 + 0.065^2 \cdot$
$0.8^2 + 0.0625^2 \cdot 0.8^2 + 0.0625^2 \cdot 0.8^2 + 0.0625^2 \cdot 0.8^2 + 0.0625^2 \cdot 0.8^2 +$
$0.0625^2 \cdot 0.8^2 + 0.0625^2 \cdot 0.8^2 + 0.0625^2 \cdot 0.8^2 + 0.065^2 \cdot 0.8^2$
$+ 0.0625^2 \cdot 0.8^2 + 0.0625^2 \cdot 0.8^2 + 0.0625^2 \cdot 0.8^2 = 0.04$, $\sigma_p = 0.2$.

(e) They don't differ. Expected portfolio returns are always a weighted average of component security expected returns, which is always 0.10 in this example.

CHAPTER 7

7.1. (a) $\begin{bmatrix} 7 \\ 0 \\ 10 \end{bmatrix}$;

(b) $\begin{bmatrix} 7 & 0 \\ 10 & 2.5 \end{bmatrix}$.

7.2. (a) $[4 \quad 6 \quad 5]$;

(b) $\begin{bmatrix} 4 & 6 \\ 5 & 2 \end{bmatrix}$.

7.3. (a) $\begin{bmatrix} 10 \\ 0 \\ 0 \\ 0 \end{bmatrix} = -\begin{bmatrix} 30 \\ 40 \\ 60 \\ 70 \end{bmatrix} + \begin{bmatrix} 40 \\ 40 \\ 40 \\ 40 \end{bmatrix} + \begin{bmatrix} 0 \\ 0 \\ 20 \\ 30 \end{bmatrix}$,

$\mathbf{P} = -\mathbf{S} + \mathbf{X} + \mathbf{C}$;

(b) $p = -50 + 40e^{-0.1 \cdot 1} + 18 = 4.19$.

7.4. (a) $\begin{bmatrix} 2 & 4 \\ 3 & 4 \end{bmatrix}\begin{bmatrix} -2 & 1 \\ \frac{3}{2} & -\frac{1}{2} \end{bmatrix} = \begin{bmatrix} -4 + \frac{12}{2} & 2 - \frac{4}{2} \\ -6 + \frac{12}{2} & 3 - \frac{4}{2} \end{bmatrix} = \begin{bmatrix} 2 & 0 \\ 0 & 1 \end{bmatrix}$;

(b) $\begin{bmatrix} 1 & 0 \\ 0 & 1 \end{bmatrix}\begin{bmatrix} -2 & 1 \\ \frac{3}{2} & -\frac{1}{2} \end{bmatrix} = \begin{bmatrix} -2 & 1 \\ \frac{3}{2} & -\frac{1}{2} \end{bmatrix}$;

(c) $\begin{bmatrix} 1 & 0 \\ 0 & 1 \end{bmatrix}$;

(d) $[4 \quad 5 \quad 6]\begin{bmatrix} 4 \\ 5 \\ 6 \end{bmatrix} = 77$;

(e) $\begin{bmatrix} 4 \\ 5 \\ 6 \end{bmatrix}[4 \quad 5 \quad 6] = \begin{bmatrix} 16 & 20 & 24 \\ 20 & 25 & 30 \\ 24 & 30 & 36 \end{bmatrix}$.

7.5. (a) The weights matrix is given as follows:

$$\mathbf{W} = \begin{bmatrix} 0.15 & 0.25 & 0.60 \\ 0.40 & 0.30 & 0.30 \\ 0.30 & 0.25 & 0.45 \end{bmatrix}.$$

(b) The returns vector is given as follows:

$$\mathbf{r} = \begin{bmatrix} 0.12 \\ 0.18 \\ 0.24 \end{bmatrix}.$$

(c) The funds' returns are computed as follows:

$$\begin{bmatrix} 0.15 & 0.25 & 0.60 \\ 0.40 & 0.30 & 0.30 \\ 0.30 & 0.25 & 0.45 \end{bmatrix} \begin{bmatrix} 0.12 \\ 0.18 \\ 0.24 \end{bmatrix} = \begin{bmatrix} 0.207 \\ 0.174 \\ 0.189 \end{bmatrix}.$$

(d) $\begin{bmatrix} \frac{1}{3} & \frac{1}{3} & \frac{1}{3} \end{bmatrix} \begin{bmatrix} 0.207 \\ 0.174 \\ 0.189 \end{bmatrix} = 0.19.$

7.6. (a) Form a returns vector as follows:

$$\mathbf{r} = \begin{bmatrix} 0.07 \\ 0.09 \\ 0.13 \end{bmatrix}.$$

(b) The covariance matrix is as follows:

$$\mathbf{V} = \begin{bmatrix} 0.04 & 0.01 & 0.02 \\ 0.01 & 0.16 & 0.08 \\ 0.02 & 0.08 & 0.36 \end{bmatrix}.$$

(c) The weights vector is as follows:

$$\mathbf{w} = \begin{bmatrix} 0.30 \\ 0.50 \\ 0.20 \end{bmatrix}.$$

(d) (a) 3×1; (b) 3×3; (c) 3×1.
(e) The expected portfolio return is given as follows:

$$E[R_p] = \begin{bmatrix} 0.30 & 0.50 & 0.20 \end{bmatrix} \begin{bmatrix} 0.07 \\ 0.09 \\ 0.13 \end{bmatrix} = 0.092,$$

$$E[R_p] = \qquad \mathbf{w}' \qquad \mathbf{r}.$$

(f) The portfolio variance is found as follows:

$$\sigma_p^2 = \begin{bmatrix} 0.30 & 0.50 & 0.20 \end{bmatrix} \begin{bmatrix} 0.04 & 0.01 & 0.02 \\ 0.01 & 0.16 & 0.08 \\ 0.02 & 0.08 & 0.36 \end{bmatrix} \begin{bmatrix} 0.30 \\ 0.50 \\ 0.20 \end{bmatrix},$$

$$\sigma_p^2 = \qquad \mathbf{w}' \qquad\qquad \mathbf{V} \qquad\qquad \mathbf{w};$$

$$\sigma_p^2 = [0.021 \quad 0.099 \quad 0.118] \begin{bmatrix} 0.30 \\ 0.50 \\ 0.20 \end{bmatrix} = 0.0794,$$

$$\sigma_p^2 = \quad \mathbf{w'} \, \mathbf{V} \quad \mathbf{w} = \sigma_p^2.$$

7.7. (a) $1/8 = 0.125$.

(b) The inverse of the identity matrix is the identity matrix:

$$\begin{bmatrix} 1 & 0 \\ 0 & 1 \end{bmatrix}.$$

(c) The inverse of a diagonal matrix is found by inverting each of the principle diagonal elements:

$$\begin{bmatrix} 0.25 & 0 \\ 0 & 2 \end{bmatrix}.$$

(d) First, augment the matrix with the identity matrix:

$$\begin{matrix} \text{row 1} \\ \text{row 2} \end{matrix} \begin{bmatrix} 1 & 2 & | & 1 & 0 \\ 3 & 4 & | & 0 & 1 \end{bmatrix}.$$

Now use the Gauss–Jordan method to transform the original matrix to an identity matrix; the resulting right-hand side will be the inverse of the original matrix:

$$\begin{matrix} 1a \\ 1b \end{matrix} \begin{bmatrix} 1 & 2 & | & 1 & 0 \\ 0 & -0.6 & | & -1 & \frac{1}{3} \end{bmatrix} \begin{matrix} \text{row } 1 \times 1 \\ \text{row } 2 \times \frac{1}{3} - (1a) \end{matrix}$$

$$\begin{matrix} 2a \\ 2b \end{matrix} \begin{bmatrix} 1 & 0 & | & -2 & 1 \\ 0 & 1 & | & 1.5 & -0.5 \end{bmatrix} \begin{matrix} (1a) - 2 \times (2b) \\ (2a) \times 1/(-0.6) \end{matrix}$$

Thus, the inverse matrix is

$$\begin{bmatrix} -2 & 1 \\ 1.5 & -0.5 \end{bmatrix}.$$

(e) Augment the matrix with the identity matrix and perform elementary row operations to obtain the inverse matrix as follows:

$$\begin{bmatrix} 0.02 & 0.04 & | & 1 & 0 \\ 0.06 & 0.08 & | & 0 & 1 \end{bmatrix},$$

$$\begin{bmatrix} 1 & 2 & | & 50 & 0 \\ 0 & \frac{2}{3} & | & 50 & -16\frac{2}{3} \end{bmatrix},$$

$$\begin{bmatrix} 1 & 0 & | & -100 & 50 \\ 0 & 1 & | & 75 & -25 \end{bmatrix}.$$

The inverse matrix is

$$\begin{bmatrix} -100 & 50 \\ 75 & -25 \end{bmatrix}.$$

(f)   The inverse matrix is

$$\begin{bmatrix} 1 & 2 \\ 3 & 4 \end{bmatrix}.$$

(g)   The inverse matrix is

$$\begin{bmatrix} 0.04 & 0.04 \\ 0.04 & 0.16 \end{bmatrix}.$$

(h)   Augment the matrix with the identity matrix and perform elementary row operations to obtain the inverse matrix as follows:

$$\left[\begin{array}{ccc|ccc} 2 & 0 & 0 & 1 & 0 & 0 \\ 2 & 4 & 0 & 0 & 1 & 0 \\ 4 & 8 & 20 & 0 & 0 & 1 \end{array}\right],$$

$$\left[\begin{array}{ccc|ccc} 1 & 0 & 0 & 0.5 & 0 & 0 \\ 0 & 4 & 0 & -1 & 1 & 0 \\ 0 & 8 & 20 & -2 & 0 & 1 \end{array}\right],$$

$$\left[\begin{array}{ccc|ccc} 1 & 0 & 0 & 0.5 & 0 & 0 \\ 0 & 1 & 0 & -0.25 & 0.25 & 0 \\ 0 & 0 & 2 & 0 & -2 & 1 \end{array}\right],$$

$$\left[\begin{array}{ccc|ccc} 1 & 0 & 0 & 0.5 & 0 & 0 \\ 0 & 1 & 0 & -0.25 & 0.25 & 0 \\ 0 & 0 & 1 & 0 & -0.1 & 0.05 \end{array}\right].$$

The inverse matrix is

$$\begin{bmatrix} 0.5 & 0 & 0 \\ -0.25 & 0.25 & 0 \\ 0 & -0.1 & 0.05 \end{bmatrix}.$$

7.8. $$\mathbf{C}^{-1} = \begin{bmatrix} 0.04 & 0.04 \\ 0.04 & 0.16 \end{bmatrix};$$

$$\begin{bmatrix} 0.04 & 0.04 \\ 0.04 & 0.16 \end{bmatrix}\begin{bmatrix} 0.05 \\ 0.10 \end{bmatrix} = \begin{bmatrix} x_1 \\ x_2 \end{bmatrix} = \begin{bmatrix} 0.006 \\ 0.018 \end{bmatrix},$$

$$\mathbf{C}^{-1} \quad \cdot \quad \mathbf{s} \quad = \mathbf{x} = \quad \mathbf{x}.$$

See 7.4(b) above for the inverse matrix.

7.9. Our original system of equations is represented as follows:

$$\begin{bmatrix} 0.08 & 0.08 & 0.1 & 1 \\ 0.08 & 0.32 & 0.2 & 1 \\ 0.1 & 0.2 & 0 & 0 \\ 1 & 1 & 0 & 0 \end{bmatrix} \begin{bmatrix} x_1 \\ x_2 \\ x_3 \\ x_4 \end{bmatrix} = \begin{bmatrix} 0.1 \\ 0.1 \\ 0.1 \\ 0.1 \end{bmatrix},$$

$$\mathbf{C} \qquad \cdot \mathbf{x} = \mathbf{s}.$$

The elements of $\mathbf{C}$ and $\mathbf{s}$ are known; our problem is to find the weights in vector $\mathbf{x}$. Thus we will rearrange the system from $\mathbf{Cx} = \mathbf{s}$ to $\mathbf{C}^{-1}\mathbf{s} = \mathbf{x}$, where $\mathbf{C}^{-1}$ is the inverse of matrix $\mathbf{C}$. So, the time-consuming part of our problem is to find $\mathbf{C}^{-1}$. We will begin by augmenting matrix $\mathbf{C}$ with the identity matrix $\mathbf{I}$:

row 1	0.08	0.08	0.1	1	1	0	0	0	
row 2	0.08	0.32	0.2	1	0	1	0	0	original system
row 3	0.1	0.2	0	0	0	0	1	0	
row 4	1	1	0	0	0	0	0	1	

1a	1	1	1.25	12.5	12.5	0	0	0	(row 1) · 12.5
2a	0	3	1.25	0	−12.5	12.5	0	0	(row 2) · 12.5 − (1a)
3a	0	1	−1.25	−12.5	−12.5	0	10	0	(row 3) · 10 − (1a)
4a	0	0	−1.25	−12.5	−12.5	0	0	1	(row 4) · 1 − (1a)

1b	1	0	0.8$\overline{3}$	12.5	16.$\overline{6}$	−4.1$\overline{6}$	0	0	(1a) − (2b)
2b	0	1	0.41$\overline{6}$	0	−4.1$\overline{6}$	4.1$\overline{6}$	0	0	(2a) · $\frac{1}{3}$
3b	0	0	−1.$\overline{6}$	−12.5	−8.$\overline{3}$	−4.1$\overline{6}$	10	0	(3a) − (2b)
4b	0	0	−1.25	−12.5	−12.5	0	0	1	(4a)

1c	1	0	0	6.25	12.5	−6.25	5	0	(1b) − (3c) · 0.83
2c	0	1	0	−3.125	−6.25	3.125	2.5	0	(2b) − (3c) · 0.416
3c	0	0	1	7.5	5	2.5	−6	0	(3b) − (3c) · −1/1.6
4c	0	0	0	−3.125	−6.25	3.125	−7.5	1	(4b) · (3c) · (−1.25)

1d	1	0	0	0	0	0	−10	2	(1d) − (4a) · 6.2
2d	0	1	0	0	0	0	10	−1	(2c) − (4d) · (−3.125)
3d	0	0	1	0	−10	10	−24	2.4	(3c) − (4d) · 7.5
4d	0	0	0	1	2	−1	2.4	−0.32	(4c) · (−1)/3.125

$$\mathbf{I} \qquad\qquad \mathbf{C}^{-1}$$

$$\begin{bmatrix} 0 & 0 & -10 & 2 \\ 0 & 0 & 10 & -1 \\ -10 & 10 & -24 & 2.4 \\ 2 & -1 & 2.4 & -0.32 \end{bmatrix} \cdot \begin{bmatrix} 0.1 \\ 0.1 \\ 0.1 \\ 0.1 \end{bmatrix} = \begin{bmatrix} x_1 \\ x_2 \\ x_3 \\ x_4 \end{bmatrix} = \begin{bmatrix} -0.8 \\ 0.9 \\ -2.16 \\ 0.308 \end{bmatrix}$$

$$\mathbf{C}^{-1} \qquad \cdot \mathbf{s} = \mathbf{x} = \mathbf{x}.$$

Now it is clear that:

$$x_1 = (0 \cdot 0.1) + (0 \cdot 0.1) + (-10 \cdot 0.1) + (2 \cdot 0.1) = -0.8,$$

$$x_2 = (0 \cdot 0.1) + (0 \cdot 0.1) + (10 \cdot 0.1) + (-1 \cdot 0.1) = 0.9,$$

$$x_3 = (-10 \cdot 0.1) + (10 \cdot 0.1) + (-24 \cdot 0.1) + (2.4 \cdot 0.1) = -2.16,$$

$$x_4 = (2 \cdot 0.1) + (-1 \cdot 0.1) + (2.4 \cdot 0.1) + (-0.32 \cdot 0.1) = 0.308.$$

7.10. Our first problem is to complete a pro-forma income statement for 2001. However, we don't know what the company's interest expenditure in 2001 will be until we know how much money it will borrow (*EFN*). At the same time, we cannot determine how much money the firm needs to borrow until we know its interest expenditure (so that we can solve for retained earnings). Therefore, we must solve simultaneously for *EFN* and interest expenditure. We know that *EFN* can be found as follows:

$$EFN = \Delta Assets - \Delta CL - RE,$$

$$EFN = \$500{,}000 - \$75{,}000 - RE.$$

Retained earnings (*RE*) can be found using the following pro-forma income statement for 2001:

Pro-forma income statement, 2001	
Sales (*TR*)	$1,125,000
Cost of Goods Sold	450,000
Gross Margin	675,000
Fixed Costs	150,000
EBIT	525,000
Interest Payments	$50,000 + (0.10 \cdot EFN)$
Earnings Before Tax	$475,000 - (0.10 \cdot EFN)$
Taxes (@ 40%)	$190,000 - (0.04 \cdot EFN)$
Net Income After Tax	$285,000 - (0.06 \cdot EFN)$
Dividends (@ 33%)	$95,000 - (0.02 \cdot EFN)$
Retained Earnings	$190,000 - (0.04 \cdot EFN)$

$$\begin{bmatrix} 1 & [0.1 \cdot (1-0.4) \cdot (1-0.333)] \\ 1 & 1 \end{bmatrix} \begin{bmatrix} RE \\ EFN \end{bmatrix} = \begin{bmatrix} [(525{,}000 - 50{,}000) \cdot (1-0.4) \cdot (1-0.333)] \\ (500{,}000 - 75{,}000) \end{bmatrix},$$

$$\mathbf{C} \qquad\qquad \cdot \quad \mathbf{x} \quad = \qquad\qquad \mathbf{s};$$

$$\begin{bmatrix} 1 & 0.04 \\ 1 & 1 \end{bmatrix} \begin{bmatrix} RE \\ EFN \end{bmatrix} = \begin{bmatrix} 190{,}000 \\ 425{,}000 \end{bmatrix},$$

$$\mathbf{C} \quad \cdot \quad \mathbf{x} \quad = \quad \mathbf{s};$$

$$\begin{bmatrix} 1.0416667 & -0.0416667 \\ -1.0416667 & 1.0416667 \end{bmatrix} \begin{bmatrix} 190{,}000 \\ 425{,}000 \end{bmatrix} = \begin{bmatrix} 180{,}208.45 \\ 244{,}791.78 \end{bmatrix},$$

$$\mathbf{C} \qquad\qquad \cdot \quad \mathbf{x} \quad = \quad \mathbf{s}.$$

Our *EFN* problem is complete. We now know that the firm must borrow $244,791.78.

7.11. (a) Solve the following system:

$$
\begin{bmatrix}
1{,}100 & 0 & 0 & 0 \\
100 & 1{,}100 & 0 & 0 \\
100 & 100 & 1{,}100 & 0 \\
100 & 100 & 100 & 1{,}100
\end{bmatrix}
\begin{bmatrix} D_1 \\ D_2 \\ D_3 \\ D_4 \end{bmatrix}
=
\begin{bmatrix} 1{,}000 \\ 980 \\ 960 \\ 940 \end{bmatrix},
$$

$$\mathbf{CF} \qquad\qquad \cdot\ \mathbf{d}\ =\ \mathbf{P};$$

$$
\begin{bmatrix}
0.000909 & 0 & 0 & 0 \\
-0.000083 & 0.000909 & 0 & 0 \\
-0.000075 & -0.000083 & 0.000909 & 0 \\
-0.000068 & -0.000075 & -0.000083 & 0.000909
\end{bmatrix}
\begin{bmatrix} 1{,}000 \\ 980 \\ 960 \\ 940 \end{bmatrix}
=
\begin{bmatrix} D_1 \\ D_2 \\ D_3 \\ D_4 \end{bmatrix},
$$

$$\mathbf{CF}^{-1} \qquad\qquad\qquad = \ \mathbf{P}\ =\ \mathbf{d}.$$

Solve first for $D_1 = 0.90909$, then $D_2 = 0.80826$, then $D_3 = 0.71660$, and finally $D_4 = 0.63328$. Then, $y_{0,1} = 0.10$, $y_{0,2} = 0.1123$, $y_{0,3} = 0.1175$, and $y_{0,4} = 0.1210$.

(b) $y_{1,3} = [(1 + y_{0,3})^3 \div (1 + y_{0,1})]^{0.5} - 1 = [(1.1175)^3 \div (1.1)]^{0.5} - 1 = 0.1264.$

7.12. (a) First, solve the following system for the discount functions $\mathbf{d}$:

$$
\begin{bmatrix}
50 & 50 & 1{,}050 \\
80 & 80 & 1{,}080 \\
110 & 1{,}110 & 0
\end{bmatrix}
\begin{bmatrix} D_1 \\ D_2 \\ D_3 \end{bmatrix}
=
\begin{bmatrix} 878.9172 \\ 955.4787 \\ 1{,}055.4190 \end{bmatrix},
$$

$$\mathbf{CF} \qquad\qquad \cdot\ \mathbf{d}\ =\ \mathbf{P}_0.$$

We find that $D_1 = 0.943396$, $D_2 = 0.857338$, and $D_3 = 0.751314$. The spot rates are obtained as follows:

$$\frac{1}{D_1} - 1 = \frac{1}{0.943396} - 1 = 0.06,$$

$$\frac{1}{D_2^{1/2}} - 1 = \frac{1}{0.857338^{1/2}} - 1 = 0.08,$$

$$\frac{1}{D_3^{1/3}} - 1 = \frac{1}{0.751314^{1/3}} - 1 = 0.10.$$

(b) The weights are found by solving for $\mathbf{w}$ as follows:

$$
\begin{bmatrix}
50 & 80 & 110 \\
50 & 80 & 1{,}110 \\
1{,}050 & 1{,}080 & 0
\end{bmatrix}
\begin{bmatrix} w_X \\ w_Y \\ w_Z \end{bmatrix}
=
\begin{bmatrix} 150 \\ 150 \\ 1{,}150 \end{bmatrix},
$$

$$\mathbf{CF} \qquad\qquad \cdot\ \mathbf{w}\ =\ \mathbf{P}_0;$$

$$
\begin{bmatrix}
-0.03996 & 0.00396 & 0.002666 \\
0.03885 & -0.00385 & -0.001667 \\
-0.00100 & 0.00100 & 0
\end{bmatrix}
\begin{bmatrix} 150 \\ 150 \\ 1{,}150 \end{bmatrix}
=
\begin{bmatrix} w_X \\ w_Y \\ w_Z \end{bmatrix},
$$

$$\mathbf{CF}^{-1} \qquad\qquad \cdot\ \mathbf{P}_0\ =\ \mathbf{w}.$$

We find that $w_X = -2.3341$, $w_Y = 3.33295$, and that $w_Z = 0$. This means that bond Q is replicated by a portfolio with a short position in 2.3341 bonds X and a long position in 3.33295 bonds Y.

7.13. The following system may be solved for **b** to determine exactly how many of each of the bonds are required to satisfy the fund's cash flow requirements:

$$\begin{bmatrix} 1,100 & 100 & 110 & 120 \\ 0 & 1,100 & 110 & 120 \\ 0 & 0 & 1,110 & 120 \\ 0 & 0 & 0 & 1,120 \end{bmatrix} \begin{bmatrix} b_1 \\ b_2 \\ b_3 \\ b_4 \end{bmatrix} = \begin{bmatrix} 80,000,000 \\ 100,000,000 \\ 120,000,000 \\ 140,000,000 \end{bmatrix},$$

$$\text{CF} \qquad\qquad \cdot \; \mathbf{b} \; = \; \mathbf{P}_0.$$

First, we invert matrix **CF** to obtain $\mathbf{CF}^{-1}$:

$$\begin{bmatrix} 0.000909 & -0.000083 & -0.00008 & -0.000079 \\ 0 & 0.000909 & -0.00009 & -0.000087 \\ 0 & 0 & 0.00090 & -0.000096 \\ 0 & 0 & 0 & 0.000892 \end{bmatrix},$$

$$\mathbf{CF}^{-1}.$$

Thus, by inverting matrix **CF** to obtain $\mathbf{CF}^{-1}$, and premultiplying vector $\mathbf{P}_0$ by $\mathbf{CF}^{-1}$ to obtain solutions vector **b**, we find that the purchase of 43,466.6 bonds 67,813.3 bonds 94,594.6 bonds 3, and 125,000 bonds 4 satisfy the fund's exact matching requirements.

7.14. (a) $120D_1 + 1,120D_2 = 957.9920$, $D_1 = 0.925925$,
       $50D_1 + 1,050D_2 = 840.2471$, $D_2 = 0.756143$,
       $y_{0.1} = 1/D_1 - 1 = 0.08$;

    (b) $y_{0.2} = (1/D_2)^{0.5} - 1 = 0.15$;

    (c) $1,000 \div (1 + y_{0.2})^2 = 756.1437$;

    (d) $120w_A + 50w_B = 0$, $w_A = -0.714285$,
       $1,120w_A + 1,050w_B = 1,000$, $w_B = 1.714285$;

    (e) $15,000 = 120\#A + 50\#B$,
       $12,000 = 1,120\#A + 1,050\#B$,
       $\#A = 216.42857$; $\#B = -219.42857$.

Thus, sell 219.42857 B bonds for $184,374.22 and pay $207,336.83 for 216.42857 A bonds.

7.15. Since the riskless return rate is 0.125, the current value of a security guaranteed to pay $1 in one year would be $1/1.125 = 0.8888889$. The security payoff vectors are as follows:

$$\mathbf{bu} = \begin{bmatrix} 20 \\ 32 \end{bmatrix}, \qquad \mathbf{b} = \begin{bmatrix} 1 \\ 1 \end{bmatrix}, \qquad \mathbf{c} = \begin{bmatrix} 4 \\ 16 \end{bmatrix}.$$

Portfolio holdings are determined as follows:

$$\begin{bmatrix} 20 & 1 \\ 32 & 1 \end{bmatrix}\begin{bmatrix} \#bu \\ \#b \end{bmatrix} = \begin{bmatrix} 4 \\ 16 \end{bmatrix}.$$

The following includes the inverse matrix:

$$\begin{bmatrix} -0.0833333 & 0.083333 \\ 2.666667 & -1.666667 \end{bmatrix}\begin{bmatrix} 4 \\ 16 \end{bmatrix} = \begin{bmatrix} 1 \\ -16 \end{bmatrix}.$$

We find that $\#bu = 1$ and $\#b = -16$. This implies that the payoff structure of a single call can be replicated with a portfolio comprising 1 share of stock for a total of $24 and short-selling 16 T-bills for a total of $14.2222222. This portfolio requires a net investment of $9.7777778. Since the call has the same payoff structure as this portfolio, its current value must be $9.7777778.

7.16.   (a)   First, we define the following payoff vectors:

$$\begin{bmatrix} 15 \\ 25 \end{bmatrix} \qquad \begin{bmatrix} 0 \\ 7 \end{bmatrix},$$

Stock   Call: $X = 18$.

We have a set of two payoff vectors in a two-outcome economy. The set is linearly independent. Hence, this set forms the basis for the two-outcome space. Since we have market prices for these two securities, we can price all other securities in this economy. First, we solve for the value of the $22-exercise price call as follows:

$$\begin{bmatrix} 15 & 0 \\ 25 & 7 \end{bmatrix}^{-1}\begin{bmatrix} 0 \\ 3 \end{bmatrix} = \begin{bmatrix} \#S \\ \#C_{X=18} \end{bmatrix},$$

$$\begin{bmatrix} 0.066667 & 0 \\ -0.238095 & 0.142857 \end{bmatrix}\begin{bmatrix} 0 \\ 3 \end{bmatrix} = \begin{bmatrix} 0 \\ 0.42857 \end{bmatrix}.$$

Thus, the call with an exercise price equal to $22 can be replicated with 0.42857 calls with an exercise price equal to $18.

(b)   The riskless return rate is determined as follows:

$$\begin{bmatrix} 0.066667 & 0 \\ -0.238095 & 0.142857 \end{bmatrix}\begin{bmatrix} 1 \\ 1 \end{bmatrix} = \begin{bmatrix} 0.066667 \\ -0.095238 \end{bmatrix}.$$

Since the riskless asset is replicated with 0.066667 shares of stock and short positions in 0.095238 calls, the value of the riskless asset is 0.666674, implying a riskless return rate equal to $1/0.666674 = 0.50$.

(c)   Solve for the value of the put as follows:

$$\begin{bmatrix} 0.066667 & 0 \\ -0.238095 & 0.142857 \end{bmatrix}\begin{bmatrix} 25 \\ 15 \end{bmatrix} = \begin{bmatrix} 1.666667 \\ -3.90952 \end{bmatrix},$$

implying that its value is $1.6666667 \cdot \$20 - 3.90952 \cdot 7 = 5.9667$. Note that this put value is lower than either of the two potential cash flows that it may generate. This is due to the particularly high riskless return rate.

Chapter 8

8.1.   Solve as follows:

$$y' = \frac{7x^2 + 2 \cdot 7x \cdot h + 7h^2 - 7x^2}{h}$$

$$= \lim_{h \to 0} \frac{14x \cdot h + 7h^2}{h} = \lim_{h \to 0} [14x + 7h] = 14x.$$

8.2.   The derivatives are found by using the power rule (polynomial rule) as follows:

(a) $dy/dx = 5 \cdot 0 \cdot x^{0-1} = 0$;
(b) $dy/dx = 3 \cdot 7 \cdot x^{3-1} = 21x^2$;
(c) $dy/dx = 4 \cdot 2 \cdot x^{4-1} + 3 \cdot 5 \cdot x^{3-1} = 8x^3 + 15x^2$;
(d) $dy/dx = 0.5 \cdot 10 \cdot x^{0.5-1} - 3 \cdot 11 \cdot x^{3-1} = 5x^4 - 33x^2$;
(e) $dy/dx = (1/5) \cdot 5 \cdot x^{1/5-1} = (5/5)x^{-4/5} = \sqrt[5]{x^4}$;
(f) $dy/dx = -2 \cdot 2 \cdot x^{-2-1} + 1/2 \cdot 2/3 \cdot x^{1/2-1} + 1/5 \cdot 3 \cdot x^{-1/5-1} - 1 \cdot 1 \cdot x^{-1-1}$;
    $= -4x + (1/3)x^{-1/2} + 0.6x^{-0.8} - 1 = -4x + (1/3)/\sqrt{x} + 0.6/x^{0.8} - 1.$

8.3.   Second derivatives are found as follows:

(a) $dy/dx = 0$;
(b) $dy/dx = 42x$;
(c) $dy/dx = 24x^2 + 30x$;
(d) $dy/dx = 20x^3 - 66x$;
(e) $dy/dx = -0.8x^{-1.8}$;
(f) $dy/dx = -4 - (1/6)/\sqrt{x^3} - 0.48/x^{-1.8}$.

8.4.   Find first derivatives, set them equal to zero, and solve for x. Then check second derivatives to ensure that they are negative:

(a) $dy/dx = 30x$; $d^2y/dx^2 = 30$; there is no finite maximum.
(b) $dy/dx = 6$; $d^2y/dx^2 = 0$; there is no finite maximum.
(c) $dy/dx = -6x + 6$; $d^2y/dx^2 = -6$; $x_{\min} = 1$.
(d) $dy/dx = 3x^2 + 6x + 2 = 0$; $d^2y/dx^2 = 6x + 6$; $x_{\max} = -3.803848$, $x_{\max} = -14.19615$.
(e) $dy/dx = 36x^2$; $d^2y/dx^2 = 72x$; there is no finite maximum; the first derivative is zero when $x = 0$, but when $x = 0$, d^2y/dx^2 is not negative.
(f) $dy/dx = 2x + 10 = 0$; $d^2y/dx^2 = 2$; the minimum occurs when $x = -5$.

8.5.   Find first derivatives, set them equal to zero, and solve for x. Then check second derivatives to ensure that they are positive:

(a) $dy/dx = 30x$; $d^2y/dx^2 = 30$; $x_{\min} = 0$.
(b) $dy/dx = 20$; $d^2y/dx^2 = 0$; there is no finite minimum.
(c) $dy/dx = 6x + 6$; $d^2y/dx^2 = 6$; $x_{\min} = -1$.
(d) $dy/dx = 6x^2 - 12x + 1$; $d^2y/dx^2 = 6x - 12$; using the quadratic formula, we find that $x = 3.1366$ and 68.86335. The second derivative is positive in both cases. This function has two minima.
(e) $dy/dx = 36x^2$; $d^2y/dx^2 = 72x$; there is no finite minimum; the first derivative is zero when $x = 0$, but when $x = 0$, d^2y/dx^2 is not positive.
(f) $dy/dx = 2x + 10 = 0$; $d^2y/dx^2 = 2$; the minimum occurs when $x = -5$.

8.6. (a) (i) First, find the yield to maturity (*ytm*) of the bond:

$$0 = NPV = \sum_{t=1}^{n} \frac{CF_t}{(1 + ytm)^t} - P_0, \qquad \text{yield to maturity} = ytm;$$

$$0 = NPV = \frac{1,000}{(1 + ytm)^1} - 900, \qquad \text{solve for } ytm;$$

$$ytm = 0.111.$$

(ii) Use *ytm* from part (i) in the duration formula:

$$Dur = \frac{\sum_{t=1}^{n} t \cdot \frac{CF_t}{(1 + ytm)^t}}{P_0}$$

(note that negative signs are omitted);

$$Dur = \frac{1 \cdot \frac{1,000}{1.111}}{900} = Dur = 1 \text{ year.}$$

(b) (i)
$$0 = NPV = \sum_{t=1}^{n} t \frac{CF_t}{(1 + ytm)^t} - P_0 = \frac{1,000}{(1 + ytm)^t} - 800;$$

$$ytm = 0.118.$$

(ii)
$$Dur = \frac{\sum_{t=1}^{n} t \cdot \frac{CF_t}{(1 + ytm)^t}}{P_0} = \frac{2 \cdot \frac{1,000}{1.118^2}}{800} = 2.$$

(c) *ytm* = 0.126:

$$Dur = \frac{3 \cdot \frac{2,000}{(1.126)^3}}{1.400} = 3.$$

(d) There are several ways to work this problem. First, consider the cash flows of the portfolio:

$$P_0 = 900 + 800 + 1,400 = 3,100;$$

$$CF_1 = 1,000, \qquad CF_2 = 1,000, \qquad CF_3 = 2,000;$$

$$0 = NPV = \frac{1,000}{(1 + ytm)^1} + \frac{1,000}{(1 + ytm)^2} + \frac{2,000}{(1 + ytm)^3} - 3,100, \qquad ytm = 0.122;$$

$$Dur = \frac{\sum_{t=1}^{n} t \cdot \frac{CF_t}{(1 + ytm)^t}}{P_0} = \frac{\frac{1 \cdot 1,000}{1.122} + \frac{2 \cdot 1,000}{(1.122)^2} + \frac{3 \cdot 2,000}{(1.122)^3}}{3,100}; \qquad Dur = 2.161 \text{ years.}$$

Second, notice that the portfolio duration is a weighted average of the bond durations: $(900/3,100) \cdot 1 + (800/3,100) \cdot 2 + (1,400/3,100) \cdot 3 = 2.161$.

(e) An equal dollar sum is invested into each portfolio. Thus, this portfolio's duration is simply an average of the three bonds' durations. The portfolio duration equals 2.

8.7. (a) (i) First find the bond's *ytm*:

$$0 = NPV = \frac{70}{(1 + ytm)^1} + \frac{70}{(1 + ytm)^2} + \frac{70 + 1,000}{(1 + ytm)^3} - 950, \qquad ytm = 0.0897.$$

(ii)   Now, use *ytm* to find Duration:

$$Dur = \frac{\frac{1 \cdot 70}{1.0897} + \frac{2 \cdot 70}{(1.0897)^2} + \frac{3 \cdot 1070}{(1.0897)^3}}{950} = 2.8027.$$

(b)
$$0 = NPV = \frac{120}{(1+ytm)^1} + \frac{120}{(1+ytm)^2} + \frac{1,120}{(1+ytm)^3} - 1,040,$$

$$ytm = 0.1038;$$

$$Dur = \frac{\frac{1 \cdot 120}{1.1038} + \frac{2 \cdot 120}{(1.1038)^2} + \frac{3 \cdot 1120}{(1.1038)^3}}{900} = 2.696.$$

(c)
$$0 = NPV = \frac{100}{(1+ytm)^1} + \frac{100}{(1+ytm)^2} + \frac{100}{(1+ytm)^3} + \frac{1,100}{(1+ytm)^4} - 900,$$

$$ytm = 0.134;$$

$$Dur = \frac{\frac{1 \cdot 100}{1.134} + \frac{2 \cdot 100}{(1.134)^2} + \frac{3 \cdot 100}{(1.134)^3} + \frac{4 \cdot 1,100}{(1.134)^4}}{900} = 3.456.$$

(d)
$$0 = NPV = \frac{100}{(1+ytm)^1} + \frac{100}{(1+ytm)^2} + \frac{1,100}{(1+ytm)^3} - 800,$$

$$ytm = 0.194;$$

$$Dur = \frac{\frac{1 \cdot 100}{1.194} + \frac{2 \cdot 100}{(1.194)^2} + \frac{3 \cdot 1,100}{(1.194)^3}}{800} = 2.703.$$

8.8.   (a) $P_1 = P_0 + Dur \cdot \Delta(1+r)/(1+r) \cdot P_0$, $P_1 = 950 - 2.8027 \cdot 0.01/1.0897 \cdot 950 = 925.57$;
(b) $P_1 = 1,040 - 2.696 \cdot 0.01/1.1038 \cdot 1,040 = 1,014.60$;
(c) $P_1 = 900 - 3.457 \cdot 0.01/1.1339 \cdot 900 = 872.56$;
(d) $P_1 = 800 - 2.703 \cdot 0.01/1.194 \cdot 800 = 781.89$.

8.9. $Dur = 2.8027 \cdot \frac{950}{3,690} + 2.696 \cdot \frac{1,040}{3,690} + 3.456 \cdot \frac{900}{3,690} + 2.703 \cdot \frac{800}{3,690} = 2.910.$

8.10.   Partial derivatives are found as follows:

(i)   (a) $\partial y/\partial x = 5$;   (d) $\partial y/\partial x = 15x^2 + 7z$;
(b) $\partial y/\partial x = 5x$;   (e) $\partial y/\partial x = 36x^2z^5 + 3z^2$;
(c) $\partial y/\partial x = 14x^6$;   (f) $\partial y/\partial x = \sum_{i=1}^n nix^{i-1}z^2$.
(ii) (a) $\partial y/\partial z = 0$;   (d) $\partial y/\partial z = 20z + 7x$;
(b) $\partial y/\partial z = 10$;   (e) $\partial y/\partial z = 60x^3z^4 + 6xz$;
(c) $\partial y/\partial z = 0$;   (f) $\partial y/\partial z = 2z\sum_{i=1}^n nx^i$.

8.11.   Derivatives are found as follows:

(a) $dy/dx = 12(4x+2)^2$;
(b) $dy/dx = 3x/\sqrt{(3x^2+8)}$;
(c) $dy/dx = 6x(12x^2+10x) + 6(4x^3+5x^2+3) = 96x^3 + 90x^2 + 18$;

(d) $dy/dx = 4.5(1.5x - 4)(2.5x - 3.5)^3 + 10(1.5x - 4)(2.5x - 3.5)^3$;

(e) $dy/dx = -50/x^3$;

(f) $dy/dx = (60x - 84) - (60x - 160)/(10x - 14)^2 = 76/(10x - 14)^2$.

8.12. First, we solve the following linear system for $z(1)$ and $z(2)$:

$$0.25z(1) + 0.05z(2) = 0.15 - 0.05;$$

$$0.05z(1) + 0.16z(2) = 0.08 - 0.05.$$

$$z(1) = 0.38666667, \qquad z(2) = 0.06666667.$$

(a) Thus, $w(1) = 0.852941$ and $w(2) = 0.147049$;

(b) $E[R(m)] = 0.139706$, $\sigma_m^2 = 0.197881$, $\sigma_m = 0.444838$.

8.13. First, we solve the following linear system for $z(1)$ and $z(2)$:

$$0.25z(1) + 0.05z(2) + 0.04z(3) = 0.15 - 0.05;$$

$$0.05z(1) + 0.16z(2) + 0.03z(3) = 0.08 - 0.05;$$

$$0.04z(1) + 0.03z(2) + 0.09z(3) = 0.06 - 0.05.$$

We multiply the following to solve for z-values:

$$\begin{bmatrix} 4.479098 & -1.09489 & -1.62575 \\ -1.09489 & 6.934307 & -1.82482 \\ -1.62575 & -1.82482 & 12.44194 \end{bmatrix} \begin{bmatrix} 0.10 \\ 0.03 \\ 0.01 \end{bmatrix} = \begin{bmatrix} z_1 \\ z_2 \\ z_3 \end{bmatrix}.$$

$$z(1) = 0.398806, \qquad z(2) = 0.080292, \qquad z(3) = -0.0929.$$

(a) Thus, $w(1) = 1.032646$, $w(2) = 0.207904$, and $w(3) = -0.24055$;

(b) $E[R(m)] = 0.157096$, $\sigma_m^2 = 0.277309$, $\sigma_m = 0.526602$.

8.14. This problem is complicated by having different borrowing and lending rates. This essentially means that there will be two "Capital Market Lines," one for lending and one for borrowing. Notice that the investor's 18% required return exceeds the return of any of the three securities. This means that the the investor will probably need to leverage up her portfolio by borrowing in order to meet her requirement for expected return. Risky asset portfolio characteristics are found from the following:

$$0.02 = 0.09z_1 + 0z_2,$$

$$z_1 = 0.2222;$$

$$0.06 = 0z_1 + 0.36z_2, \qquad z_2 = 0.1667,$$

$$w_1 = 0.571, \qquad w_2 = 0.429;$$

$$E[R_m] = 0.097, \qquad w_f = (1 - w_m),$$

$$E[R_p] = 0.18 = (1 - w_m) \cdot 0.06 + w_m \cdot 0.097.$$

Now, the allocations of funds to the stock portfolio and to the bonds are made:

$$0.18 = 0.06 + w_m \cdot 0.037,$$

$$w_m = 3.243, \qquad 1 - w_m = w_f = -2.243.$$

Borrow $1,121,500.

Invest $1,621,500 in the market: $925,876.5 in security 1 and $695,623.5 in security 2.

8.15. (a) $dy/dx = 0.05e^{0.05x}$;
(b) $dy/dx = e^x(x - 1)/x^2$;
(c) $dy/dx = 5/x$;
(d) $dy/dx = e^x(1/x + \ln(x))$ (using the product rule).

8.16. Durations and convexities are as follows:

(a) $ytm = 0.052612$
$Dur = [57.00064 + 108.3024 + 2,726.544]/1,020 = -2.8351446$;
$Con = [102.8885 + 293.2354 + 9,843.047/1,020 = 10.0384$;
(b) $ytm = 0.0610701$;
$Dur = [84.82003 + 159.8764 + 226.012 + 3,439.618]/1,100 = -3.554842$;
$Con = [150.6747 + 426.0077 + 802.9775 + 15,275.38]/1,100 = 15.1409455$.

8.17. (a) $P_{1A} = 944.78$, $P_{1B} = 1,030.24$;
(b) $P_{1A} = 948.62$, $P_{1B} = 1,033.22$;
(c) $P_{1A} = 948.56$, $P_{1B} = 1,033.12$.

The new bond values given in 8.17(c) are precise (subject to rounding). Note how much better the bond convexity model in 8.17(b) estimates revised bond prices than the duration model in 8.17(a). The duration model will tend to underestimate bond prices; the convexity model will tend to overestimate bond prices. However, the convexity model is normally closer to the true value.

8.18. First, set up the Lagrange function:

$$L = 50x^2 - 10x + \lambda(100 - 0.1x).$$

Next, find the first order conditions:

$$\partial y/\partial x = 100x - 0.1\lambda = 10;$$

$$\partial y/\partial \lambda = -0.1x \qquad = -100.$$

We find that $x = 1,000$ and $\lambda = 999,900$.

8.19. First set up the Lagrange function:

$$L = (25 + 3x + 10x^2) + \lambda(100 - 5x).$$

Next, find the first order conditions:

$$\frac{\partial L}{\partial x} = 3 + 20x - 5\lambda = 0, \qquad 20x - 5\lambda = -3;$$

$$\frac{\partial L}{\partial z} = 100 - 5x = 0, \qquad -5x - 0\lambda = -100.$$

(3) Next, solve the above system of equations for x and λ:

$$\begin{bmatrix} 20 & -5 \\ -5 & 0 \end{bmatrix} \cdot \begin{bmatrix} x \\ \lambda \end{bmatrix} = \begin{bmatrix} -3 \\ -100 \end{bmatrix},$$

$$\mathbf{C} \qquad \cdot \mathbf{x} = \mathbf{S};$$

$$x = 20, \qquad \lambda = 80\tfrac{3}{5}.$$

8.20. (a) (i) Our problem is defined as:

$$min: \sigma_p^2 = 0.04w_A^2 + 0.16w_B^2 + 0.08w_Aw_B \quad \text{(objective function)}$$

$$s.t.: 0.15 = 0.1w_A + 0.2w_B \quad \text{(constraint 1)},$$

$$1 = 1w_A + 1w_B \quad \text{(constraint 2)}.$$

First, set up the Lagrange function:

$$L = (0.04w_A^2 + 0.16w_B^2 + 0.08w_Aw_B) - \lambda_1(0.15 - 0.1w_A - 0.2w_B) - \lambda_2(1 - 1w_A - 1w_B).$$

Find first order conditions:

$$\partial L/\partial w_A = 0.08w_A + 0.08w_B + 0.1\lambda_1 + 1\lambda_2 = 0;$$

$$\partial L/\partial w_B = 0.32w_B + 0.08w_A + 0.2\lambda_1 + 1\lambda_2 = 0;$$

$$\partial L/\partial \lambda_1 = 0.15 - 0.1w_A - 0.2w_B = 0;$$

$$\partial L/\partial \lambda_2 = 1 - 1w_A - 1w_B = 0.$$

Now, we have four equations with four unknowns, which can be arranged as follows:

$$0.08w_A + 0.08w_B + 0.1\lambda_1 + 1\lambda_2 = 0;$$

$$0.08w_A + 0.32w_B + 0.2\lambda_1 + 1\lambda_2 = 0;$$

$$0.1w_A + 0.2w_B + 0\lambda_1 + 0\lambda_2 = 0.15;$$

$$1w_A + 1w_B + 0\lambda_1 + 0\lambda_2 = 1.$$

We structure matrices to solve this system as follows:

$$\begin{bmatrix} 0.08 & 0.08 & 0.1 & 1 \\ 0.08 & 0.32 & 0.2 & 1 \\ 0.1 & 0.2 & 0 & 0 \\ 1 & 1 & 0 & 0 \end{bmatrix} \begin{bmatrix} w_A \\ w_B \\ \lambda_1 \\ \lambda_2 \end{bmatrix} = \begin{bmatrix} 0 \\ 0 \\ 0.15 \\ 1 \end{bmatrix},$$

$$\mathbf{C} \qquad \cdot \mathbf{x} = \mathbf{S}.$$

Step-by-step, we invert the coefficients matrix (augmented by the identity matrix) as follows:

row 1	0.08	0.08	0.1	1	1	0	0	0	
row 2	0.08	0.32	0.2	1	0	1	0	0	original system
row 3	0.1	0.2	0	0	0	0	1	0	
row 4	1	1	0	0	0	0	0	1	

1a	1	1	1.25	12.5	12.5	0	0	0	(row 1) · 12.5
2a	0	3	1.25	0	−12.5	12.5	0	0	(row 2) · 12.5 − (1a)
3a	0	1	−1.25	−12.5	−12.5	0	10	0	(row 3) · 10 − (1a)
4a	0	0	−1.25	−12.5	−12.5	0	0	1	(row 4) · 1 − (1a)

$$
\begin{array}{l}
\text{1b} \\
\text{2b} \\
\text{3b} \\
\text{4b}
\end{array}
\left[
\begin{array}{cccc|cccc}
1 & 0 & 0.8\overline{3} & 12.5 & 16.\overline{6} & -4.1\overline{6} & 0 & 0 \\
0 & 1 & 0.41\overline{6} & 0 & -4.1\overline{6} & 4.16 & 0 & 0 \\
0 & 0 & -1.\overline{6} & -12.5 & -8.\overline{3} & -4.1\overline{6} & 10 & 0 \\
0 & 0 & -1.25 & -12.5 & -12.5 & 0 & 0 & 1
\end{array}
\right]
\begin{array}{l}
(1a)-(2b) \\
(2a)\cdot 1/3 \\
(3a)-(2b) \\
(4a)
\end{array}
$$

$$
\begin{array}{l}
\text{1c} \\
\text{2c} \\
\text{3c} \\
\text{4c}
\end{array}
\left[
\begin{array}{cccc|cccc}
1 & 0 & 0 & 6.25 & 12.5 & -6.25 & 5 & 0 \\
0 & 1 & 0 & -3.125 & -6.25 & 3.125 & 2.5 & 0 \\
0 & 0 & 1 & 7.5 & 5 & 2.5 & -6 & 0 \\
0 & 0 & 0 & -3.125 & -6.25 & 3.125 & -7.5 & 1
\end{array}
\right]
\begin{array}{l}
(1b)-(3c)\cdot 0.83 \\
(2b)-(3c)\cdot 0.416 \\
(3b)\cdot[-1/(1.6)] \\
(4b)-(3c)\cdot(-1.25)
\end{array}
$$

$$
\begin{array}{l}
\text{1d} \\
\text{2d} \\
\text{3d} \\
\text{4d}
\end{array}
\left[
\begin{array}{cccc|cccc}
1 & 0 & 0 & 0 & 0 & 0 & -10 & 2 \\
0 & 1 & 0 & 0 & 0 & 0 & 10 & -1 \\
0 & 0 & 1 & 0 & -10 & 10 & -24 & 2.4 \\
0 & 0 & 0 & 1 & 2 & -1 & 2.4 & -0.32
\end{array}
\right]
\begin{array}{l}
(1c)-(4d)\cdot 6.2 \\
(2c)-(4d)\cdot -3.125 \\
(3c)-(4d)\cdot 7.5 \\
(4b)\cdot[-1/(3.125)]
\end{array}
$$

$$
\qquad\qquad \mathbf{I} \qquad\qquad\qquad \mathbf{C}^{-1}
$$

$$
\begin{bmatrix}
0 & 0 & -10 & 2 \\
0 & 0 & 10 & -1 \\
-10 & 10 & -24 & 2.4 \\
2 & -1 & 2.4 & -0.32
\end{bmatrix}
\begin{bmatrix}
0 \\ 0 \\ 0.15 \\ 1
\end{bmatrix}
=
\begin{bmatrix}
w_A \\ w_B \\ \lambda_1 \\ \lambda_2
\end{bmatrix}.
$$

$$
\qquad \mathbf{C}^{-1} \qquad\qquad \cdot \quad \mathbf{s} \ = \ \mathbf{x}
$$

We multiply to find the following:

$$
w_A = (0\cdot 0)+(0\cdot 0)+(-10\cdot 0.15)+(2\cdot 1)=0.5;
$$

$$
w_B = (0\cdot 0)+(0\cdot 0)+(10\cdot 0.15)+(-1\cdot 1)=0.5;
$$

$$
\lambda_1 = (-10\cdot 0)+(10\cdot 0)+(-24\cdot 0.15)+(2.4\cdot 1)=-1.2;
$$

$$
\lambda_2 = (2\cdot 0)+(-1\cdot 0)+(2.4\cdot 0.15)+(-0.32\cdot 1)=0.04.
$$

Notice that since only two securities will be included in the portfolio, we can infer immediately from the expected return constraint that w_A must equal w_B, which must equal 0.5. This simple algorithm will not work when the number of securities in the portfolio exceeds 2.

(ii)
$$
min:\ \sigma_p^2 = 0.04w_A^2 + 0.16w_B^2 + 0.08w_Aw_B
$$

$$
s.t.:\ 0.12 = 0.1w_A + 0.2w_B,
$$

$$
1 = 1w_A + 1w_B.
$$

$$
L = 0.04w_A^2 + 16w_B^2 + 0.08w_Aw_B - \lambda_1(0.12 - 0.1w_A - 0.2w_B) \\
- \lambda_2(1 - 1w_A - 1w_B).
$$

First order conditions are:

$$
\partial L/\partial w_A = 0.08w_A + 0.08w_B + 0.1\lambda_1 + 1\lambda_2 = 0;
$$

$$
\partial L/\partial w_B = 0.08w_A + 0.32w_B + 0.2\lambda_1 + 1\lambda_2 = 0;
$$

$$\partial L/\partial \lambda_1 = 0.1 w_A + 0.2 w_B + 0\lambda_1 + 0\lambda_2 = 0.12;$$

$$\partial L/\partial \lambda_2 = 1 w_A + 1 w_B + 0\lambda_1 + 0\lambda_2 = 1.$$

Thus, our system is:

$$
\begin{bmatrix}
0.08 & 0.08 & 0.1 & 1 \\
0.08 & 0.32 & 0.2 & 1 \\
0.1 & 0.2 & 0 & 0 \\
1 & 1 & 0 & 0
\end{bmatrix}
\begin{bmatrix}
w_A \\
w_B \\
\lambda_1 \\
\lambda_2
\end{bmatrix}
=
\begin{bmatrix}
0 \\
0 \\
0.12 \\
1
\end{bmatrix}.
$$

$$\mathbf{C} \qquad \cdot \mathbf{x} = \mathbf{S}$$

Notice that the coefficients matrix (**C**) is identical to that in 21.a.i above. Thus, its inverse is identical to $\mathbf{C}^{-1}$ in part 8.19(a,i). Notice also that only element three in the solutions vector has changed. Thus, we determine our weights as follows:

$$
\begin{bmatrix}
0 & 0 & -10 & 2 \\
0 & 0 & 10 & -1 \\
-10 & 10 & -24 & 2.4 \\
2 & -1 & 2.4 & -0.32
\end{bmatrix}
\begin{bmatrix}
0 \\
0 \\
0.12 \\
1
\end{bmatrix}
=
\begin{bmatrix}
w_A \\
w_B \\
\lambda_1 \\
\lambda_2
\end{bmatrix}
=
\begin{bmatrix}
0.8 \\
0.2 \\
-0.48 \\
-0.032
\end{bmatrix},
$$

$$\mathbf{C}^{-1} \qquad \cdot \quad \mathbf{S} = \mathbf{x} \qquad
\begin{aligned}
w_A &= 0.8, \\
w_B &= 0.2.
\end{aligned}$$

(iii) Notice that only the third element in **x** has changed. Thus:

$$
\begin{bmatrix}
w_A \\
w_B \\
w_C \\
w_D
\end{bmatrix}
=
\begin{bmatrix}
0.2 \\
0.8 \\
1.92 \\
0.112
\end{bmatrix},
$$

$$\mathbf{x} \qquad
\begin{aligned}
w_A &= 0.2, \\
w_B &= 0.8.
\end{aligned}$$

(b) Our asset returns and standard deviations are as follows:

Asset	E(R)	σ	
A	0.10	0.20	$\sigma_{A,B} = 0.04$
B	0.20	0.40	$\sigma_{A,rf} = 0$
r_f	0.09	0	$\sigma_{B,rf} = 0$

(i) The Lagrange function is now:

$$L = (0.04 w_A^2 + 0.16 w_B^2 + 0.08 w_A w_B) - \lambda_1(0.15 - 0.1 w_A - 0.2 w_B - 0.09 w_{rf}) - \lambda_2(1 - 1 w_A - 1 w_B - 1 w_{rf}).$$

Because $\sigma_{rf} = \sigma_{B,rf} = \sigma_{A,rf} = 0$, w_{rf} terms are dropped from the first set of parentheses. The first order conditions are:

$$\partial L/\partial w_A = 0.08w_A + 0.08w_B + 0.1\lambda_1 + 1\lambda_2 = 0;$$

$$\partial L/\partial w_A = 0.32w_B + 0.08w_A + 0.2\lambda_1 + 1\lambda_2 = 0;$$

$$\partial L/\partial w_{rf} = -0.09\lambda_1 - 1\lambda_2 = 0;$$

$$\partial L/\partial \lambda_1 = 0.15 - 0.1w_A - 0.2w_B - 0.09w_{rf} = 0;$$

$$\partial L/\partial \lambda_2 = 1 - 1w_A - 1w_B - 1w_{rf} = 0.$$

Now we have a (5 × 5) coefficient matrix:

$$
\begin{bmatrix}
0.08 & 0.08 & 0 & 0.1 & 1 \\
0.08 & 0.32 & 0 & 0.2 & 1 \\
0 & 0 & 0 & 0.09 & 1 \\
0.1 & 0.2 & 0.09 & 0 & 0 \\
1 & 1 & 1 & 0 & 0
\end{bmatrix}
\begin{bmatrix}
w_A \\
w_B \\
w_{rf} \\
\lambda_1 \\
\lambda_2
\end{bmatrix}
=
\begin{bmatrix}
0 \\
0 \\
0 \\
0.15 \\
1
\end{bmatrix},
$$

$$\mathbf{C} \qquad\qquad \cdot \ \mathbf{x} \ = \ \mathbf{s}.$$

Simply solve this system, to obtain:

$$
\begin{bmatrix}
14.68447 & -1.33495 & -13.3495 & -6.79612 & 0.61165 \\
-1.33495 & 0.121359 & 1.213592 & 9.708738 & -0.87379 \\
-13.3495 & 1.213592 & 12.13592 & -2.91262 & 1.262136 \\
-6.79612 & 9.708738 & -2.91262 & -23.301 & 2.097087 \\
0.61165 & -0.87379 & 1.262136 & 2.097087 & -0.18874
\end{bmatrix}
\begin{bmatrix}
0 \\
0 \\
0 \\
0.15 \\
1
\end{bmatrix}
=
\begin{bmatrix}
w_A \\
w_B \\
w_{rf} \\
\lambda_1 \\
\lambda_2
\end{bmatrix},
$$

$$\mathbf{C}^{-1} \qquad\qquad\qquad \cdot \ \mathbf{s} \ = \ \mathbf{x}.$$

Thus, we have

$$w_A = -0.40777,$$

$$w_B = 0.582524,$$

$$w_{rf} = 0.825243.$$

(ii) If the return constraint were to decrease to 0.12, only the fourth element in the solutions vector would change:

$$
\begin{bmatrix}
0 \\
0 \\
0 \\
0.12 \\
1
\end{bmatrix},
\quad \text{which results in the following weights:}
\quad
\begin{aligned}
w_A &= -0.20388, \\
w_B &= 0.291262, \\
w_{rf} &= 0.912621.
\end{aligned}
$$

(iii) Increasing the return constraint to 0.18 results in the following weights:

$$w_A = -0.61165, \qquad w_B = 0.873786, \qquad w_{rf} = 0.737864.$$

8.21. $L = 0.16w_2^2 + 0.64w_3^2 + \lambda_1(0.20 - 0.05w_1 - 0.15w_2 - 0.25w_3) + \lambda_2(1 - w_1 - w_2 - w_3);$

$$\partial L/\partial w_1 = -0.05\lambda_1 - 1\lambda_2 = 0,$$

$$\partial L/\partial w_2 = 1.00w_2 - 0.07\lambda_1 - 1\lambda_2 = 0,$$

$\partial L/\partial w_3 = 1.62w_3 - 0.11\lambda_1 - 1\lambda_2 = 0,$

$\partial L/\partial \lambda_1 = -0.05w_1 - 0.07w_2 - 0.11w_3 = -0.10,$

$\partial L/\partial \lambda_2 = -w_1 - w_2 - w_3 = -1;$

$w_1 = -0.27451, \qquad w_2 = 0.661765, \qquad w_3 = 0.612745.$

CHAPTER 9

9.1.   (a) $F(x) = k;$
       (b) $F(x) = 5x + k;$
       (c) $F(x) = 5x^3 + k;$
       (d) $F(x) = 5x^3 + 5x + k;$
       (e) $F(x) = e^x + k;$
       (f) $F(x) = e^{0.5x} + k;$
       (g) $F(x) = 5^x + k;$
       (h) $F(x) = \ln(x) + k.$

9.2.   (a) $\int_0^1 x\,dx = \frac{1}{2}x^2 \big|_0^1 = (\frac{1}{2} + k) - (0 + k) = \frac{1}{2};$

       (b) $\int_2^4 (x + 5)\,dx = [\frac{1}{2}x^2 + 5x]\big|_2^4 = (\frac{1}{2}\cdot 16 + 5\cdot 4 + k) - (\frac{1}{2}\cdot 4 + 5\cdot 2 + k) = 16;$

       (c) $\int_0^{20} 100{,}000e^{0.10t}\,dt = 100{,}000\left[\dfrac{e^{0.10t}}{0.10}\right]\Bigg|_0^{20}$

           $= 1{,}000{,}000e^2 - 1{,}000{,}000e^0 = 1{,}000{,}000(e^2 - 1) = 6{,}389{,}056.$

9.3.   (a) $(0.2\cdot 0.2) + (0.2\cdot 0.4) + (0.2\cdot 0.6) + (0.2\cdot 0.8) + (0.2\cdot 1) = 0.04 + 0.08 + 0.12$
          $+ 0.16 + 0.20 = 0.6;$
       (b) $2.96 + 3.12 + 3.28 + 3.44 + 3.6 = 16.4;$
       (c) $596{,}730 + 890{,}216 + 1{,}328{,}047 + 1{,}981{,}213 + 2{,}955{,}622 = 7{,}751{,}828.$

9.4.   (a) $P(x) = \int p(x)\,dx = 0.5x^3 + 0.5x^2.$
       (b)   The distribution function for x will be $\int f(x)p(x)\,dx$, which, since $f(x) = x$, equals $\int(x \cdot 1.5x^2 + x \cdot x)\,dx = \int(1.5x^3 + x^2)\,dx = 0.375x^4 + 0.3333x^3$. The probability that x will be in the range 0.2–1.0 equals $P[0.2 < x < 1] = (0.5x^3 + 0.5x^2)|_{0.2}^1 = [(0.5\cdot 1^3 + 0.5\cdot 1^2) - (0.5\cdot 0.2^3 + 0.5\cdot 0.2^2)][1 - 0.024] = 0.976$. The expected value of x given that it falls within this range is a conditional distribution determined by:

          $E[x|0.2 < x < 1] = \{\int_{0.2}^1 xp(x)\}/\{P[0.2 < x < 1]\}$

          $= [(0.375\cdot 1^4 + 0.3333\cdot 1^3) - (0.375\cdot 0.2^4 + 0.3333\cdot 0.2^3)]/0.976$

          $= 0.7050666/0.976 = 0.7224043.$

       (c)   The probability that x will be in the range 0–0.2 equals $(0.5x^3 + 0.5x^2)|_0^{0.2} = [(0.5\cdot 0.2^3 + 0.5\cdot 0.2^2) - 0] = 0.024$. The expected value of x given that it falls within this range is a conditional distribution determined by:

$$E[x|0 < x < 0.2] = \{\int_0^{0.2} xp(x)\}/\{P[0 < x < 0.2]\}$$

$$= (0.375 \cdot 0.2^4 + 0.3333 \cdot 0.2^3) - (0.375 \cdot 0^4 + 0.3333 \cdot 0^3)]/0.024$$

$$= 0.0032667/0.024 = 0.136111.$$

(d) $E[x] = \int_0^1 xp(x)dx = [(0.375 \cdot 1^4 + 0.3333 \cdot 1^3) - (0.375 \cdot 0^4 + 0.3333 \cdot 0^3) = 0.7083333.$

(e) $\sigma^2 = \int_0^1 [f(x)]^2 p(x)dx - (\int_0^1 f(x)p(x)dx)^2$
$= \int_0^1 x^2 p(x)dx - (\int_0^1 xp(x)dx)^2 = \int_0^1 x^2 \cdot (1.5x^2 + x)dx - [\int_0^1 x \cdot (1.5x^2 + x)dx]^2.$

And since the term to the right of the minus sign is the expected value squared:

$$\sigma^2 = \int_0^1 (1.5x^4 + x^3)dx - 0.7083333^2$$

$$= (0.3x^5 + 0.25x^4)|_0^1 - 0.7083333^2$$

$$= 0.55 - 0 - 0.5017 = 0.0483.$$

9.5.   (a) $P(x) = \int p(x)dx = x.$

  (b) $E[S|50 \le S \le 100] = \{\int_{0.5}^1 100xp(x)dx\}/\{P[50 \le S \le 100]\} = \{\int_{0.5}^1 100x \cdot 1 \, dx\}$
     $/\{\int_{0.5}^1 p(x)dx\} = \{50 \cdot 1^2 - 50 \cdot 0.5^2\}/0.5 = 75.$

  (c) $E[S|0 \le S \le 50] = \{\int_0^{0.5} 100xp(x)dx\}/\{P[0 \le S \le 50]\} = \{\int_0^{0.5} 100x \cdot 1 \, dx\}/\{\int_0^{0.5} p(x)dx\}$
     $= \{50 \cdot 0.50^2 - 50 \cdot 0^2\}/0.5 = 12.5.$

  (d) $E[S] = \int_0^1 f(x)p(x)dx = \int_0^1 100x \, dx = 50x^2|_0^1 = 50.$

  (e) $\sigma^2 = \int_0^1 [f(x)]^2 p(x)dx - (\int_0^1 f(x)p(x)dx)^2 = \int_0^1 10,000x^2 p(x)dx - (\int_0^1 100xp(x)dx)^2$
     $= \int_0^1 10,000x^2 dx - (\int_0^1 100x \, dx)^2.$

     Since the term to the right of the minus sign is the expected value squared:

$$\sigma^2 = \int_0^1 10,000x^2 dx - 50^2 = (3333.33)x^3|_0^1 - 50^2$$

$$= (3,333.33) \cdot 1 - 0 - 2,500 = 833.33.$$

  (f) $E[S - 50|50 \le S \le 100] = 25.$

  (g) $E[CF_t] = \{0.5 \cdot 0\} + \{0.5 \cdot E[S - 50|50 \le S \le 100]\} = 12.5.$

  (h) $PV(E[CF]) = 12.5e^{-0.1 \cdot 1} = 11.31.$

9.6.   We integrate the density functions as follows:

$$P_f(x) = \int 4x^3 = x^4 \qquad \text{for } 0 \le x \le 1,$$

$$P_g(x) = \int (3x^4 + 0.08x) = \tfrac{3}{5}x^5 + \tfrac{2}{5}x^2 + k \qquad \text{for } 0 \le x \le 1.$$

9.7.   The amount of dividend payment to be received at any infinitesimal time interval dt equals $f(t)dt = 3,000,000dt$. The present value of this sum equals $f(t)e^{-kt}dt = 3,000,000e^{-0.06t}$. To find the present value of a sum received over a finite interval beginning with $t = 0$, one may apply the definite integral as follows:

$$PV[0,T] = \int_0^T f(t)e^{-kt}dt,$$

$$PV[0,10] = \int_0^{10} 3,000,000e^{-0.06t}dt = 3,000,000\left[-\frac{e^{-0.06t}}{0.06}\right]\Bigg|_0^{10}$$

$$= \frac{3,000,000}{0.06}(1 - e^{-0.6}) = \$22,559,418.$$

9.8.   The dividend stream is evaluated as follows:

$$PV[0,2] = \frac{10,000}{0.05 - 0.03}(1 - e^{(0.03 - 0.05) \cdot 2}) = 19,605.28.$$

9.9. (a) The differential equation for this problem can be created in two steps. First, the account should generate interest continuously (including interest on any payments deducted from the account) as follows:

$$\frac{\mathrm{d}FV_t}{\mathrm{d}t} = iFV_0.$$

However, deductions will be made continuously from the account. The interest that these deductions would have accumulated must be deducted from the total interest given above. These deductions will reduce the amount of interest that the account will draw in the future. Assume $T - t$ relevant years in the future. The payments deducted from the account continuously are $PMT\mathrm{d}t$. These payments plus $T - t$ years of interest that would otherwise have accumulated on those payments are as follows:

$$PMTe^{i(T-t)}\mathrm{d}t.$$

The difference between these is the differential equation representing the evolution of the account:

$$\mathrm{d}FV_t = [iFV_0 - PMTe^{i(T-t)}]\,\mathrm{d}t.$$

(b) To find the state of the account (system) at any time T, integrate over t the final equation from part 9.9(a) as follows:

$$FV_T = \int_0^T [iFV_0 - PMTe^{i(T-t)}]\,\mathrm{d}t,$$

$$FV_T = FV_0 e^{iT} - \int_0^T [PMTe^{i(T-t)}]\,\mathrm{d}t,$$

where $FV_0 = \$1,000,000$. This integral is solved as follows:

$$FV_T = FV_0 e^{iT} - \frac{1}{-i}[PMTe^{i(T-t)}]|_0^T,$$

$$FV_T = FV_0 e^{iT} + \frac{PMT}{i}[e^{i(T-T)}] - \frac{PMT}{i}[e^{i(T-0)}],$$

$$FV_T = FV_0 e^{iT} + \frac{PMT}{i}[1 - e^{iT}].$$

(c) Substitute numbers in the solution to part 9.9(b) as follows:

$$FV_{10} = \$1,000,000e^{0.06 \cdot 10} + \frac{\$75,000}{0.06}[1 - e^{0.06 \cdot 10}]$$

$$= \$1,822,118.8 - \$1,027,648.5 = \$794,470.3.$$

(d) Solve the following for T, to find that the retiree runs out of money in approximately 26.83 years:

$$FV_T = 0 = \$1,000,000e^{0.06 \cdot T} + \frac{\$75,000}{0.06}[1 - e^{0.06 \cdot 10}]$$

$$= -\$250,000e^{0.06 \cdot T} + \$1,250,000;$$

$$\ln(1,250,000) = \ln(250,000) + 0.06T, \qquad T = 26.82397.$$

9.10. (a) First, the account should generate interest continuously (including interest on any payments deducted from the account) as follows:

$$\frac{\mathrm{d}FV_t}{\mathrm{d}t} = iFV_0.$$

However, deductions will be made continuously from the account. The interest that these deductions would have accumulated must be deducted from the total interest given above. These deductions will reduce the amount of interest that the account will draw in the future. Assume $T - t$ relevant years in the future. The payments deducted from the account continuously are $PMT_t e^{gt} dt$. These payments plus $T - t$ years of interest that would otherwise have accumulated on those payments are as follows:

$$PMT_0 e^{gt} e^{i(T-t)} dt.$$

The difference between these is the differential equation representing the evolution of the account:

$$dFV_t = [iFV_0 - PMT_0 e^{gt} e^{i(T-t)}] dt.$$

(b) To find the state of the account (system) at any time T, integrate over t the final equation from part 9.10(a) as follows:

$$FV_T = \int_0^T [iFV_0 - PMT_0 e^{gt} e^{i(T-t)}] dt,$$

$$FV_T = FV_0 e^{iT} - \int_0^T [PMT_0 e^{gt} e^{i(T-t)}] dt,$$

where $FV_0 = \$1,000,000$. This integral is solved as follows:

$$FV_T = FV_0 e^{iT} - \frac{1}{g-i} [PMT_0 e^{gt+i(T-t)}]|_0^T,$$

$$FV_T = FV_0 e^{iT} + \frac{PMT_0}{i-g} [e^{gT+i(T-T)}] - \frac{PMT_0}{i-g} [e^{g \cdot 0 + i(T-0)}],$$

$$FV_T = FV_0 e^{iT} + \frac{PMT_0}{i-g} [e^{gT} - e^{iT}].$$

(c) Substitute numbers in the solution to part 9.10(b) as follows:

$$FV_{10} = \$1,000,000 e^{0.06 \cdot 10} + \frac{\$75,000}{0.06 - 0.02} [e^{0.02 \cdot 10} - e^{0.06 \cdot 10}]$$

$$= \$1,822,118.8 - \$1,126,342.6 = \$695,776.22.$$

(d) Solve the following for T, to find that the retiree runs out of money in approximately 19.05 years:

$$FV_T = 0 = \$1,000,000 e^{0.06 \cdot T} + \frac{\$75,000}{0.06 - 0.02} [e^{0.02T} - e^{0.06 \cdot T}]$$

$$= -\$875,000 e^{0.06 \cdot T} + \$1,875,000 e^{0.02T};$$

$$\ln(1,875,000) = \ln(875,000) + 0.04T, \qquad T = 19.0535.$$

CHAPTER 10

10.1. (a) $c_T = MAX[0, S_T - X]$; $c_T = \$0$ or $\$15$.

   (b) One can construct a one period hedge for a call option by shorting α shares of stock per option contract such that $c_u - \alpha u S_0 = c_d - \alpha d S_0$. We solve for the hedge ratio α as follows:

$$\alpha = \frac{C_u - C_d}{S_0(u - d)},$$

$$\alpha = \frac{15 - 0}{50(1.4 - 0.6)} = 0.375.$$

(c) Since shorting α shares of stock ensures that the portfolio is perfectly hedged, the hedged portfolio must earn the riskless rate of return $c_u - \alpha u S_0 = c_d - \alpha d S_0 = (c_0 - \alpha S_0)e^{-r_f T}$. Thus, the current value of the call can be solved for as follows:

$$C_0 = \frac{1 + r_f \alpha S_0 + C_d - \alpha d S_0}{1 + r_f},$$

$$C_0 = \frac{(1.1111) \cdot 0.375 \cdot 50 + 0 - 0.375 \cdot 0.6 \cdot 50}{1.1111} = 8.68.$$

10.2. The hedge ratio for the call equals 1. Since the riskless return rate is 0.125, the call's current value must be $4.8888889.

10.3. The following are call and put values:

n	c_0	p_0
2	4.62	29.96
3	3.91	29.25
8	3.87	29.21

10.4. $c_0 = \$5.10$; $p_0 = \$11.61$.

10.5. (a) $d_1 = 0.6172$; $d_2 = 0.1178$; $N(d_1) = 0.7314$; $N(d_2) = 0.5469$; $c_0 = 11.05$; with put–call parity, $p_0 = 4.34$.
(b) Use $X = 30$; $d_1 = 0.925$; $d_2 = 0.4245$; $N(d_2) = 0.6644$; $1 - N(d_2) = 0.3356$.

10.6. First, value the calls using the Black–Scholes model, then use put–call parity to value the puts:

$$p_0 = Xe^{-rT} + c_0 - S_0.$$

Thus, we will first compute d_1, d_2, $N(d_1)$, and $N(d_2)$ for each of the calls; then we will compute each call's value. Finally, we will use put–call parity to value each of the puts.

	Option 1	Option 2	Option 3	Option 4
d_1	0.957739	−0.163836	0.061699	0.131632
d_2	0.657739	−0.463836	−0.438301	−0.292626
$N(d_1)$	0.830903	0.434930	0.524599	0.552365
$N(d_2)$	0.744647	0.321383	0.330584	0.384904
Call	7.395	2.455	4.841	4.623
Put	0.939	5.416	7.803	5.665

10.7. First, value the calls using the Black–Scholes model, then use put–call parity to value the puts. Thus, we will first compute d_1, d_2, $N(d_1)$, and $N(d_2)$ for each of the calls; then we will compute each call's value. Finally, we will use put–call parity to value each of the puts.

First, find for each of the 15 call values for d_1:

X	March	April	May
50	1.412245	1.147191	1.020949
55	0.733636	0.625012	0.578796
60	0.114115	0.148301	0.175142
65	−0.455789	−0.290231	−0.196184
70	−0.983438	−0.696249	−0.539978

Next, find for each of the 15 calls values for d_2:

X	March	April	May
50	1.271796	0.964667	0.805390
55	0.593187	0.442488	0.363237
60	−0.026334	−0.034223	−0.040417
65	−0.596239	−0.472755	−0.411743
70	−1.123888	−0.878773	−0.755537

Now, find $N(d_1)$ for each of the 15 calls:

X	March	April	May
50	0.921061	0.874349	0.846361
55	0.768415	0.734019	0.718637
60	0.545427	0.558947	0.569516
65	0.324271	0.385820	0.422233
70	0.162696	0.243137	0.294606

Next, determine $N(d_2)$ for each of the 15 calls:

X	March	April	May
50	0.898277	0.832644	0.789703
55	0.723472	0.670932	0.641786
60	0.489495	0.486350	0.483880
65	0.275508	0.318194	0.340264
70	0.130530	0.189762	0.224963

Finally, use $N(d_1)$ and $N(d_2)$ to value the calls and use put–call parity to value the puts:

Calls

X	March	April	May
50	10.626	<u>11.260</u>	11.866
55	<u>6.558</u>	7.522	8.329
60	3.536	<u>4.658</u>	5.557
65	1.658	2.681	3.536
70	<u>0.681</u>	<u>1.442</u>	2.156

Puts

X	March	April	May
50	0.319	0.742	<u>1.145</u>
55	1.220	1.952	2.536
60	3.168	<u>4.037</u>	4.692
65	<u>6.259</u>	7.008	7.599
70	<u>10.251</u>	10.717	11.147

The options whose values are underlined are overvalued by the market; they should be sold. Other options are undervalued by the market; they should be purchased.

10.8. Implied volatilities are given as follows:

(a) $X = 40$, $\sigma = 0.2579$;
(b) $X = 45$, $\sigma = 0.3312$;
(c) $X = 50$, $\sigma = 0.2851$;
(d) $X = 55$, $\sigma = 0.2715$;
(e) $X = 60$, $\sigma = 0.2704$.

Standard normal distribution

z	0.00	0.01	0.02	0.03	0.04	0.05	0.06	0.07	0.08	0.09
0.0	0.0000	0.0040	0.0080	0.0120	0.0159	0.0199	0.0239	0.0279	0.0319	0.0358
0.1	0.0398	0.0438	0.0478	0.0517	0.0557	0.0596	0.0636	0.0675	0.0714	0.0753
0.2	0.0793	0.0832	0.0871	0.0909	0.0948	0.0987	0.1026	0.1064	0.1103	0.1141
0.3	0.1179	0.1217	0.1255	0.1293	0.1331	0.1368	0.1406	0.1443	0.1480	0.1517
0.4	0.1554	0.1591	0.1628	0.1664	0.1700	0.1736	0.1772	0.1808	0.1844	0.1879
0.5	0.1915	0.1950	0.1985	0.2019	0.2054	0.2088	0.2123	0.2157	0.2190	0.2224
0.6	0.2257	0.2291	0.2324	0.2356	0.2389	0.2421	0.2454	0.2486	0.2517	0.2549
0.7	0.2580	0.2611	0.2642	0.2673	0.2703	0.2734	0.2764	0.2793	0.2823	0.2852
0.8	0.2881	0.2910	0.2939	0.2967	0.2995	0.3023	0.3051	0.3078	0.3106	0.3133
0.9	0.3159	0.3186	0.3212	0.3238	0.3264	0.3289	0.3315	0.3340	0.3365	0.3389
1.0	0.3413	0.3437	0.3461	0.3485	0.3508	0.3531	0.3554	0.3577	0.3599	0.3621
1.1	0.3643	0.3665	0.3686	0.3708	0.3729	0.3749	0.3770	0.3790	0.3810	0.3830
1.2	0.3849	0.3869	0.3888	0.3906	0.3925	0.3943	0.3962	0.3980	0.3997	0.4015
1.3	0.4032	0.4049	0.4066	0.4082	0.4099	0.4115	0.4131	0.4147	0.4162	0.4177
1.4	0.4192	0.4207	0.4222	0.4236	0.4251	0.4265	0.4279	0.4292	0.4306	0.4319
1.5	0.4332	0.4345	0.4357	0.4370	0.4382	0.4394	0.4406	0.4418	0.4429	0.4441
1.6	0.4452	0.4463	0.4474	0.4484	0.4495	0.4505	0.4515	0.4525	0.4535	0.4545
1.7	0.4554	0.4564	0.4573	0.4582	0.4591	0.4599	0.4608	0.4616	0.4625	0.4633
1.8	0.4641	0.4649	0.4656	0.4664	0.4671	0.4678	0.4686	0.4693	0.4699	0.4706
1.9	0.4713	0.4719	0.4726	0.4732	0.4738	0.4744	0.4750	0.4756	0.4761	0.4767
2.0	0.4772	0.4778	0.4783	0.4788	0.4793	0.4798	0.4803	0.4808	0.4812	0.4817
2.1	0.4821	0.4826	0.4830	0.4834	0.4838	0.4842	0.4846	0.4850	0.4854	0.4857
2.2	0.4861	0.4864	0.4868	0.4871	0.4875	0.4878	0.4881	0.4884	0.4887	0.4890
2.3	0.4893	0.4896	0.4898	0.4901	0.4904	0.4906	0.4909	0.4911	0.4913	0.4916
2.4	0.4918	0.4920	0.4922	0.4925	0.4927	0.4929	0.4931	0.4932	0.4934	0.4936
2.5	0.4938	0.4940	0.4941	0.4943	0.4945	0.4946	0.4948	0.4949	0.4951	0.4952
2.6	0.4953	0.4955	0.4956	0.4957	0.4959	0.4960	0.4961	0.4962	0.4963	0.4964
2.7	0.4965	0.4966	0.4967	0.4968	0.4969	0.4970	0.4971	0.4972	0.4973	0.4974
2.8	0.4974	0.4975	0.4976	0.4977	0.4977	0.4978	0.4979	0.4979	0.4980	0.4981
2.9	0.4981	0.4982	0.4982	0.4983	0.4984	0.4984	0.4985	0.4985	0.4986	0.4986
3.0	0.4986	0.4987	0.4987	0.4988	0.4988	0.4989	0.4989	0.4989	0.4990	0.4990

APPENDIX C
NOTATION

The notation used in this book is defined in this appendix. Since this book discusses a wide range of topics, a few symbols will have more than one definition. In a few instances, certain notation used only in a short portion of the text will be defined in the text only and not here.

GREEK LETTERS

β Beta in the capital asset pricing model.
Γ The sensitivity of an option delta to a change in underlying security price.
Δ (1) Change; (2) Option sensitivity to underlying asset price change.
Θ The slope of the Capital Market Line.
λ Lagrange multiplier.
μ (1) Continuously compounded security return; (2) population mean.
Π Product operation.
π (1) The number pi, with approximate value 3.141; (2) in chapter 2, profits; (3) in chapter 10, probability of up-jump.
ρ (1) Correlation coefficient; (2) in chapter 10, option sensitivity to interest rates.
Σ Summation operation.
σ_i Standard deviation.
$\sigma_{i,j}$ Covariance.
σ_i^2 Variance.

LATIN LETTERS

a The number of price upjumps required for option exercise in the binomial framework.
APY   Annual percentage yield.
b Beta in the capital asset pricing model.
C Call value.
c (1) Constant or coefficient; (2) call value; (3) coupon rate.
CF_t Cash flow at time t.
conv.   Convexity.

COV	Covariance.
cy	Current yield.
d	Multiplicative downward movement.
D_t	Discount function for time t.
d_1	Parameter in the Black–Scholes formula.
d_2	Parameter in the Black–Scholes formula.
DD	Demand deposits.
Dur	Duration.
E[*]	Expected value of [*].
e	The number e, with an approximate value equal to 2.7182818.
F	Face value of debt instrument.
$f(*)$	Function of (*).
FC	Fixed costs.
FV_n	Future value of cash flow received in n periods.
g	Growth rate.
i	(1) Interest rate; (2) counter in a summation or product.
INT	Interest payment.
IRR	Internal rate of return.
K	The currency in an economy.
k	(1) Discount rate; (2) constant of integration.
L	Lagrange function.
lim	Limit.
ln	Natural log.
m	The number of compounding intervals per period.
n	(1) Ending or stopping value or time; (2) number of securities in portfolio.
N[*]	Cumulative normal density function for [*].
NPV	Net Present value.
P	Price.
P	Probability.
p	(1) Put value; (2) probability or density.
P_i	The probability associated with outcome i.
P_0	The purchase price of an asset.
P_t	The price of an asset at time t.
PV	Present value.
Q	Quantity.
R	Return.
r	(1) Usually denotes rate of return or interest rate; (2) in application 3.8, represents reserve requirement.
r_f	Risk-free rate of return.
ROI	Return on investment.
S	(1) Stock price; (2) In chapter 3, denotes the value of a series.
S_t	Stock value at time t.
T	Usually denotes the maturity or expiration date of an instrument.
t	Usually denotes time.
u	Multiplicative upward movement.
U	Utility.
V	Value.
VC	Variable costs.
w_i	The portfolio weight for security i.
W_0	Initial wealth.

X	(1) Usually denotes the striking price of an option; (2) in chapter 4, denotes a cash flow.
X_0	Cash flow, time zero.
x	Usually denotes a variable.
y	Yield to maturity.
$y_{0,t}$	The spot rate over t periods.
$y_{i,t}$	The forward rate on a note originated at time i and maturing at time t.
ytm	Yield to maturity.
z	$[(r_m - r_f)/\sigma_m^2] \cdot w_i$.

OTHER MATHEMATICS SYMBOLS

∂	Partial derivative notation.
$\mid$	Given.
$!$	Factoral.
$\rightarrow$	Approaches.

APPENDIX D
GLOSSARY

American option   An option that can be exercised prior to expiration.

annuity   A series of equal payments made at regular intervals.

antidifferentiation   The inverse process of differentiation.

arbitrage   The simultaneous purchase and sale of assets with identical cash flow structures.

arbitrage pricing theory   A theory of market equilibrium where expected security returns are linearly related to a series of factors.

bankrupt   The situation arising when a firm is unable to fulfill its obligations and its assets are surrendered to a court for management and distribution.

basis   The set of n or more vectors which can, through linear combinations, express any other vector in that n-dimensional space.

beta   A coefficient that measures the risk of a security relative to the risk of some factor (usually the market).

binomial process   A process which results in one of two potential outcomes at each stage or vertex.

Black–Scholes option pricing model   A continuous time–space option pricing formula.

bond   Financial security which makes fixed payment(s) at specified interval(s).

call   A security or contract granting its owner the right to purchase a given asset at a specified price on or before the expiration date of the contract.

capital asset pricing model   A theory of market equilibrium where security expected returns are related to their covariances (or betas) with the market portfolio.

capital market   The market for financial resources.

Capital Market Line   The line plotting risk and return combinations of the most efficient portfolios of assets, including the riskless asset.

central limit theorem   This states that the distribution of the mean of n independent and identically distributed random variables tends to a normal distribution as n approaches infinity.

coefficient of correlation   A measure of the strength and direction of the relationship between two sets of variables. It ranges between zero and one and may be regarded as a "standardized" covariance (dividing covariance by the product of the standard deviations of the two variable sets).

coefficient of determination   Correlation coefficient squared (often called "r-squared" or "ρ-squared"). These may be interpreted as the proportion of variability in one data set which may be "explained" be a second data set.

convexity (1) The slope of the slope of a function; (2) the sensitivity of the duration of a bond to changes in the market rate of interest.

correlation The strength and the direction of the relationship between two variables. *See* **coefficient of correlation**.

coupon The interest rate on debt as a percentage of its face value.

covariance A statistical measure of the co-movement between two sets of variables.

degree (of a differential equation) The power to which its highest order derivative is raised.

density The probability that a continuous random variable assumes a value between y^* and $y^* + dy$, where $dy \rightarrow 0$.

derivative The instantaneous slope of a function.

derivative security An instrument whose payoff or value is a function of that of another security, index, or value.

diagonal matrix A symmetric matrix whose elements off the principal diagonal are zero.

differential equation A function that represents the derivative of another function.

discount rate A rate used to discount (usually reduce) future cash flows to express their values relative to current cash flows.

discrete A variable that can be assigned only a countable number of values.

distribution function The probability that a continuous random variable assumes a value no greater than y^*.

diversify To accumulate a variety of different types of assets.

drift The predictable change component of a stochastic process.

duration Measures the proportional sensitivity of a bond to changes in the market rate of interest.

efficient (1) Produces maximum profit relative to investment amount; (2) has highest return given risk; (3) has least risk given return.

Efficient Frontier The curve plotting risk and return combinations of the most efficient portfolios of risky assets.

efficient market Security prices instantly adjust to fully reflect all available information.

efficient portfolio (1) The portfolio with the highest return at its risk level, or (2) the portfolio with the lowest risk level at its return level.

European option An option that can be exercised only at expiration.

expected return A weighted average return, where the weights are determined by probabilities associated with potential return outcomes.

expected value Weighted averages, where weights are probabilities associated with outcomes.

face value The principal or par value of debt.

forward contract A contract for the future purchase, sale, and/or exchange of an asset at a price that is set when the contract is agreed to.

function A rule that assigns a unique second number to each number in a set.

futures contract A publicly (exchange) traded forward contract providing for the exchange or transfer of an asset or assets at a price that is set when positions are taken in the contract.

future value The value of a sum of money after it has been invested for a period of time.

gamble To take a risk.

geometric mean return The nth root minus one of the product of the sum of one plus periodic returns, where n is the number of returns to be averaged. It is an average return that has been adjusted for the impact of compounding.

hedge To take a position to reduce risk.

identity matrix A diagonal matrix consisting of ones along the principal diagonal.

immunization A fixed income strategy concerned with matching the present values of asset portfolios with the present values of cash flows associated with future liabilities.

index   An indicator (for example, the Dow Jones Industrials Average may be regarded as a market index).

infinitesimal   Value approaching zero.

interest   A charge imposed on borrowers by lenders.

internal rate of return   The discount rate which sets the Net Present Value (*NPV*) of an investment equal to zero. It is a measure of the profitability of an investment.

inverse matrix $\mathbf{A}^{-1}$ exists for the square matrix $\mathbf{A}$ if the product $\mathbf{A}^{-1}\mathbf{A}$ or $\mathbf{AA}^{-1}$ equals the identity matrix $\mathbf{I}$.

Law of One Price   Assets or portfolios with identical cash flow structures must have the same market price.

linear combinations   Combinations of vector addition and scalar multiplication.

linear dependence   This exists when a vector in a given *n*-dimensional space can be expressed as a linear combination of a set of other vectors in the same space.

liquid   Easily converted into cash or sold.

market   The arena for buying and selling.

market portfolio   The combination of all assets held by investors and institutions.

matrix   An ordered rectangular array of numbers.

maturity   Payments cease on a debt security. The maturity date is the date on which payments cease.

mean   Average; sum of data points divided by the number of data.

median   The value in the middle of a ranked data set.

mutual fund   An institution that pools investors' funds into a single portfolio.

objective function   The function whose value is to be minimized or maximized in an optimization problem.

option   A security that grants its owner the right to buy or sell an asset at a specific price on or before the expiration date of the security. *See* **call**; **put**.

portfolio   A collection of investment holdings.

present value   The value of a future cash flow or series of cash flows expressed in terms of money received now.

principal diagonal   This contains the series of elements where row i = column j.

probability   Likelihood; likely to be expressed in percentage or decimal terms.

pure discount note   A debt security paying no interest; it only pays its face value or principal.

put   A security or contract granting its owner the right to sell a given asset at a specified price on or before the expiration date of the contract.

random walk   A process whose future behavior, given by the sum of independent random variables, is independent of its past.

range   The difference between high and low values in a data set.

return   Profit relative to initial investment amount.

risk   Uncertainty.

risk premium   A return offered or demanded as compensation for accepting uncertainty.

scalar   A matrix with exactly one element.

security   A marketable certificate denoting a financial claim; that is, a paper or contract with underlying value which can be bought and sold.

set   A collection of any type of objects.

short sell   To borrow and sell. Presumably, the short-sold security will be repurchased and returned to its original owner.

skewness   The asymmetry of a distribution. The third moment about the mean of a distribution.

solution (to a differential equation)   A function which, when substituted for the dependent variable, satisfies the equality.

space   A system of entities such as outcomes or points in time.

spot rate   The yield at present prevailing for zero coupon bonds of a given maturity.

square matrix   A matrix with the same number of rows and columns.

standard deviation   A measure of dispersion, risk, and uncertainty. It is the square root of variance.

state space   The set of values generated by a process.

statistics   A branch of mathematics concerning the collection, organization, interpretation, and presentation of numerical facts and data.

stochastic   Random.

stochastic processes   Processes generating outcomes that are influenced by random effects over time.

symmetric matrix   A square matrix, where $c_{i,j}$ equals $c_{j,i}$ for all i and j.

systematic risk   Risk that is common to the market or a large number of securities.

Taylor series   The expression of the value of a function $f(x)$ near x in terms of $f(x)$ and its first and higher order derivatives.

technical stock analysis   This concerns the examination of historical price sequences.

terminal value   The value of a sum of money after it has been invested for a period of time.

term structure of interest rates   The relationship between yields to maturity of debt securities and the length of time before the securities mature.

transpose   To interchange the rows and columns of a matrix.

Treasury bill   A short-term pure discount note issued by the Treasury of the United States federal government, and considered to be relatively free of risk.

unit matrix   *See* **identity matrix**.

unsystematic risk   Risk that is unique or specific to one firm.

variance   A measure of dispersion, risk, and uncertainty. It is the expected value of the squared deviation of a data point from the expected value of the data set. It is the square of the standard deviation.

vector   A matrix with either only one row or one column.

vector space   The set of all vectors with n real valued elements or coordinates.

warrant   An option on the treasury stock of a firm.

yield to maturity   The internal rate of return for a bond.

zero coupon bond   A bond that makes no interest payments. *See* **pure discount note**.

INDEX

Printed and bound by CPI Group (UK) Ltd, Croydon, CR0 4YY

24/04/2025

14661399-0001